Get More Out of

Your PC and Add-Ons

First Edition

Preston Gralla, Walter Glenn, Tom Bunzel, et al.

que®

201 W. 103rd Street
Indianapolis, Indiana 46290

AUG 1 9 2004

Get More Out of Your PC and Add-Ons

First Edition

Copyright © 2003 by Que

International Standard Book Number: 0-7897-2942-3

Library of Congress Catalog Card Number: 2003101769

Printed in the United States of America

First Printing: May 2003

06   05   04   03   4   3   2   1

Trademarks

Warning and Disclaimer

Bulk Sales

Que offers excellent discounts on this book when ordered in quantity for bulk purchases or special sales. For more information, please contact:

U.S. Corporate and Government Sales
1-800-382-3419
corpsales@pearsontechgroup.com

For sales outside of the U.S., please contact:

International Sales
+1-317-581-3793
international@pearsontechgroup.com

Associate Publisher
Greg Wiegand

Acquisitions Editor
Angelina Ward

Development Editor
Kevin Howard

Managing Editor
Charlotte Clapp

Project Editor
Tonya Simpson

Production Editor
Benjamin Berg

Indexer
Erika Millen

Team Coordinator
Sharry Gregory

Interior Designer
Anne Jones

Cover Designer
Anne Jones

Page Layout
Kelly Maish

Contents at a Glance

Contents at a Glance

Table of Contents

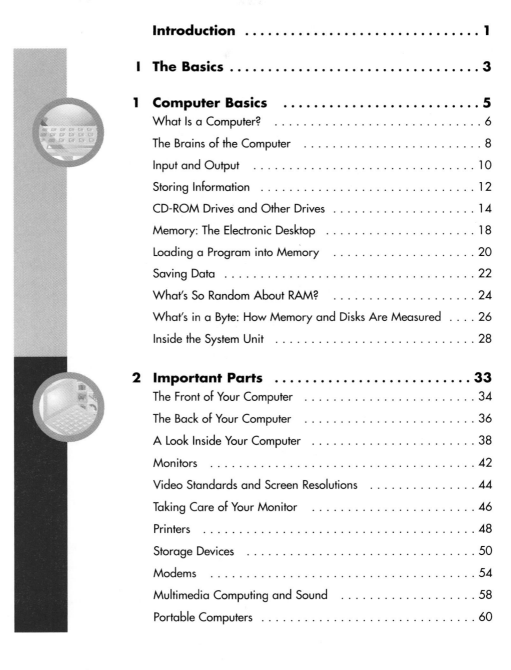

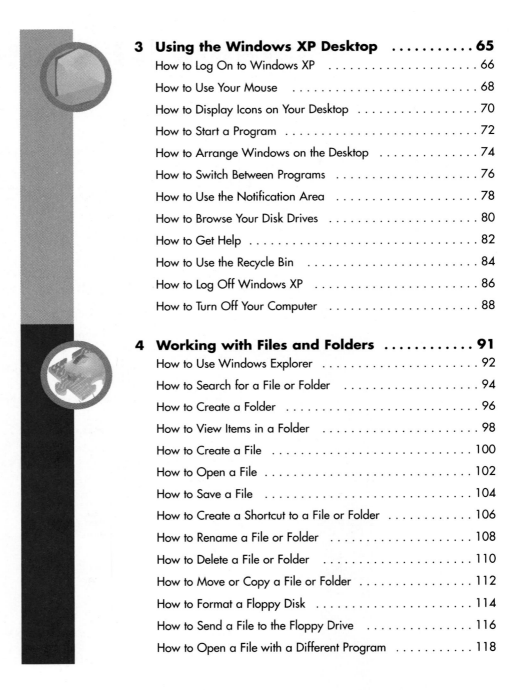

We Want to Hear from You!

As the reader of this book, *you* are our most important critic and commentator. We value your opinion and want to know what we're doing right, what we could do better, what areas you'd like to see us publish in, and any other words of wisdom you're willing to pass our way.

As an associate publisher for Que, I welcome your comments. You can email or write me directly to let me know what you did or didn't like about this book—as well as what we can do to make our books better.

Please note that I cannot help you with technical problems related to the *topic* of this book. We do have a User Services group, however, where I will forward specific technical questions related to the book.

When you write, please be sure to include this book's title and author as well as your name, email address, and phone number. I will carefully review your comments and share them with the author and editors who worked on the book.

Email: feedback@quepublishing.com

Mail: Greg Wiegand
Que Publishing
201 West 103rd Street
Indianapolis, IN 46290 USA

For more information about this book or another Que title, visit our Web site at www.quepublishing.com. Type the ISBN (excluding hyphens) or the title of a book in the Search field to find the page you're looking for.

The Complete Visual Reference

Each chapter of this book is made up of a series of short, instructional tasks, designed to help you understand all the information that you need to get the most out of your computer hardware and software.

 Click: Click the left mouse button once.

 Double-click: Click the left mouse button twice in rapid succession.

 Right-click: Click the right mouse button once.

 Drag: Click and hold the left mouse button, position the mouse pointer, and release.

 Pointer Arrow: Highlights an item on the screen you need to point to or focus on in the step or task.

 **Selection:** Highlights the area onscreen discussed in the step or task.

 Type: Click once where indicated and begin typing to enter your text or data.

 **Drag and Drop:** Point to the starting place or object. Hold down the mouse button (right or left per instructions), move the mouse to the new location, and then release the button.

Each task includes a series of easy-to-understand steps designed to guide you through the procedure.

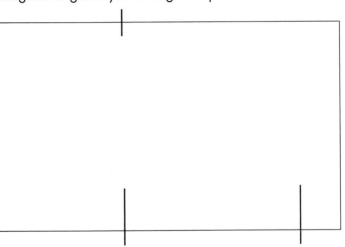

Each step is fully illustrated to show you how it looks onscreen.

Extra hints that tell you how to accomplish a goal are provided in most tasks.

⌐Enter) **Key icons:** Clearly indicate which key combinations to use.

Menus and items you click are shown in **bold**. Words in *italic* are defined in more detail in the glossary. Information you type is in a `special font`.

Introduction

If you are new to computers, you might seem overwhelmed by everything there is to know. Don't worry; with this book you're off to a great start. We'll begin by learning the basics of Windows, move on to security and recovery, what to do when things go wrong, and then delve into adding and changing hardware. Imagine: You wake up one morning, turn on the computer, and the thing simply won't start. Or, you can't install any new programs because your hard disk is full. You want to play a great new game, but you don't have the right graphics card.

And it's not just that things go wrong with them. You're always looking for ways to get your computer to do more, or you want to buy new equipment. Maybe you'd like to install a scanner, a new modem, or a new hard disk. You find yourself wading through technical manuals written in a language resembling Sanskrit. You find fast-talking salesmen getting you to buy equipment you don't need. Computer technicians charge an arm and a leg to do something such as installing a hard disk—that's if you can even find someone to install it for you.

Those are the types of problems to which this book is devoted—helping you expand and upgrade your computer yourself. You'll find there's no need to hire someone to do it for you. Even if you've never picked up a screwdriver, you can do it yourself.

Many books offer advice on how to upgrade and expand PCs but are written for people with advanced technical skills. This book is different. This book is written for everyone, at every skill level, not just those who already know what USB stands for. Whether you've never opened up your PC or you're a pro at installing SCSI devices, you'll find this book helpful because it takes a different approach to helping you upgrade and expand computers. It's devoted to the time-honored idea that a picture is worth a thousand words. So, we don't just tell you how to do something—we *show* you in easy-to-follow pictures and step-by-step instructions.

Many people who buy this book may buy it for a single reason—for example, to learn how to install a scanner. But I hope that even if you buy it for that single reason, you'll soon gain enough confidence to install other devices and to do computer repairs yourself. You'll be surprised how easy it is, and not only will you be saving money and getting a more powerful computer, you'll be having fun. And you'll have the satisfaction of knowing you did it all yourself.

I suggest that you spend at least a little time perusing several chapters in the front of the book. There, you'll learn the basics that will bring you a long way as you delve into your PC and add-ons.

Most chapters start with an illustration showing how the peripheral or device addressed works and how it connects to your computer. It's good to check out the illustration before reading the rest of the chapter, so you'll know what to expect ahead of time and how everything fits together.

After the opening illustration, you'll find step-by-step instructions with clear images describing how to repair and upgrade that particular computer component. Then, you'll read the steps themselves. At the end of the steps, you'll find something to which you should pay particular attention: "Watch Out!" and "How-to Hints." These give advice on common problems you'll face and offer suggestions for making your upgrade or repair easier. Many chapters also include an "Upgrade Advisor" section that gives advice on what to know before buying and installing that particular piece of hardware.

The Basics

Task

Computer Basics

Learning to use computers is like learning a new language. Along with the new vocabulary and skills, you will inevitably acquire some new ways of thinking about and interacting with the world. Even if all you learn to do is plug in the computer and compose letters, the computer may change your writing process by making it much easier to revise what you've written.

Learning about computers will also give you access to new ways of obtaining and working with information. After you know how to operate a computer, you can easily use it to chat with people across the country or the globe, about everything from international politics to recipes for bouillabaisse to Chinese word processing programs. If you have an office job, computer literacy may enable you to carry out some or all of your work from home—letting you communicate with the office computer using your own computer and a telephone. Finally, you may gain glimpses of what the future will be like, when computers are sure to be even more ubiquitous and more capable than they are today.

Most of this book concentrates on the maintenance and performance of your PC. The most obvious analogy to illustrate how regular maintenance can enhance your productivity on the PC would in the fields of personal health or automotive repair. In both cases, doing *preventive maintenance* on a regular basis, and making sure that the various parts of your car or body are working with *regular checkups*, can avoid serious problems.

For example, your hard drive is the brains of your computer—but this $75 peripheral can hold *thousands of dollars worth of data*. Optimizing its performance, and *backing up data*, just makes good practical and business sense. In fact, you can think of a regular data backup as business life insurance.

Caring for the rest of the system is just as important, but the speed and performance you need may depend upon how you use the PC. If you do heavy graphics or video, you may need the peak performance of an athlete, and provide your PC with the maximum amount of RAM and CPU speed. If your needs are more modest, you can use a lower performance machine, but it will still be in your best interest to do regular maintenance, understand how to solve problems when they come up, and maximize its performance. We'll start with the basics, familiarizing yourself with computers, and move on from there. Enjoy!

What Is a Computer?

A computer is a general-purpose machine for storing and manipulating information. Beyond this, there are two very different schools of thought: 1) Computers are dumb but very fast machines equivalent to extremely powerful calculators. 2) Computers are thinking machines capable of awe-inspiring, almost limitless feats of intelligence. Actually, both statements are true.

You see text and images and hear sound.

Fa La La!

April is the cruelest month

1010110101011
0101001100110
10100100010110

Inside, all information is handled as numbers.

1 How Computers Work

By themselves, computers have a very limited set of skills. They can add, compare, and store numbers. This probably seems very strange because the computers we see each day seem to do far more than this. They manipulate text, display graphical images, generate sounds, and do lots of other things that seem nonmathematical.

2 Information Is Numbers

Internally, the computer handles all information as numbers, and everything it does involves storing and manipulating those numbers. In this sense, computers are like fancy adding machines. But if you know how to "talk" to a computer in the language of numbers, as programmers do, you can get it to do some amazing things. Any kind of information that can be represented numerically—from music to photographs to motion picture videos—can be manipulated via a computer, assuming someone knows how to provide the computer with the proper instructions.

3 You Don't Need to Learn Programming

This does not mean that you need to know how to program computers (write your own instructions) to use them. You will buy and use programs that other people have created. You need to learn how to use those programs—a task that is far easier and less demanding than learning to write programs of your own.

4 Computers Are Everywhere

You probably deal with computers on a daily basis, whether you want to or not. Every time you use an ATM, or watch the checker scan the bar code on your milk carton into an electronic cash register, or use a hand-held calculator, you are using a computer. Some of those computers—such as the calculator—are designed to do a specific task, and the instructions for performing that task are built into the equipment itself. The type of computer you will be using at your home or office is probably more general-purpose. It can do just about anything, provided it is given appropriate instructions.

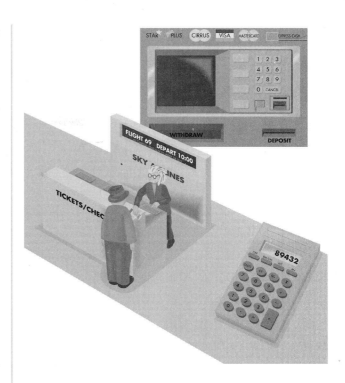

5 Shapes and Sizes of Computers

Computers come in a multitude of shapes, sizes, and types, ranging from those that fit in the palm of your hand or hide in the corner of your microwave or VCR to those that occupy entire rooms; from ones generally used by one person at a time to those simultaneously used by dozens or even hundreds of people. This book is about personal computers—computers primarily designed for use by one person at a time.

6 Personal Computers

Personal computers are relative newcomers to the computer scene. Although the first computers were built in the 1940s, the first personal computers were only introduced in the 1970s and didn't come into widespread use until the 1980s. The speed and capacity of the machines has continued to increase almost as quickly as their size and price shrinks, making them all the more practical and popular. Today's personal computers are hundreds of times more powerful than those sold 10 or 15 years ago, cost less, and can fit in packages the size of a notebook.

How-to Hint

The First Friendly Computer

In 1984, Apple introduced the original Macintosh computer, specifically designed to be easy to learn, fun to use, and unintimidating for the nontechnical user. Although not all this technology was original with Apple, this "user friendly" computer design has come to be the standard for most personal computers.

How-to Hint

Computer Networks

Just because personal computers are "personal" doesn't mean they can't talk to each other. Computer networks are groups of computers that are linked together so they can share information, programs, and/or equipment. Today, a PC can talk to millions of other computers over the Internet as well.

The Brains of the Computer

At the core of every computer is a device roughly the size of a large postage stamp. This device, known as the central processing unit, or CPU, is the "brain" of the computer; it reads and executes program instructions, performs calculations, and makes decisions. The CPU is responsible for storing and retrieving information on disks and other media. It also handles moving information from one part of the computer to another like a central switching station that directs the flow of traffic throughout the computer system.

When placed under a microscope, a CPU chip resembles an aerial photograph of a city.

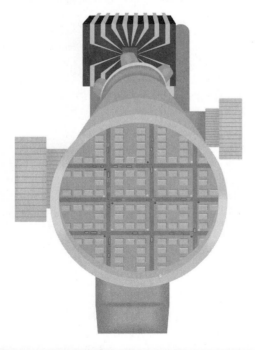

① Integrated Circuits and Transistors

In personal computers, the CPU (also known as the microprocessor) consists of a single integrated circuit. An integrated circuit, or IC, is a matrix of transistors and other electrical components embedded in a small slice of silicon. (Transistors are essentially microscopic electronic switches: tiny devices that can be turned on and off.)

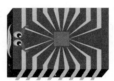

② Where the CPU Lives

Like the dozens of other integrated circuits that inhabit your computer, from the outside a CPU chip looks something like a square ceramic bug with little metal legs. These "legs" are designed to fasten the chip to a fiberglass circuit board that sits inside your computer and to carry electrical impulses into and out of the chip.

③ The Chip

Inside the ceramic case is the chip itself, a slice of silicon about the size of a fingernail. At first glance, it's hard to imagine how this tiny device can run your entire computer. But under a microscope, the slice of silicon reveals an electronic maze so complex that it resembles an aerial photograph of a city, complete with hundreds of intersecting streets and hundreds of thousands of minuscule houses. Most of the "houses" are transistors, and there are usually somewhere between a million and several million of them on a single CPU chip.

④ How Fast Is Your CPU?

The type of CPU that a computer contains determines its processing power—how quickly it can execute various instructions. These days, most CPUs can execute on the order of millions of instructions per second. The type of CPU also determines the precise repertoire of instructions the computer understands and, therefore, which programs it can run.

⑤ Chip Models

In the PC world, people often categorize computers by the model of CPU chip they contain. The CPU chips most commonly used in new PCs are the Pentium III, the Celeron, and Pentium 4. These chips are all made by a company named Intel. Intel's main competitor is AMD, which makes a line of chips called Athlon.

⑥ The System Unit

The CPU resides inside a box known as the system unit, along with various support devices and tools for storing information. You will learn about these other residents of the system unit later in this chapter. For now, just think of the system unit as a container for the CPU. The system unit case—that is, the metal box itself—can either be wider than it is tall, in which case it usually sits on top of your desk, often underneath the screen, or it can be taller than it is wide, in which case it generally sits underneath your desk and is referred to as a tower case.

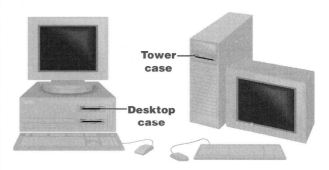

Tower case

Desktop case

How-to Hint

Measuring CPU Speed

Within each class of CPU, speed is measured in terms of the cycle time at which the computer was designed to operate. All computers have built-in clocks that help regulate the flow of information from one part of the computer to another, rather like a metronome. Each pulse of this clock is known as a cycle, and a CPU can perform, at maximum, one operation per cycle. Every CPU is designed to work with a clock that "ticks" at a particular rate. A CPU may be designed to run at 800 megahertz (MHz) for example, meaning 800 million cycles per second.

Input and Output

The other parts of the computer system—that is, the parts outside the system unit—are primarily used as a means of communicating with the CPU, to send in instructions and data and get out information. Devices used to communicate with the CPU are known, collectively, as input and output devices, or I/O devices. Input devices are all those things that allow you to "talk" to your computer—to pose questions and issue commands. Output devices are what allow the computer to talk back, providing you with answers, asking you for additional information, or, at worst, informing you that it has no idea what you are talking about.

1 Keyboard

In personal computers, one of the two most common input devices is the keyboard. Using a keyboard, you can type text and issue commands.

2 Mouse

The other most common input device is a mouse. The mouse is a hand-held pointing device that allows you to point to words or objects on the computer screen. Pressing the buttons on the mouse (called pressing or clicking, depending on how fast you do it) lets you make selections on your screen. A mouse can also be used to move around items onscreen.

You can also communicate with your computer using an input device called a trackball, which is a pointing device that resembles a ball nestled in a square cradle and serves as an alternative to a mouse.

3 Scanner

Another input device is a scanner, which allows you to copy an image (such as a photograph, a drawing, or a page of text) into your computer, translating it into a form that the computer can store and manipulate.

4 Game Controllers

A number of different types of game controllers are commonly used. A joystick is an input device that lets you manipulate the various people, creatures, and machines that populate computer games. Other game controllers include game pads (similar to controllers for video game units) and steering wheel simulators.

5 Digital Camera

A digital camera lets you capture a photographic image in digital (that is, computer-readable) form and then lets you transfer that image directly from camera to computer. Digital video cameras allow you to do the same with video and sound.

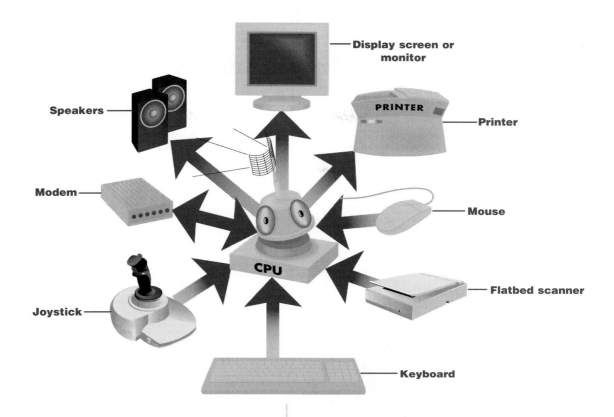

Display screen or monitor

Speakers

Modem

Joystick

PRINTER

Printer

Mouse

CPU

Flatbed scanner

Keyboard

---

6 Monitor

The most common output device is the monitor, which the computer uses to display instructions and present information. There are many types of computer monitors including LCD (liquid crystal display) and CRT (for cathode ray tube, the technology used in most desktop computer screens).

7 Printer

A printer generates paper copies of your data. Like monitors, printers come in many shapes and sizes and generate output ranging from the old grainy-looking computer printouts to color printouts that rival the clarity of offset printing.

8 Speakers

These days, many computers also come equipped with a sound board—a device that resides inside the system unit and allows your computer to generate sounds and music. Most computers have some kind of speakers, which are the output device for the sound board.

How-to Hint

What Are Peripherals?

You may also hear the term *peripherals* applied to I/O devices. Technically, the term peripheral means everything outside the CPU (including I/O devices).

Storing Information

Now you know a little about the CPU of the computer and the devices that you use to communicate with that "brain." There is still one large gap in our image of a computer system, however—storage space.

① What Is Storage?

Although the CPU is terrific at manipulating data and following instructions, it has almost no capacity for storing information. (Think of it as a brilliant but extremely absent-minded professor.) Your computer needs a place to store both programs (the instructions that tell the CPU what to do) and data. You need, in other words, the electronic equivalent of a closet or filing cabinet.

② Disks

In most computers, the primary storage places are disks—which are flat, circular wafers. (You may be used to thinking of computer disks as square because they are always housed inside square plastic jackets, but the disks themselves are round.)

③ Disk Drives

Like compact discs, these computer disks store information that can be "played" by devices known as disk drives. They are in several respects the equivalent of CD players. Like CD players, disk drives have components designed to access the information on a specific area of the disk. These parts are called read/write heads and are equivalent to the laser in a CD player. Disk drives spin the disk so different parts of the surface pass underneath the read/write heads. Most disk drives have at least two read/write heads—one for each side of the disk.

④ Reading and Writing to Disks

Unlike record players or CD players, however, disk drives can record new information on disks as well as play existing information. (In this sense, they're more like cassette tapes than music CDs.) In computer terminology, the process of playing a disk is called reading and the process of recording onto a disk is called writing. (Hence the term read/write head.)

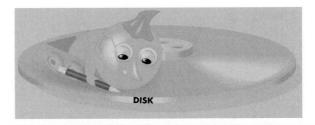

DISK

⑤ Types of Disks

Computer disks come in three basic types: floppy, CD-ROM, and hard. Floppy disks generally hold less information and are slower than hard disks. They can also be removed from their disk drives, so you can "play" different floppy disks in the same drive by removing one and inserting another. CD-ROM discs are similar to floppies in that they are portable. However, CDs hold many times more data than floppies.

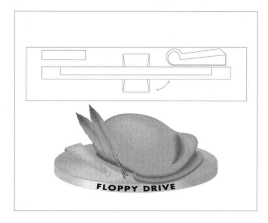

FLOPPY DRIVE

⑥ Floppy Disks

The word floppy refers to the disk itself, which is a thin, round piece of plastic on which information is magnetically recorded (much as music is recorded on the surface of plastic cassette tapes). This decidedly floppy disk is enclosed inside a sturdier, unfloppy plastic jacket to protect it. The disks used in personal computers are usually 3 1/2 inches in diameter.

Inside the floppy disk's jacket is the floppy itself: a very thin piece of plastic.

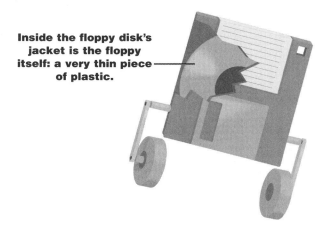

⑦ Hard Disks and Drives

Hard disks hold more information and spin much faster than floppies. They are also permanently enclosed within their disk drives, so the disk and its drive are essentially a single unit. Contrary to what you may think, hard disks are not always physically larger than floppies; they're capable of packing information more tightly, and therefore can store more data in the same amount of space. Most hard drives contain multiple disks, often called platters, that are stacked vertically inside the drive. Typically, each disk has its own pair of read/write heads. Because you never remove hard disks, hard-disk drives do not contain doors or slots, as do their floppy counterparts. This means that the drive itself is completely invisible (and sometimes hard to locate) from outside the system unit.

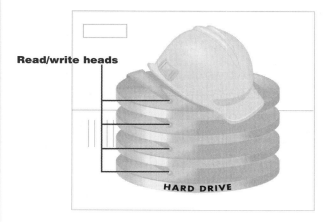

Read/write heads

HARD DRIVE

How-to Hint

What's Data?

In computerese, the term *data* refers to whatever type of information you are trying to manipulate. Data, therefore, includes far more than numbers; it includes any information that you type or otherwise input into the computer. You can also think of data as the raw material that is processed or manipulated by applications programs. If you are using a word processing program, data means the document (letter, memo, poem, novel, legal brief, whatever) you are typing or editing. If you are working with a database program, it may be a set of names and addresses you are adding to your company mailing list.

CD-ROM Drives and Other Drives

These days, most PCs have one hard-disk drive, one floppy disk drive, and a CD-ROM drive. In general, you'll use hard disks as the primary repository of data and programs—the place you store the information that you work with day to day. You'll use floppy drives mainly as a means of getting information into and out of your computer, by transferring information to and from floppy disks.

Most programs are also stored on CD-ROMs instead of floppy disks, and new computers generally come equipped with a CD-ROM drive. As mentioned, a CD-ROM is a type of compact disc that is "meant to be "played" in a computer. CD-ROM stands for compact disc–read-only memory.

① Installing Programs from CD-ROMs or Floppies

When you purchase a new program, it is usually stored on CD-ROMs or floppies. You must copy the program to your hard disk before you can use it. This process of copying these disks to your hard disk is known as installing.

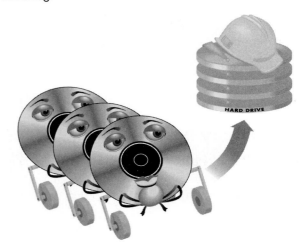

HARD DRIVE

② Backing Up Your Data

You can use floppy disks to ake extra copies of programs or data for safekeeping by copying from the hard disk to floppies. This is known as making backups. If you are working on the great American novel, for example, you will keep your main, working copy on the hard disk but keep an extra copy on a floppy disk, in case there is a mechanical problem with the hard-disk drive or you accidentally erase the original. If you want to be completely safe, you might even keep this duplicate copy in a safe deposit box or a fireproof safe.

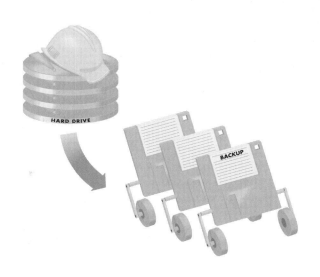

③ Archiving Data

You can use floppy disks to archive data that you don't use regularly (and therefore don't want taking up space on your hard disk) but that you don't want to discard altogether.

④ Transferring Data

You can use floppy disks to transfer data from one computer to another by copying information from one computer's hard disk to a set of floppies, taking the floppies over to the other computer, and copying from those floppies onto the hard disk.

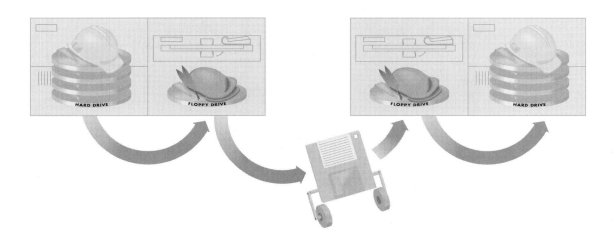

5 CD-ROMs Are Read-Only

You'll learn more about ROM (read-only memory) soon. For now, you just need to know that "read only" means that while you can "read" (access) the programs or data stored on CD-ROMs, you cannot easily "write" (store) your own data or programs on them using most CD-ROM drives. (Recording information on a CD-ROM requires a special type of drive.)

CD-ROM DRIVE

6 CD-ROMs Hold More Data

The reason that so many programs are now stored on CD-ROMs is that CD-ROMs can hold much more information than floppy disks: A single CD-ROM can hold more data than 300 floppies.

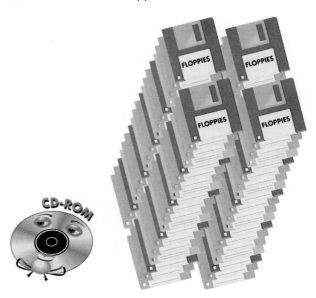

7 Internal CD-ROM Drives

You can only use CD-ROMs if your computer has a CD-ROM drive. Most CD-ROM drives sit inside the system unit and, from the outside, look pretty similar to floppy disk drives. These types of drives are known as internal CD-ROM drives.

8 External CD-ROM Drives

It's also possible to buy external CD-ROM drives. These drives work the same as the internal ones, but they come in their own little boxes that sit outside the system unit and are attached to the system unit via a cable.

9 CD-R and CD-RW Drives

Plain-vanilla CD-ROM drives are just one of many types of drives on the market these days. One special kind of CD-ROM drive is called a CD-Recordable (or CD-R) drive. What's special about these drives is that they are not read-only. That is, you can not only read information from the disks, but can write information to them as well. This feature makes these discs excellent for storage purposes. Another drive, called CD-RW (CD-Rewritable) allows you to write and rewrite to the same CD many times, making it the equivalent of a high-powered floppy disk.

Memory: The Electronic Desktop

6

Given what you've learned so far, you might assume that when you run a program, the CPU fetches instructions from the disk one at a time and executes them, returning to the disk drive every time it finishes a single step. If this were actually the way computers worked, they would be too slow to use.

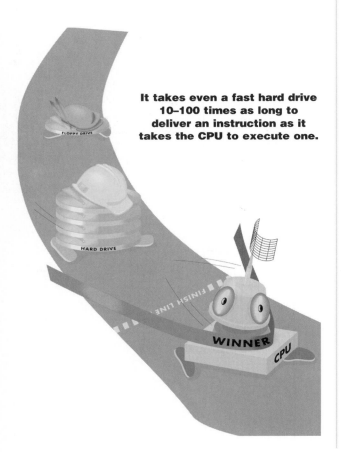

It takes even a fast hard drive 10–100 times as long to deliver an instruction as it takes the CPU to execute one.

1 CPU Speed Versus Disk Drive Speed

Left to their own devices, most personal computer CPUs are capable of executing between one million and one hundred million instructions per second. But because the disk drive is mechanical—that is, composed of moving parts—it cannot deliver program instructions anywhere near that fast. Reading an instruction from the disk involves rotating the disk so that the proper section is below one of the read/write heads and then moving the head closer to or farther from the center of the disk until it is positioned directly above the spot where the instruction is recorded. Even on a hard-disk drive, this process generally takes between 7 and 25 milliseconds (thousandths of a second). CD-ROM drives and floppy drives are slower still.

2 Random Access Memory (RAM)

For the computer to function efficiently, it needs some repository of information that is capable of keeping pace with the CPU. This extra piece is called random access memory, usually referred to as RAM or memory for short.

③ How RAM Works

Physically, RAM consists of a set of separate integrated circuits (each of which looks something like a small CPU chip) that are often mounted on fiberglass boards; in practice, however, memory is treated as a single, contiguous set of storage bins. One useful way to envision memory is as a set of mailboxes, like those inside a post office. Each mailbox holds a single character, and the entire collection of boxes is numbered sequentially. (In computer jargon, the mailboxes are called *bytes* and their numbers are known as *memory addresses*.)

MEMORY MAILBOXES

| 0 | 1 | 2 | 3 | 4 |
| 5 | 6 | 7 | 8 | 9 |

④ Memory Chips

Like the CPU chip, memory chips store and transmit information electronically. Sending an instruction from memory to the CPU is therefore a simple matter of transmitting electrical impulses. There is no waiting for a disk to spin or a read/write head to move to the proper position.

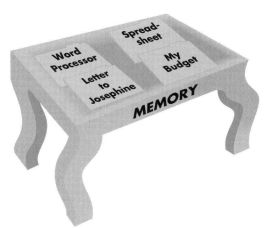

Memory is like an electronic desktop on which you can place the programs and other files you are working with at the moment.

⑤ The Electronic Desktop

Because the CPU can move information into and out of memory so quickly, it uses memory as a kind of electronic desktop—the place it stores whatever it is working on this instant or plans to work with shortly. When you tell your computer that you want to use a particular program, for example, the first thing it does is find the program on your hard disk and copy it into memory. This process is known as loading a program. This gets the comparatively slow process of reading instructions from disk over with at the start. After the entire program has been loaded, the CPU can quickly read instructions from memory as needed.

How-to Hint

Placing Programs in Memory

Although you can compare placing a program in memory to moving it from a file cabinet (the disk) to your desktop (memory), there is also one important difference: Placing something on your desktop entails removing it from its usual storage place in the file cabinet. In contrast, when you place a program in memory, you copy the program and place the copy in memory. The original program stays on the disk, ready to load again whenever you need it.

Loading a Program into Memory

The first program that is loaded into memory in every work session is the operating system. In fact, just about the first thing your CPU does when you turn on your computer is hunt for and load the operating system program. This program then remains in memory until you turn off your computer. When you load application programs, they always share the electronic desktop with the operating system, and, in fact, application programs need to have an operating system around to function. Loading an application program into memory involves several steps.

When you are using an application program, there are three layers of information stored in memory.

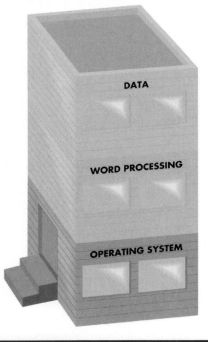

① You Start the Program

You select an option from a menu (onscreen list), type a command, or double-click an icon (picture) to tell the CPU that you want to start the program.

② The Read/Write Head Searches the Hard Disk

The read/write head finds your program on the hard disk.

3 Your Computer Copies the Program into Memory

Your computer copies the program from disk into memory (alongside the operating system).

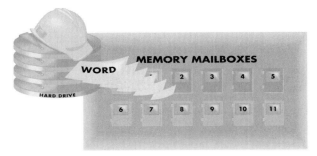

4 The Program Appears Onscreen

The program appears on your screen and you can start using it.

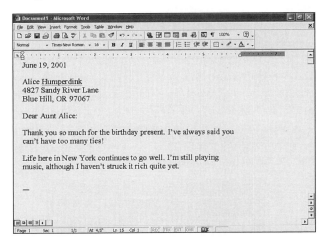

5 Entering Data

When you type in new data while working in an application program or retrieve data from disk, the data is placed in memory as well, alongside the application program and the operating system. The data remains in memory until you either issue a command to close the file (remove it from memory) or leave the application program. Whenever you leave an application program, both the program itself and any data that goes with it are removed from memory. The operating system stays put until you turn off your computer.

Layers of Information

You might find it helpful to think of these three different types of information as a set of layers, each of which depends on the one below. The operating system is the bottom layer, followed by the application program, followed by the data. If you unload any one layer, the layers above are erased as well. If you unload the operating system—for example, by turning off or restarting your system—memory is completely erased. If you unload an application program from memory, by issuing that program's exit or quit command, both the program and the data you were working on inside that program are erased from memory. If you unload just the top layer—the data you are working with—by closing a particular word processing document, for example, both the application program (in this case, the word processing program) and the operating system remain loaded and ready to use.

Don't Confuse Memory with Disk Storage

Don't confuse erasing a program from memory with removing it from disk. Even if you erase an application program or a data file from memory, it should still be present on your hard disk (assuming you saved it there), and you can go back and retrieve it another time.

Saving Data

As you just learned, programs are not the only things that the CPU places in memory. It stores data there as well. As shown in this figure, each character that you enter, including any spaces, occupies a single "mailbox" of storage space.

Every character of data that you enter (including a space) occupies a single "mailbox" (byte) in memory.

MEMORY MAILBOXES

0 D	**1** E	**2** A	**3** R	**4**	**5** M
6 S	**7** .	**8**	**9** P	**10** R	**11** U
12 N	**13** D	**14** I	**15** M	**16** P	**17** L
18 E	**19** :	**20**	**21** Y	**22** O	**23** U
24	**25** H	**26** A	**27** V	**28** E	**29**
30 W	**31** O	**32** N	**33**	**34** T	**35** E
36 N	**37**	**38** T	**39** R	**40** I	**41** L
42 L	**43** I	**44** O	**45** N	**46**	**47** D

① Storing Data in Memory

There is one fundamental problem with housing data in memory: As soon as your computer is turned off, the contents of memory are erased. This means that if you accidentally kick your computer's power cord in the midst of typing a letter, for example, everything you have typed is lost. It also means that you can't rely on memory if you want to return to a piece of work the next day or next week, because you will undoubtedly turn off your computer in between.

② Erasing Data from Memory

Data is also erased from memory whenever you leave an application program, because the CPU assumes you'll need to use the space for the next task you choose to tackle. If you are using a spreadsheet program, for example, the CPU erases the spreadsheet you were using from memory as soon as you exit that program, just as you might clear your desk when you finish a particular project.

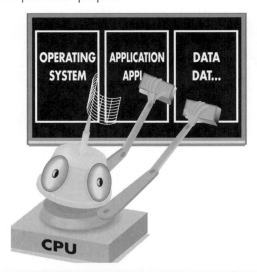

OPERATING SYSTEM | APPLICATION APPL... | DATA DAT...

CPU

③ Saving Your Data

To protect your work and to store it for use in future work sessions, you need to copy it from memory to a more secure storage place—namely, a disk. This process is known as saving your data. Don't worry about how, exactly, you tell your computer to save data; the procedure may vary from one application program to another or, at minimum, from operating system to operating system. For now, just focus on when you need to save and why.

④ When to Save

In general, you should save your data whenever you are done working with it and are ready to start on another project (if you finish typing one letter and want to start another one, for example). You should also save your data when you are ready to leave an application program.

⑤ Saving Automatically

For your convenience, most programs automatically ask whether you want to save when you give the command to exit or to close a document. You should also save to disk whenever you have been working for a while and want to protect the work you have done so far. This protects your data against power failures, kicked power cords, or drastic mistakes.

⑥ Retrieving Data

After something is stored on disk, you can copy it back into memory when you want to use it again. This is known as retrieving data or opening a document or file. As soon as the data is copied back into memory, the data reappears on your screen and you can modify it if you like. In general, any data that appears onscreen while you're using an application program is currently in memory, although not all the data in memory may fit on your screen at one time.

How-to Hint

Save Early, Save Often

How often should you save? A good rule of thumb is that you should save your work every time you'd be unhappy if you had to do it over again. For some people, this will be once an hour; for others, it will be every two minutes. Bear in mind that when you save something, you are not removing it from memory. You are making a copy and then storing that copy on disk. You can then continue modifying the original if you like.

How-to Hint

When Not to Save

Occasionally, you will enter some data that you have no need or desire to save. For example, you may use a word processing program to type a short letter that you need to print but don't need to store for future reference. Or you may load your spreadsheet program to perform a few calculations and have no need to save the results. In such cases, you can close the document without saving your data and it won't take up space on your hard disk.

What's So Random About RAM?

As mentioned, the type of memory we have been discussing—that is, the memory used to temporarily house programs and data—is called random access memory, or RAM for short. To understand where this name comes from, you need to know more about how information is stored in memory.

1 Sequential Access

Remember, the CPU treats memory as a set of numbered storage bins, rather like a collection of mailboxes, each one of which holds a single character. In early computers, the CPU had to access the mailboxes (bytes) in numerical order, starting from the first mailbox and moving forward until it reached the one that actually contained the desired information. This is known as sequential access. With the development of random access memory, the CPU can go directly to whichever mailbox it is interested in.

2 Random Access Versus Sequential Access

You can conceptualize the difference between random access memory and this older type of sequential access memory by comparing music CDs to cassette tapes. If you want to listen to the fifth song on a cassette tape (sequential access), you have to start at the beginning of the tape and move past the first four songs, even if you fast-forward the tape. With a music CD (random access), you can go directly to song five. Disks are random access devices, too. Rather than starting from the outside of the disk and reading inward, or from the inside and reading outward, the read/write head can jump directly to the spot where the desired data is stored.

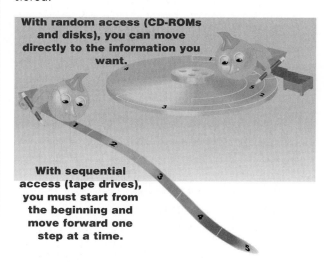

With random access (CD-ROMs and disks), you can move directly to the information you want.

With sequential access (tape drives), you must start from the beginning and move forward one step at a time.

③ What Is ROM?

There is actually a second type of memory used in personal computers, in addition to RAM. This second type of memory is named read-only memory, or ROM (rhymes with Tom). Unlike RAM chips, ROM chips have software (program instructions) etched into their circuitry. For this reason, ROM is often referred to as firmware—because it's kind of halfway between hardware and software.

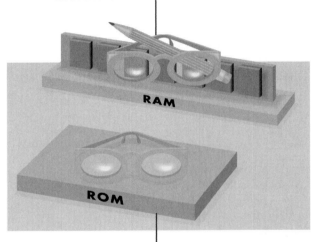

RAM is read/write memory. The CPU can store information in it as well as retrieve the information it holds.

ROM is read-only memory. The CPU cannot change its contents.

④ RAM Versus ROM

Both RAM and ROM allow random access. If the point were to distinguish RAM from ROM, then RAM would more properly be called read/write memory, meaning that you can both retrieve (read) information from RAM, and record (write) information to it. In contrast, with read-only memory (ROM), instructions are frozen into the circuitry. The feature that sets RAM apart from ROM is its changeability: the fact that you can alter its contents at will.

⑤ Short-Term and Long-Term Memory

The other difference between RAM and ROM is how long their memories last. RAM is short-term memory; it forgets everything it knows as soon as you turn off your computer. ROM is long-term memory; it remembers everything it has ever known as long as it lives. It's the elephant of the memory kingdom.

⑥ ROM Stores Part of the Operating System

In personal computers, ROM is generally used to store some part of the operating system. In IBM-type PCs, only a small part of the operating system is stored in ROM—just enough to get the hardware up and running and to tell the CPU how to locate and load the rest of the operating system from disk.

How-to Hint

You Don't Have to Worry About ROM

ROM is changeable, but chances are you will never have to deal with it yourself. It's just another part of your computer to know about, even if you never need to see it, touch it, or think about it much at all. Don't worry about changing it unless a qualified technician informs you that it is necessary.

What's in a Byte: How Memory and Disks Are Measured

As mentioned, the term byte means the amount of space required to represent a single character—a letter, a number, or even a space. (In our mailboxes analogy, it's a single mailbox.) This term is used regardless of whether you're talking about space in memory, on a disk, or on any other storage medium. Because many, many bytes are often required to accommodate an entire word processing document, spreadsheet, database, or program, computerese includes terms for several larger units of measurement.

❶ Kilobyte

A kilobyte (often abbreviated as KB or K) is 1,024 bytes. To a computer's way of thinking, 1,024 is a nice round number. (Computers "think" in units of two, and 1,024 is 2 to the 10th power.) To us, however, it's a little unwieldy, so most people think of a kilobyte as "around 1,000" bytes. In other words, 100KB equals approximately 100,000 characters.

❷ Megabyte

The term megabyte (abbreviated as MB or meg) means a kilobyte squared (1,024 times 1,024), or approximately one million bytes. A floppy disk whose capacity is 1.44MB can hold 1,440,000 characters. (This is a standard capacity for high-density 3 1/2-inch floppies.)

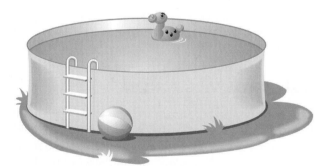

A megabyte would fill a small swimming pool (1,500 gallons).

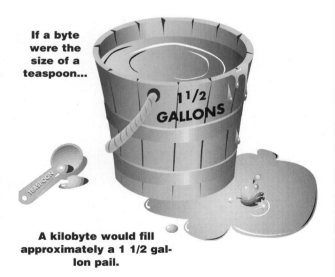

If a byte were the size of a teaspoon...

A kilobyte would fill approximately a 1 1/2 gallon pail.

3 Gigabyte and Terabyte

The term gigabyte (abbreviated GB or gig) means a kilobyte to the third power (1,024 times 1,024 times 1,024), or approximately one billion bytes. The term terabyte (abbreviated TB or T) means a kilobyte to the fourth power (1,024 times 1,024 times 1,024 times 1,024). Right now, there are no reasonably priced terabyte hard drives.

A gigabyte would fill an entire lake (1.5 million gallons).

4 How Much Memory Is Enough?

Although a few years ago most computers had less than 1MB of RAM, these days most new computers have 128MB or more. Hard disks typically hold several gigabytes. Just to give you a measuring stick, a typical printed page of text, using single spacing, contains 2,500 to 3,000 characters. Therefore, 1MB holds close to 400 pages of single-spaced text.

5 Why Is Memory Important?

So why do you care how much memory your computer has? Because it determines what kinds of work you can do. The amount of memory in your computer dictates which programs you can run. Many Windows programs, for example, run best with 64MB or more of memory and cannot run at all on computers with less than 32MB.

6 Memory for Programs

The size of your hard disk is important because it defines how many programs and how much data you can store on your computer at once. In general, you will want enough room on your hard disk to accommodate all the programs and data that you work with regularly. Otherwise, you'll waste time copying data or programs to and from floppies. These days, each program you install requires 80MB or more of disk space, not including room for data. (Check the documentation that comes with the program if you're not sure.)

How-to Hint

Upgrading Memory

Bear in mind that you can almost always add memory to your computer by buying additional memory chips and having them installed. If you are brave and have a good upgrading book, you may even be able to install the memory chips yourself. You can also add an additional hard drive if your current drive runs out of room.

Inside the System Unit

Now that you know what the CPU, memory chips, and disk drives do, you're ready to learn about where they reside and how they're connected. In most computer systems, all three of these components are housed inside the system unit. (Some computer systems have an external disk drive instead of, or in addition to, the ones inside the system unit.)

1 The Motherboard

The centerpiece of the system unit is a printed circuit board, known as the motherboard, which holds the CPU chip and its support circuitry. (You may also hear the motherboard referred to as the system board.) The motherboard generally lies face up at the bottom of the system unit.

2 Support Chips

The motherboard contains several other types of chips, in addition to the CPU, that help the CPU perform its job. One such support chip is the clock chip, which serves as the computer's metronome, setting the pace at which the various components function. There are also one or more ROM chips containing some part of the operating system software.

3 Memory Chips

Finally, the motherboard usually includes sockets for memory chips. In most cases, memory comes in the form of small, plug-in boards called SIMMs (single inline memory modules) or DIMMs (dual inline memory modules), each of which includes eight or nine memory chips.

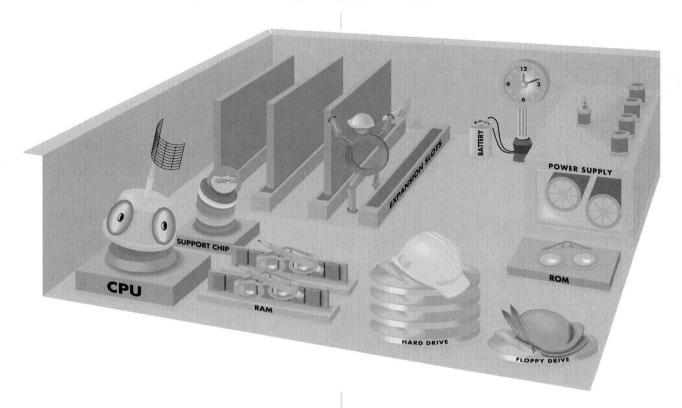

The illustration is labeled with: CPU, SUPPORT CHIP, RAM, EXPANSION SLOTS, BATTERY, POWER SUPPLY, ROM, HARD DRIVE, FLOPPY DRIVE

④ Disk Drives and the Power Supply

Aside from the motherboard, the system unit includes disk drives (usually one or two floppy drives and one hard drive) and a power supply. The power supply brings in power from the wall socket and supplies it to the motherboard. It also contains your computer's on/off switch and a place to attach the power cord that connects the system unit to a power outlet. The power supply unit usually contains a fan, to prevent the various chips from overheating. If your system includes an internal CD-ROM drive, modem, or tape drive, it probably resides in the system unit as well.

⑤ Expansion Boards

Most computers also contain additional circuit boards, commonly known as expansion boards, that fit into slots on the motherboard. (The slots themselves are known as expansion slots; think of them as parking spaces for circuit boards.) Expansion boards sit at the back of the system unit at a right angle to the motherboard itself. The purpose of most expansion boards is to allow an I/O (input/output) device—such as a display monitor or a scanner—to communicate with the CPU.

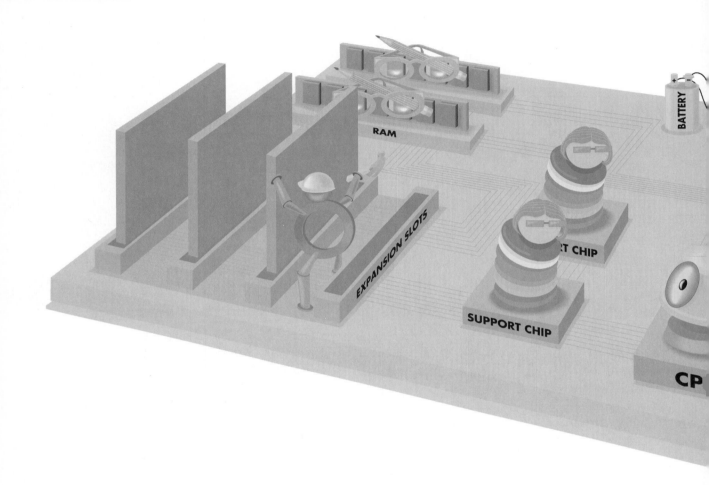

RAM

EXPANSION SLOTS

BATTERY

RT CHIP

SUPPORT CHIP

CP

6 Ports

Expansion boards that are designed to serve as intermediaries between the CPU and some device outside the system unit have ports on one end. Ports are sockets that protrude from the back of the system unit. You can think of them as places where you can "dock" various external devices, plugging them into a circuit board that, in turn, connects them to the CPU. (Expansion boards that are designed for components inside the system unit—such as disk drives—do not include ports.)

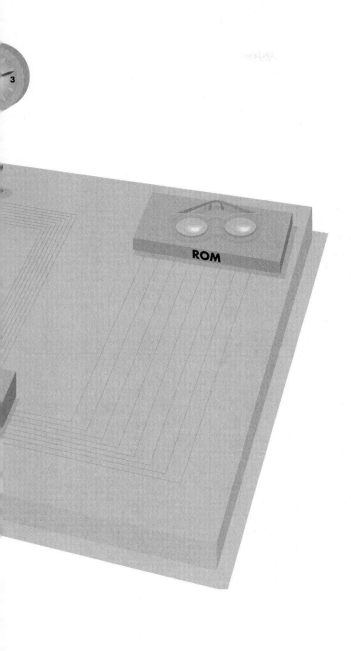

ROM

7 The Bus

Finally, all motherboards contain a bus: a set of circuitry designed to carry data and instructions back and forth between various devices on the board itself. You might think of the bus as a collection of elaborate, high-speed conveyor belts. The bus not only carries data and instructions back and forth between the CPU and memory (both RAM and ROM), it also connects the CPU and memory to any expansion boards that are plugged into the motherboard.

How-to Hint

Customizing Your System

The advantage of this design—a motherboard containing all the standard circuitry of the computer and a set of expansion slots that allow you to plug in additional circuitry as needed—is that it allows you to customize your system. Two people can buy essentially the same computer but add on different sets of peripherals. This design also allows you to easily add new parts to your computer as your needs change or as new forms of computer paraphernalia are invented.

2

Important Parts

In Chapter 1, "Computer Basics," you were introduced to computer hardware. In this chapter you'll go a little further, learning some of the finer points about peripherals.

In many cases, this chapter discusses some piece of hardware that you already have, either at work or at home. If instead you're in the market for either a new computer or new peripherals, there are several ways to research which model is best. Computer magazines regularly review various types of hardware, presenting articles on the latest printers or newest storage devices. These are excellent sources of comparative information because they frequently present tables comparing price, features, speed, and other criteria. Friends and coworkers can also be a good source of information, or at least a source of information on which models to stay away from. You can also shop online by calling up the Internet sites for various computer manufacturers and comparing features and prices yourself. You can also compare computers at online review sites such as CNET (www.cnet.com).

The Front of Your Computer

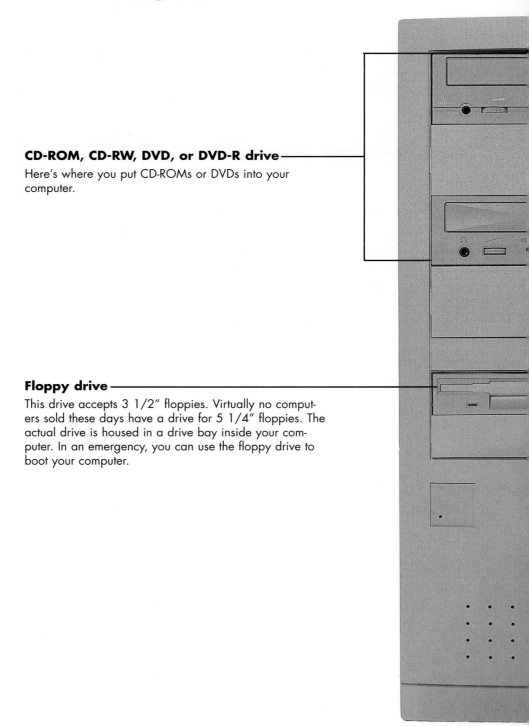

CD-ROM, CD-RW, DVD, or DVD-R drive

Here's where you put CD-ROMs or DVDs into your computer.

Floppy drive

This drive accepts 3 1/2" floppies. Virtually no computers sold these days have a drive for 5 1/4" floppies. The actual drive is housed in a drive bay inside your computer. In an emergency, you can use the floppy drive to boot your computer.

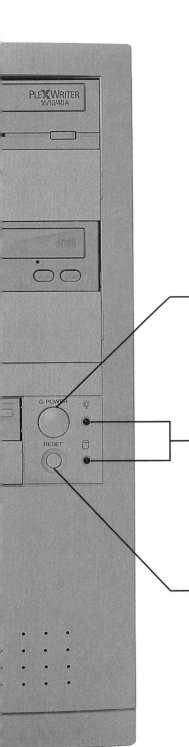

On/off switch

You use this switch to turn your PC on and off. Although your PC often will turn off automatically when you shut it down in Windows, you can use this switch to turn off your computer if it locks up for some reason. You may need to press the button for several seconds.

Indicator lights

You'll find a variety of lights on the front of your computer that give you vital information about its operation. A power light tells you when the power is on; a hard disk light flashes on when the hard disk is being accessed; and a reset light goes on when the computer is reset.

Reset switch

Use this switch to shut down and restart your computer. Use it only in case of an emergency; it's a better idea to shut down your computer in the normal manner, by using software or the on/off switch.

The Back of Your Computer

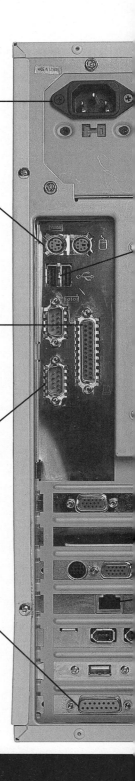

Power cord plug

Here's where you plug your power cord into your computer. The cord sends electricity from the wall outlet to the power supply inside your PC.

Mouse and keyboard ports

Your keyboard and mouse plug into ports that generally look exactly like each other. There is usually a small picture of a mouse next to the mouse port and a small picture of a keyboard next to the keyboard port. Sometimes the ports and plugs are color-coded, to make figuring out where to plug in the keyboard and the mouse even easier.

Parallel port

The printer plugs into the parallel port, sometimes called the printer port. Pictured here is the common 25-pin printer port. Other devices, such as scanners, also plug into the parallel port. Your computer often calls the parallel port LPT, such as LPT1 or LPT2.

Serial port

Different kinds of devices can plug into a serial port, such as modems and mice. Most serial ports are 9-pin and are a male connector—in other words, the pins stick up and plug into a female plug that has 9 holes in it. Some serial ports, however, are larger and have 25 pins in them. Serial ports are also called COM ports. Converters are available to convert a 9-pin port to a 25-pin port, or vice versa.

Game port

A variety of devices, such as joysticks, plug into the game port—a 15-hole female port usually attached to the portion of the sound card that sticks outside the back of your computer. On some machines, you might find two game ports: one on the sound card and one above either the serial port or the parallel port. It's best to use the sound card game port.

Fan

Your power supply can get hot and need to be cooled off. A fan in it cools it off by blowing air out the back of the computer. There might also be other fans in your computer. These can be fan cards that plug into a expansion slot, are built into the case, or are on the microprocessor itself.

Universal Serial Bus (USB) port

These ports enable you to connect devices such as scanners, printers, monitors, keyboards, MP3 players, and more to your computer. They enable you to hook them up without having to open the case of your computer. Older PCs don't have USB ports, whereas newer ones usually have one or two.

Modem jack

If your computer has an internal modem (this one does not), it will have modem jacks, into which a phone line can plug to give you access to the Internet. A modem typically has two jacks, so if you want to share a phone line with your telephone, you can run a wire from the jack labeled phone to the telephone and a wire from the other jack, labeled line, to the phone line.

Video port

Your monitor plugs into the video port. In most cases, it is a 15-hole female port, which is for a VGA or Super VGA monitor. Other devices, such as projectors, can be attached to the video port as well. In addition, other ports might be associated with the video port, such as a TV-out port.

LAN connection

Some computers connect to the Internet through a local area network (LAN) card. The card is in turn connected to a cable. In homes, this cable can be connected to a DSL or cable modem for a high-speed connection to the Internet.

Audio port

Speakers or headphones plug into an audio port, typically connected to a sound card.

A Look Inside Your Computer

Microprocessor (CPU)

This is the brains of your PC, also called a CPU (central processing unit). It does most of the processing and computations. On many PCs, you can replace the microprocessor with a faster one—although the motherboard has to specifically enable the new, faster microprocessor to be plugged in at a specific speed.

CPU fan

CPUs can run hot and need to be cooled down so they don't get damaged. Fans cool them off.

Expansion slots

These hold the expansion cards, also called adapters, that expand how your PC can be used, such as video cards, disk controllers, and similar add-ins. Among the common standards for expansion slots are the Advanced Graphics Port (AGP) for graphics cards, and PCI and ISA for many types of devices. ISA slots are becoming less common than PCI slots.

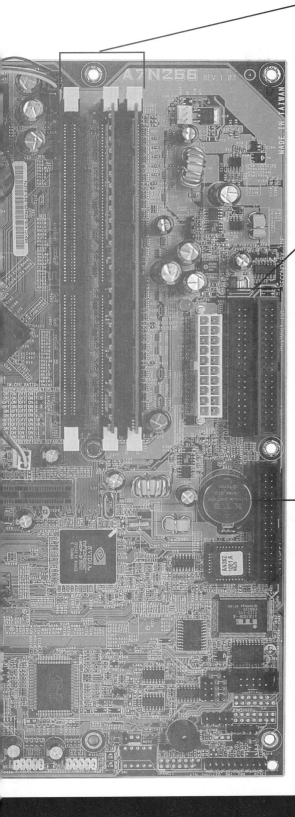

RAM (random access memory)

This is the memory where programs are run and data is stored while the data is being manipulated. When you turn off your computer, any information in RAM is lost. The more RAM you have, the more programs you can run at once.

IDE connectors

These connect hard disks and other devices to the motherboard.

CMOS battery

A small battery that provides power to the CMOS chip.

Power supply

Provides power to your PC by converting the current from your wall outlet to the type of power that can be used by your PC and all its components. Some power supplies also have a second plug for attaching your monitor.

Ports

These let you plug in devices such as a keyboard, modem, printer, and mouse. Some ports are connected to the motherboard, whereas others are connected to expansion cards. Ports stick through the back of the PC, where they are accessible.

Motherboard

This contains the main circuitry of the computer and provides the way in which all components communicate with one another. All components of a PC plug into the motherboard in one way or another.

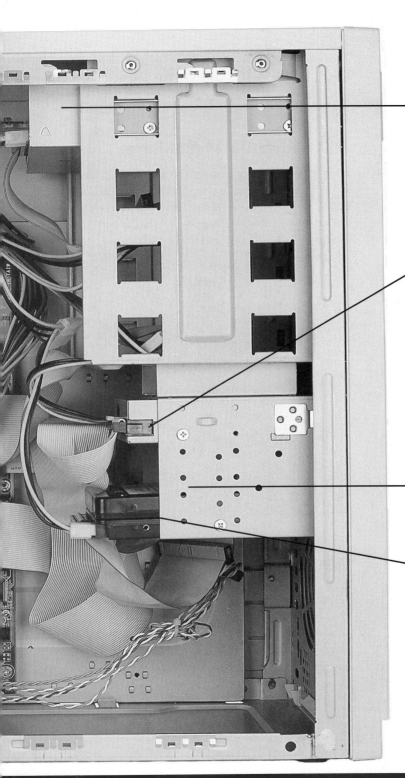

Removable drive

Removable drives such as CD-ROMs, DVDs, and Zip drives store data permanently like a hard drive but hold data on removable disks. These disks commonly hold several hundred megabytes of data or even several gigabytes of data. The drives are visible from the front of your PC.

Floppy drive

The floppy drive stores data in the same way as does a hard drive, but it stores information on removable disks that hold only 1.44MB of data. In an emergency, you can start your computer from the floppy drive.

Drive bays

These are where you put hard drives, CD-ROM drives, floppy drives, and similar add-ins.

Hard drive

This is where the operating system, the programs, and your data are stored. Hard disks commonly have several gigabytes or more of space.

Monitors

The monitor is your computer's primary output device—it's a tool for displaying information, soliciting information, and responding to your requests. It's also likely to be the center of your attention most of the time you are using the computer. As a result, it's hard to overestimate the importance of a good monitor, meaning one that's clear, easy to read, and free of glare and flicker. A good monitor can make staring at the screen for eight hours bearable. A bad one can cause headaches, fatigue, and eye strain (not to mention grumpiness).

❶ Varieties of Monitors

New PCs have color monitors. Most are enclosed in a large box, similar to a small TV. Some desktop computers now use flat-panel displays, which use LCD (liquid crystal display) technology similar to that used by laptops. Flat-panel displays can be expensive, but they do save space.

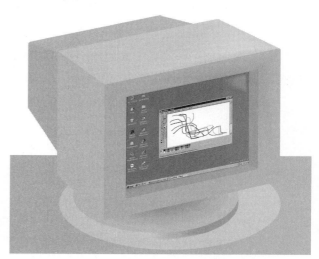

Monitors come in all shapes and sizes.

❷ Monitor Sizes

Monitors also come in a wide range of sizes. (Monitor size is almost always measured diagonally across the screen.) At the small end are the standard 14-inch screens found on most low-end PCs. At the large end are 21-inch screens. Some specialty screens are even larger.

③ The Video Adapter

The monitor works with a video adapter that translates instructions from your computer into a form your monitor can use. Many systems now have the video adapter embedded on the motherboard. In others, the video adapter is an expansion board that fits into a slot on your computer's motherboard. Video adapters are also called display adapter cards, video cards, or video hardware. You might also hear the acronyms for various types of video cards, such as VGA and SVGA.

④ What Comes with Your Computer?

When you buy a new computer, it almost always contains a video adapter. (You probably will only need to buy a new video adapter if you buy a larger monitor or start running more graphics-intensive programs, either of which may require a more powerful and expensive video adapter.) The monitor itself may either be sold as part of the system or purchased separately.

⑤ What's a Cathode Ray Tube?

The monitors for most desktop computers work just like television sets: They use something called a cathode ray tube (CRT) to project images onto a screen. A CRT is essentially a vacuum tube with an electron gun at one end and a flat screen at the other. The electron gun "shoots" a single stream of electrons at the screen. The inside of the screen is coated with special particles, known as phosphors, that glow when struck by the electrons.

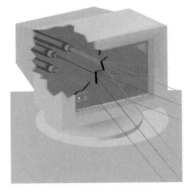

Inside a CRT, one or more electron guns at the back of the monitor shoot electrons toward the screen. When the electrons hit phosphors on the inside of the screen, the phosphors glow, creating patterns of dots on your screen.

⑥ How Monitors Work

In color monitors, there are three electron guns, and each screen dot consists of three phosphor dots: one red, one green, and one blue. The color of the dot onscreen depends on the intensities of the various electron streams. In both types of monitors, each of the electron beams is directed at one spot at a time, but the beams themselves move, scanning horizontally across a single line of the screen, then dropping down a line and scanning across that one, and so on. As various phosphors are struck by the electron beam(s), they glow for a fraction of a second and then fade again. To keep the image from fading or flickering, the monitor must hit the same phosphors with electrons dozens of times in one second. The term refresh rate means the amount of time it takes the monitor to scan across and down the entire screen, "re-zapping" all the phosphors.

How-to Hint

Refresh Rates

If you are shopping for a new monitor, you'll want to compare the highest refresh rate that your monitor can support at various resolutions. (You'll learn all about screen resolution and how to change it shortly.) The higher the refresh rate, the better.

How-to Hint

Check the Display

Never buy a monitor until you see it running the software you plan to use. Some monitors are great at displaying color photographs and horrible at displaying text, and vice versa. Make sure your monitor is well-suited to the particular task you have in mind.

Video Standards and Screen Resolutions

Most new monitors and video adapters are capable of displaying images at various resolutions by using different numbers of dots per inch. When you use a lower resolution, the image expands: You see less on the screen but everything you do see is larger, as if you were looking through a magnifying glass. When you use a higher resolution, everything on the screen shrinks, allowing you to see more information at once. Screen resolution depends on three things: your monitor, your video adapter, and your software. As you already know, the monitor determines whether you can display images in color. It also sets the upper limit of the screen resolution—that is, how many dots per inch you can display onscreen. Some older monitors were designed to display images at only one resolution. Most newer monitors are multisync monitors, meaning that they can display images at various resolutions.

1 Pixels

Resolution is described in terms of number of pixels. A *pixel*, which is short for *picture element*, is a dot used to construct screen images. In the PC world, resolution is usually described in terms of the number of pixels displayed horizontally by the number of pixels displayed vertically across the entire screen.

A spreadsheet at 800×600 resolution.

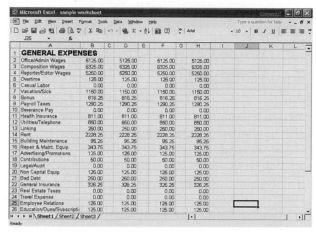

The same spreadsheet at 1024×768 resolution.

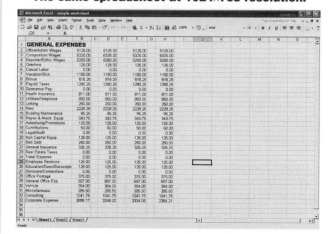

2 Video Standards

The video adapter you are using determines whether you can display graphics and, if so, which of several video standards and resolutions you can use. There are several standards for PC video cards, including VGA (Video Graphics Array). A regular VGA adapter displays images at 640×480 resolution (meaning 640 dots horizontally by 480 vertically). Super VGA is an enhancement of the VGA standard. It allows for higher resolutions (800×600, 1024×768, and in some cases 1280×1024). Virtually all computer systems sold today feature Super VGA adapters.

3 The Default Windows Resolution

By default, Windows displays information in 800×600 resolution. Increasing the resolution can dramatically increase the amount of information you can see at one time. However, because more pixels mean more work for your computer, you may notice a corresponding decrease in performance, particularly on slower systems. Additionally, the higher the resolution, the smaller the individual characters and pictures on the screen.

4 How Many Colors Should You Use?

There is a similar trade-off with colors. Windows displays images using a 16-bit color palette by default (or 65,536 colors). You can increase the number of colors (sometimes called the color depth) to 16.8 million colors (referred to as true color, and sometimes also called 24-bit color) or even higher. The greater the number of colors, the clearer your graphic images will be. The downside, again, is speed. The more colors your computer has to display, the longer it will take to display images on the screen. If you are displaying pictures, photographs, or videos, you might want to use a setting higher than 16-bit color. But if all you're doing is word processing, manipulating a database, or creating spreadsheets, 16-bit color should be adequate and may give you better performance.

5 Changing Your Screen Resolution

To change the resolution of your screen display, right-click the desktop, choose Properties from the context menu to open the Display Properties dialog box, and click the Settings tab. Drag the Screen Resolution slider to the right for higher resolution (more pixels per inch) or to the left for lower resolution (fewer pixels per inch); the precise resolution setting (800×600 pixels, or whatever) will appear below the slider. Then click OK. (A few video adapters have their own utility programs for changing screen resolution, which you use instead of the Windows Display Properties dialog box.) If Windows asks you to restart your machine, go ahead and follow the instructions.

6 Adjusting the Number of Display Colors

To adjust the number of colors used in your display, open the Settings tab of the Display Properties dialog box (as described previously) and use the Colors drop-down list to select the number of colors. Remember that the more colors you use, the greater the demand on your system. The range of choices you have for resolution, font size, and color density depends on your monitor, your display adapter, and the video drivers you have. If you are unable to drag the Desktop Area slider, for example, then either your monitor or display adapter only supports a single resolution, or you only have a video driver for that one resolution.

Taking Care of Your Monitor

Although monitors tend to be fairly low-maintenance machines, there are a few basics you should know about their care.

① Power Saving Monitors

Some monitors feature an energy-saving mode, which both reduces the monitor's power consumption and minimizes wear and tear on the monitor itself. If you have a "green" monitor—that is, a monitor that features an energy-saving mode—whenever you haven't touched the keyboard or mouse for a while, the screen goes blank and only a bare minimum of electricity continues to flow to the monitor. As soon as you touch your keyboard or mouse, the monitor returns to normal mode (and the normal amount of energy consumption).

② Using a Screen Saver

Whether or not you have a green monitor, you might elect to use a screen saver, a special program that either blanks out the screen or displays a moving image (like fish swimming or toasters flying) whenever you haven't touched the keyboard or mouse for a certain amount of time. After the screen saver image appears, you can always restore the previous screen image by moving your mouse or pressing any key. Screen savers got their name because they used to help prolong the life of a monitor. With today's monitors, that's no longer necessary; now they are mostly for fun!

③ Configuring Your Screen Saver

First, right-click the screen and select Properties. Next, select the Screen Saver tab. Use the pull-down menu to select the particular screen saver that interests you. With some screen savers, you can adjust settings such as how fast the image moves. Do this by clicking the Settings button and making your selections.

④ Taking Care of Your Monitor

Another way to pamper your monitor is to clean the screen periodically. Most monitors pick up an inordinate amount of dust, not to mention fingerprints. You can often get rid of both by wiping the screen with a soft, dry cloth. You can also safely clean most monitors with a glass cleaner, provided you spray the cleaner on a cleaning cloth rather than directly on the screen. A few monitors have special coatings, designed to cut down on glare, that may not take kindly to cleaners. If you have an expensive monitor, be sure to check the monitor manual for warnings and advice before you apply anything but a dry cloth to the screen.

⑤ Taking Care of Yourself

Then there's the issue of taking care of yourself while you use a monitor. Most monitors have contrast and brightness controls, usually on the front of the monitor but sometimes on the side or back. Use these to make the image as clear and easy on your eyes as possible. And remember that a badly positioned monitor can be, literally, a pain in the neck. You can minimize neck strain by positioning the monitor so that its upper edge is at or just below eye level. Most monitors also have swivel stands that you can use to adjust the angle of the screen to eliminate glare and/or neck strain. Finally, to prevent eye strain, look away from your monitor every few minutes, letting your eyes settle on a person or object that's further away.

How-to Hint | Using Power-Saving Measures

In an effort to save electricity and reduce wear and tear on your monitor, you can set it to shut off automatically after a certain amount of time without use. Right-click the screen and select Properties, then select the Screen Saver tab. Click the Power button, and you'll be able to create settings for when the monitor should automatically power down.

How-to Hint | Screen Saver Options

In addition to the screen savers that are included within Windows, there are a large number of commercially available screen saver programs and some that can be downloaded for free off the Internet.

Printers

For years, people have predicted that computers would make paper obsolete. Although this may be true in the long run, in the short run they seem to be having the opposite effect. By giving people the power to endlessly manipulate and analyze their data, computers have facilitated the production of mountains of reports and memos that we had somehow previously managed to live without. For most of us, printing is still the final step in any project we undertake on the computer. When you finish the letter, you print and send it. When you get done calculating how much money you could make if only you did X, you print the spreadsheet and show it to your spouse, boss, or coworkers. Sooner or later, you'll want a hard copy, if for no other reason than that it's easy to carry around and show to others.

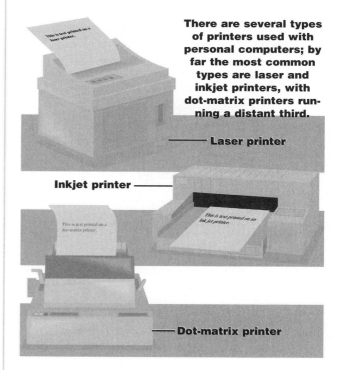

There are several types of printers used with personal computers; by far the most common types are laser and inkjet printers, with dot-matrix printers running a distant third.

Laser printer

Inkjet printer

Dot-matrix printer

❶ Laser Printers

Laser printers print better, faster, and more quietly than other printers, producing output that looks close to type-set. Laser printers are also more expensive, ranging from about $300 all the way up to $6,000 (with most falling in the $400 to $1,000 range). Like photocopiers, they produce images by electrically charging a metal drum that then attracts particles of toner in a specific pattern. The drum rolls across a piece of paper that has an even greater electrical charge, causing the toner to jump from drum to page.

❷ Benefits and Drawbacks of Laser Printers

Laser printers involve no impact—that is, there are no wires or other moving parts that strike the paper, making laser printers extremely quiet. Laser printers also cannot print on continuous forms of any kind, including sticky mailing labels. The advertised speeds for laser printers typically range from 12 to 24 pages per minute. Take these ratings with a grain of salt, however, since they measure the speed it takes to print a single page of text (sans graphics) over and over. When you're printing different pages, and especially when you're printing graphics, you can expect less speed.

❸ Laser Printer Resolution

The quality of laser printer output is typically measured in terms of resolution. Resolution refers to the density of dots used to construct characters or symbols on the page. Laser printers typically print at a resolution of somewhere between 300 and 1,800 dots per inch (dpi). (Typesetting machines typically print at 1270 dpi and up.) Bear in mind that 300 dpi means 300 dots per inch horizontally by 300 dots per inch vertically, for a maximum of 90,000 dots in any square inch of a page. This is more than adequate for most business correspondence. You may want a higher resolution for desktop publishing or printing graphics.

❹ Inkjet Printers

Unlike laser printers, which print an entire page at once, inkjet printers have print heads that move horizontally across the page, applying ink one line at a time. Although the resolution offered by inkjet printers is similar, the ink tends to spread through the fiber of the paper as it dries, giving characters a slightly fuzzy quality. Inkjet printers also tend to be a bit slower than laser printers, producing 1–12 pages per minute, and cheaper ($75 to $500 as of this writing, with the higher prices reserved for high-end color inkjets). Most color printers currently sold are inkjets. There are some color laser printers as well, but they are generally too expensive for use in homes or small offices.

❺ Dot-Matrix Printers

Dot-matrix printers work by striking a cloth, nylon, or mylar ribbon with a set of small wires. The resulting characters are composed of a pattern of dots, just like characters displayed on a monitor. Because dot-matrix printers are impact printers—that is, they have components that actually strike the page through an ink-laden ribbon—they are perfect for printing multipart forms. They can print labels, checks, and other continuous forms designed to be fed through a printer in a single stream. (Such forms have little holes on the edges that fit over sprockets in the printer's tractor feed mechanism so they can be pulled through the printer.) Dot-matrix printers aren't often used by individuals anymore, but they are still used in some businesses, particularly in accounting departments.

How-to Hint

Specialized Printers

There are several less commonly used types of printers. Label printers are small, specialized printers designed solely to print labels—directly from the screen, from a mailing list file, or from the printer program's own built-in database. If you use a laser printer for most of your work, you might consider buying a label printer as a relatively low-cost means of printing labels.

Storage Devices

Most computer hard disks contain too much data to back up onto floppy disks easily. (A modest 1GB hard disk would require almost 100 disks to back up in its entirety, even if you use a backup program that compresses data as it goes.) If you're going to make regular backups of your data and programs (and you definitely should), you'll need some other mechanism for storing data long term. This section discusses some of the possibilities, including tape drives, magnetic removable-media drives, CD-Recordable drives, and magneto-optical drives.

Floppy disks

Zip disks

Jaz disks

DAT tape

❶ Tape Drives

DAT tape drives (that is, tape drives that use Digital Audio Tape) can record up to 8GB or more on a single cassette tape. Just like more conventional tape recorders, however, they access data sequentially and are therefore suited for backup rather than regular data storage.

❷ What Are Magnetic Removable Drives?

Magnetic removable-media drives combine the best features of floppy and hard drives. Like floppy drives, they use disks that are removable. Like hard drives, they store anywhere from dozens of megabytes to over a gigabyte on a single disk. This makes them perfect for backing up data and transferring large amounts of data from one computer to another. In addition, removable-media drives allow you to keep expanding your computer's storage capacity at a relatively low cost. Every time you run out of space, you just buy another cartridge.

3 The Types of Magnetic Removable Drives

Magnetic removable-media drives can be grouped into two categories: small-format and large-format. The most popular small-format drives are Iomega ZIP drives. These drives store a relatively small amount of data per cartridge (the smallest ZIP stores 100MB) and are relatively inexpensive (under $200 these days). They are well suited to transferring large files or groups of files from one computer to another—from home computer to office computer, for example, or between friends or colleagues. (You might think of these drives as high-capacity floppy disk drives.) The most popular large-format drive is currently the Iomega Jaz drive. A good middle ground is the 250MB.

4 ZIP Drives and Small-Format SyQuest Drives

ZIP drives are becoming extremely popular and common. They have the additional advantage of coming in a parallel port version, meaning a version that can be plugged into the parallel port you usually use for your printer. This means that if you're working with someone who doesn't happen to have a ZIP drive, you can potentially take your own drive over to their home or office and plug it into the parallel port on their computer to transfer the files. Other ZIP drives use a SCSI port connection, which is less commonly used on home or small office PCs but which allows you to save and retrieve files faster. SyQuest EZ135 drives are faster than ZIP drives, which makes them more suited to storing programs and data you use often.

5 Difficulties in Backing Up Your System

The low-capacity drives don't store a lot of data per cartridge, so you cannot easily use them to back up your entire hard disk; most new computers have hard drives that hold far more than 100MB of data. (They are sufficient if you're willing to back up just your data, in 100 or 135MB chunks, and reinstall all your software from scratch should your hard drive fail.)

(6) Jaz Drives and Large-Format SyQuest Drives

If what you need is a drive you can use both for backup and as an extension of your hard drive—one that is capable of running your favorite programs at the speed to which you've grown accustomed—you're better off with a large-format drive, such as the Jaz drive or high-end SyQuest drives, or even with a PD/CD drive or a magneto-optical drive (described shortly). Most large-format drives are almost as fast as most hard drives and can store between 540MB and 1.3GB per cartridge. (This means that even if you can't back up your entire hard drive onto one cartridge, you probably can fit it on two or three.) The prices for these drives run from about $300 to $700, with cartridges costing between $50 and a little over $100.

(7) CD-Recordable Drives

Another technology, called CD-Recordable (CD-R for short), lets you create CDs in a format that can be read by a regular CD-ROM drive (as well as by a CD-R drive). CD-R drives cost more than regular CD-ROM drives, although their prices have been dropping rapidly. (CD-R drive prices are now starting to dip below $75.) Although most CD-R drives only let you record data once on a CD, some let you add more data in separate sessions, adding to what's been previously recorded. One of the main attractions of this type of drive is that discs you record on using a CD-R drive can be read in any regular CD-ROM drive.

(8) Using CD-R Drives for Backups

CD-R and CD-RW drives are a viable mode of backing up data. Because they are much slower than hard disks, however, they're likely to be used primarily for backup and long-term storage rather than for storing data or programs that will be used regularly. Another advantage is the cost of discs themselves—usually less than $1 each.

9 Magneto-Optical Drives

Magneto-optical (MO) drives use both a laser and an electromagnet to record information on a cartridge, the surface of which contains tiny embedded magnets. These cartridges can be written to, erased, and then written to again. They are slightly more expensive than CD-R drives but hold more data (typically in the 1–2.5GB range, although sometimes less). The drives can range anywhere from $500 dollars to thousands of dollars.

10 DVD Drives

DVDis a type of disc destined to replace videotape as the medium of choice for recording and distributing movies for home viewers. They're also expected to supplant CD-ROM drives in the coming years. The first DVD players can read existing CD-ROM discs as well as DVDs, which range from 4.7GB to 17GB. Prices range from $50 to $1000. The first applications for DVDs are things like countrywide phone and address listings.

Modems

To send or receive data via regular phone lines, you need a device called a modem. The main purpose of a modem is to translate data from a form palatable to a computer into a form palatable to a telephone and vice versa. Most computers are digital devices. They store and manipulate information by turning on and off sets of tiny electronic switches. (When turned on, a switch represents the number 1; when off, it represents the number 0.) Transmitting digital data is therefore a bit like sending Morse code: At any given instant, the signal must represent either a dot or a dash. There are no gradations. Telephones, in contrast, transmit data as an analog signal (sound wave) that varies in frequency and strength, rather like the line drawn by an electrocardiograph machine.

For two computers to communicate, they must both have modems and be running some form of communication program. After your modem has successfully established a connection to another modem, you are said to be online. When no such connection exists, you are offline.

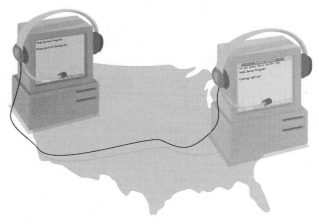

The purpose of modems is to transform digital information generated by a computer into an analog form that can be transmitted over phone lines (modulation) and to transform analog signals received over the phone line into digital codes that your computer knows how to use (demodulation).

0101100010011110001001011

FROM/TO COMPUTER

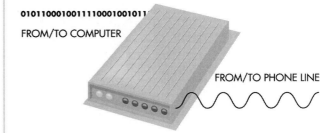

FROM/TO PHONE LINE

① How Modems Work

Modems translate digital signals into analog ones and vice versa. When you send data, the modem converts the digital information from the computer into analog signals that can be transmitted over phone wires: a process known as modulation. When you receive data, the modem converts the analog signals received from the phone into digital codes that your computer can manage (a process known as demodulation). The term modem is a hybrid of the terms modulate and demodulate.

② Internal Modems

There are basically two types of modems. Internal modems are expansion boards that are installed in expansion slots inside your system unit. Internal modems are often cheaper and consume none of your precious desk space. Most new computer systems are sold with internal modems already installed.

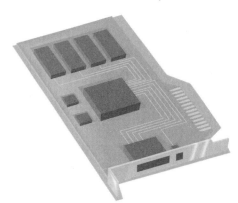

③ External Modems

External modems look like flat plastic or metal boxes (about the size of a rather thin hardback book) that usually plug into the back of your computer with a cable. External modems offer the advantage of visible status lights—little lights on the front end of the device that can help you (or the expert you get on the phone) figure out where the problem lies if you have trouble establishing a connection with another computer. External modems are also easily transferred from one computer to another, and they are usually faster than a comparable internal modem.

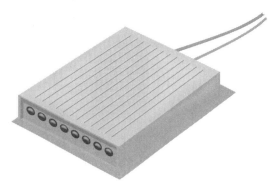

④ Data Transmission Speed

Aside from living quarters, what distinguishes one modem from the next is the speed at which it can transmit data. The speed at which modems send and receive data is typically measured in kilobits per second (Kbps). Most modems now in use transmit data at a maximum of 56Kbps. (It takes 8 bits to represent each byte of data. There is more information on bits and bytes in the Notes section.) Another type of modem, Digital Subscriber Line (DSL), transfers data many times faster. Cable modems, offered through cable television companies, are also faster. These high-speed connections can range from 500Kbps to 1,000Kbps.

5 Determining How Fast a File Will Transfer

As a rule of thumb, you can multiply the Kbps rate by 100 to determine the number of characters (bytes) transferred per second. A 60KB (60,000-character) file will take approximately 10 seconds to transmit at 57.6Kbps (60,000 divided by 5,760). This rule of thumb is only approximate because the actual transmission rate varies slightly depending on the amount of interference on the phone line (if any) and other factors.

6 When You Need Speed

Modem speed doesn't matter that much if you are using your modem strictly to send short messages via email or carry on online conversations with friends or colleagues. Speed does matter, however, when you are sending or receiving files. It takes almost twice as long to transmit a file at 28.8Kbps as it does at 56Kbps. Try transmitting a file that's 1MB or more and the difference will be very noticeable. Modem speed also makes a big difference when you're accessing the Internet, particularly if you're using the graphics-intensive World Wide Web.

7 The Fax Modem

A final factor to consider when choosing a modem is whether it has fax capabilities. See the upcoming section on fax modems for details.

How-to Hint

How Computers Store Information

Computers store and manipulate information as numbers, regardless of whether that information consists of numbers, letters, pictures, or any other type of data. Internally, computers represent all numbers using base 2, a numbering system that employs only two digits—0 and 1. (Humans, in contrast, like to think in base 10, which involves ten digits: 0 through 9.) Base 2 is often referred to as binary notation or a binary numbering system. The reason computers "think" in base 2 is that they represent information in terms of the presence or absence of an electrical or magnetic charge. The number 1 is used as the numeric equivalent of on, or charged. Zero means off, or uncharged.

How-to Hint

Bits and Bytes

In computer terminology, the electronic representation of a 0 or a 1 is known as a bit (short for binary digit) and there are eight bits to each byte of information. (That is, it takes eight 0s and/or 1s to represent a single character.) For example, the pattern used to represent a lowercase "a" on a personal computer is 01100001. As mentioned, when bits are stored inside a computer, they are stored as electrical or magnetic charges. When information is transmitted from one part of the computer to another or from a computer to a modem, bits are represented by small bursts of electricity—where a single burst represents an on bit (a number 1) and a pause between bursts represents an off bit (a number 0). A lowercase "a," for example, is represented by a pause, two bursts of electricity, four pauses, and another burst of electricity.

Multimedia Computing and Sound

A few years ago, multimedia became one of the biggest buzzwords in the computer industry. Computer systems are regularly advertised as "multimedia PC," games are touted as being multimedia, and so on.

By themselves, most PCs are only capable of beeps and a few whirring sounds. Today's computers come equipped with sound and video cards designed to maximize your enjoyment of the Internet and software programs. They allow you to hear the music, speech, and other sounds and see the images clearly.

1 What Is a Multimedia Program?

A multimedia program is a program that communicates in more than one medium. In practical terms, this means any program that employs any combination of text, pictures, sound, and full motion video. The first multimedia computer programs were encyclopedias that mixed text and graphics. Today's multimedia applications often feature full-motion video and sound and range from elaborate and visually stunning games to sophisticated interactive training programs.

2 What Is a Multimedia Computer?

A multimedia computer is any computer that can take full advantage of multimedia programs—that is, it can generate sounds, display pictures, and store large quantities of data. (Both sounds and pictures consume a great deal of disk space.) In terms of hardware requirements, this means a computer with a reasonably fast processor, a color monitor, plenty of memory, a sound card, speakers or headphones, and a CD-ROM drive. Virtually all packaged computers sold today are multimedia computers.

③ What Is a Sound Card?

sound card (also known as sound board) is a circuit board that is capable of translating program instructions into sounds. When you hear sound from a CD-ROM program (such as a game) on a PC, the sounds are actually being generated by the computer's sound card. The CD-ROM is simply delivering instructions to the sound card about what sounds to produce and when.

④ Using Sound Cards

A sound card fits into an expansion slot inside your computer's system unit. If your computer doesn't already have a sound card, you can add one (if you're not afraid to open up your computer and if your system unit has an available expansion slot). Sound cards range in price from about $50 dollars to several hundred dollars. As you might guess, the more expensive boards can produce richer, more complex tones.

⑤ Speakers

If you want your computer to communicate in sound, you'll probably want speakers as well. Although it is possible to hook up the sound card to your stereo system, for most people a pair of inexpensive computer speakers is adequate and more convenient. A pair of computer-compatible speakers will cost you anywhere from $25 to several hundred dollars.

⑥ 3D Graphics

The latest video cards are 3D graphics accelerators that allow you to see objects and moving pictures in 3D. These are great for serious game players who want a more "realistic" experience.

How-to Hint

Keep Disks Away from Your Speakers!

Speakers contain magnets that can destroy the data stored on floppy disks. Unless your speakers are designated as "magnetically shielded," keep them at least a few inches from your floppies. You don't have to worry about CD-ROMs, because information on CD-ROMs is recorded with lasers rather than magnets.

Portable Computers

In the world of computers, the smaller the package, the larger the price tag. If you compare two computer systems—one a desktop system and the other a portable—with the same CPU speed, hard-disk capacity, amount of RAM, and extras (CD-ROM drive, sound card, speakers), the portable will generally cost much more. (The portable's price can be as much as double the desktop's.) However, if you travel a lot or if you want a computer you can easily carry from office to home and back, the convenience of a portable may outweigh the price.

❶ Running on Batteries

For travelers, portable computers not only offer the advantage of coming in a small, lightweight package, they can also run on batteries, for at least a few hours. This means you can write a report or a couple of letters on your coast-to-coast flight or do your homework in your favorite café. Most portable computers provide you with some kind of warning when your battery is running out of juice—either a warning on the screen or a continual beeping. This gives you a chance to save your work and turn off the computer before it runs out of power. You can easily recharge a portable's battery by plugging it into an electrical outlet for an hour or two.

❷ Laptops and Notebooks

The term *laptop computer* used to indicate a subcategory of portable computers—those that were small enough and light enough to fit on your lap. Then the term *notebook computer* was invented to mean laptop computers that were almost as small as a notebook. These days, just about all portable computers are notebook sized, and the terms portable computer, laptop, and notebook are used almost interchangeably.

③ Handhelds

There are even smaller computers known as handheld computers that typically weigh about 1/2 lb. These tend to be used primarily for scheduling programs and address books, and often come with hardware and software that enables you to synchronize the scheduling/address data on the palmtop and your desktop PC. (This allows you to make changes from either computer.) Most of the higher-end handheld designed to talk with PCs use an operating system called Pocket PC. Pocket PC-based computers can run special Pocket PC versions of standard Windows software, such as word processing, spreadsheet, and presentation programs.

④ PDAs

There's yet another term for pint-size computers: PDA, for Personal Digital Assistants. Some people use the terms palmtop and PDA interchangeably; others reserve PDA for devices that combine limited computing capabilities with other talents, including the capability to act as a cellular phone and send faxes. Most PDAs use a pen and stylus rather than a keyboard for input, and feature handwriting recognition and, in some cases, voice recognition.

⑤ Portable Screens

If you're shopping for a portable computer, you'll want to consider screen type and size. Portable screens vary widely in both size (from about 12 inches to slightly over 15, measured diagonally) and clarity. They also support different ranges of screen resolutions: Some support regular VGA resolution only (640×480); others can go as high as 1024×768. (If you're thinking that high resolution seems impractical for a small screen, bear in mind that you may want to plug a full-sized desktop monitor into your portable when you're not on the road.) Be aware that some, but not all, portables can power both the portable screen and either a full-size desktop monitor or overhead display simultaneously. This feature is a must if you plan to use your portable to deliver presentations.

⑥ Portable Speed

You also need to take speed into account when hunting for a portable. At any given moment, the fastest desktop computers are always faster than the fastest portables. (As of this writing the high end for desktop computers is around 3GHz for a desktop PC and 2.5GHz for a portable.) As with desktop computers, the faster the CPU, the higher the price. If you already have a desktop computer and plan to use the portable only when traveling, you may be willing to compromise on speed, unless you plan to use the portable to do demanding multimedia presentations. If you plan to use it as your one and only computer, however, you may need to pay the extra price.

⑦ Storage and Memory

Storage space and memory are also important in a laptop. The size of hard disks in portable computers varies quite a bit. You're more likely to need more disk space if you're using a lot of graphical images or different programs or are planning to use your portable as your sole computer. As in a desktop computer, the amount of RAM you have will impact the speed of your computer and the number of programs you can comfortably run at once. (256MB to 512MB is becoming standard on new computers. 128MB may be sufficient if you don't run graphics-intensive programs or use multiple programs at once.)

⑧ Battery Life

Battery life is another important consideration. All portable computers sport batteries that let you use your computer when there's no electrical outlet in sight, a feature that's especially important when you're in transit. (When an electrical outlet is available, you can also plug into that, sparing your battery.) If you spend a lot of time working on long airplane flights, you might want to invest in a second battery pack so you can swap batteries. Two types of batteries are commonly used in portables: nickel hydride batteries and longer-running lithium-ion batteries. Most batteries can power from one to three hours of continuous computer use before they need recharging.

9 Pointing Devices

Different laptops have different pointing devices. Using a mouse is impractical when traveling, because mice require a fairly large flat surface. (On a plane, you'd probably knock over your neighbor's drink trying to click the Close button!) All portables therefore feature an alternative pointing device that you can use on the road; some have trackballs, some pointing sticks, some touchpads, and a few offer both a pointing stick and a touchpad. Most portables also have either a mouse port or a regular serial port into which you can plug a mouse when you're not traveling.

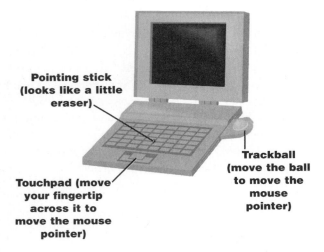

Pointing stick (looks like a little eraser)

Trackball (move the ball to move the mouse pointer)

Touchpad (move your fingertip across it to move the mouse pointer)

10 Weight

Portable computers weigh from under two pounds for mini-portables to more than eight pounds. Weight makes a lot of difference if you plan to frequently lug your computer, along with all your other bags, through airports. It makes less difference if your computer will mostly travel from home to work and back.

11 Keyboards

All portable keyboards differ a bit from desktop keyboards. At the least, they usually forego a numeric keypad and rearrange some of the cursor-movement keys. On some keyboards, the keys are slightly closer together than on regular desktop computers. Some portables let you have your cake and eat it too, by featuring a fold-out keyboard that fits inside a small case when closed but that opens to a more comfortable and familiar size when in use.

12 Portable Extras and Accessories

You should also investigate which components and accessories a laptop has. These days, most portables feature a modem and a CD-ROM drive; some come with a sound card and speakers. Some include DVD players, so you can watch a movie while on the go. In some cases, you can pick and choose the extras you want, like buying a car. Bear in mind that extra features usually mean at least a little extra weight. Some portables keep their weight down by foregoing an internal floppy disk drive. On these systems, there's usually an external floppy disk drive that you can plug in when needed. Some portables let you replace the CD-ROM drive with other components, such as the battery, a floppy disk drive, or a second hard drive.

13 Ports and Port Replicators

Most portable computers have ports that allow you to plug in a regular desktop monitor, keyboard, and mouse. Some have only a few ports; if you want more, you need to purchase a separate port replicator, a device that lets you connect to several peripherals at once. Rather than plugging all your peripherals back in every time the portable returns to your office, you can leave the peripherals plugged into the port replicator and then simply plug in your portable.

14 Docking Stations

Docking stations are port replicators with some extras—often providing additional components, such as a CD-ROM drive, speakers, or network card, and sometimes including a hutch where you can stash the portable (the monitor sits on top), leaving your desk free for a full-size keyboard and a mouse. Some portable computers are equipped with an infrared port, which allows you to connect with an infrared-equipped printer or network without using cables.

15 Liquid Crystal Displays

The screens on most laptop computers use a technology known as liquid crystal display (LCD). In LCD screens, liquid crystals (a fluid that reflects light) are sandwiched between two polarized pieces of glass or plastic. These polarized sheets shut out all light waves except those that are parallel to their particular plane. Inside the display, tiny electrodes pass current through the crystals, causing them to form spirals that bend the light to a greater or lesser degree. The amount of current determines the amount of spiraling, which in turn determines how much of the light actually makes it through the front of the screen. (In areas where the light is not bent at all, the beam is completely blocked and the screen remains dark.) In the case of color LCD screens, the light passes through various color filters.

16 Active Versus Passive Matrix Displays

LCD screens are often characterized as either passive or active matrix displays. In passive matrix displays, groups of pixels (screen dots) share the same electrodes. In active matrix displays, which are more expensive, each pixel gets a transistor of its own. The resulting images are much clearer and easier to read. Active matrix displays also drain batteries much faster than passive matrix displays, making them less appropriate for long airplane flights and other work sessions conducted without the benefit of an electrical outlet.

How-to Hint
Battery Power Check

Most portable computers display the amount of battery power remaining, either on the screen or on a panel built into the computer. If you are using Windows, check the tray at the right edge of the taskbar for a battery status utility program icon. In some cases, you only need to point to the icon to see the amount of battery life remaining.

How-to Hint
Energy-Saving Mode

Don't panic if your screen blacks out when you haven't even touched the machine. Some portables automatically go into energy-saving mode when you haven't touched the keyboard or pointing device for a while. This feature is designed to prolong battery life. In most cases, you can turn the energy-saving mode on and off. (You might prefer to have it off when you're using an electrical outlet.) See your computer's user's manual for details.

How-to Hint
PCMCIA Cards

If possible, purchase a computer that has one or more PCMCIA slots so you can easily upgrade the system later. There are three types of PCMCIA cards available—Type I, Type II, and Type III. Type I cards are typically used to add RAM or ROM to a computer; Type II cards are most often used for modems or fax modems; and Type III cards can be used for disk drives. Most new portables have a PCMCIA slot that can accept either a Type II or Type III card.

Task

Using the Windows XP Desktop

The Windows desktop works much like its real-world counterpart; it is a place where you organize files, run programs, and coordinate your work. When you run a program or open a folder, these items open in a window on the desktop. You can keep multiple windows open at once, arrange them how you like, and switch between them easily.

In the following tasks, you will explore some of the basic features of the Windows desktop—features that you will use daily. You will learn how to log in and out of Windows, how to use a mouse, how to run a program, and how to get help when you need it. You will also learn techniques for arranging windows and switching between open programs. Finally, you will learn the proper way to shut down your computer.

How to Log On to Windows XP

Windows XP is a secure system. If more than one user account is configured on your computer, or if your computer is on a network, you must log on so that Windows knows who you are and what you are allowed to do on the computer and network. If your computer is on a network, your logon information is supplied by your network administrator. When you install Windows XP on your own computer, you supply the information during setup. Depending on how your computer is set up, you may see the new Windows XP logon screen (Steps 1–3) or the traditional logon screen (Steps 4–7).

❶ Select the User Account

From the list of available users, click the user account with which you want to log on. If a password is not assigned to the account (that is, if the password field was left blank when Windows was installed), you will enter directly into Windows. Otherwise, you'll be asked for a password.

❷ Enter Your Password

Type your password in the box that appears. As you type, the characters appear as dots. This prevents people looking over your shoulder from discovering your password. Note that the password is case-sensitive.

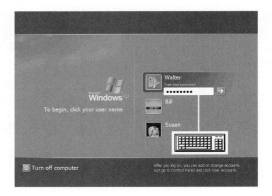

❸ Log On

Click the arrow next to the password box (or press the Enter key on your keyboard) to submit the password and log on to Windows.

④ Press Ctrl+Alt+Del

An alternative way to log on to Windows is to use the traditional logon screen. To get to the main logon screen, you must press the **Ctrl**, **Alt**, and **Del** keys all at once. This special key combination informs Windows that you want to enter a username and password.

⑤ Enter Your Username and Password

Type your username and password into the appropriate boxes. As you type the password, the characters you enter appear on the screen only as dots. Passwords are case-sensitive. You must enter the correct combination of uppercase and lowercase characters and numbers.

⑥ Show Extra Login Options

Most of the time, a username and password are enough for you to log on to Windows XP. However, you can click the **Options** button for more choices, including choosing a different domain and logging on to just the computer instead of a network. For more information on domains and networking, see Chapter 7, "Working on a Network."

⑦ Shut Down

You can also shut down your computer from the logon screen. Clicking the **Shutdown** button opens a dialog box from which you can choose to shut down or restart the computer. These options are great when you need to shut down the system but don't want to wait through the logon process.

How to Use Your Mouse

Your mouse allows you to get tasks done quicker than with the keyboard. Sliding the mouse on your desk moves the pointer on the screen. The pointer usually appears as an arrow pointing up and to the left—just point it to the item you want to use. The pointer shape changes as you move over different areas of the screen—a vertical bar shows where you can enter text, for example. The shape also changes to indicate system status. An hourglass means that Windows is busy. An hourglass with an arrow means that Windows is working on something but that you can continue to do other things in the meantime.

❶ Point to an Object

An object refers to an item on your screen, usually an icon, that represents a program, file, or folder. You can point to an object by sliding the mouse so that the tip of the mouse pointer arrow is over that object.

❷ Click an Object

Clicking your left mouse button one time selects an object. When you select the object, its icon and text become highlighted with a dark blue background. Then you can perform another action on the object, such as deleting it.

❸ Double-Click an Object

Double-clicking means to move the mouse pointer over an object and click the left mouse button twice in quick succession. Double-click an object to launch it. Double-click a folder to open it; double-click a program to run it.

④ Right-Click an Object

When you click once on an object with the right mouse button, a shortcut menu pops up that lets you perform various actions associated with the object. The command in boldface is the action that would be performed by double-clicking the object.

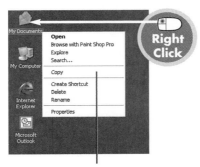

The shortcut menu

⑤ Drag an Object

To drag an object, point to the item, click and hold the left mouse button, and move the mouse to reposition the item. Release the mouse button to drop the object. The drag-and-drop approach is the way to move files to new folders and to move whole windows on your desktop.

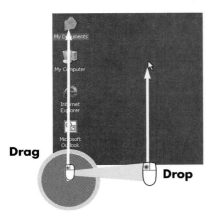

Drag

Drop

⑥ Open a Menu

Many windows, such as open folders and programs, have menus that provide access to different commands for working in the window. To open a menu, click the menu's name once.

Click

⑦ Select a Menu Command

After a menu is open, you can click any command on the menu to have Windows perform that action.

Click

How to Display Icons on Your Desktop

In previous versions of Windows, icons representing important parts of your system were always shown on your desktop. This may or may not be the case with Windows XP. If you buy a copy of Windows XP and install it yourself (see the Appendix), your desktop will be empty except for the Recycle Bin. If you buy your computer with Windows XP already installed, the icons may or may not be on the desktop, depending on the manufacturer of your computer. Throughout this book, many tasks assume that these icons are displayed on the desktop. If you don't see them on your desktop, you can find them on the Start menu. You can also tell Windows to show the icons on the desktop using the following steps.

❶ Open the Start Menu

The **Start** menu lets you access all your programs and most of the Windows settings available for configuration. The first time you start a computer with Windows XP, the **Start** menu opens automatically. After that, you must open it yourself by clicking its button once.

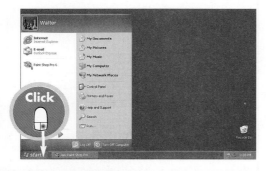

❷ Find the Icon You're Looking For

The icons that used to appear on the Windows desktop now appear in the upper-right part of the **Start** menu.

❸ Click an Icon to Open Its Window

To open the window for any of the icons in the **Start** menu, click the icon once with the left mouse button. The **Start** menu closes and a window opens on your desktop.

④ Open an Icon's Shortcut Menu

Right-click any icon to open a shortcut menu with special commands for working with that icon.

⑤ Show the Icon on the Desktop

Click the **Show on Desktop** command in the shortcut menu to have that icon appear on the Windows desktop. (The icon will still appear on the **Start** menu, as well.) If you decide you don't want the icon on your desktop after all, open the **Start** menu, right-click the icon in the menu, and choose **Show on Desktop** again to remove the icon from the desktop.

⑥ Open the Desktop Icon

After the icon is shown on your desktop, double-click it to open it.

⑦ Turn on Other Icons

Each of the icons shown in the upper-right portion of the **Start** menu can appear as icons on your desktop. Just right-click each one in turn and choose the **Show on Desktop** command from the shortcut menu.

How to Start a Program

Windows XP provides several ways to run your programs. To begin with, all your programs are conveniently located on the Start menu. This menu includes some simple programs that come with Windows (such as a calculator and a notepad) and any other programs you have installed.

1 Click the Start Button

Click the **Start** button to open the **Start** menu. Directly under your logon name, you'll find shortcuts to your Web browser and email program (Internet Explorer and Outlook Express, by default). Under these shortcuts, you'll find shortcuts to any programs you've run recently. On the right side of the **Start** menu, you'll find shortcuts to various important folders on your system and access to the help and search features.

2 Click the More Programs Button

If you don't see the program you are looking for on the **Start** menu, click the **All Programs** button to see a list of all the programs installed on your computer. Some might be listed in folders within the **All Programs** folder; just point to a subfolder to open it. Programs that have recently been installed are highlighted. When you find a program you want, click the shortcut to run it.

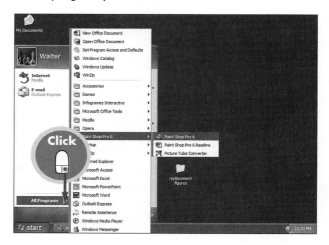

3 Click a Quick Launch Shortcut

Some programs have shortcuts on the **Quick Launch** toolbar, just to the right of the **Start** button. Click any of these shortcut buttons to launch the program. The program opens in a new window on the desktop.

4 Maximize a Program Window

Click the **Maximize** button to make the program window take up the whole screen (except for the space occupied by the taskbar).

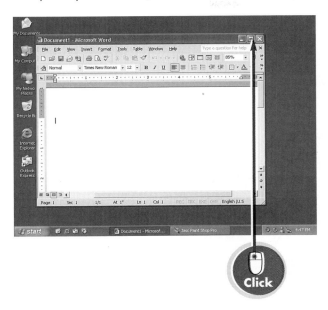

5 Restore a Program Window

After a window is maximized, the **Maximize** button turns into a **Restore** button. Click the **Restore** button to shrink the window back to its previous size.

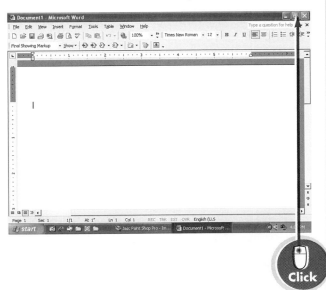

6 Minimize a Program Window

Click the **Minimize** button to remove the window from the desktop but leave the program running. You can tell the program is still running because its button remains in the taskbar at the bottom of the screen. Click the taskbar button to restore the window to the desktop.

7 Close a Program Window

Click the **Close** button to end the program and remove its window from the desktop. The program displays a dialog box asking you to save any unsaved work before it closes. You can also close a program by choosing the **Exit** command from the **File** menu.

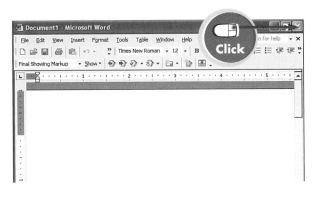

How to Arrange Windows on the Desktop

Windows offers the ability to keep many windows open at the same time. Although having multiple windows open at the same time provides the ability to easily move between tasks, using multiple windows can become confusing. Fortunately, Windows offers some clever tools for working with and arranging the windows on your desktop.

1 Resize a Window

When you move your pointer to the outer edge or corner of a window, the pointer changes into a double-headed arrow. When the pointer changes, click and drag the edge of the window to change its size.

2 Move a Window

You can move an entire window to a different location on the desktop by dragging its title bar. You can even move the window off the edges of your screen.

3 Cascade Windows

You can line up Windows in a cascade by right-clicking the taskbar and choosing **Cascade Windows** from the shortcut menu.

④ Tile Windows Vertically

Another way to arrange multiple windows on your desktop is to tile them. Right-click the taskbar and choose **Tile Windows Vertically** to arrange them from left to right on your screen.

⑤ Tile Windows Horizontally

You can also tile windows horizontally. Right-click the taskbar and choose **Tile Windows Horizontally**.

⑥ Minimize All Windows

You can minimize all open windows on your desktop at once (and thus clear them from your desktop) by right-clicking the taskbar and choosing **Minimize All Windows**. This is a great way to get to your desktop quickly.

How-to Hint

Showing the Desktop

A better way to get to your desktop quickly instead of using the **Minimize All Windows** command is to use the **Show Desktop** button on the **Quick Launch** toolbar. This button effectively minimizes all windows, even if some windows are showing dialog boxes (something the **Minimize All Windows** command can't do). Click **Show Desktop** again to reverse the action and return all the minimized windows to their previous states.

How to Switch Between Programs

When you run several programs at once, you must be able to switch between these programs easily. Windows offers three great methods for switching between open applications—two using the mouse and one using the keyboard.

① Click the Program's Window

The easiest way to switch to an open program is simply to click the program's window, if some portion of the window is visible. Inactive windows have a slightly dimmer title bar than the active window. Clicking anywhere on an inactive window brings it to the front and makes it active.

Click to make the inactive window active

The active window

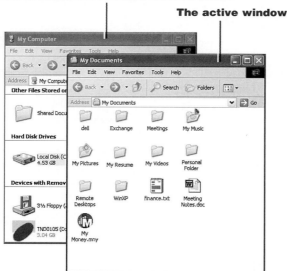

② Click the Taskbar Button

When you can't see the window you want, the simplest way to switch to it is to click that window's button on the taskbar. This action brings that window to the front of the desktop in whatever size and position you left it.

③ Resize the Taskbar

When there are a lot of open windows, the buttons on the taskbar might get too small to be of much value in determining which window is which. You can hold your pointer over a button to see its full description, or you can drag the top edge of the taskbar up to make it bigger.

Drag

④ Use Grouped Taskbar Buttons

When more than one window is open for a single program, Windows XP groups those windows using a single taskbar button instead of multiple taskbar buttons. For example, you may be looking at a few different Web sites in different windows using Internet Explorer. A single taskbar button for Internet Explorer is displayed and the number of active Internet Explorer windows (five in the example shown here) is shown on the button. Click the button once to open a menu from which you can choose a specific window to activate.

⑤ Press Alt+Tab

You can also switch between open windows using your keyboard. Press and hold the **Alt** key and then press the **Tab** key once (without letting go of the **Alt** key). A box appears, displaying icons for each window. Press the **Tab** key to cycle through the windows. When you get to the window you want, release the Alt key to switch to it.

Getting Out of Alt+Tab

If you use **Alt+Tab** to open the box that lets you switch between windows and then decide that you don't want to switch, just press **Esc** while you're still holding down the **Alt** key. The box disappears and puts you right back where you were.

Unlocking the Taskbar

If you find that you cannot resize the taskbar, it is probably locked. A locked taskbar cannot be resized or moved. Some people prefer to keep their taskbar locked so that no accidental changes are made to it. Others prefer to leave it unlocked so that they can easily resize it. Right-click anywhere on the taskbar and click the **Lock the Taskbar** command to deselect that command and unlock the bar.

How to Use the Notification Area

The notification area is the part of the taskbar at the far right side that holds your clock and probably several other small icons. These icons show information about programs that are running in the background on your computer. Some of the icons provide access to certain functions of the programs they represent. For example, the speaker icon lets you set your system's volume and configure audio properties.

① Expand the Notification Area

The notification area collapses automatically to show only the clock and any recently used icons. To view the entire notification area, click the button with the double-left arrow at the left side of the notification area. A few seconds after you move your pointer away from the area, the notification area collapses again.

② Viewing the Date

Hold the mouse pointer over the clock for a moment to view a pop-up balloon with the current date.

③ Setting the Clock

Double-click the clock to open a dialog box that lets you set the current date and time, as well as configure time-zone settings.

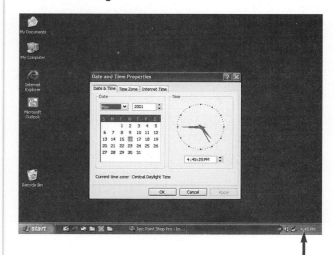

④ Setting the Volume

Click the speaker icon in the notification area to open the volume control. Slide the control up or down to change the volume of your system. A beep sounds to let you know how loud the volume is set.

⑤ Using Other Notification Area Icons

Unfortunately, the notification area icons for different programs behave in different manners. Sometimes, right-clicking or left-clicking the icon once opens a dialog box for configuration of some sort (as was the case with the volume control). Sometimes, right-clicking the icon opens a shortcut menu with program options. You'll have to experiment or read the documentation for the appropriate program.

How-to Hint

Keeping the Notification Area Open

To keep the notification area open and showing all its icons all the time, right-click the taskbar and choose **Properties**. On the **Taskbar** tab of the dialog box that opens, disable (that is, remove the check mark next to) the **Hide inactive icons** option.

Turning Off Icons

You can turn off some icons in the notification area by right-clicking the icon and choosing the **Exit** command, if one exists. There also might be a command for setting options or preferences. Sometimes these settings contain an option for permanently turning off the icon. Another place you might look is in the **Startup** folder on your **Start** menu. Often, programs that are configured to start with Windows place icons on the notification area. For more about using the Startup folder, see Chapter 5, "Changing Windows XP Settings."

Updating the Clock Automatically

If you have Internet access and are not behind a firewall, Windows XP can update your clock automatically. Double-click the clock. In the dialog box that opens, select the **Internet Time** tab. Select the **Automatically synchronize with an Internet time server** option and then choose an available server.

How to Browse Your Disk Drives

Your disk drives hold all the information on your computer: all the files, folders, and programs, as well as all your documents. The My Computer window gives you access to these drives, whether they are hard drives, floppy drives, CD-ROM drives, or something else. My Computer also provides a shortcut to the Windows Control Panel, which is discussed more in Chapter 5, "Changing Windows XP Settings."

1 Open My Computer

Double-click the **My Computer** icon on the desktop or Start menu to open the **My Computer** window.

2 Select a Disk Drive

The **My Computer** window shows any drives present on your computer. Click the icon for the drive you want to investigate to select it. Your floppy drive is usually named **A:** and your main hard drive is usually named **C:**. Information about the capacity and free space on any selected drive is shown in the **Details** pane to the left.

③ Open a Drive

Double-click the drive icon to open that drive.

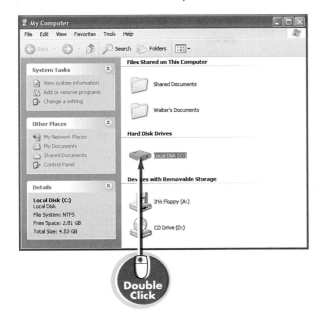

④ Open a Folder

Objects on a drive are organized into folders. *Folders* can contain both files and other folders. Double-click a folder to open it.

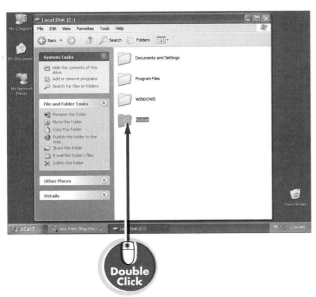

⑤ Open a File

When you select a file, a description of that file appears on the left side of the window. Double-click a file to launch the program that created the file (that is, the program *associated* with the file) and open that file within the program.

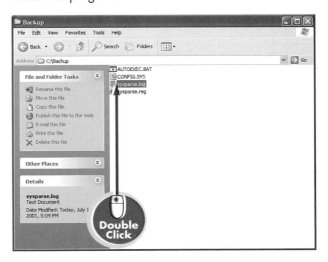

⑥ Navigate Folders

Click the **Back** button in the toolbar at the top of the folder window to go back to the folder you just came from. Click the down arrow next to the **Back** button to view a list of previous locations you can jump back to.

How to Get Help

Windows XP boasts a comprehensive Help system that lets you get details on Windows concepts and performing specific tasks. You can browse the contents of Windows Help, search for specific terms, or even ask questions in plain English.

① Open Help

To open the Windows Help system, click the **Start** button and then choose **Help and Support**. The **Help and Support Center** window opens.

② Enter a Search Term

If you know what topic you are looking for, type a word, phrase, or question in the **Search** box and click the **Search** button.

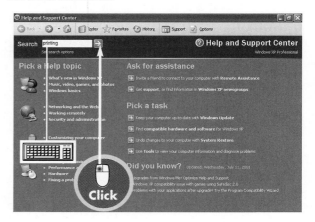

③ Select a Result

Windows shows a list of articles that match your search. Click one of the results in the left pane to view the article in the right pane. Buttons above the article let you print the article or add it to a list of favorites.

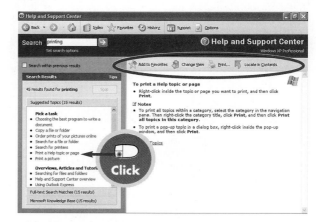

4   Pick a Help Topic

If you are not sure what the name of the topic you're looking for is, or if you just want to browse the Help system, click the link for a help topic on the main **Help and Support Center** page.

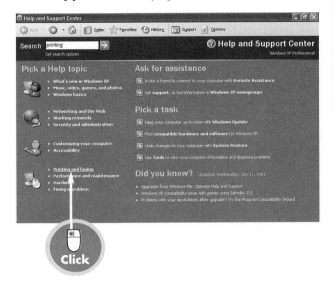

5   Pick a Category

In the left pane, Windows displays the categories for the topic you selected in Step 4. Click a category to display a list of help articles related to that category in the right pane.

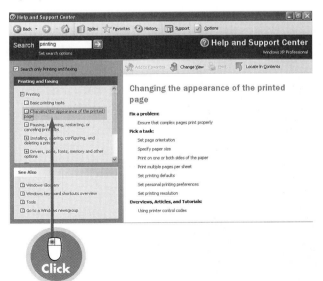

6   Pick an Article

Click the article in the list you want to view. Windows opens the selected article in a new window. When you're done reading the article, click the window's **Close** button to close the window and return to the **Help and Support Center** window.

How-to Hint

Using the F1 Key

Press the **F1** key at any time while using Windows to open a help page related to your current activity. Many programs also support the F1/Help feature.

Using the Index

Click the **Index** button on the help window's toolbar to view a searchable index of all help articles. Some people find it easier to browse the Help system this way.

How to Use the Recycle Bin

You can delete files, folders, and programs from your computer at any time. However, when you delete an item, Windows does not immediately remove it from your computer. Instead, the item is placed into the **Recycle Bin**. You can restore an item from the **Recycle Bin** later if you decide you would rather not delete it. When the **Recycle Bin** becomes full (depending on the amount of disk space allocated to it), Windows deletes older items permanently to make room for newer items. You can think of the **Recycle Bin** as sort of a buffer between your files and oblivion.

❶ Drag an Object to the Recycle Bin

The easiest way to delete an object is to drag it to the **Recycle Bin**. You can drag an item from the desktop or from any open folder. You can also delete a file by selecting it and pressing the **Delete** key on your keyboard.

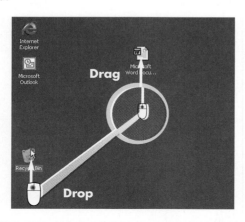

❷ Confirm the Deletion

When you try to delete an object, Windows asks you to confirm that you really want to delete it. Click **Yes** if you're sure; click No if you made a mistake and don't want to delete the object.

❸ Open the Recycle Bin

Double-click the **Recycle Bin** icon on the desktop to open it. All files in the **Recycle Bin** are listed with their original locations and the date on which they were deleted.

4 Restore Files

To remove a file from the **Recycle Bin** and restore it to its original location, select the file and click the **Restore this item** link that appears on the left.

5 Delete Files

Right-click a file in the **Recycle Bin** list and choose **Delete** from the shortcut menu to permanently delete that file from your hard disk.

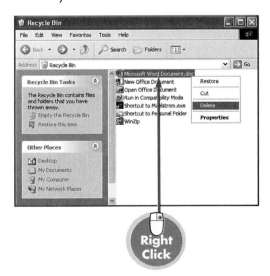

6 Empty the Recycle Bin

To permanently delete all the files from the Recycle Bin (which you might want to do to regain some disk space), make sure that no files are selected and click the **Empty Recycle Bin** link on the left.

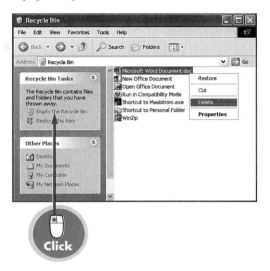

How-to Hint

Another Way to Empty the Bin

You can empty the **Recycle Bin** without opening it by right-clicking its icon on the desktop and choosing **Empty Recycle Bin** from the shortcut menu.

Allocating Recycle Bin Space

By default, 10% of your hard drive space is reserved for use by the **Recycle Bin**. You can change the amount of space used by right-clicking the **Recycle Bin** and selecting the **Properties** command from the shortcut menu. On the Global tab of the Recycle Bin Properties dialog box, drag the slider to change the maximum size of the **Recycle Bin**.

How to Log Off Windows XP

As you learned earlier in this chapter, logging on (providing Windows with your username and maybe a password) tells Windows who is using the computer. Logging off tells Windows that you are finished with your computer session. You should log off whenever you plan to be away from the computer for a length of time (such as for lunch or at the end of the day).

1 Click Log Off

Click the **Start** button and then choose **Log Off**.

2 Switch User

If you are not finished using Windows and just want to let someone else use the computer for a short time, you can simply switch users. Click the **Switch User** button if you want to leave all your programs running and your documents open while the other person uses the computer. The logon window (shown in Task 1) opens so that the other person can log on. When that person logs off, you can switch back to your account and continue working.

3 Log Off

Logging off closes any running programs. Although Windows usually gives you the chance to save any unsaved documents before it actually logs off, you should save your files manually before you log off to make sure that your data is safe.

Log On Another User

As soon as you log off, Windows presents the logon screen. You can now log back on as described in Task 1.

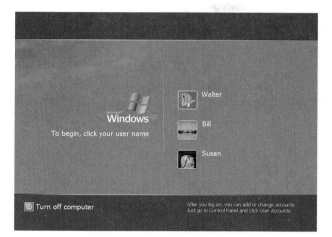

How-to Hint

Using a Screen Saver Password

Screen saver passwords let your computer automatically lock itself whenever the screen saver activates. To access the computer again, you'll have to type the password to deactivate the screen saver. For more on this feature, see Chapter 9, "Protecting Your Files."

How to Turn Off Your Computer

While running, Windows keeps a lot of its information in system memory—memory that is not sustained when the computer is turned off. For this reason, you should never simply turn your computer off using the power button. You should always use the **Turn Off Computer** command to allow Windows to gracefully shut itself down.

1 **Click Turn Off Computer**

Click the **Start** button and then choose **Turn off Computer**. The **Turn Off Computer** window opens.

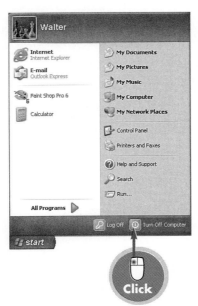

2 **Choose the Turn Off Option**

Click the **Turn Off** button. Windows closes all open programs (giving you the opportunity to save unsaved documents) and tells you when it is safe to turn off the power. This is the option you will likely choose at the end of the day or when the computer will be unused for a lengthy period.

3 **Choose the Restart Option**

Click the **Restart** button to have Windows shut itself down and then automatically restart the computer. After the computer is restarted, you can log on to Windows again. Restarting your computer is the first thing you should try if you find that Windows, another program, or a hardware component isn't working as you think it should.

④ Choose Hibernate or Standby

Some computers offer additional logoff options, including **Hibernate** and **Standby**. The **Hibernate** option saves all the information in your computer's memory to hard disk and then shuts the computer down. When you restart the computer, all your programs and windows are restored to the same state in which you left them. The **Standby** option turns off the power to most of the components of your computer, but keeps enough power going to your computer's memory that it can remember its current state. When you restore a computer from **Standby** (usually by pressing the power button, but different computers can vary in the method), the computer returns to the state in which you left it.

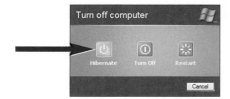

⑤ Save Any Open Files

If you attempt to shut down Windows while programs are running with unsaved documents, you are given the chance to save those documents before shut-down proceeds. Choose **Yes** if you want to save the changes to the named document; choose **No** if you don't want to save the changes; choose **Cancel** if you want to abort the shut-down process altogether.

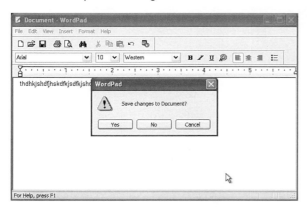

How-to Hint

Other Active Users

Because Windows XP now allows multiple user accounts to be logged on at the same time, you may find that when you try to shut down or restart the computer, other user accounts are still logged on. Windows XP informs you that the accounts are still active and gives you a chance to cancel your request to shut down. You should log off the other accounts (or have the people to whom the accounts belong log off); if you don't, any documents open in those accounts will be lost. Windows does not give you the option of saving other people's files the way it lets you save your own when shutting down or restarting.

Task

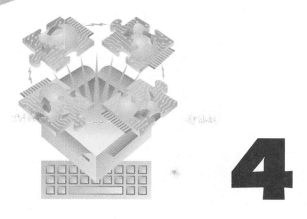

4

Working with Files and Folders

Everything on your computer is made up of files on your hard drive. Windows itself is just thousands of different files that interact with one another. Your programs are also collections of files that interact with one another and with Windows files. Finally, all the documents you create are themselves files.

Files are organized into folders that can hold both files and other folders. For example, suppose your C: drive contains a folder named Backup, which in turn holds a folder named July, which in turn holds a file named smith.jpg. The full description of the location of a file on a drive is called a path and includes the name of the disk drive, the names of each folder, and the name of the file—each name separated by a backslash (\). For the smith.jpg document mentioned earlier, the path would be C:\Backup\July\smith.jpg.

The name of a file can be 256 characters long and has a three-character extension (the three characters after the dot) that identifies the type of file it is. By default, extensions are not shown for file types that your system knows about.

How to Use Windows Explorer

Chapter 3, "Using the Windows XP Desktop," explained how to use the **My Computer** window to browse through the folders and files on a disk drive. In truth, you can use the **My Computer** window to get to any file on your computer and do anything you want with it. However, Windows offers another utility, **Windows Explorer**, that you might find more useful for working with the files and folders on your computer. It's really a matter of personal style.

❶ Open Explorer

You run Windows Explorer just like you do any other program. Click the **Start** button and select **All Programs**, **Accessories**, **Windows Explorer**.

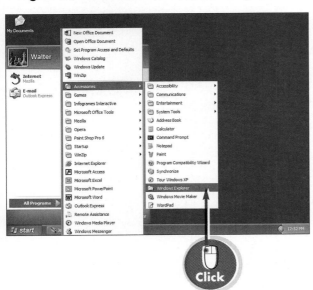

❷ Browse Folders

The left pane of the Explorer window shows a hierarchy of all the drives, folders, and desktop items on your computer. A drive or folder that contains other folders has a plus sign to the left of the icon. Click the **plus sign** to expand it and see the folders inside.

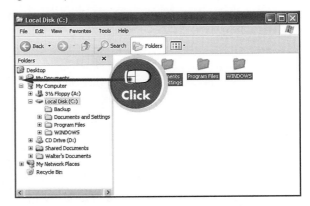

❸ Open a Folder

Click any folder in the list in the left pane; all the files and folders in that folder are shown in the right pane.

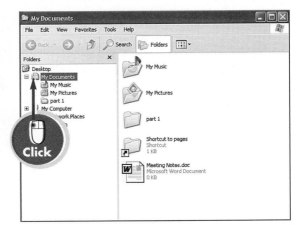

④ Open a File

The right pane works the same way as the **My Computer** window. You can double-click any file or folder in this pane to open it.

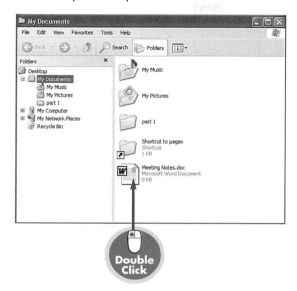

⑤ Move a File to Another Folder

One of the advantages of using Windows Explorer is that you can easily move a file to any other folder on your computer. Drag a file from the right pane and drop it on any folder icon in the left pane to move the file there.

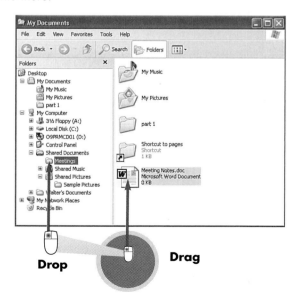

⑥ Copy a File to Another Drive

Copying a file to another drive is as easy as moving it. Just drag a file from the right pane to another disk drive (or a folder on another drive) to copy it there. Notice that the icon you are dragging takes on a small plus sign to let you know that the file will be copied, but not moved.

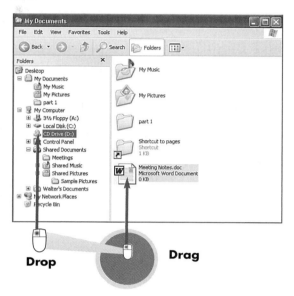

How-to Hint

Auto-Expanding

When you move a file to another folder in Windows Explorer, the folder doesn't have to be visible already. While dragging the file, hold the mouse pointer over a folder's plus sign for two seconds to automatically expand that folder.

Auto-Scrolling

While dragging a file, hold the mouse pointer at the top or bottom of the left pane for two seconds to automatically scroll up or down.

Copying or Moving to Other Locations

For more on how to move or copy files between folders and drives, see Task 11, "How to Move or Copy a File or Folder," later in this chapter.

② How to Search for a File or Folder

Using Windows Explorer is great if you know where the file or folder you want is located. Sometimes, however, it's hard to remember just where you put something. Fortunately, Windows has a great search function built right in that helps you find files and folders. You can search for folders by all or part of their names, by text they might contain, or by their location. You can even search using all three of these criteria at once.

① Open the Search Window

Click the **Start** button and select **Search**. You'll also find a **Search** button on the toolbar of most windows that performs the same function. A search window opens.

② Select the Type of Document

The left pane holds the interface you will use for searching. Results of any search you perform are displayed in the right pane. Choose the type of document you want to search for from the list in the left pane. The pane changes to show additional search questions based on the type of file you choose.

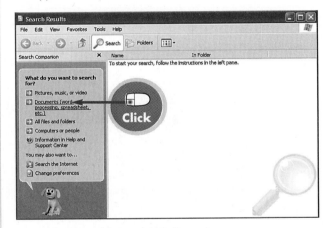

③ Type the Document Name

Type all or part of the name of the file or folder you want to search for in the text box. When you search, Windows shows all of the file and folder names that contain the text you enter.

④ Select a Time Frame

If you know approximately when the document was last modified, select one of the time options. If you don't remember, just leave the **Don't remember** option selected.

⑤ Click Search

After you have entered your search criteria, click **Search** to have Windows begin the search.

⑥ View the Results

The results of your search are displayed in the right pane. You can double-click a file to open it right from the search window.

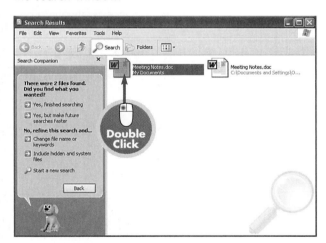

How-to Hint

Quickly Open a File's Folder

You can quickly open the parent folder of a file you've found by right-clicking the file in the results pane and choosing **Open Containing Folder** from the shortcut menu.

How to Create a Folder

Folders help you organize your files. You create a folder using the **My Computer** window or **Windows Explorer**. You can create a folder in any existing disk drive or folder or on the Windows desktop itself.

1 Find the Place to Make the Folder

The first step in creating a folder is to decide where you want to create it. Use the **My Computer** window or **Windows Explorer** to find the place you want to be.

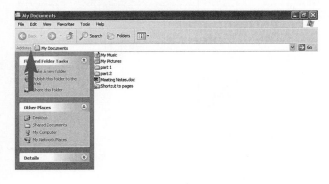

2 Create the New Folder

In the **Tasks** list, select **Make a new folder**. Alternatively, pull down the **File** menu and select **New**, **Folder**.

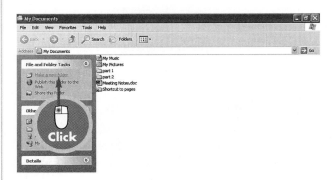

3 Rename the Folder

The new folder appears in the current location with the default name **New Folder**. The name is already highlighted; you can rename it by typing the name you want and pressing **Enter** or clicking somewhere outside the name field (here I've named the folder **Personal Folder**). You can also rename the folder later by selecting it and choosing **File**, **Rename** and then typing the new folder name. Note that renaming the folder does not affect any files contained in that folder.

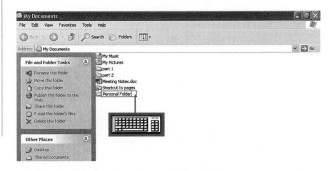

④ Create a Folder on the Desktop

To create a new folder directly on your desktop, right-click any empty area of the desktop. Point to **New** on the shortcut menu and then choose **Folder**.

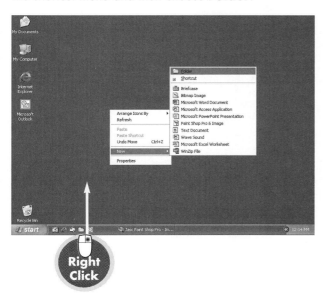

⑤ Name the New Folder

As you did in Step 3, type a new name for the folder (its default name is **New Folder**) and press **Enter**.

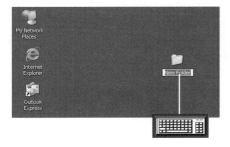

Saving a Document

Some programs let you create a new folder from the same dialog box you use to save a document. There is usually a button named **Create New Folder**. Just click the button, name the new folder, and open it to save your document there.

Creating a Folder in the Start Menu

The Start menu is really a folder on your hard disk; you can create new folders in it to help organize your files. Right-click the **Start** button, choose **Open** from the shortcut menu, and create the folder in the window that opens using the methods described in this task. The new folder appears on your Start menu. For more on customizing your Start menu, see Chapter 5, "Changing Windows XP Settings."

How to View Items in a Folder

Normally, both the My Computer window and Windows Explorer show you the contents of a folder as large icons that represent other folders and files. This is a friendly way to view folders, but not always the most useful, especially if a folder contains large numbers of files or many files with similar names. You can also view the contents of a folder as small icons, as a list, as a list with file details, or even as thumbnails.

1 Open a Folder

First, you need to find a folder to view. You can do this in either the **My Computer** window or in **Windows Explorer**. In this **Windows Explorer** example, notice that the regular large icon view looks pretty cluttered.

2 Change to List View

Choose **View**, **List** to view the folder contents as a list. The contents are listed in alphabetical order. You can also use the **View** button on the toolbar to change views.

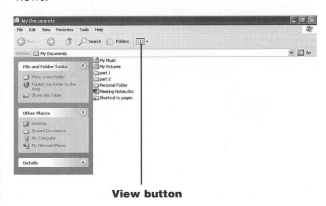

View button

3 Change to Details View

The **Detail** view is perhaps the most useful way to view the contents of a folder. Choose **View**, **Details**. Contents are presented in a list with columns that include file details, such as the size and type of the file and when the file was last modified.

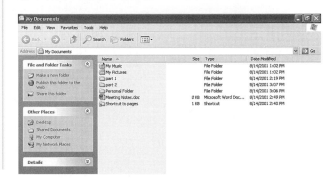

④ Change to Thumbnail View

Thumbnail view presents the contents of a folder as small thumbnails, or previews, of the actual documents. Only certain file types, such as JPEG images, support this type of viewing. Choose **View**, **Thumbnail** to display the folder contents as thumbnails. Other types of documents are displayed as larger versions of their normal icons.

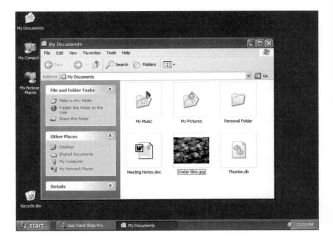

⑤ Arrange Icons

In addition to choosing how to view the contents of a folder, you can also choose how those contents are arranged. Choose **View**, **Arrange Icons By** and then choose **Name**, **Type**, **Size**, or **Modified** (the date the files were last modified) to order the contents of the folder. You can also have the folder arrange the icons automatically.

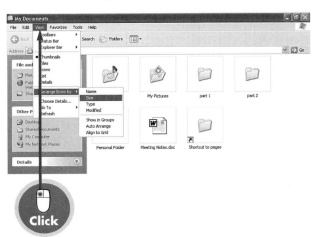

How-to Hint

Arranging in Details View

You can easily arrange the contents of a folder in the Details view by clicking the column heading by which you want to order the contents. For example, click the **Type** column heading to group the files in the current folder by type. You can choose the columns that are shown in Details view by choosing **View**, **Choose Columns** from the menu bar. A window opens with lots of different choices for columns to display. Just select the ones you want.

Other Arrangements

Select **View**, **Arrange Icons By**, **Show in Groups** to divide a folder's window into different sections that show different types of items, such as folders, drives, and files. Within each group, icons are arranged according to your other settings on the View menu. The Auto Arrange option on the same menu automatically arranges the icons in a window by alphabetic and numerical order and groups them together at the beginning of a window. The Align to Grid option gives you the freedom to arrange your icons as you like, while making sure that they all uniformly align to an invisible grid in the window.

Cleaning Up Your Windows

Many users find that the common tasks shown on the left side of most windows take up too much space and really aren't that useful anyway. You can turn the task list off for all folders by going to **Start**, **Control Panel**, **Folder Options**. On the **General** tab of the **Folder Options** dialog box, choose the **Use Windows classic folders** option. To turn the task list back on, come back to the **Folder Options** dialog box and choose the **Show common tasks in folder** option. Unfortunately, you cannot enable the list for some folders and disable it for others.

How to Create a File

Most of the time, you will create new documents from within a particular program. For example, you usually use Microsoft Word to create a new Word document. However, Windows does offer the ability to quickly create certain types of documents without opening the associated program at all. This can be quite useful when you are creating a large number of new documents that will be edited later.

1 Locate the Parent Folder

First, you must find the folder in which you want to create the new file. You can create a file directly in any folder on your computer. Here I used **Windows Explorer** to navigate to the new **Personal Folder** folder I created in Task 3, "How to Create a Folder."

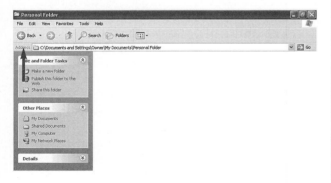

2 Create the File

Choose **File**, **New**, and then select the type of file you want to create. Note that the list of file types presented in the submenu covers basic Windows objects (such as folders, shortcuts, and text files) and objects that depend on additional software you have installed (such as Microsoft Word documents).

3 Locate the New Document

The new document appears in the selected folder with a generic name, such as **New Microsoft Word Document**. If you don't see the new file immediately, use the window's scrollbars to find it.

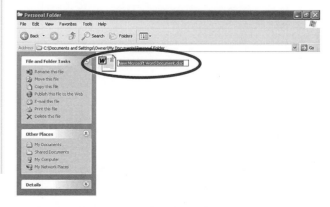

④ Rename the File

The new file appears with the name already high-lighted. Just start typing to enter a new name for the file. When you're done, press Enter or click somewhere outside the text box.

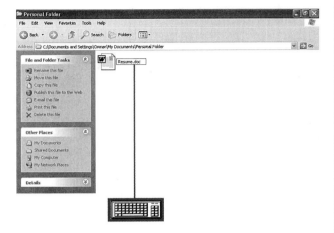

⑤ Open the File to Edit

After you have created and renamed your new file, double-click it to launch the appropriate program and open the new file with it. Now that the file is open in the appropriate application, you can work with it just as you would any other file created in that application.

How-to Hint

Renaming Files

Files can have names of up to 256 characters, including spaces. There are several special characters you cannot use in your file's name, including \ / : * ? " < >

Preserving the File Type

When you create a new file, Windows automatically gives it the right three-letter file extension (the three letters after the dot) to indicate the file type. If your Windows settings allow you to see the file extension (by default, they don't), be sure that you don't change the extension when you rename the file. If you do, the file won't open with the right program. Windows warns you if you try to change the file extension.

Populating a Folder Quickly

In Windows Explorer or My Computer, you can create as many new documents as you need and then go back and rename them later. To create files even more quickly, create one file, copy it by selecting it and pressing **Ctrl+C**, and then paste as many new files in the same folder as you need by pressing **Ctrl+V**. Each new file has the text **Copy of** and a number prepended to the filename to distinguish it from its siblings (for example, if the original file is named **resume.doc**, the first copy is named **Copy of resume.doc**; the second copy is named **Copy [2] of resume.doc**, and so on).

How to Open a File

There are several different ways to open a file in Windows. One way is to locate the file in the **My Computer** window or **Windows Explorer** and open it from there. You can also open a file from within the program that created it. Windows even keeps track of the files you have opened recently so that you can reopen these in one simple step using the **Start** menu.

1 Double-Click the File

Find the file you want to open by using the **My Computer** window or **Windows Explorer**. Double-click the file to launch the file's program and open the file with it. Here, the file **Resume.doc** will open in Microsoft Word.

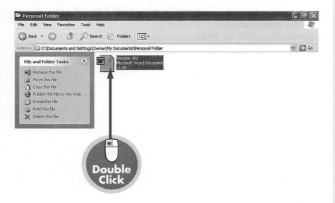

2 Open a Recently Used File

Windows keeps track of the most-recent 15 documents you have opened. To open any of these documents, click the **Start** button and point to the **My Recent Documents** option to see a list of the documents most recently opened on your computer. Select the document you want to open. If the My Recent Documents option does not show up on your **Start** menu, see Chapter 5, "Changing Windows XP Settings," for details on how to add it.

③ Run a Program

Yet another way to open a file is from within the program that created it. The first step is to run the program. Click the **Start** button, point to **More Programs**, and find the program you want to run in the submenus that appear.

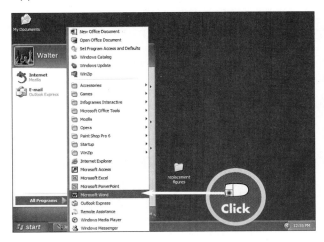

④ Choose Open from the File Menu

After the selected program opens, choose **File**, **Open** from the menu bar. The **Open** dialog box appears.

⑤ Find the File to Open

For most programs, the Open dialog box works a lot like the **My Computer** window. Navigate through the folders on your computer system to find the file you want to open, select it, and click **Open**.

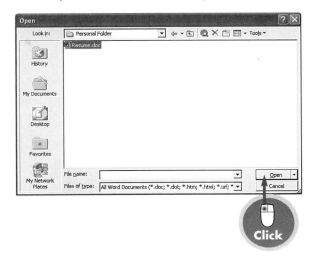

How-to Hint

Removing Recently Used Files

You can clear the list of recently used files from the **Recent Documents** folder by right-clicking the taskbar and choosing **Properties** from the shortcut menu. In the **Properties** dialog box that opens, click the **Start Menu** tab and then click **Customize**. In the dialog box that opens, click the **Advanced** tab and then click **Clear List**.

Searching for Files

When you search for files using the **Search** command on the **Start** menu, you can open any of the files you find just by double-clicking them. For more information about searching for files, see Task 2, "How to Search for a File or Folder," earlier in this chapter.

How to Save a File

Saving your work is one of the most important things you'll do. After all, if you don't save your work, what's the point of doing it in the first place? Saving a file is always done while you are working on it within a program. There are two save commands in most programs. Save As lets you choose a location and name for your file. Save simply updates the file using its current location and name. The first time you save a new file, the program uses the Save As function no matter which command you choose.

1 Open the Save As Dialog Box

If you want to save a file using a particular name or to a particular location, click the **File** menu and then choose **Save As**. Note that you can use this command to save a copy of the file you are working on with a new name or to save versions of a file. The **Save As** dialog box opens.

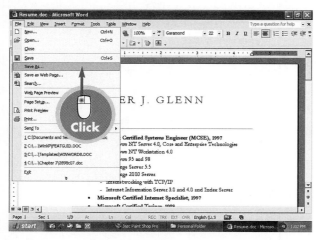

2 Choose a Location

The **Save As** dialog box works just like the **My Computer** window. Choose the disk drive to which you want to save the file using the **Save in** drop-down list. After you choose the drive, navigate to the desired folder.

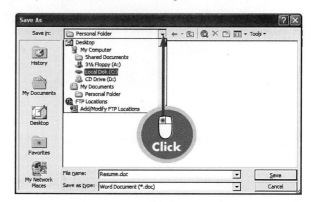

3 Choose a Favorite Place

Instead of using the drop-down list, you can choose a favorite place by clicking the icon for a folder in the bar on the left of the dialog box. You can then save your file in that folder or browse to another folder inside the folder.

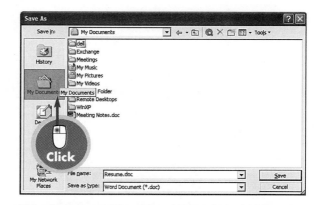

4 Create a New Folder

If you want to save the file you're working on in a new folder, navigate to the folder in which you want to store the new file, then click the **Create New Folder** button in the **Save As** dialog box toolbar. Type a name for the new folder and press **Enter**. Open the new folder by double-clicking it.

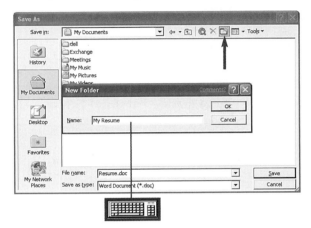

5 Name the File

Type the name for the document in the **File name** box. Note that, in most applications, you do not have to include the file extension when you type the filename. The application supplies the extension for you. If you do include an extension, the application accepts it.

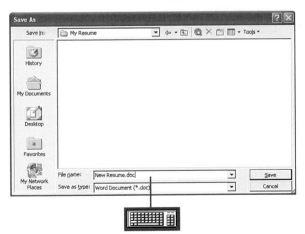

6 Save the File

Click **Save** to save the new file in the selected folder with the name you specified.

7 Save the File as You Work

Periodically as you work, save any changes to your document using the **Save** button on the program's main toolbar (or the **Save** command on the **File** menu). If you click **Save** and it is the first time you are saving a new document, the **Save As** dialog box opens and prompts you for a filename. Otherwise, the file is saved in the current location with the current filename, overwriting the last version of the file you had saved.

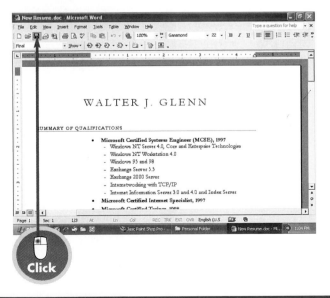

How to Create a Shortcut to a File or Folder

A shortcut is an icon that points to a file or folder somewhere on your computer. The shortcut is merely a reference to the actual object and is used to access the object without having to go to the object's location. For example, on your desktop you could place a shortcut to a frequently used document. You could then double-click the shortcut to open the file without having to go to the folder where the actual file is stored.

① Open Windows Explorer

The first step in creating a new shortcut is to use the **My Computer** window or **Windows Explorer** to find the file or folder to which you want to make a shortcut. To open Windows Explorer, click **Start** and select **All Programs**, **Accessories**, **Windows Explorer**.

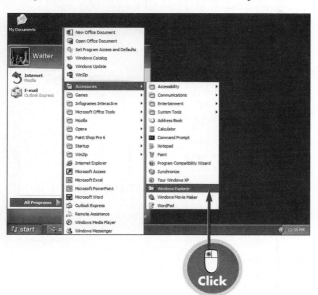

Click

② Select a File or Folder

In Windows Explorer, navigate to the object to which you want to make a shortcut. In this example, I want to create a shortcut to my new **Personal Folder** folder.

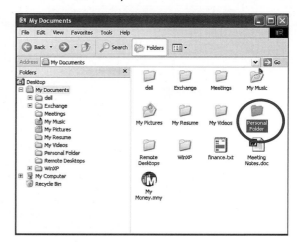

③ Drag the File to Your Desktop

Click and hold the *right* mouse button and drag the object to a blank space on the desktop. Release the right mouse button to drop the icon on the desktop.

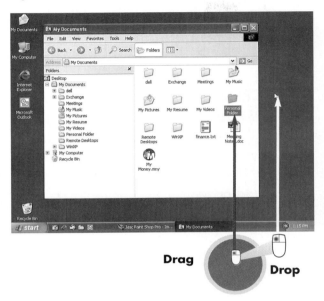

Drag   **Drop**

④ Choose Create Shortcuts Here

When you release the right mouse button, a shortcut menu appears. Choose **Create Shortcuts Here**.

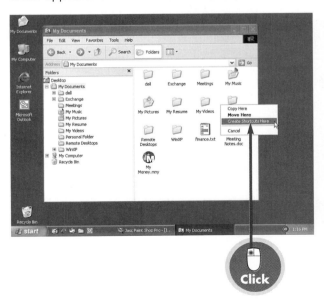

Click

⑤ Rename the Shortcut

Notice that the shortcut icon has a small arrow on it, indicating that it is a shortcut. You can rename the shortcut to anything you like by right-clicking the shortcut icon and choosing **Rename** from the shortcut menu.

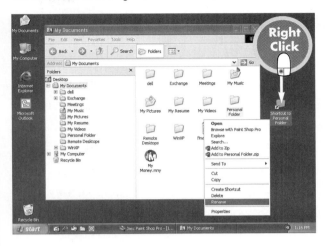

Right Click

⑥ Double-Click the Shortcut

To open the original object to which you made the shortcut, double-click the shortcut icon. In this example, double-clicking the **Shortcut to Personal Folder** shortcut opens the **Personal Folder** folder in Windows Explorer.

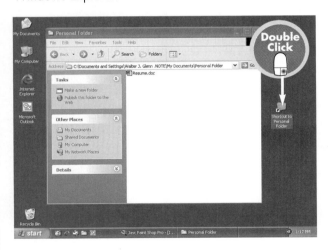

Double Click

How to Rename a File or Folder

In Windows XP, you can name files or folders just about anything you want. Names are limited to 256 characters, including spaces, but there are a few special characters you are not allowed to use, including the following: \ / : * ? " < >. You can rename files and folders at any time. Note that you should be very careful to rename only those files and folders that you created in the first place. Windows and Windows programs are composed of many folders and files that have special names. Changing the names of these files can often cause a program, or even Windows itself, to malfunction.

1 Select the File

To rename a file in the **My Computer** window or **Windows Explorer**, first select the file with a single click.

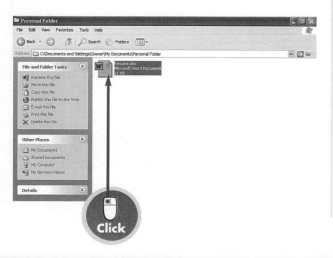

2 Choose Rename from the File Menu

From the menu bar, choose **File**, **Rename**. A box appears around the name of the file or folder you selected in Step 1 and the filename itself is highlighted.

3 Type a New Name

Type a new name for the selected file. Note that as you type, the highlighted filename is replaced by the text you type. If you want to edit (and not replace) the current filename, use the arrow keys or mouse pointer to position the insertion point, then add and delete characters from the filename as desired. When you're done with the filename, press **Enter**.

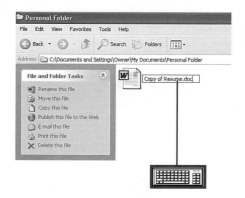

④ Click the Name Twice Slowly

A quicker way to rename a file (and one that also works on files on the desktop) is to first select the file with a single click and then click the name of the file a second later—not so fast as to suggest a double-click. You can also select the file and press the **F2** key. When the filename is highlighted, you can then type a new name.

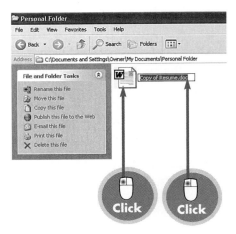

⑤ Right-Click the File

Yet another way to rename a file is to right-click the file and choose **Rename** from the shortcut menu. You can then type a new name as explained in Step 3.

How-to Hint

Keeping Names Simple

Although you can create very long filenames in Windows, it is usually better to keep them short and simple. The reason for this is that when you view the contents of a folder, filenames are often cut off after the first 15–20 characters so that you can view more files in the folder. Keep the filenames short so that you can view the contents of a folder without having to switch to details view and adjust the default column size to see the entire filename. For more on adjusting window views, see Task 4, "How to View Items in a Folder."

How to Delete a File or Folder

When you delete a file or folder in Windows, the object is not immediately removed from your computer. It is first placed into the **Recycle Bin**, where it is kept temporarily before being permanently deleted. The **Recycle Bin** gives you the chance to recover files you might have accidentally deleted. For more information about the **Recycle Bin**, see Chapter 3, Task 10, "How to Use the Recycle Bin." There are a few ways to delete objects in Windows, including dragging them to the Recycle Bin or deleting them directly using the keyboard or Windows Explorer.

❶ Select a Group of Files

Place the mouse pointer in a blank spot near a group of objects you want to delete. Click and hold the left mouse button and drag the pointer toward the objects. A dotted rectangle (named the lasso) appears behind the pointer. Drag the lasso over all the objects to select them all at once.

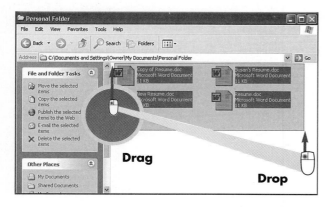

❷ Drag to the Recycle Bin

After you have selected a group of files, drag them to the **Recycle Bin** by clicking any single selected file and holding the mouse button while you drag the pointer over the **Recycle Bin**. Release the mouse button when the **Recycle Bin** icon becomes highlighted to drop the selected files into the **Recycle Bin**.

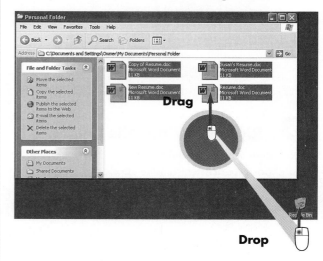

3 Select a File

It is also easy to delete files without using the **Recycle Bin**, which is helpful when you can't see your desktop. First, select the file you want to delete by clicking it once.

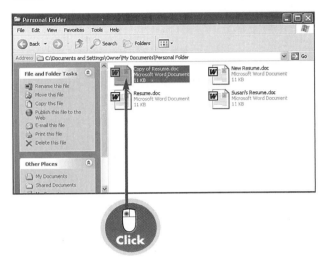

4 Use the Delete Key

Press the **Delete** key on your keyboard to send the selected file (or files) to the **Recycle Bin**.

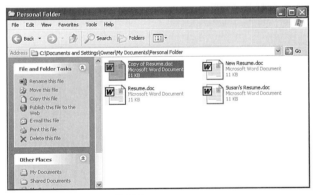

Del

5 Choose Delete from the File Menu

After a file is selected, you can also open the **File** menu and choose **Delete** to send the file to the **Recycle Bin**.

How-to Hint

Disabling the Recycle Bin

If you would rather not use the **Recycle Bin**, right-click the **Recycle Bin** icon on the desktop and choose **Properties** from the shortcut menu. Select the **Do not move files to the Recycle Bin** option. Be careful, though. When this option is selected, files that you delete are permanently removed from your system, giving you no chance to recover them.

Changing the Recycle Bin Settings

There are several ways you can customize the operation of your **Recycle Bin**. For more information on this, see Chapter 3, "Using the Windows XP Desktop."

How to Move or Copy a File or Folder

Most people move objects around from folder to folder by simply dragging them using the left mouse button. This usually works fine, but it might not provide the exact results you want. Depending on where you drag an object, you can move the object or you can copy it to the new location. For better results, try using the right mouse button instead of the left when you drag files to a new location.

① Find the Parent Folder

Use the **My Computer** window or **Windows Explorer** to find the folder that contains the object you want to move or copy.

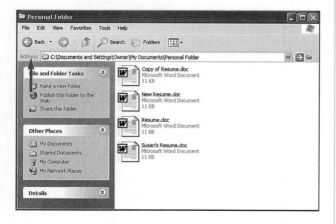

② Locate an Object

Locate an object you want to move. The object can be a file or a folder. Note that if you move a folder, you move the contents (all the files and folders contained in that folder) as well. If you copy a folder, you copy the contents of the folder as well.

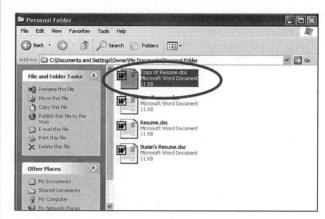

③ Drag the File to a New Location

Place the mouse pointer over the object, click and hold the right mouse button, and drag the object to the target location. In this example, I am dragging the document file to the desktop. Release the right mouse button to drop the object in its new location.

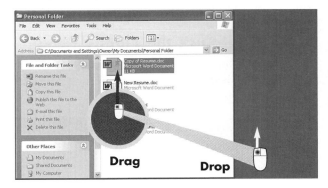

Drag **Drop**

④ Choose Copy Here

When you release the right mouse button, a shortcut menu appears. Choose **Copy Here** to place an exact copy of the selected item in the new location and keep the original object in the old location.

Click

⑤ Choose Move Here

Choose **Move Here** from the shortcut menu to move the object to the new location and remove it from the old location.

Click

How-to Hint

Left-Dragging

When you use the left mouse button to drag a file, the icon you drag changes to reflect what action will be performed. If the icon has a small plus sign on it, the file will be copied when you release the mouse button. If the icon has a small arrow, a shortcut will be created. If the icon has nothing extra on it, the object will be moved.

Right-Dragging

A better way to move files is to drag them using the right mouse button (instead of the left). When you release a file or folder you have dragged with the right button, a menu pops up asking whether you want to copy, move, or create a shortcut.

Dragging with Keys

When you drag using the left mouse button, you can hold down the **Shift** and **Ctrl** keys to get different effects. For example, hold down the **Shift** key while dragging a file to move the file instead of copying it. Hold down the **Ctrl** key while dragging a file to copy the file instead of moving it.

How to Format a Floppy Disk

When you buy floppy disks from a store, they are usually formatted. Make sure that you buy disks formatted for your system. The package should read **"IBM Formatted"** if the floppy disks are to work with Windows. If you have an unformatted disk, it is easy enough to format in Windows. Formatting is also a quick way to erase all the files that you don't need anymore from a disk. Before you start the steps in this task, insert the floppy disk to be formatted in your floppy drive.

① Open My Computer

Double-click the **My Computer** icon on your desktop to open the **My Computer** folder.

② Right-Click the Floppy Drive

Right-click the drive labeled **3½ Floppy (A:)** and select the **Format** command from the shortcut menu. The **Format** dialog box opens.

③ Choose a Capacity

Almost all computers today use 1.44MB floppy drives, which is the default choice in this dialog box. If you are formatting an older floppy (or one for an older computer), choose the 720K size from the **Capacity** drop-down list.

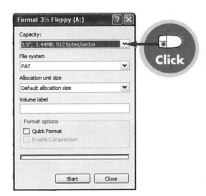

⑤ Perform a Quick Format

If you are formatting a disk that has been previously formatted by Windows (as you would do when erasing a disk), choose the **Quick Format** option to significantly shorten the time needed to format the disk.

④ Enter a Volume Label

Type a label into the **Volume Label** box. The volume label is the name of the floppy disk. You can leave this blank if you do not want a label (most people do leave this field blank).

⑥ Format the Disk

Click **Start** to begin formatting the disk. A progress indicator at the bottom of the dialog box shows the formatting progress. Another dialog box opens to inform you when the format is done.

How-to Hint

Be Careful When Selecting a Drive

The **Format** dialog box lets you select any drive on your system to format. Be sure that the correct drive is selected before formatting. Formatting a hard drive erases all its contents!

How to Send a File to the Floppy Drive

Floppy disks are often used to back up files or transfer files to another computer. In Windows, the floppy drive is always labeled A: in the **My Computer** window and **Windows Explorer**. As with most other tasks, Windows offers a couple different ways to send files to a floppy disk. Before you begin this task, make sure that a properly formatted floppy disk is in the floppy disk drive.

❶ Open My Documents

Double-click the **My Documents** icon on your desktop to open the **My Documents** folder. If you don't see the **My Documents** icon on your desktop, you can find it on the **Start** menu or add it to your desktop as explained in Chapter 3, "Using the Windows XP Desktop."

❷ Open My Computer

Double-click the **My Computer** icon on your desktop to open the **My Computer** window.

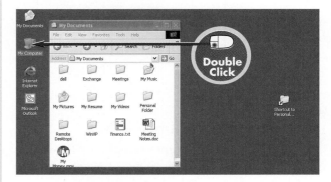

❸ Tile Your Windows

Right-click the taskbar and choose **Tile Windows Vertically** so that you can see both the **My Computer** and the **My Documents** windows at the same time.

④ Drag the File to the Floppy Drive

Place the mouse pointer over the file in the **My Documents** window that you want to copy. Click and hold the left mouse button while dragging the file to the floppy drive icon in the **My Computer** window.

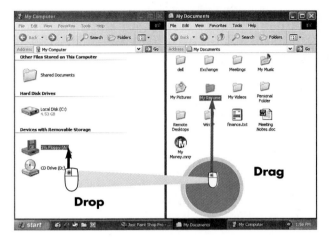

⑤ Copy the File

Release the left mouse button to drop the file on the floppy drive icon. A dialog box appears to track the progress of the copy operation.

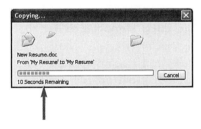

⑥ Select a File

Another way to send a file to the floppy drive is to choose a command rather than dragging and dropping the file. Start by selecting the file (click it once).

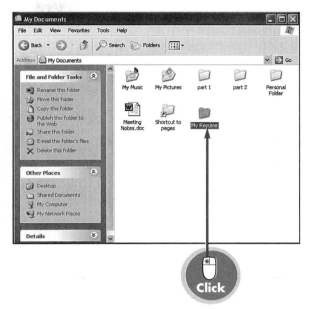

⑦ Choose Send to Floppy Drive

Right-click the selected file, point to the **Send To** command on the shortcut menu, then choose the floppy drive option. Windows copies the file to the floppy disk in the drive.

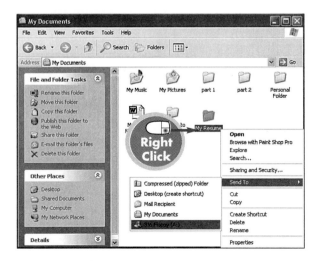

How to Open a File with a Different Program

Files usually have a certain program associated with them, normally the program that created them. A text file, for example, is associated with Notepad. Windows knows what program to use to open a file because of the three-character extension following the file's name. For example, a text file might be named Groceries.txt. Windows knows that files with the .txt extension should be opened in Notepad. Sometimes, however, you might want to open a file with a different program or even change the program associated with the file altogether.

❶ Right-Click the File

Right-click the file you want to open with a special program and choose **Open With** from the shortcut menu. The **Open With** dialog box opens.

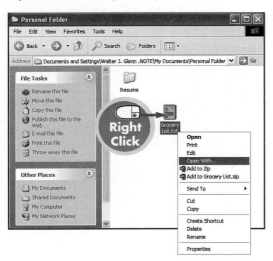

❷ Choose the Program

Select the program you want to use to open the file.

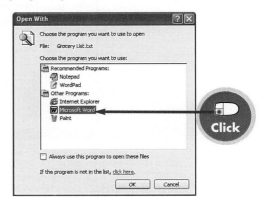

❸ Find Another Program

If the program you want to use does not appear in the list, click the **Click Here** link to find the program file on your computer yourself. Most of the programs installed on your computer are located in the **Program Files** folder on your C: drive. If you don't find the program there, consult the documentation for the program to get more information.

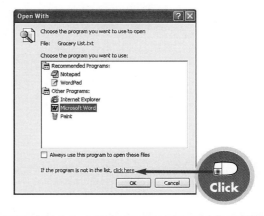

④ Make It the Default Choice

If you want to change an extension's association (that is, to make all files of that type open with the new program you've selected from now on), enable the **Always use this program to open these files** option.

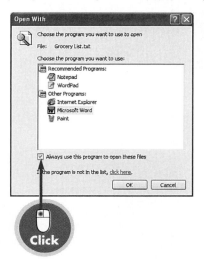

⑤ Open the File

Click **OK** to open the file in the selected program.

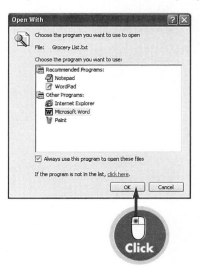

How-to Hint

Viewing File Associations

You can view a complete list of file associations in Windows. Click **Start** and choose **Control Panel**. In the **Control Panel** window, double-click **Folder Options**. In the dialog box that appears, click the **File Types** tab. All associations are listed here. You can create new associations and change existing ones.

Task

Changing Windows XP Settings

After you have worked with Windows XP for a while and gotten used to the way things work, you might find that there are changes you would like to make. Windows XP is wonderfully customizable and provides many options for changing its interface to suit the way you work.

Most of the changes you will make take place using the Windows Control Panel, which is a special folder that contains many small programs that adjust settings for a particular part of your system. For example, Display lets you change display settings such as background color, window colors, screen saver, and screen size. You can access the Control Panel through either the Start menu or the My Computer window, as you will see in the tasks in this chapter.

You'll also find that many of the Control Panel settings are also directly available from the shortcut menu of various desktop items. For example, right-clicking the desktop and choosing Properties from the shortcut menu that opens is exactly the same as opening the Display applet from the Control Panel. You'll see several such ways for accessing common controls in the following tasks.

How to Change the Volume

If you have speakers hooked up to your computer, you've probably noticed that some programs and certain things that Windows does (called events) make sounds. Many speakers have physical volume control knobs on them, but there is also a convenient way to change the volume from within Windows itself.

1 Click the Volume Icon

A small volume icon that looks like a speaker appears in the system tray next to your clock to indicate that sound is configured on your computer. Click the icon once with your left mouse button to open the **Volume** dialog box.

2 Change the Volume Setting

Click and drag the slider with your left mouse button to adjust the volume. Your computer beeps when you release the slider to give you an idea of the volume you've set.

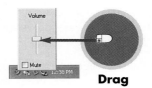

Drag

3 Mute Your Speakers

Click the **Mute** option to silence your speakers. While your speakers are muted, the volume icon is overlaid with a red circle and slash. When you want the speakers to play again, open the **Volume** dialog box again and deselect the **Mute** option.

④ Close the Dialog Box

Click anywhere out on your desktop once to close the **Volume** dialog box.

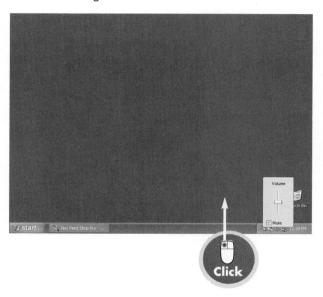

How-to Hint

Double-Clicking

The main volume control adjusts the volume for all the sounds on your computer, no matter where that sound comes from. Double-click the **Volume** dialog box to open a more sophisticated volume control that lets you adjust the volume for each audio device configured on your system. For example, you might want to lower the volume for CD-ROMs but leave the volume for Wave files (which are used for Windows system events) alone.

Where's My Volume Icon?

On some computers, the volume icon on the system tray may be disabled. If you don't see one, but would like to, first open the **Start** menu and click **Control Panel**. In the **Control Panel** window, double-click the **Sounds and Audio Devices** icon. On the **Volume** tab of the **Sounds and Audio Devices Properties** dialog box that opens, select the **Place Volume icon in the taskbar** option.

How to Set Up a Screen Saver

On older monitors (those more than ten years old), screen savers help prevent a phenomenon called burn-in, where items on your display can actually be permanently burned in to your monitor if left for a long time. Newer monitors don't really have a problem with this, but screen savers are still kind of fun and do help prevent passers-by from seeing what's on your computer when you're away. Windows XP provides a number of built-in screen savers.

❶ Open the Display Properties

Right-click any open space on your desktop and choose the **Properties** command from the shortcut menu. The **Display Properties** dialog box opens.

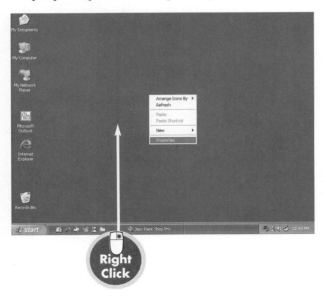

❷ Switch to the Screen Saver Tab

Switch to the **Screen Saver** tab by clicking it once.

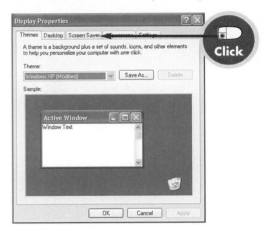

❸ Choose a Screen Saver

By default, Windows comes with no screen saver active. Click the arrow next to the **Screen saver** drop-down list to choose from the available screen savers.

④ Preview the Screen Saver

When you choose a screen saver, Windows displays a small preview of it right on the picture of a monitor in the dialog box. To see how the screen saver will look when it's actually working, click the **Preview** button. Move the mouse or press a key during the preview to get back to the dialog box.

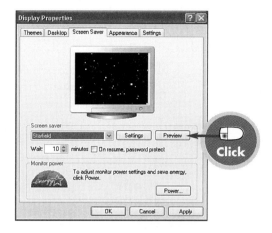

⑤ Adjust Settings

Each screen saver has its own specific settings so that you can change how the screen saver behaves. Settings for the **Starfield** screen saver, for example, let you control how many stars are displayed and how fast they move. Click the **Settings** button to experiment with options for any screen saver.

⑥ Adjust Wait Time

The **Wait** field specifies how long your computer must be idle before the screen saver kicks in. By default, this value is 15 minutes, but you can change it to whatever you want by using the scroll buttons. You can make a screen saver password protected by clicking the **password protect** option on the **Screen Saver** tab. See Chapter 9, "Protecting Your Files," for more information. Click **OK** when you're done setting up the screen saver.

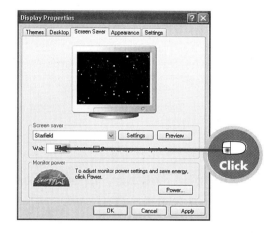

Getting Back to Work

After the screen saver kicks in, you won't be able to see the work that was on your screen because the screen saver "takes over." To get back to work, banish the screen saver simply by moving the mouse or pressing any key on the keyboard. The screen saver will come back on after the next lull in your activity.

Getting New Screen Savers

New screen savers are available for purchase at most software stores; many are available for free on the Internet. When you download a screen saver, it usually appears as a file with the extension .scr. Just copy the file to the **System32** folder inside your **Windows** folder to have it show up on the list in Step 3.

How to Change Your Desktop Theme

A desktop theme determines the overall look and feel of your desktop. A theme includes a background picture, a set of desktop icons, a color scheme for window elements, a predetermined set of sounds for Windows events, and a set of display fonts. All these aspects of the theme are customizable.

❶ Open Display Properties

Right-click any open space on your desktop and choose the **Properties** command from the shortcut menu. The **Display Properties** dialog box opens.

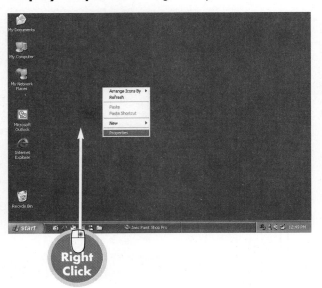

❷ View the Current Theme

On the **Themes** tab of the dialog box, the name of the current theme is displayed along with a sample of what the theme looks like on your desktop.

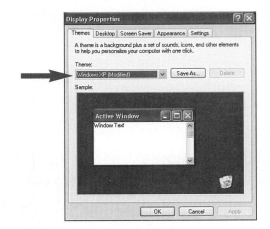

❸ Select a Theme

Click the arrow next to the **Theme** drop-down list and choose a different theme.

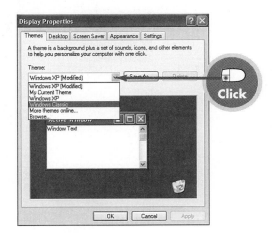

④ Sample the New Theme

A sample of the selected theme is displayed in the **Sample** window so that you can see what the theme will look like before actually applying it to your desktop.

⑤ Set the New Theme

To apply the new theme to your desktop and close the **Display Properties** window, click **OK**. To apply the theme and keep the dialog box open, click **Apply**.

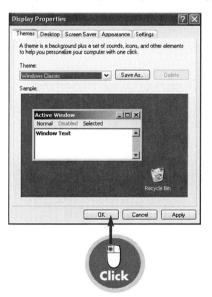

How to Change Your Wallpaper

Wallpaper is a pattern or picture that is displayed on your desktop just to make things a bit more fun. By default, Windows uses no wallpaper; you see only the standard blue desktop color. Windows XP includes a number of interesting wallpapers you can use to spruce up your display.

1 Open Display Properties

Right-click any open space on your desktop and choose the **Properties** command from the shortcut menu. The **Display Properties** dialog box opens.

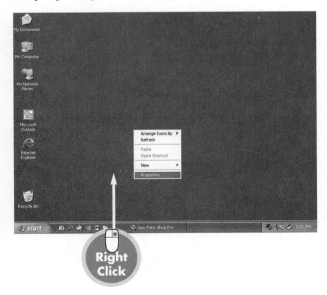

2 Switch to the Desktop Tab

Click the **Desktop** tab once to bring that page to the front.

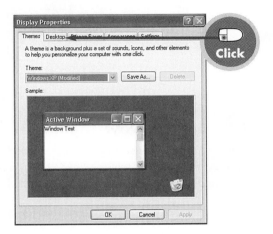

3 Choose a Wallpaper

Choose any wallpaper from the **Background** list by clicking it once. Whatever wallpaper you choose is displayed in the picture of a monitor in the dialog box.

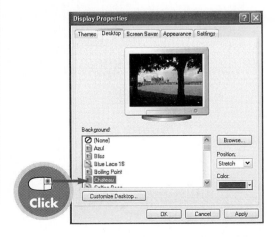

4 Use Your Own Picture

If you have a picture file on your computer that you want to use as wallpaper, click the **Browse** button to open a dialog box that lets you locate the file. Background pictures can have the following extensions: .bmp, .gif, .jpg, .dib, and .htm.

5 Adjust the Picture Display

You can display background pictures in one of three ways. You can **Center** a picture on the screen, **Stretch** a picture so that it fills the screen, or **Tile** a small picture so that it appears multiple times to fill the screen. Click the **Position** drop-down list to experiment with these options.

6 Set a Color

If you would rather not use a picture, but are tired of staring at a blue desktop, try setting a different color. Click the down-arrow next to the current color to open a palette for choosing a new color.

7 Apply the Settings

Click the **Apply** button to apply any new wallpaper to your desktop and keep the **Display Properties** dialog box open so that you can more easily experiment with backgrounds. After you find a background you like, click the **OK** button to get back to work.

How to Change Desktop Appearance

Changing your desktop appearance can really affect how you work. Windows lets you change the colors used on your desktop background, parts of windows, and even menus. For example, if you find yourself squinting at the text on the monitor, you can adjust the point size of the display font. If you don't like blue title bars on dialog boxes, you can change the color of that element, too.

❶ Open Display Properties

Right-click any open space on your desktop and choose the **Properties** command from the shortcut menu. The **Display Properties** dialog box opens.

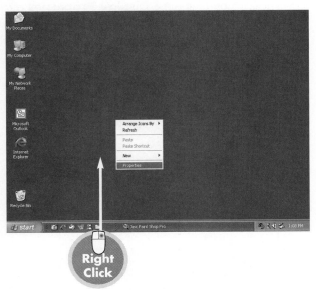

❷ Switch to the Appearance Tab

Switch to the **Appearance** tab by clicking it once.

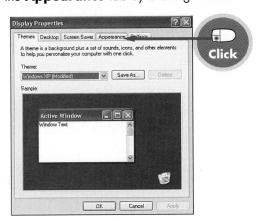

❸ Choose a Style

The Windows XP style uses the new rounded windows and stylized buttons. **Windows Classic** uses windows and buttons that look like previous versions of Windows. In **Windows Classic** style, the **Advanced** button (not available in the Windows XP style) lets you set colors for the different window elements.

④ Choose a New Color Scheme

If you're using the **Windows XP** style, you have only a few choices for the color scheme, including blue (the default), olive, and silver. If you're using the **Windows Classic** style, you can choose from many predefined color schemes. Choose a scheme using the **Color scheme** drop-down list. The sample window in the dialog box changes to show you what a color scheme will look like.

⑤ Adjust Font Size

Some of the color schemes allow for more than one font size to be used when displaying menus, window text, and dialog boxes. Use the **Font size** drop-down list to choose a **Normal**, **Large**, or **Extra Large** display font.

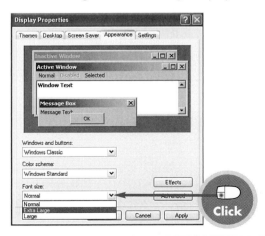

⑥ Open the Effects Dialog Box

Click the **Effects** button to open a separate dialog box for adjusting special desktop settings.

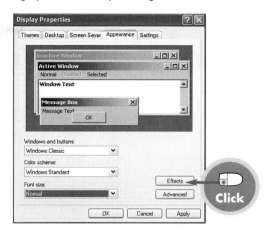

⑦ Adjust Effects

Many of the effects you can choose in this dialog box affect the speed with which windows are displayed on your computer. Using transition effects for menus, showing window contents while dragging the windows, and showing shadows under menus all make displaying windows on the desktop take just a little longer. Consider turning them off if you have a slower computer. Click **OK** twice to close both dialog boxes and apply the settings.

How to Change Display Settings

Display settings control various aspects of your video adapter and monitor. You can change the display settings to control the screen resolution (how many pixels are shown on your screen) and the color quality (how many colors are available for the display to use). Using a higher resolution lets you fit more on your desktop. Using better color quality makes things look better. However, both options depend on the quality of your video card and monitor, and using higher settings can slow down your system a bit.

① Open Display Properties

Right-click any open space on your desktop and choose the **Properties** command from the shortcut menu. The **Display Properties** dialog box opens.

② Switch to the Settings Tab

Switch to the **Settings** tab by clicking it once.

③ Choose a New Color Depth

Color depth refers to the number of colors your screen can display. Click the **Color quality** drop-down list to choose a new color setting. And although using the highest available color quality is usually the better choice, it can slow down your system just a bit. You'll have to play with the settings to find what you like best.

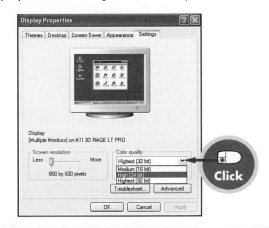

④ Choose a New Screen Resolution

Screen resolution refers to the size of items displayed on your screen. Increasing the area means that you can see more items on your screen at once, but also means that those items will appear smaller. Adjust the screen area by dragging the **Screen resolution** slider.

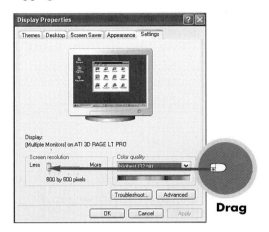

Drag

⑤ Start the Display Troubleshooter

If you are having display problems, click the **Troubleshoot** button to open the Windows Help system and go directly to the display troubleshooter.

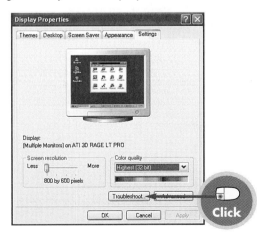

Click

⑥ Open Advanced Properties

Click the **Advanced** button to open a separate dialog box with controls for changing the video adapter and monitor drivers your computer is using, along with other advanced display settings.

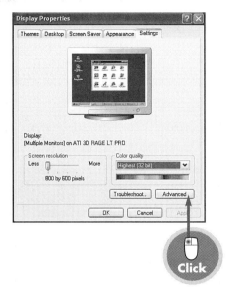

Click

How to Change Mouse Settings

Because the mouse will likely be your main tool for getting around in Windows, it should come as no surprise that Windows allows you to change the way your mouse works. Among other things, you can change the clicking speed that makes for a successful double-click and the speed at which the pointer moves across the screen.

❶ Open the Control Panel

Click **Start** and then select **Control Panel** to open the **Control Panel** window.

❷ Open the Mouse Icon

Double-click the **Mouse** icon to open the **Mouse Properties** dialog box.

❸ Change Button Configuration

Choose the **Switch primary and secondary buttons** option to swap the functions of the left and right buttons. This option is useful if you use your mouse with your left hand.

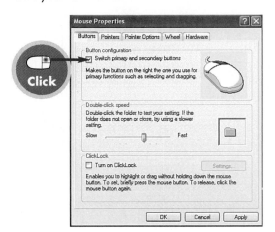

④ Adjust Double-Click Speed

The **Double-click speed** option refers to how close together two clicks of the mouse button must be for Windows to consider them a double-click rather than two single clicks. Drag the slider with your left mouse button to adjust the speed and then test it by double-clicking the folder icon in the test area.

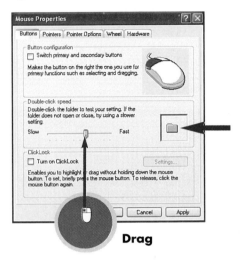

Drag

⑤ Adjust the Pointer Speed

Click the **Pointer Options** tab to switch to that page. Here you can set several options relating to how the mouse pointer moves. Drag the **Motion** slider to set how fast the pointer moves across the screen when you move the mouse. Click the **Apply** button to experiment with any settings you make while keeping the **Mouse Properties** dialog box open.

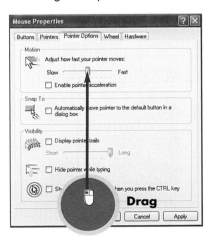

Drag

⑥ Enable Acceleration

Acceleration refers to whether the movement of your pointer accelerates if you begin moving your mouse more quickly. Without this option, the pointer keeps moving at a single speed no matter how quickly you move your mouse. Usually, you want this option enabled so that the speed you move the mouse on the table top is mimicked in the speed at which the mouse pointer moves onscreen. However, you sometimes may find that the mouse pointer moves too quickly or acts erratically with this option enabled.

Click

⑦ Snap to Default

Normally, when a new dialog box opens, the mouse pointer stays right where it is; you must move it to the buttons on the dialog box to do anything. With the **Snap To** option enabled, the mouse pointer automatically jumps to whatever the default button is.

Click

How to Change Keyboard Settings

Windows allows you to change a number of settings related to how your keyboard works. You can change the delay that occurs between when you press a key and when the key starts to repeat from holding it down. You can also change the rate at which the key repeats. Finally, you can change the blink rate for your cursor (the little vertical line that blinks where you are about to type something).

❶ Open the Control Panel

Click **Start** and then choose **Control Panel** to open the **Control Panel** window.

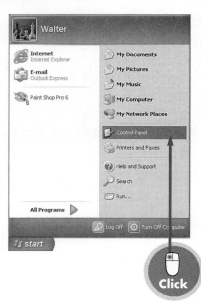

❷ Open the Keyboard Icon

Double-click the **Keyboard** icon to open the **Keyboard Properties** dialog box.

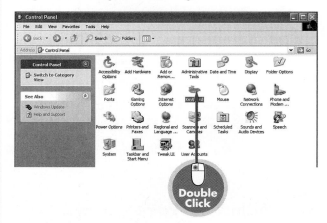

❸ Change the Repeat Delay

The **Repeat delay** option specifies the delay that occurs between when you press a key and when the key starts to repeat from holding it down. Drag the slider to change the rate.

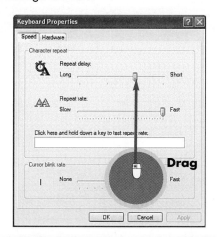

④ Change the Repeat Rate

When you hold a key down longer than the repeat delay you specified in the previous step, the key begins to repeat. Drag the **Repeat rate** slider to change the repeat rate.

Drag

⑤ Test Your Settings

Click in the test box and then press and hold any key to test your repeat delay and repeat rate settings.

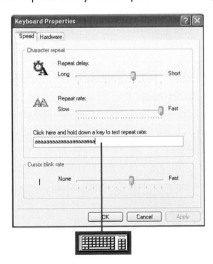

⑥ Change the Cursor Blink Rate

Whenever you click in a text box to type a value or to type a document, a little vertical line called a cursor blinks to let you know where the characters you type will appear. The cursor is sometimes also called the insertion point. Drag the **Cursor blink rate** slider to change the rate at which the cursor blinks. A sample cursor to the left of the slider blinks according to your settings.

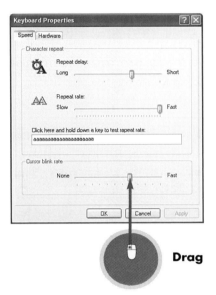

Drag

How to Customize the Taskbar

The taskbar is one of the more important tools you use when working in Windows XP. There are several ways you can customize its use, as you will see in the following steps.

1 Open Taskbar Properties

Right-click anywhere on the taskbar and click **Properties**. The **Taskbar and Start Menu Properties** dialog box opens.

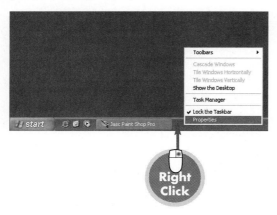

2 Lock the Taskbar

By default, you can drag the taskbar to other edges of the screen, resize the taskbar, and adjust the size of the system tray and Quick Launch portions of the taskbar. Enable the **Lock the taskbar** option to prevent this from happening.

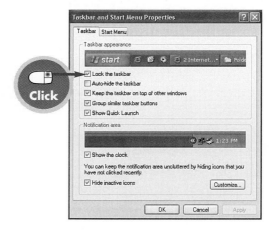

3 Make the Taskbar Autohide

Enable the **Auto-hide the taskbar** option to have the taskbar automatically scroll off the edge of the screen when it's not in use. Move your pointer to the edge of the screen to make the taskbar scroll back into view. This option cannot be used when the taskbar is locked.

④ Keep the Taskbar on Top

By default, the taskbar is always on the top of your display. Thus, when you move a window into the same space occupied by the taskbar, the taskbar still appears in front of the window. Disable the **Keep the taskbar on top of other windows** option so that other items can appear in front of the taskbar.

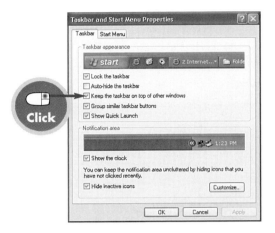

⑤ Group Similar Buttons

When you start a program (such as Internet Explorer) more than once, a separate button appears on the taskbar for each instance of the program. When you enable the **Group similar taskbar buttons**, only one button appears for each program and a number to the side indicates how many documents for that program are open.

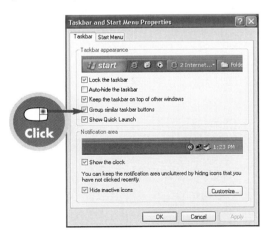

⑥ Show the Clock

The **Show the clock** option causes Windows to display the clock in the system tray at the far right of your taskbar. Disable this option to hide the clock. Double-click the clock to open a dialog box that lets you set the time and date.

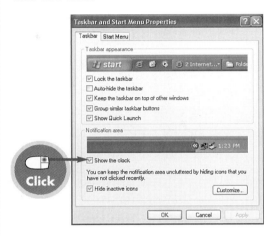

⑦ Hide Inactive Icons

By default, the system tray is collapsed so that only the most frequently used icons are shown. If you don't like this space-saving feature, turn it off by disabling the **Hide inactive icons** check box.

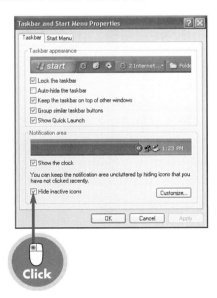

How to Change Folder Options

Windows XP handles folders in much the same way as previous versions of Windows. You have the option of viewing a folder as a Web page, in which a pane on the left side of the folder view gives you information about any selected item. You also have the option of having Windows open a new window for each folder you want to open. The following steps explain how to access these options using the **Control Panel**. You can also access the **Folder Options** dialog box from the **View** menu at the top of any open folder.

❶ Open the Control Panel

Click the **Start** button and then choose **Control Panel**. The **Control Panel** window opens.

❷ Open the Folder Options Icon

Double-click the **Folder Options** icon to open the **Folder Options** dialog box.

❸ Use Web View

Web View is an option that shows Web content in folders. Normally, this just means that a pane at the left of a folder window shows information about selected items in that folder. Some folders, however, might have more specialized content. Enable the **Use Windows classic folders** option to disable this feature.

④ Change Folder Browsing

Normally when you open a folder, that folder opens in whatever window you are using at the time. If you would rather Windows open a whole new window for each folder you open, select the **Open each folder in its own window** option here.

⑤ Change Click Settings

By default, you single-click items to select them and double-click items to open them. If you prefer, enable the **Single-click to open an item (point to select)** option so that you only have to single-click items to open them, much like you do in Internet Explorer. With this option enabled, holding the mouse pointer over an item for a second selects the item.

⑥ Restore Defaults

If you find that you don't like the folder settings you have already made, click the **Restore Defaults** button to change the settings back to their original configuration.

Advanced Options

The **View** tab of the **Folder Options** dialog box features a long list of specific settings relating to how folders work, such as whether hidden system files should be displayed, whether file extensions should be displayed or hidden, and whether Windows should remember the view for each folder you open. After you are familiar with using Windows, you may want to check the options on this list and see whether any appeal to you.

How to Change Power Options

You might find it useful to adjust the way Windows handles your power settings. To save energy, Windows can automatically turn off parts of your computer, such as the hard drive and monitor, after a certain amount of time. The next time you try to access these devices, the power is immediately restored and you can proceed with your tasks without delay.

1 Open Control Panel

Click **Start** and then choose **Control Panel**. The **Control Panel** window opens.

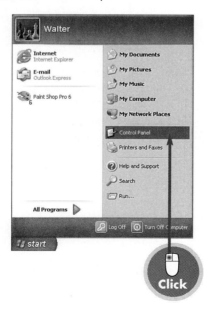

2 Open the Power Options Icon

Double-click the **Power Options** icon to open the **Power Options Properties** dialog box.

3 Choose a Power Scheme

The easiest way to configure power settings is to choose a custom scheme designed to fit the way you use your computer. Click the **Power schemes** drop-down list to choose from a number of schemes.

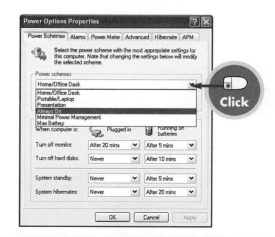

④ Turn Off Monitor

If you want to customize power settings beyond just choosing a scheme, you can choose how long the computer should be idle before certain devices are turned off. Click the **Turn off monitor** drop-down menu to specify how long the computer should be idle before your monitor is turned off. Note that you can specify a different delay time if your computer is running on batteries.

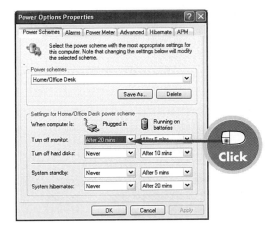

⑤ Turn Off Hard Disks

Click the **Turn off hard disks** drop-down menu to specify how long the computer should be idle before your hard drive is turned off. Note that you can specify a different delay time if your computer is running on batteries.

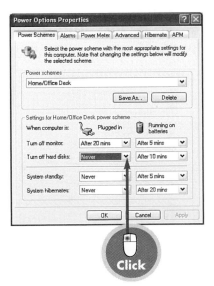

⑥ Send System to Standby

Some computers have the capability to go into standby, where only a trickle of power is used to keep track of what's in your computer's memory. When you come back from standby, everything should be as you left it. Use the drop-down menu to specify how long the computer should be idle before it goes into standby. Note that you can specify a different delay time if your computer is running on batteries.

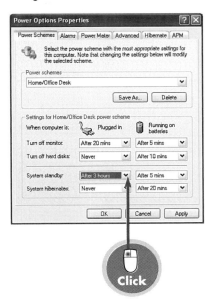

How-to Hint

Where Are All Those Options?

Depending on the type of computer and type of hardware installed, the **Power Options Properties** dialog box you see may be different than the one shown in this task. Notebook computers, for example, have settings both for when the computer is plugged in and when it is running on batteries. Notebooks also boast several more tabs on the dialog box to configure such things as advanced standby and hibernation modes. The best place to find out information about these advanced options is in the documentation for the computer itself.

How to Change System Sounds

If you have speakers on your computer, you might have noticed that certain things you do in Windows (such as emptying the Recycle Bin, starting Windows, and logging off) make certain sounds. These things are called events. Windows events also include things you don't do yourself, such as when an error dialog box is displayed or when e-mail is received. You can easily change the sounds associated with Windows events by using the following steps.

① Open the Control Panel

Click **Start** and then choose **Control Panel**. The **Control Panel** window opens.

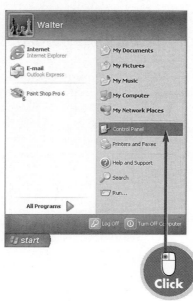

② Open the Sounds and Audio Devices Icon

Double-click the **Sounds and Audio Devices** icon to open the **Sounds and Audio Devices Properties** dialog box.

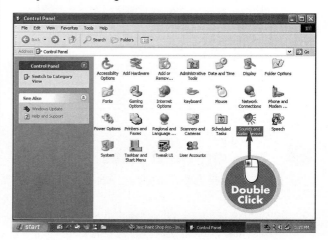

③ Switch to the Sounds Tab

Click the **Sounds** tab to bring it to the front.

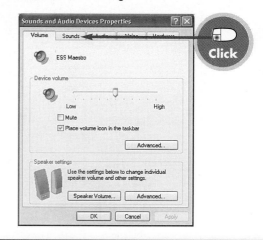

4 Choose an Event

From the **Program** events list, select any system event, such as **Default Beep**.

5 Choose a Sound File

Click the arrow next to the **Sounds** drop-down list to select a sound to associate with the selected event. You can also use your own sound file (any .wav file) by clicking the **Browse** button.

6 Play the Sound

Click the **Play** button to hear the selected sound.

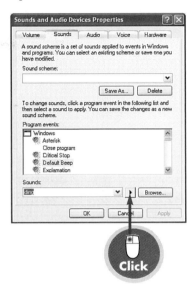

7 Choose a Sound Scheme

Windows comes with a couple of different sound schemes, which are sets of sounds similar in effect that are applied to all the major system events at once. Use the **Sound Scheme** drop-down list to choose a scheme.

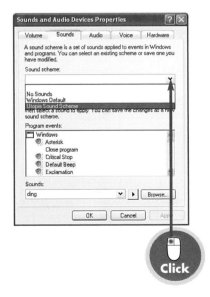

How to Add an Item to the Start Menu

The Start menu is loaded with shortcuts to various programs and folders on your computer. Whenever you install a new program, that program usually adds a shortcut of its own to the **Start** menu automatically. You can also add items of your own. You can add shortcuts to programs, documents, or even folders.

1 Find the Item You Want to Add

Use the **My Computer** or **My Documents** window to find the item you want to add to the **Start** menu. This item can be a document, a program, or even a folder.

2 Drag the Item over the Start Menu

Using the left mouse button, click and drag the item over the **Start** button, but *do not* release the mouse button yet.

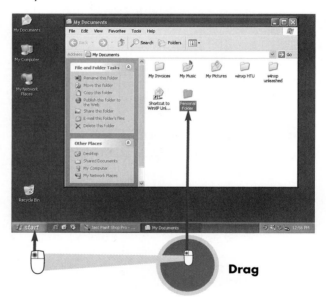

Drag

③ Place the Item in the More Programs Folder

After holding the item over the **Start** button for about two seconds, the **Start** menu opens. Continue dragging the item over the **All Programs** folder and then onto the **All Programs** menu that appears. When you find where you want to place the item (a horizontal line appears to guide placement), let go of the mouse button. After you have placed the shortcut, just click it to launch the original program.

④ Rename the Shortcut

Right-click the new shortcut and choose **Rename** from the shortcut menu to give the shortcut a new name. This name appears in a pop-up window when you hold your pointer over the shortcut for a second.

⑤ Delete the Shortcut

Right-click the shortcut in the **Start** menu and choose **Delete** from the shortcut menu to remove the shortcut from the **Start** menu.

How to Hint
Adding Shortcuts

Unfortunately, you can only add shortcuts to the **All Programs** menu and not to the main **Start** menu itself, as you could in previous versions of Windows. Still, this does provide an easier way to open programs, folders, and files than by browsing for them on your hard drive.

How to Add an Item to the Quick Launch Bar

The **Quick Launch** bar is handy feature located in the task bar next to the **Start** button. You can use it to open certain programs with a single click. Only three shortcuts appear by default on the **Quick Launch** bar: one to launch Internet Explorer, one to launch Outlook Express, and one to show your desktop when there are windows in the way. Fortunately, it's pretty easy to add new shortcuts for programs, documents, and folders. In fact, many programs (such as Microsoft Outlook) add their own shortcuts during installation.

1 Find the Item You Want to Add

Use the **My Computer** or **My Documents** window to find the item to which you want to make a Quick Launch shortcut.

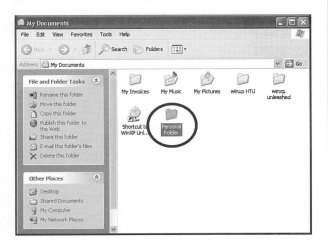

2 Drag the Item to the Quick Launch Bar

Click the item with your left mouse button and, while holding the button down, drag the item into a blank space on the **Quick Launch** bar. You can even drag the item between two existing shortcuts to put it exactly where you want.

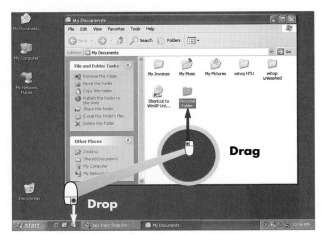

3 Rename the Shortcut

Right-click the new shortcut and choose **Rename** from the shortcut menu to give the shortcut a new name. This name appears in a pop-up window when you hold the mouse pointer over the shortcut icon for a second.

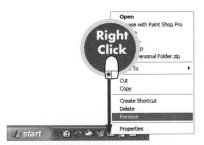

Delete the Shortcut

Right-click the shortcut and choose **Delete** from the shortcut menu to remove the shortcut from the **Quick Launch** bar and place it in the **Recycle Bin**. Hold the **Shift** key down when selecting **Delete** to permanently delete the shortcut without sending it to the **Recycle Bin**.

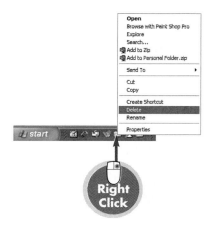

How-to Hint

Rearranging Shortcuts

You can rearrange existing shortcuts in the **Quick Launch** bar by simply dragging them to new locations on the **Quick Launch** bar.

Moving the Quick Launch Bar

You can move the **Quick Launch** bar separately from the taskbar by clicking at the leftmost edge of the **Quick Launch** bar (marked by two rows of small, dimpled dots) and dragging it. You can move the bar to one of the other edges of your display or into the center of the window.

Don't See a Quick Launch Bar?

On some computers, the **Quick Launch** bar may be disabled. If you don't see the **Quick Launch** bar and want to add it, right-click anywhere on your taskbar and choose **Properties**. On the **Taskbar** tab of the **Taskbar and Start Menu Properties** dialog box that opens, choose the **Show Quick Launch** option.

How to Start a Program When Windows Starts

Windows maintains a special folder named **Startup** that lets you specify programs, folders, and even documents that open every time Windows starts. You can see the **Startup** folder and what's in it by selecting **Start**, **All Programs**, and **Startup**. The following steps show you how to add shortcuts to that folder.

❶ Find the Item You Want to Add

Use the **My Computer** or **My Documents** window to find the item you want to add to the Startup folder menu. This item can be a document, program, or even a folder.

❷ Drag the Item over the Start Menu

Using the left mouse button, click and drag the item over the **Start** button, but *do not* release the mouse button yet.

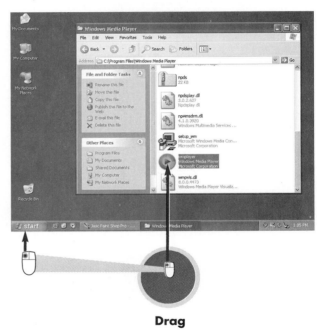

Drag

③ Drag the Item over the All Programs Folder

Continue dragging the item and hold it over the **All Programs** option on the **Start** menu. Do not release the mouse button yet.

④ Place the Item in the Startup Folder

When the **All Programs** folder opens, drag the item to the **Startup** folder and drop it there.

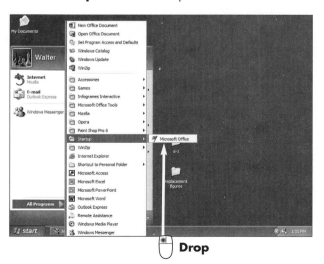

Drop

How-to Hint

Removing Startup Programs

Many of the programs you install (and even Windows itself) have small associated programs that are configured to start when your computer starts. For example, Windows Messenger starts automatically and so does the AOL Instant Messenger when you install AOL. You can usually tell these programs have started because you can see icons representing them in the system tray at the right side of the taskbar. If you have programs starting automatically that you would rather did not, try checking the **Startup** folder first. If there is a shortcut in there for the program, you can delete it and the program will not start automatically anymore. If you're not sure whether it's necessary that the program start when Windows starts, try moving the shortcut to your desktop and restarting Windows to see what happens. You can always move the shortcut back into the **Startup** folder if you decide you need it. If a program is starting and you don't see a shortcut for it in the **Startup** folder, try clicking or right-clicking the icon in the system tray. Sometimes you will find an option to exit the program or even prevent it from starting with Windows.

How to Set Accessibility Options

Windows includes a number of accessibility options intended for people with disabilities (some people without disabilities find these settings useful, as well). These options include a small window that magnifies whatever part of the screen your mouse pointer is on and the ability to make Windows flash the display instead of making sounds. All these options are available through the Windows **Control Panel**.

❶ Open the Control Panel

Click the **Start** button and then choose **Control Panel**. The **Control Panel** window opens.

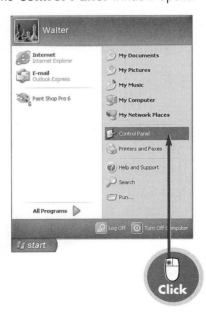

❷ Open Accessibility Options

Double-click the **Accessibility Options** icon. The **Accessibility Options** dialog box opens.

❸ Set Keyboard Options

Switch to the **Keyboard** tab to set various accessibility options for working with the keyboard. The **StickyKeys** option lets you press one key at a time (**Ctrl** and then **Shift**, for example) instead of having to press them simultaneously. The **FilterKeys** option tells Windows to ignore brief or quickly repeated keystrokes that may be caused by unsteady hands on the keyboard. The **ToggleKeys** option plays sounds to indicate when the **Caps Lock**, **Num Lock**, and **Scroll Lock** keys are turned on or off.

④ Set Sound Options

Switch to the **Sound** tab to set options for using sound in addition to the visual feedback your computer gives you in certain circumstances. The **SoundSentry** option generates visual warnings (such as flashes) when your system would otherwise just play a sound. The **ShowSounds** option generates captions for the speech and sounds made by certain programs.

⑤ Set Display Options

Switch to the **Display** tab to find settings that make it easier to read the screen. The **High Contrast** option causes Windows to display the desktop using colors and fonts that are easier to read. The **Cursor Options** adjust the size and blink rate of the cursor that appears where text is about to be typed.

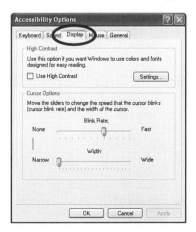

⑥ Set Mouse Options

Switch to the **Mouse** tab to enable **MouseKeys**, a feature that lets you use your keyboard's number pad to control the mouse pointer. Click the **Settings** button to open a dialog box that lets you control the pointer speed and turn on and off the **MouseKeys** feature using the **Num Lock** key on your keyboard.

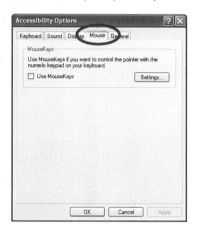

⑦ Set General Options

Switch to the **General** tab to set options that pertain to all accessibility features, such as when they are used and whether they are automatically turned off after a period of time. When you have specified all the options you want, click **OK** to apply the settings and close the dialog box.

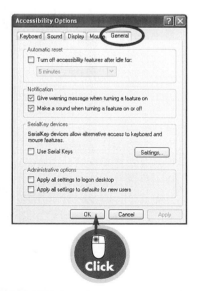

Task

6

Using the System Tools

Computers are pretty complicated. A lot of things can happen during the course of normal use that can slow a computer down or keep certain things from working as they should. If you are connected to a network, the chances are that you have a network administrator to rely on for fixing problems when they occur. If you don't have an administrator, you'll have to take things into your own hands. There are a few things you can do to help make sure that your computer is performing well and your work is not lost if something does go wrong. Windows XP provides a number of important system tools to help you protect your files and maintain your computer.

How to Free Up Space on Your Hard Disk

Even with the size of today's large hard drives, you might still find conservation of disk space an issue. During normal operation, Windows and the programs you run on it create temporary and backup files. Unfortunately, these programs (Windows included) are sometimes not very good at cleaning up after themselves. Windows includes a tool named Disk Cleanup that you can use to search for and delete unnecessary files.

① Run Disk Cleanup

Click the **Start** button and choose **All Programs**, **Accessories**, **System Tools**, and **Disk Cleanup**.

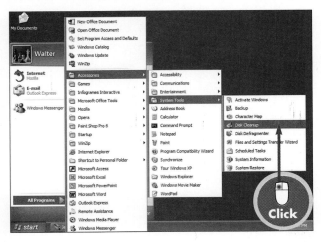

② Select the Drive to Clean Up

Use the drop-down list to select the hard drive on which you want to free up space. Click the **OK** button after you have chosen your drive. Disk Cleanup scans the specified drive for files. This process might take a few minutes.

③ Select the Items to Remove

After Disk Cleanup has finished scanning your drive, it presents a list of categories for files it has found. Next to each category, Windows shows how much drive space all the files in that category take up. You can mark categories for deletion by clicking the check boxes next to them.

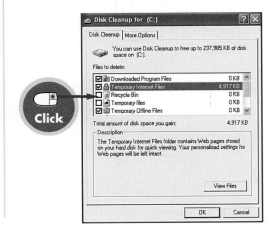

④ View Files

Categories that are already checked, such as Downloaded Program Files, are always safe to delete. Other categories might contain important files, and it is up to you to decide whether they should be deleted. Select a category by clicking its name once and click the **View Files** button to see what's contained in that category.

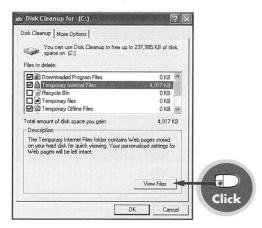

⑤ Click OK

When you have selected all the categories for files you want to delete, click the **OK** button to proceed. Windows asks whether you are sure you want to delete the files. If you are, click the Yes button.

How-to Hint

Taking Out the Trash

One way to keep space free on your hard drive is to regularly empty your Recycle Bin. Right-click the bin and choose **Empty Recycle Bin** from the shortcut menu to delete all the files it holds. You can also double-click the **Recycle Bin** to display a list of the files it contains and then delete individual files.

Deleting Only Certain Files

When you click the **View Files** button (as described in Step 4), a standard window opens showing the files in that location. If you want to delete only some of the files, select them in this window and delete them by pressing the **Delete** key. Make sure that you deselect the folder when you return to the Disk Cleanup Wizard or you'll end up deleting all the files anyway. Also, when you delete selected files using the View Files method, the files are moved to the Recycle Bin. You must empty the Recycle Bin to finish freeing the disk space. When you remove files using the Disk Cleanup Wizard, the files are permanently deleted.

How to Defragment Your Hard Disk

When you delete a file on your computer, Windows doesn't really remove it. It just marks that space as available for new information to be written. When a new file is written to disk, part of the file might be written to one available section of disk space, part might be written to another, and part to yet another space. This process fitting files in pieces on the disk is called fragmentation. It is a normal process, and Windows keeps track of files just fine. The problem is that when a drive has a lot of fragmentation, it can take Windows longer to find the information it is looking for. You can speed up drive access significantly by periodically defragmenting your drive.

1 Run Disk Defragmenter

Click the **Start** button and choose **All Programs**, **Accessories**, **System Tools**, and **Disk Defragmenter**.

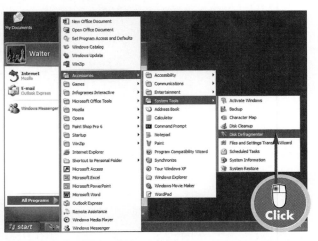

2 Choose a Drive

The window at the top of the screen lists all the hard drives on your computer. Select the drive you want to defragment by clicking it once.

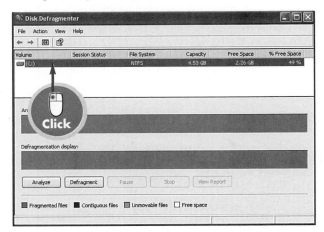

③ Analyze Drive

Click the **Analyze** button to have Disk Defragmenter analyze the selected drive for the amount of fragmentation on it. This process might take a few minutes, and the process is depicted graphically for you while you wait.

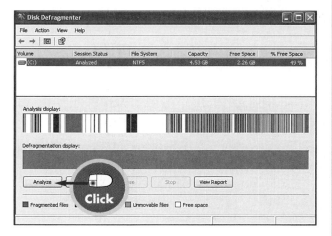

⑤ Defragment Drive

Should the analysis and report prove that your drive needs to be defragmented, you can start the procedure by clicking the **Defragment** button. This process can take a while—even an hour or so—depending on the size of your hard drive and how fragmented it is.

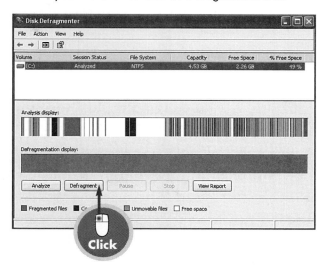

④ View Report

When the analysis is done, a dialog box appears that lets you view a report or go ahead with defragmentation. You can also perform these actions from the main program window itself. Click the **View Report** button to view a detailed report of the fragmented files that the analysis has discovered.

Some Helpful Tips

Make sure that you close all programs before beginning the defragmentation process. Also make sure that all documents are finished printing, scanning, downloading, and so on. In other words, your computer should not be busy doing anything else. During the defragmentation process, you will not be able to run any other programs. Unless you enjoy watching the defragmentation process, take a coffee break.

How to Schedule a Task to Occur Automatically

Windows XP includes a task scheduler that lets you schedule certain programs to run automatically. This can be particularly useful with programs such as Disk Cleanup and Disk Defragmenter, although you can schedule virtually any program. You might, for example, schedule Disk Cleanup to run automatically every Friday night after work and Disk Defragmenter to run once a month or so, saving you the time of running these programs when you have better things to do.

① Start Scheduled Tasks

Click the **Start** button and choose **All Programs**, **Accessories**, **System Tools**, and **Scheduled Tasks**.

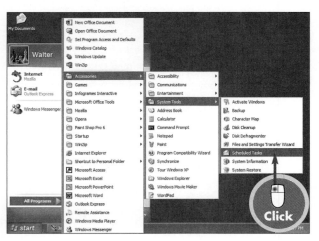

② Add a Scheduled Task

Double-click the **Add Scheduled Task** icon to start the Scheduled Task Wizard. The first page of the wizard is just a welcome page. Click the **Next** button to go on.

③ Choose a Program to Run

Select the program you want to schedule from the list by clicking it once. If you don't see the program on the list, you can try to locate it by clicking the **Browse** button. After you've selected the program, click the **Next** button to go on.

④ Choose When to Run the Program

If you want to change the default name of the task, type a new name in the text box. Choose when you want to perform the task by enabling that option. When you're done, click the Next button to go on.

⑥ Enter a Username and Password

To run a program in Windows, Task Scheduler must have your username and password. Type this information into the boxes on this page, and then click the Next button to go on.

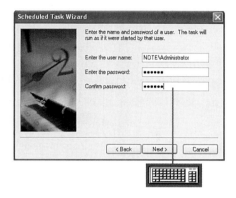

⑤ Choose a Time and Day

If you chose to run the program daily, weekly, or monthly, you must also specify the time of day to run the program. Type in a time or use the scroll buttons. You must also select the day or days you want the program to run by clicking the appropriate check boxes. Click the **Next** button to go on.

⑦ Finish

Click the **Finish** button to schedule your new task. When the specified day and time roll around, the selected program starts and runs with the default settings. If you want the selected program to start using any other settings, you'll have to consult the Help file for the program to see whether it supports changing settings in a scheduled task.

How to Use the Windows Troubleshooters

If your computer is on a corporate office network, you are probably fortunate enough to have a network administrator to call when your computer has problems. In a home office situation where you are the network administrator, or for a standalone installation, you will be relieved to know that Windows includes a few useful troubleshooters that can help you diagnose and repair problems.

① Start Help

Click the **Start** button and then choose **Help and Support**.

② Open Fixing a Problem Category

Click the **Fixing a problem** subject once to expand it.

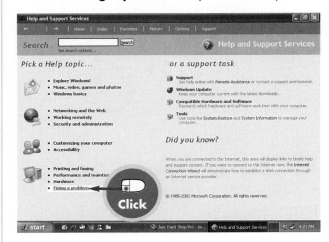

③ Choose a Type of Problem

From the list on the left side of the window, choose the type of problem you are having by clicking it once.

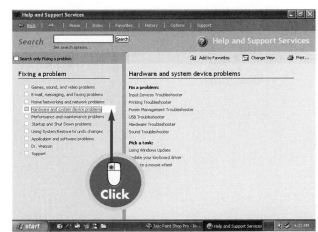

④ Choose a Troubleshooter

From the window on the right, locate the troubleshooter you want to run. After you find the troubleshooter you want, **Printing** for example, click it once to start it.

⑤ Work Through the Steps

Troubleshooters work just like wizards. Each page asks a question. Choose the answer by clicking it once, and then click the **Next** button to go on. Some pages offer steps for you to try to fix your problem. If the steps work, you're done. If the steps don't work, the troubleshooter continues. If the troubleshooter can't fix your problem, it recommends where you should go (Web sites and Microsoft technical support) for more information.

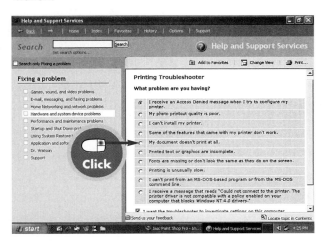

⑤ How to Get System Information

Often, fixing a problem requires that you find more information about your computer or your installation of Windows than is normally necessary. Fortunately, Windows includes a useful tool named System Information that lets you browse all kinds of useful information. Some of this information can be useful to you in determining why something is not working. For example, you can determine whether an existing piece of hardware is conflicting with the new piece you just installed. Much of the information is technical and will be useful when you're speaking with a technical support person.

❶ Start System Information

Click the **Start** button and choose **More Programs**, **Accessories**, **System Tools**, and **System Information**.

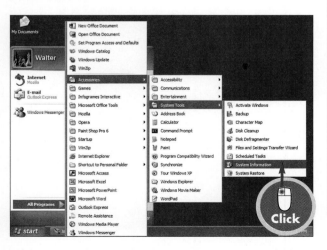

❷ View System Summary

The right side of the Help and Support Services window that opens contains a brief summary of your system, including the exact version of Windows installed and a snapshot of your basic hardware.

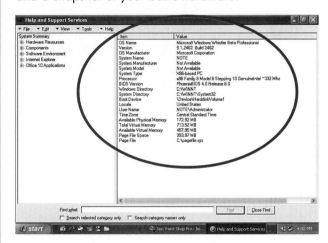

3 View Hardware Resources

Expand the **Hardware Resources** item in the left side of the window by clicking the plus sign next to it. Inside, you'll find various types of resources you can check on. Click any of these resources, such as **IRQs**, to view details on that resource.

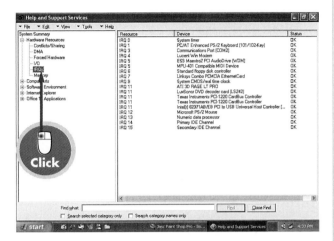

4 View Components

Expand the **Components** item to view details about many of the hardware components on your system. Click any subcategory, such as **CD-ROM**, to view details about that particular component.

5 Access Tools

Many useful tools are available on the Tools menu in the Help and Support Services window. Some of the tools are not available anywhere else in Windows. A good example is the DirectX Diagnostic Tool, which can help you diagnose video problems related to the Windows DirectX drivers.

How-to Hint

Printing and Exporting System Information

The File menu of the Help and Support Services window offers the ability to print and export your system information. When exporting, a text file is created. The entire set of system information (not just the page you're looking at) is printed or exported.

How to Use System Restore

Windows XP automatically creates system restore points at regular intervals. These restore points are basically backups of vital system settings and information. If you make a major change to your system, such as installing a new application or hardware driver, and then discover that the change has caused unwanted side effects, you can return to a previous restore point. The System Restore tool is used both to restore the computer to a previous point and to manually create a restore point.

❶ Start System Restore

Click the **Start** button and choose **All Programs**, **Accessories**, **System Tools**, and **System Restore**.

❷ Create a Restore Point

Although Windows creates restore points automatically, you can manually set a restore point before you make some change to your system that you think might adversely affect system performance. In the System Restore window that opens, select the **Create a restore point** option and then click **Next**.

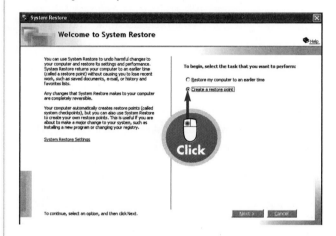

③ Name the Restore Point

Type a name for the restore point that describes it well enough to help you remember it. For example, you might name the restore point after the date, an action you just performed (or are about to perform), or after the fact that you have installed Windows and have everything working the way you want.

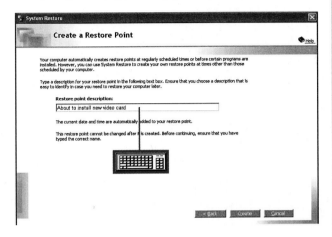

⑤ Close System Restore

When Windows has successfully created the restore point, it displays a message to that effect. To return to the Welcome to System Restore screen shown in Step 2, click **Home**. Otherwise, click **Close**.

④ Create the Restore Point

When you have named the new restore point, click **Create**.

How-to Hint

Restoring a Restore Point

Returning your computer to a restore point is just as easy as setting one. On the initial page of the System Restore Wizard, select the **Restore my computer to an earlier time** option. The wizard will guide you through choosing the restore point to which you want to return your system. The necessary files will be restored, your computer will be restarted, and you'll be back in business in no time. If you use System Restore to return your computer settings to a point before a software installation that went bad, note that System Restore just returns your Windows settings to the restore point—it does not remove the software from your computer. To do that, use the procedure described in Chapter 40, Task 2, "How to Change or Remove a Program."

How to Compress Files and Folders

Windows XP includes a built-in compression tool. You can compress files and folders to help save hard disk space. While compressed, the items are still accessible. In fact, you probably won't notice any difference between files you've compressed and those you haven't. On large files, however, you may notice that access is a bit slower than normal because of the compression. But if disk space is an issue, you may decide that it's better to have the large file and wait through the file-access hesitation.

1 Open an Item's Properties

In the My Documents or My Computer window, right-click the file or folder you want to compress and choose the **Properties** command from the shortcut menu.

2 Open Advanced Options

On the General tab of the Properties dialog box, click the **Advanced** button to open the Advanced Attributes dialog box.

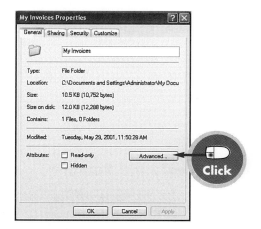

3 Compress the Item

Select the **Compress contents to save disk space** option. Note that there is also an option here that lets you encrypt the item. You cannot use both compression and encryption at the same time.

4 Close the Dialog Boxes

Click the **OK** button to close the Advanced Attributes dialog box. Click the **OK** button on the General tab of the folder's Properties dialog box to close it.

5 Compress Files and Subfolders

A dialog box appears that lets you choose whether to compress only the selected folder or also to compress the files and subfolders within that folder. Choose the option you want and click the **OK** button. The file or folder is compressed.

How-to Hint

Decompressing a Folder

To decompress a folder, simply follow the preceding steps and disable the Compress Contents to Save Disk Space option on the Advanced Attributes dialog box in Step 3.

Visual Indicator

When you compress a file or folder, by default Windows gives no visual indicator that compression is present. To see whether an item is compressed, you must open its Properties dialog box and see whether the Compress Contents to Save Disk Space option is enabled. However, you can tell Windows to display compressed files in a different color: Open the Control Panel and double-click **Folder Options**. On the View tab of the dialog box that opens, enable the **Display compressed files and folder in alternate color** option.

Sending Compressed Files

If you send a compressed file as an e-mail attachment or transfer a compressed file or folder to another computer using a network or a removable disk, the compression is removed on the copy that is sent. For example, if you e-mail a compressed file to a friend, the file remains compressed on your drive but the attachment is not compressed when your friend receives it.

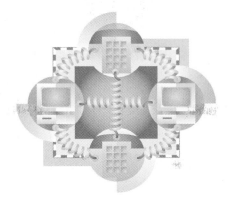

Working on a Network

A network is really just a bunch of computers (and sometimes other devices) that are connected together—a setup often referred to as a local area network, or LAN. Sometimes these LANs are connected together over different types of telephone lines to form one large network—often called a wide area network, or WAN.

When your computer is part of a network, you can share files, folders, and printers on one computer with other computers on the network. On a Windows network, computers and users are grouped together in one of two ways: domains or workgroups. Domains are fairly complicated networks, often used by large companies. Powerful computers called servers provide security, Internet access, file storage, and much more to less powerful computers called workstations. Workgroups are used on smaller networks and are usually groups of workstations networked together with no servers. Each of the workstations takes an equal part in the network and is often called a peer. If you are setting up your own network, you'll almost certainly use a workgroup.

How to Set Up a Small Network

Windows XP makes it easy to configure a small network after all the networking hardware is in place and the computers are physically connected. The installation instructions that come with the hardware you're using to create the network will help you physically connect your computers. Windows XP is all you need to handle the communications between the connected devices. This task provides an overview of setting up your network.

❶ Buy Your Networking Hardware

The majority of networks installed today use a type of cable called *twisted pair*. Twisted pair cable looks like a thick phone cable with jacks on the ends that are slightly wider than normal phone jacks. Cables and hardware are rated based on industry standards. As of the publication of this book, the highest standard officially available is Category 5e, although standards for Category 6 are in the works. Make sure that all the hardware and cables you use are rated at least Category 5e.

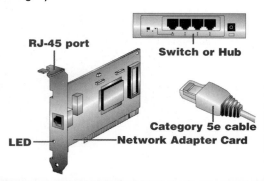

RJ-45 port
Switch or Hub
Category 5e cable
Network Adapter Card
LED

❷ Install Network Cards

A network adapter card must be installed into each computer that will be on the network. The card translates information back and forth between your computer and the network cable attached to the card.

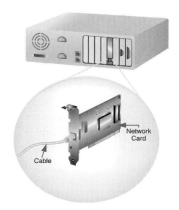

Network Card
Cable

❸ Set Up a Hub or Switch

If you have only two computers to network, you can connect them directly together using a crossover cable (a cable in which some of the wires are switched). Connect one end of the cable to each computer and that's it. If you have more than two computers, each computer must be connected to a central hub or switch with a normal cable (that is, not a crossover cable). Switches offer some advantages over hubs (including speed and ease of configuration), and are only about 15–20% more expensive. Use a switch when possible.

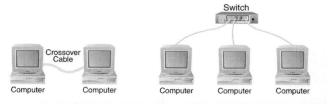

Switch
Crossover Cable
Computer   Computer   Computer   Computer   Computer

④ Set Up a Router

If you have a broadband Internet connection, such as a cable modem or DSL line, routers are available that can connect directly to your cable or DSL modem and then share your Internet connection automatically with the rest of your network. Many of these routers contain a built-in switch so that you can simply connect your computers right to it without using a separate hub or switch. Some routers even contain built-in firewalls that protect your computers from the Internet. If you don't want to use a router, you can still share an Internet connection with other computers on the network using Windows XP.

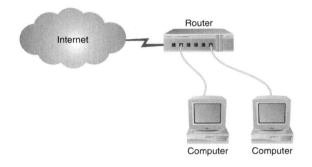

⑤ Set Up Other Networking Devices

Devices such as printers and fax machines can connect directly to the network cable in the same way that a computer with a network card does. These devices can then be shared by all computers on the network. On a small network, you probably won't use such devices. Instead, you might want to share the printer (or other device) attached to one of your computers with the rest of the network. For now, just make sure that the device is hooked up to the computer in the location you desire. You'll configure it later.

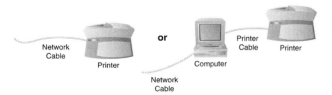

⑥ Connect Cables

After you've decided where the computers (and other network hardware) will be located, it's time to hook up the cables. Just plug one end of a cable into each computer and plug the other end into one of the jacks on your switch or hub. When the cables are connected, the physical part of setting up the network is finished. Next, you'll be working with Windows.

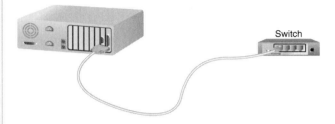

⑦ Install Windows XP

You'll have to install Windows XP on each of the computers on the network. It doesn't matter which edition of Windows XP you use—Home Edition or Professional. You can even use one edition on some computers and the other edition on other computers. In fact, you can even use previous versions of Windows on some of the computers (although you might have to do a little more configuring than with Windows XP). All editions and versions of Windows will talk to one another on the network. For details on installing Windows XP, see the Appendix.

8 Name the Computers

During the installation of Windows XP, you will be asked to provide a name for your computer. The setup program suggests one for you, but it is usually a somewhat convoluted name with lots of numbers in it. The name of the computer distinguishes it from the other computers on the network. For this reason, it is best to use simple names that help you identify each computer. For example, you might want to name the computers after the people who use them.

9 Join the Same Workgroup

During the installation of Windows XP, you will be asked to make the computer a member of either a domain or workgroup. For a small network, you will want to choose the **Workgroup** option and type in the name of the workgroup. It doesn't matter what workgroup name you use, as long as all the computers on the network use the same workgroup name.

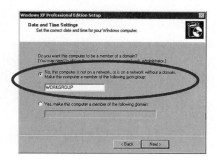

10 Set Up Network Cards

After you have installed Windows on each computer, turn on the computers. It is likely that Windows XP figured out what type of network adapter card you are using and configured it for you during installation. If Windows could not determine the network card, you will be asked the first time you start Windows after the installation to insert the disk that came with your network adapter card. Windows then finishes configuring your card.

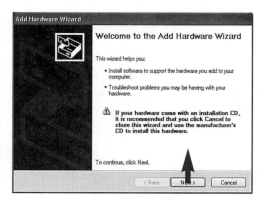

11 Make Sure the Network Works

Double-click the **My Network Places** icon on your desktop and then click the **View workgroup computers** link on the left side of the window. The resulting window should show a list of computers on the network. If no computers are shown, try another computer on the network. If none of the computers show any other computers, something is probably wrong with your switch or hub. If some computers show up and some don't, something is probably wrong with those computers. Double-check your installation.

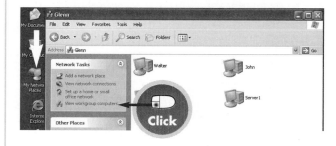

12 Share Folders and Files

When you know that the network is working, it's time to set up a few things. The first thing you'll want to do is go to each computer and share the folders and files you want other computers to be able to access. You learn how to do this in Task 8, "How to Share a File or Folder with Others."

13 Share Printers

You'll also want to share any printers that you want other computers to use. This process is covered in Chapter 16, "Printing."

14 Share an Internet Connection

If one of your computers has an Internet connection (whether it be a dial-up modem connection or a broadband connection such as cable or DSL), you can share the connection with all the computers on the network. Sharing an Internet connection is covered in Task 3, "How to Share an Internet Connection."

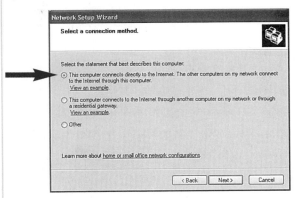

15 Get to Work

Your network should now be ready to use. Remember to check the rest of this chapter and the other chapters of this book (particularly Chapter 9, "Protecting Your Files") for more on using your network.

How to Set Up Additional User Accounts

User accounts provide an easy and secure way to share a single computer with more than one person. Although you could let different people share the same user account, creating different accounts has some advantages. When you first install Windows, two accounts are created. One is named by whatever name you provide to Windows during installation. The other is called a **Guest** account. This task shows you how to set up additional user accounts.

① Open User Accounts

Click the **Start** button and choose **Control Panel** to open the **Control Panel** window. Double-click the **User Accounts** icon to open the **User Accounts** window. It's possible that your **Control Panel** window will open in category view, which groups the various icons in the **Control Panel** according to their use and even hides some of the more useful ones. If your **Control Panel** is in category view, click the **Switch to Classic View** link.

② Create a New Account

The **User Accounts** window shows the accounts currently configured on the computer. Click **Create a new account**.

③ Name the New Account

Type a name for the new account. With a small number of users, it is usually best to use the first name of the person for whom you are creating the account. If two people have the same first name, you might want to use a last initial or some other variation of the name.

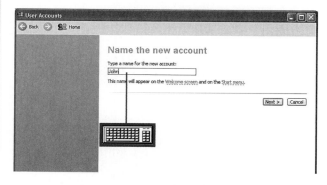

4   Choose the Type of Account

Each user account you create can be one of two types. A person with a **Computer Administrator** account can add, change, and delete other user accounts. That user can also install and remove software and make changes that affect all users of the computer. A person with a **Limited** account can change his own password, work with programs already installed by a **Computer Administrator**, and make limited configuration changes. After you choose the type of account you want to create, click **Create Account**.

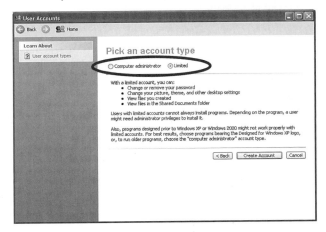

5   Change an Account

From the main **User Accounts** window, you can also change existing user accounts if you are allowed to do so (you must be using an account of the **Computer Administrator** type to make these kinds of changes). Click the **Change an account** link.

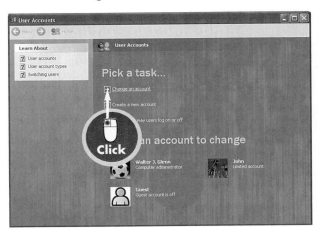

6   Choose an Account to Change

Click the account to which you want to make changes.

7   Select Changes to Make

Click the link for the change you want to make. You can change the name of the account, the picture that appears beside it, the type of account, and the password. You can also delete the account altogether.

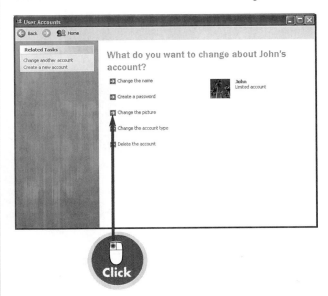

How to Share an Internet Connection

One of the biggest advantages of a home network (aside from playing games together and transferring large files easily) is the ability to share a single Internet connection among several computers. This task explains how to set up the computer that has the Internet connection so that the connection is shared with the other computers on the home network.

1 Start the Home Networking Wizard

These steps should be performed on the computer that has the Internet connection. Refer to the How-To Hints at the end of this task for instructions on setting up the other computers in your network. Click **Start** and choose **All Programs**, **Accessories**, **Communications**, **Network Setup Wizard**.

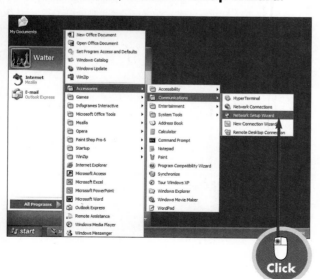

2 Click Next Twice

Click **Next** to go past the **Welcome** page of the wizard. Click **Next** again to go past the page that tells you that your computers must be connected together before starting the wizard.

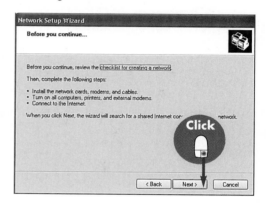

3 Select the Connection Method

Select the first listed option—**This computer connects directly to the Internet**. When you set up the other computers on your home network (as explained in the How-To Hints at the end of this task), you'll select one of the other options in this list. Click **Next** to go on.

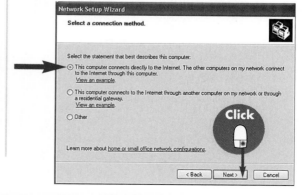

④ Choose the Internet Connection

Choose the specific connection that your computer uses to connect to the Internet. This connection could be a modem or it might be a networking card if you are directly connected. Click **Next** to continue.

⑥ Apply Network Settings

The wizard presents a summary of the settings you have chosen. When you have reviewed them and are sure that you want to apply them, click **Next**. When you are done, the wizard will let you know that the process has been successful; click **Finish** to exit the wizard.

⑤ Enter a Description for the Computer

Optionally, you can type a description for the computer that makes it easier for others on the network to identify it as the computer sharing an Internet connection. Click **Next** to go on.

How-to Hint

Setting Up Other Computers on the Network

After you have set up the computer with the Internet connection, run the **Home Networking Wizard** from each of the other computers on the network. On those computers, select the **This computer connects to the Internet through another computer on my network** option when asked for a connection method in Step 3.

Configuring a Firewall

When you set up a network connection that Windows recognizes as an Internet connection Windows automatically configures firewall software on the connection. For the most part, this software requires no configuration on your part. If you suspect that the firewall is not active for a connection, click the **Start** button and choose **Network Connections**. Right-click the connection that is used for the Internet, choose **Properties**, and select the **Advanced** tab. You can enable or disable the firewall for the connection on this tab.

How to Use My Network Places

Most of what you do on the network is done using the **My Network Places** icon on your desktop. If you do not see the **My Network Places** icon on your desktop, you can find it on your **Start** menu or add it to your desktop using the procedure described in Chapter 3. With it, you can access all the shared resources your network has to offer, add new network places of your own, and even search for computers and documents on the network.

1 Open My Network Places

Double-click the **My Network Places** icon on your desktop to open the **My Network Places** window.

2 View Workgroup Computers

The **My Network Places** window shows a list of all the shared folders on the local network. You can double-click any of them to open the folder and look for files. If you are in a workgroup, you'll also see a **View workgroup computers** link in the left column; if you are in a domain, you'll see an **Entire Network** link. Both links work the same way and let you further browse the resources on a network. Click the appropriate link or icon to begin browsing.

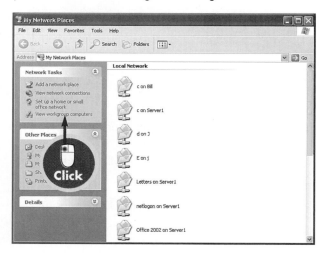

③ Open a Computer

The workgroup window shows all the other computers in your workgroup. Double-click a computer to open its window.

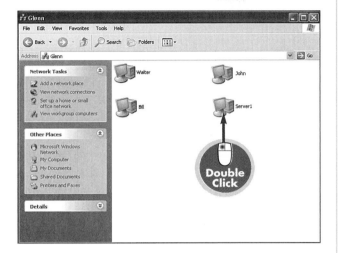

④ Open a Shared Folder

When you open a particular computer, all the resources shared on that computer are listed in this window. The computer's "resources" include shared folders, files, and printers. Double-click any shared object to open it.

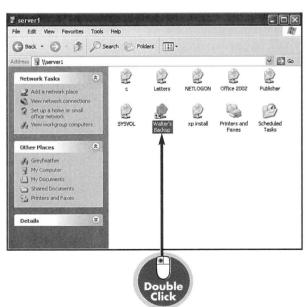

⑤ Open a File

You can use items in a shared folder just as you use items on your own computer. Double-click a file to open it.

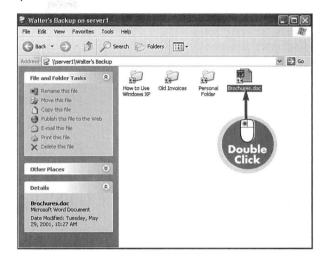

⑥ Copy a File to Your Computer

Instead of just opening and modifying a file on someone else's computer, you might want to copy it to your computer. To do that, just drag the file directly onto your desktop or into any open folder.

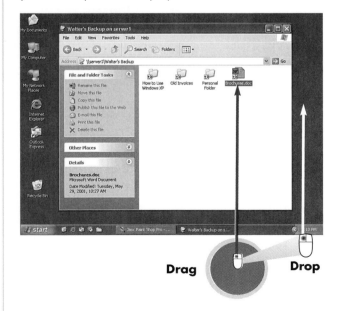

How to Add a Network Place

Although you can use **My Network Places** to browse the network looking for the right folder, you might want to add frequently used shared folders on your network, Web sites, or even FTP sites directly to the My **Network Places** window. Doing so lets you quickly get to files you use often.

① Add a Network Place

In the **My Network Places** window, click the **Add a network place** link to launch the **Add Network Place Wizard**. On the welcome page of the wizard, click **Next** to continue.

② Select Other Location

You can configure a remote storage location on the Microsoft Network if you have an account there, or you can configure a shortcut to a place on your local network. In this example, you'll create a shortcut to a place on your local network. Select the **Choose another network location** option and click **Next**.

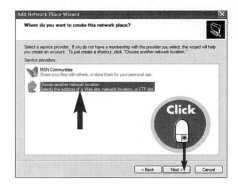

③ Browse for a Computer

If you know the exact path to the network resource you want, enter it in the text box. Don't be concerned that the text asks for the "name of a server." Type the path of any resource for which you are creating a network place. If you don't know the exact path, click the **Browse** button.

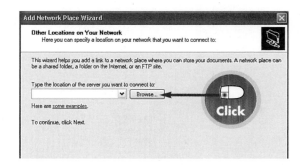

4 Select the Network Resource You Want

The **Browse** window lists all the computers in your domain or workgroup. Select the computer that contains the shared resource you want from the list, select the folder in that computer, and click **OK**. Note that you can select an entire computer if you want to make a network shortcut.

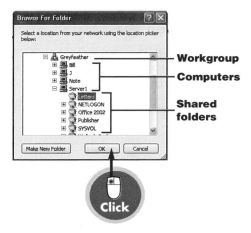

Workgroup
Computers
Shared folders

Click

5 Click Next

The path for the resource you've chosen appears in the **Type the location** text box on the wizard page. Click **Next** to go on.

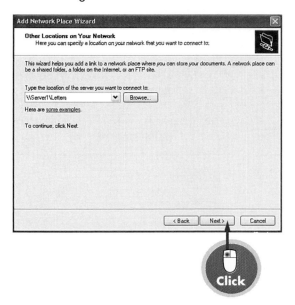

Click

6 Enter a Name for the Network Place

A name for the new shortcut is suggested for you. If you want to name it something different, type the new name in the **Enter a name for this network place** box and click **Next**.

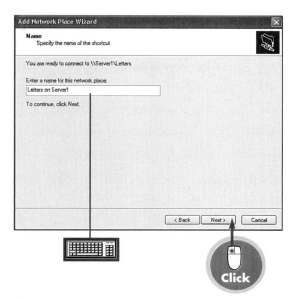

Click

7 Finish

Click **Finish**. When you are done, the new shortcut is available in the **My Network Places** window.

Click

How to Find a Computer on the Network

Using the **My Network Places** window to browse your network and locate a computer works fine if there are not a lot of computers on your network. Sometimes, however, the list of computers can be so long that scrolling around looking for a particular computer can be quite time consuming. Fortunately, Windows lets you quickly find a computer on the network, even if you know only part of its name.

1 Open My Network Places

Double-click the **My Network Places** icon on your desktop to open the **My Network Places** window.

2 Open the Search Pane

Click the **Search** button on the toolbar to open the **Search Companion** pane on the left side of the **My Network Places** window.

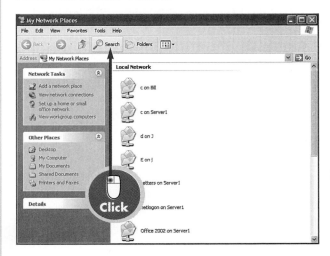

Auto-filling

As it does in many other places throughout the system, Windows remembers searches you have performed in the past. As you type your search term, Windows will try to fill in the rest of the search term for you based on what it remembers.

③ Enter a Computer Name

Type the name of the computer you are looking for in the **Computer name** text box. You can type just part of a name if you don't remember the whole thing.

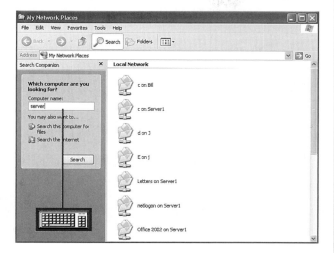

④ Search for the Computer

Click the **Search** button or press Enter to begin the search. Results of your search are displayed in the right pane of the **My Network Places** window.

⑤ Open the Computer

You can open any computer displayed in the search results list simply by double-clicking it. In this example, my search for a computer with the partial name "**server**" turned up only one match: **Server1**.

⑥ Close the Search Pane

Click the **Search** button on the toolbar again to close the **Search Companion** pane and get back to work.

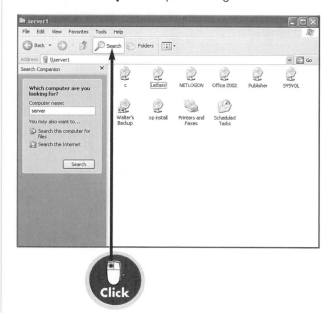

How to Find a File on the Network

Windows does not really have the built-in capability to search an entire network full of computers for a particular file. However, it is easy enough to perform a regular search on a shared folder. This, at least, saves you from having to rummage through the shared folder and its sub-folders yourself. The trick is to know at least the names of the computer and shared folder holding the document for which you are looking.

1 Open Computers Near Me

In the **My Network Places** window, click the **View workgroup computers** link to open the workgroup window. If you are on a domain, click the **Entire Network** link instead. Both links work the same way.

2 Open a Computer

Double-click the computer on which you want to search for a file.

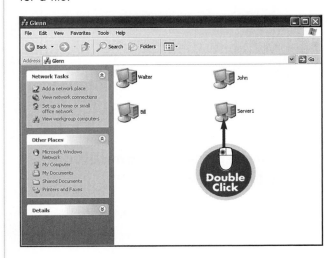

Searching from the Start Menu
You can also get to the **Search Results** window by choosing **Search** from the **Start** menu. When the Search Results window appears, select the type of file for which you want to search. Next, enter the filename and use the **Look In** drop-down list to browse to the shared folder you want to search. Learn more about the windows search feature in Chapter 4, "Working with Files and Folders."

How-to Hint

③ Search a Shared Folder

Find the shared folder in which you want to search for a file. Right-click the folder and choose **Search** from the shortcut menu that appears. The **Search Results** window opens with the **Search Companion** pane on the left.

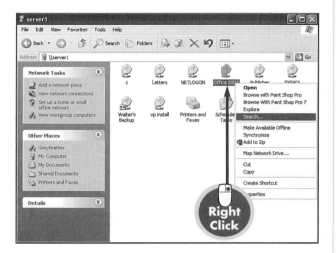

⑤ Search for the File

Click the **Search** button or press Enter to begin the search. Results are displayed in the right pane of the Search Results window.

④ Enter the Name of a File

Type the name of a file for which you want to search in the text box. You can also enter part of a name if you don't remember the whole thing.

⑥ Open the File

After you find the file for which you are looking, double-click it to open it, or drag it to your desktop to copy it from the shared folder to your computer.

How to Share a File or Folder with Others

In addition to giving you access to other user's files, folders, and printers, networks allow you to share your resources with other users. To share resources, your computer must be on a network and your network administrator must have already set up your computer so that you can share items with others.

1 Open the Sharing Dialog Box

Using the **My Computer** or **My Documents** window, find the folder or file you want to share. Right-click it and choose **Sharing and Security** from the shortcut menu to open the **Sharing** tab of the item's **Properties** dialog box. This task focuses on sharing a folder, but the process of sharing a file is the same.

2 Share the Folder

Click the **Share this folder on the network** option to enable sharing of the folder.

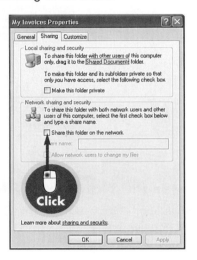

How-to Hint

How Do You Know It's Shared?

A shared file or folder shows up on your computer as a standard icon with a hand underneath the icon.

---

③ Change the Share Name

Windows names the shared folder the same as the original name of the folder. If you want, type a new share name in the text box for the folder you are sharing.

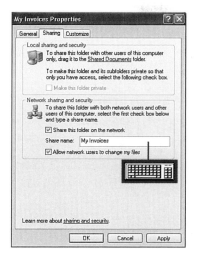

④ Allow Network Users to Change Files

When you share the file, Windows automatically turns on the **Allow network users to change my files** option. If you would rather other people be able to view your files, but not change them, disable this option.

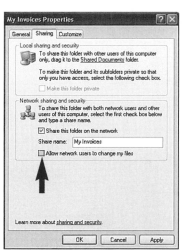

⑤ Learn More

The Windows XP Help system contains a large amount of useful information on sharing files. To access this information quickly, click the **sharing and security** link at the bottom of the tab.

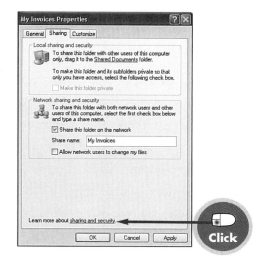

⑥ Close the Properties Dialog Box

Click **OK** to close the **Properties** dialog box. Users can now access the folder you just shared.

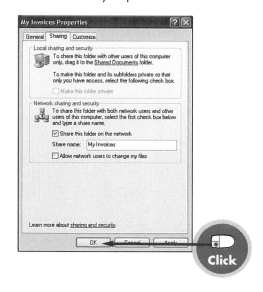

How to Map a Network Drive

When you map a network drive, you essentially tell your computer to treat a shared resource as a drive on your computer—the resource even gets its own drive letter and shows up in the **My Computer** window. Older programs sometimes don't know how to use Network Places and can only open files on real disk drives. By mapping a network drive, you can fool these programs into thinking that a shared folder is a real disk drive.

❶ Open Computers Near Me

In the **My Network Places** window, click the **View workgroup computers** link. If you are on a domain, click the **Entire Network** link instead. Both links work the same way.

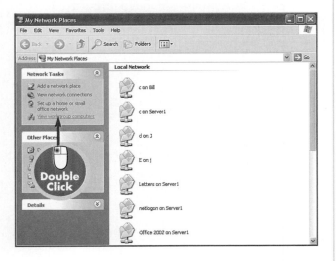

❷ Open a Computer

Find the computer that contains the shared folder you want to map as a network drive and double-click it.

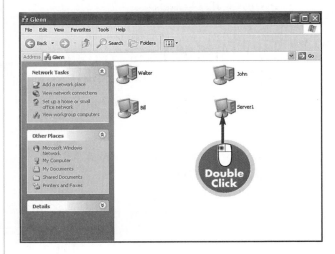

❸ Select a Shared Folder

Find the shared folder you want to map and select it by clicking it once.

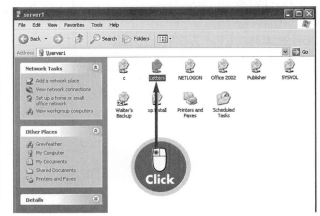

4 Choose Map Network Drive

From the File menu, choose the **Map Network Drive** command. The **Map Network Drive** dialog box opens.

5 Select a Drive Letter

Select a drive letter using the **Drive** drop-down menu. Only letters that are not already used on your computer are listed here, so you don't have to worry about conflicts.

6 Reconnect at Logon

If you want the network drive to be remapped to the same drive letter each time you log on to your computer, click the **Reconnect at logon** option. When you're done, click **Finish**.

7 View the New Drive

In the **My Computer** window, the new network drive appears using the drive letter you assigned it in Step 5. Network drives look like a regular disk drive with a network cable attached.

Task

Working Away from the Network

Many people work when away from the network by connecting to the network over a modem or by taking work home with them on a disk. Some even take their computers off the network and on the road with them. Windows XP offers two ways to work when you are away from the network.

The Windows briefcase is a special folder designed for users to take work home with them on a removable disk, work on the files, and then synchronize the updated files with the originals on the hard drive back at work.

Offline folders are for users who take their computers away from the network, as with a notebook, or who dial into the network with a modem. You can mark any shared folder on a network to be available offline. The contents of the folders are copied to the hard drive on your computer. Once disconnected from the network, you can still work on these files. When reconnected, the files are synchronized with the originals.

How to Create and Fill a Briefcase

Creating a briefcase in Windows is pretty easy. After it is created, you can move files into and out of it the same way you move other folders on your computer. You can create a briefcase directly on the desktop or in any folder using the method described in this task.

① Create the New Briefcase

Right-click any empty space on your desktop, point to **New** on the shortcut menu, and then choose **Briefcase**. A new icon with the label **New Briefcase** appears on the desktop.

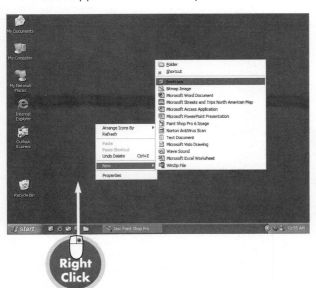

② Open the New Briefcase

Double-click the **New Briefcase** icon to open it. The first time you open any new briefcase, you are shown a welcome screen that gives you a brief introduction to using it.

③ Open My Documents

To place objects in the briefcase, you must first locate those objects. Double-click the **My Documents** icon on the desktop to open the **My Documents** window.

④ Tile Windows Vertically

Right-click a blank space on the taskbar and choose **Tile Windows Vertically** so that you can see both the **My Documents** and the **New Briefcase** windows side by side.

Right Click

⑤ Drag a File to the Briefcase

Copy any file or folder to your briefcase by simply dragging it to the **New Briefcase** window. You can copy as many files and folders as you want to the briefcase.

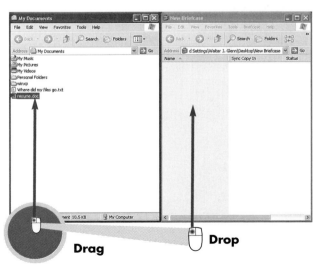

Drag

Drop

How-to Hint

Watch Your Disk Space

If you are using a floppy disk to carry your briefcase, do not copy more files to your briefcase than the disk can hold. Find out how big a briefcase is by right-clicking it and choosing **Properties** from the shortcut menu. If you routinely place more files in the briefcase than will fit on a typical 1.44MB floppy disk, consider investing in a Zip disk drive. Zip disks hold 100MB or 250MB of data (depending on which drive you buy). You'll need a Zip drive at home and at work.

Renaming Your Briefcase

Rename your briefcase the same way you do any folder. Right-click its icon and choose **Rename** from the shortcut menu. See Chapter 4, "Working with Files and Folders," for more on renaming folders.

How to Take a Briefcase with You

Taking a briefcase with you is as simple as copying it to a floppy disk (or other removable disk). Any computer running Windows 95/98/Me, Windows NT 4.0, Windows 2000, or Windows XP will recognize the briefcase for what it is.

1 Open My Computer

Double-click the **My Computer** icon on your desktop to open the **My Computer** window.

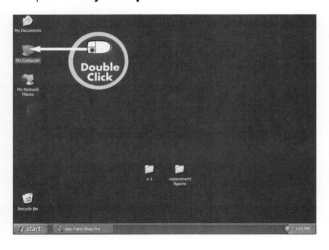

2 Move the Briefcase to Your Floppy Drive

Move the mouse pointer over the briefcase icon. Click and hold the left mouse button, then drag the briefcase over the floppy drive icon in the **My Computer** window. Release the mouse button to move the briefcase. You can also right-click the briefcase and choose the **Send To**, **3-½" floppy A**: command from the shortcut menu.

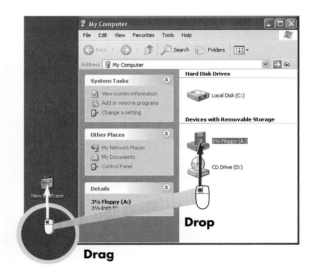

③ Open the Briefcase on Your Home Computer

When you're at the computer away from the network, pop the floppy disk into the computer. Open the **My Computer** window, open the floppy drive, and double-click the **New Briefcase** icon to open the briefcase.

④ Open a File from the Briefcase

In the briefcase, find the file you want to work on and double-click to open it.

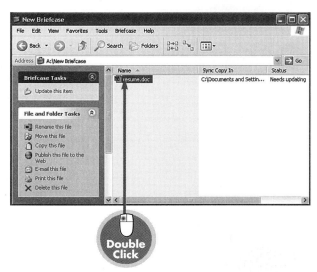

⑤ Save the File

The file opens in whatever application was used to create it. To open a Word file from the briefcase, for example, you must have Microsoft Word installed on your home computer. When you're done working, save the file. The file is updated in the briefcase on the floppy disk.

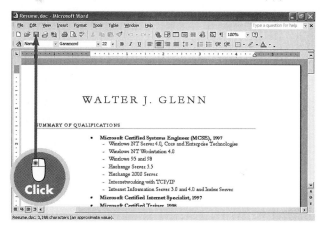

⑥ Move the Briefcase to Your Work Computer

When you get back to your main computer, insert the floppy disk in the drive, open the **My Computer** window, open the floppy drive, and drag the briefcase onto your desktop. In Task 3, you'll see how to update the files on your main computer with the files in the briefcase.

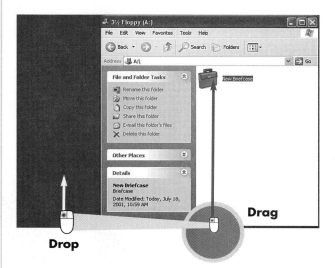

How to Update Files in a Briefcase

Now that you are back at work, you have files in your briefcase that have changed from the originals that are still on your work computer. The next step is to update the original files. You do this from within your briefcase.

1 Open Your Briefcase

Double-click the **New Briefcase** icon to open the **New Briefcase** window. If the briefcase is still on a floppy disk, you should move it back to your desktop first for quicker access.

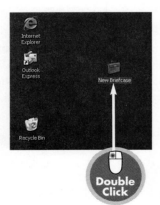

2 Note the Status of Files

In the **New Briefcase** window, choose **View**, **Details** from the menu bar to switch to **Details** view. The **Status** column tells you which files on your work computer's hard disk need to be updated.

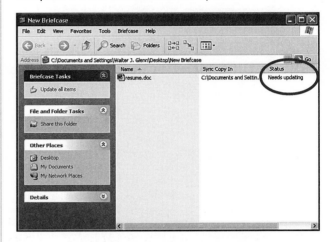

3 Select a File to Update

Select any file you want to update by clicking it once. You can select additional files by holding down the **Ctrl** key while you click other files.

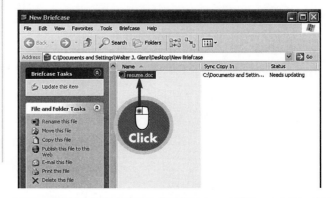

4 Update Selection

From the **Briefcase Tasks** list on the left side of the window, choose the **Update this item** link to update the selected files.

5 Review the Update

After you choose the **Update** this item link, you are given the chance to review the updates in the **Update** window. The version of the file in the briefcase is shown on the left. The original file on your hard disk is shown on the right. The arrow in between indicates which version should be updated.

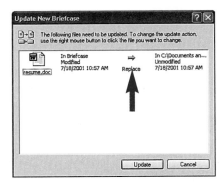

6 Update the File

When you are ready to begin the update, just click the **Update** button. Windows replaces the file on the hard disk with the file in the briefcase. Now both files are identical.

Updating All

Use the **Update All** button on the toolbar in the **New Briefcase** window to update all the files in the briefcase that need to be updated. A link of the same name is available on the left side of the window if no files are selected.

Resolving Conflicts

If the **Update** window shows a red arrow pointing down between the two versions of a file, it means that both versions have been updated since the original was copied to the briefcase. When this happens, you should open both versions of the file and figure out for yourself which is the most recent.

How to Make Items Available Offline

If you are running Windows XP Professional, you can make any shared folder on the network available as an offline folder so that you can use those files when you disconnect from the network. Windows does this by copying the files in the shared folder to a temporary location on your computer's hard disk. When you are connected to the network, you can work on the original files. When you disconnect from the network, you work on the temporary copies. When you connect again, any temporary files you worked on are copied back to the original location and replace the older originals.

❶ Open My Network Places

While still connected to the network (either through a direct cable connection or remotely with a dial-up connection), double-click the **My Network Places** icon to open the **My Network Places** window.

❷ Open Computers Near Me

Browse for a shared folder on the network using the techniques in Chapter 7, "Working on a Network." If you don't see the shared folder that contains the files you want make available offline in the **My Network Places** window, click the **View workgroup computers** link to browse all the computers on your network for the shared folder. If you are in a domain instead of a workgroup (such as on a large corporate network), you'll see a link named **Entire Network** instead of **View workgroup computers**. Both links work the same way.

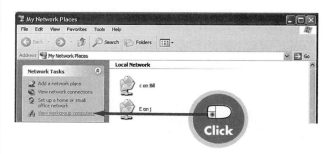

How-to Hint

Making an Item Unavailable

After you make a folder available offline, you can make it unavailable again by right-clicking the folder and choosing the **Make Available Offline** command from the shortcut menu. The temporary files are removed from your hard drive. When you no longer need offline access to a folder, you should make the folder unavailable to reclaim the disk space taken up by the temporary files.

③ Open a Computer

When you find the computer on the network that holds the shared folder you want to change into an offline folder, double-click to open its window.

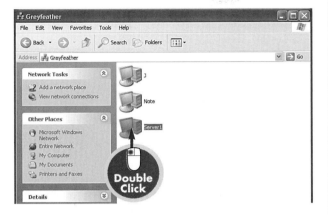

④ Locate a Shared Folder

Scroll through the computer window to find the shared folder you want to make available offline. Click once to select it.

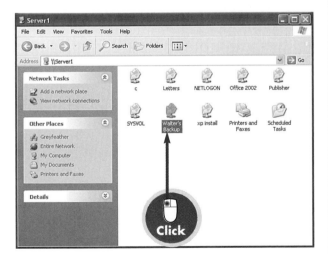

⑤ Make It Available Offline

Right-click the folder you want to make available offline and choose **Make Available Offline** from the short-cut menu.

⑥ Make Subfolders Available

You can decide whether to make just the folder you selected available offline or all of its subfolders available, as well. Choose the appropriate option and click **OK**. Files from the network folder are copied as temporary files to your computer's hard disk. Should you disconnect from the network, you can work on these temporary files until you reconnect. To use the folder offline, refer to the next task.

How to Use Offline Items

After you set up a folder to be available offline, that folder is surprisingly easy to use. All you have to do is open **My Network Places** and browse to the folder the same way you do when you are connected to the network. When you are offline, only the folders configured for offline use are visible.

❶ Open My Network Places

On the computer that you have taken off the network (your laptop or the remote computer that is no longer connected to the workplace through a telephone connection), double-click the **My Network Places** icon to open the **My Network Places** window. Note that you cannot access items offline unless you have first made those items available as described in the preceding task.

❷ Open Computers Near Me

Click the **View workgroup computers or Entire Network** link (depending on the type of network you're on) to browse for the computer that contains the offline folders you want to access.

③ Open a Computer

When you are disconnected from the network, only computers that have shared folders configured for offline use are visible in the window. Double-click the computer's icon to open it.

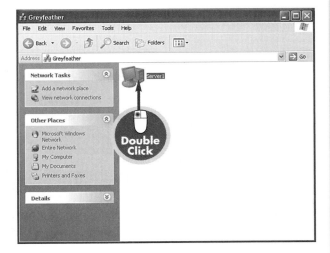

④ Open an Offline Folder

When you open a computer, only the shared folders configured for offline use show up in the computer's window—these folders are called, appropriately enough, *offline folders*. Double-click any offline folder to open it.

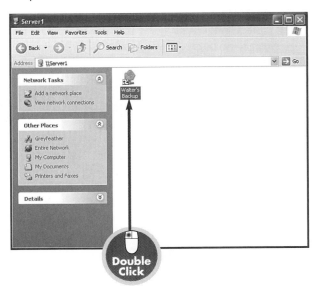

⑤ Open a File

Folders and files in an offline folder have two small arrows at the bottom left of their icons to show that they are offline copies of original files on the network. Double-click any file or folder to open it, just as you would with any regular file or folder.

How-to Hint

Offline Permissions

When you are using offline folders and files, the same permissions (such as only being able to read and not change a file) apply to you that would apply if you were using the actual shared folders or files on the network. So don't think that you can bypass security just by using offline folders. For more information on permissions, see Chapter 9, "Protecting Your Files."

Your Network Places

If you have added any of your own Network Places that point to a shared folder (see Chapter 7, "Working on a Network," for more on this) you might notice that there is no **Make Available Offline** command on the **Network Places** shortcut menu. To make that shared folder available offline, you actually have to browse to the real shared folder the Network Place represents.

How to Synchronize Offline Items

When you have been working on files offline, all you have to do is log back on to the network to automatically synchronize all the files you worked on while you were disconnected. If you are working with offline folders while you are still connected to the network, you have to synchronize files manually. In this task, you learn to synchronize files manually.

1 Synchronize a Specific Folder

Use the **My Network Places** icon on your desktop to browse to the offline folder or file you want to synchronize. Right-click the folder or file and choose **Synchronize** from the shortcut menu. The item is automatically synchronized with the original shared item on the network.

2 Synchronize Multiple Folders

To synchronize multiple folders, open the **Tools** menu of any open folder and choose **Synchronize**. This method also gives you more control over synchronization by opening an **Items to Synchronize** dialog box.

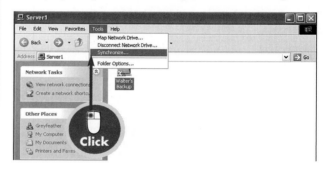

3 Choose Items to Synchronize

The **Items to Synchronize** dialog box shows a list of offline items you can synchronize with their online versions. Select the items you want to synchronize and click **Synchronize**. Remember, when you synchronize an offline item, newer versions of files replace older versions of files.

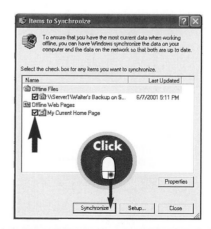

4 Set Up Automatic Synchronization

There are a few ways in which you can configure the automatic synchronization of your files. In the **Items to Synchronize** dialog box, click the **Setup** button to open the **Synchronization Settings** dialog box.

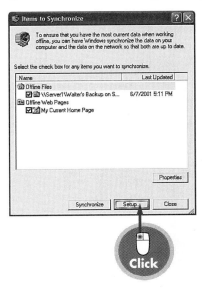

5 Set Up Logon/Logoff Synchronization

From the list, select the items you want to be automatically synchronized when you log on or log off the network. Then choose whether you want the selected items to synchronize during logon, logoff, or both. You can also have Windows ask you before synchronizing any items.

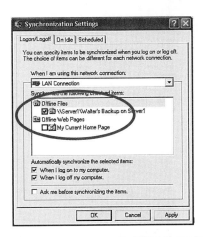

6 Switch to On Idle Tab

In the **Synchronization Settings** dialog box, click the **On Idle** tab to configure your computer to synchronize offline files during idle time—when your computer is connected to the network but is not being used.

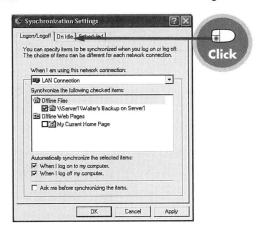

7 Set Up Idle Synchronization

Choose the folders you want to be synchronized during idle time from the list and enable the **Synchronize while my computer is idle** option. You can also click the **Advanced** button to specify how many minutes should pass before your computer is considered idle.

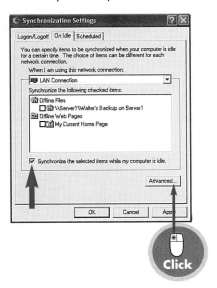

How to Change Offline Settings

For the most part, the default settings for offline folders should work pretty well. However, there are a few settings that might be useful to you. For example, you can change when files are synchronized, how much disk space offline files can use, and whether Windows continuously reminds you when you are using offline instead of online files.

① Open the Control Panel

Click the **Start** button and then click **Control Panel**. The Control Panel window opens.

② Open Folder Options

Double-click the **Folder Options** icon to open the **Folder Options** dialog box.

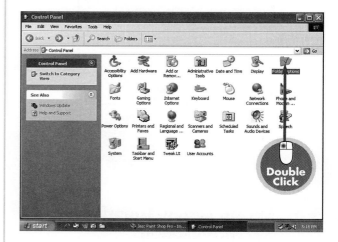

③ Open Offline Files Tab

In the **Folder Options** dialog box, click the **Offline Files** tab.

④ Synchronize at Log Off/On

By default, the **Synchronize all offline files when logging on** and **Synchronize all offline files before logging off** options are enabled. If you prefer not to wait through this process each time you log off and on, disable these options. If you disable these options, remember to synchronize your files for offline use (as explained in Task 4, "How to Make Items Available Offline," before disconnecting from the network.

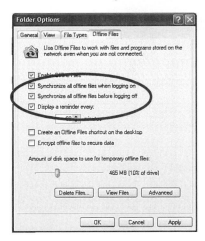

⑤ Enable Reminders

When the **Display a Reminder every** option is enabled, a small icon appears in the notification area next to your clock to indicate that offline files are being used. In addition, a text bubble appears once in a while as yet another reminder. You can specify the interval at which this reminder appears.

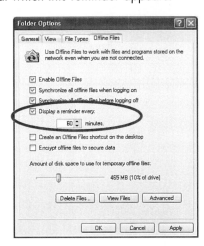

⑥ Place a Shortcut on the Desktop

When you enable the **Create an Offline File shortcut on the desktop** option, a shortcut named **Shortcut to Offline Files** appears on the desktop. Double-clicking this shortcut opens a window that displays all the files you have configured for offline use.

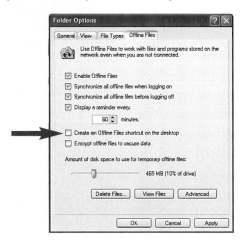

⑦ Choose Amount of Disk Space to Use

By default, offline folders are allowed to use 10% of the space on your hard drive. You can change this to any amount you like by simply dragging the slider to adjust the percentage. When you're done changing the settings for the offline folder, click **OK** to close the dialog box.

Drag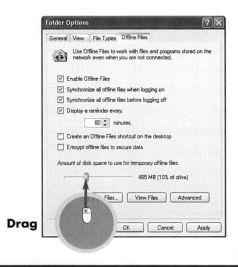

Security and Recovery

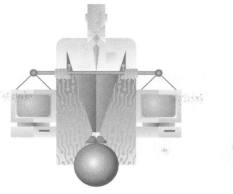

9

Protecting Your Files

Part of Windows XP's claim to fame is that it is built on Windows NT technology, which is a more secure operating system than most. Security is most important when your computer is part of a networking environment (including the Internet) where it is possible that other users can access your system. Windows XP security is a complicated topic. Fortunately, there are only a few things with which you really have to be concerned. If you're using a computer at home, the default security settings are probably fine; changing them is fairly simple.

How to Set Local Permissions on a Domain-Based Network

For each person in the domain who might use your computer, you can assign a specific set of permissions to use an object. Permissions you assign to files and folders differ slightly, but each allows you to assign a certain level of control to the object. To assign permissions to a folder or file, you must be the creator of the file, have administrative permissions on the computer (as the special **Administrator** user account does), or have been given special permission to change permissions.

① Open a Folder's Properties

Find the folder for which you want to assign permissions. Right-click it and choose **Properties** from the shortcut menu.

② Switch to the Security Tab

Switch to the **Security** tab of the **Properties** dialog box by clicking it once.

③ Select a User or Group

Select a user or group by clicking the entry once. If you don't see the person on the list, you can add users by clicking the **Add** button and choosing from a list of available users.

④ Set Permissions

After you have selected a user or group account, set permissions by clicking the check boxes. Sometimes, objects inherit permissions from the folder they are in; when that happens, the permissions check boxes are shaded. Select the opposite permission (**Allow** or **Deny**) to override the permission. If a box is clear (unchecked), it means that no permissions have been inherited or explicitly assigned to the object, and permissions could be inherited in the future should the permissions for a parent folder change.

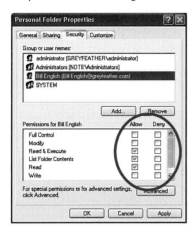

⑤ Configure Advanced Settings

Click the **Advanced** button to set other security options, such as whether files and folders inside the current folder will inherit the permissions set for the folder.

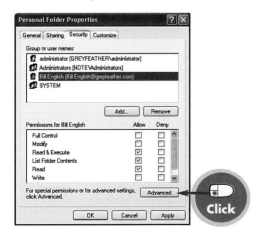

How-to Hint

NTFS

The use of local file permissions requires that your disk be formatted using the NTFS file system, which is Windows XP's native file system. Unless you are on a computer that also runs a previous version of Windows such as Windows 98 or Me, the chances are that your disk uses the NTFS system. If you don't see any of the dialog boxes mentioned in the previous steps on your computer, you probably don't use NTFS. Check the instructions in your Windows documentation for steps on how to convert an existing drive to NTFS.

Windows Help

If you want to know more about Windows security, including what each of the permissions means and how they interact with one another, consult Windows Help system (as discussed in Chapter 1, "Using the Windows XP Desktop").

How to Set Shared Permissions on a Domain-Based Network

Permissions are also set on folders you share over the network in a domain. The actual process for sharing a folder is discussed in Chapter 7, "Working on a Network." The following steps show you how to change permissions on a folder that is already shared.

❶ Open the Sharing Dialog Box

You can identify shared folders on your computer by the small picture of a hand that looks like it's holding the folder. Right-click a shared folder and choose the **Sharing and Security** command from the shortcut menu.

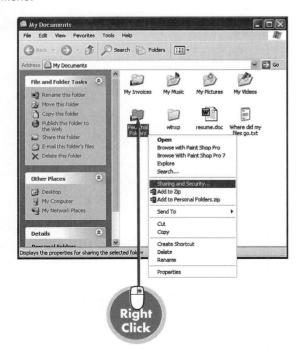

❷ Open the Permissions Dialog Box

In the folder's **Properties** dialog box, click the **Permissions** button to open the **Permissions** dialog box for the folder.

③ Remove the Everyone Group

By default, a special group named **Everyone** is given the **Full Control** permission over a shared folder. It is best to remove this group altogether. Just select it and click the **Remove** button.

⑤ Set Permissions

New users and groups you add are given only **Read** permission by default, meaning that these people can open files in the folder, but cannot change or delete them. You can allow or deny other actions by enabling the check boxes.

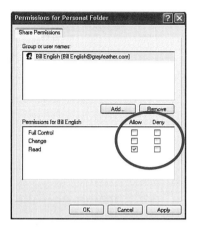

④ Add a New User

Click the **Add** button on the **Permissions** dialog box to open a dialog box that helps you find users in the domain. Type the name of a user (or group) in the **Enter the object names to select** box or click the **Advanced** button to browse for certain types of user. Click **OK** when you're done.

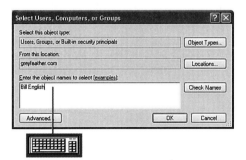

How-to Hint

Standalone Computers

If your computer is not on a network and part of a **Windows** domain, you probably will not see the **Sharing** command on the shortcut menu, or be able to assign shared permissions. Of course, if you're not part of a network, why would you want to share folders?

How to Encrypt a File or Folder

Windows XP allows you to encrypt files or folders so that other people who use your computer cannot make sense of the files even if they manage to bypass permissions and gain access to them. The whole process of encryption is pretty transparent on your end. After you encrypt a file or folder, you can continue to use it normally. You only need to decrypt it if you want to share it with others or if you want to take it to another computer to use yourself.

1 Open a File's Properties

Right-click the file or folder you want to encrypt and choose the **Properties** command from the shortcut menu. The **Properties** dialog box opens.

2 Open Advanced Options

On the **General** tab of the **Properties** dialog box, click the **Advanced** button to open the **Advanced Attributes** dialog box.

3 Encrypt the Folder

Enable the **Encrypt contents to secure data** check box. Note that there is also an option here that lets you compress files and folders to save disk space. You cannot use both encryption and compression on an object at the same time.

④ Close the Dialog Boxes

Click the **OK** button to close the **Advanced Attributes** dialog box; click the **OK** button on the **General** tab of the folder's **Properties** dialog box to close it.

⑤ Encrypt Files and Subfolders

A dialog box appears that lets you choose whether to encrypt only the selected folder or also to encrypt the subfolders within that folder. Whether or not you encrypt the subfolders, the files directly inside the selected folder are encrypted. Choose the option you want and click the **OK** button.

Decrypting a Folder

To decrypt a folder, simply follow the preceding steps and disable the **Encrypt contents to secure data** check box on the **Advanced Attributes** dialog box in Step 3.

When It Doesn't Work

As is true with local file permissions, encryption is available only if you are using the NTFS file system. Also note that Windows XP system files cannot be encrypted. Finally, note that encrypted files become unencrypted if you copy or move the file to another computer or to a removable disk (such as a floppy disk).

No Visual Indicator

When you encrypt a file or folder, Windows XP gives no visual indicator that encryption is enabled. To see whether an object is encrypted, you must open its **Properties** dialog box and see whether the **Encrypt contents to secure data** check box is enabled.

How to Lock Your Workstation

When you leave your desk for any period of time, it is best to log off of Windows XP using the procedure described in Chapter 3, Task 11, "How to Log Off Windows XP." Sometimes, however, you might want to prevent even other authorized users from gaining access to your computer (which they can do if you have logged off). If you are part of a domain, Windows XP Professional lets you lock your workstation. When your workstation is locked, only you or a system administrator can unlock the computer. Windows XP Home Edition does not allow you to lock your computer.

❶ Press Ctrl+Alt+Delete

Press the **Ctrl**, **Alt**, and **Delete** keys all at once. You can perform this action no matter where you are in the system, even if you have programs running.

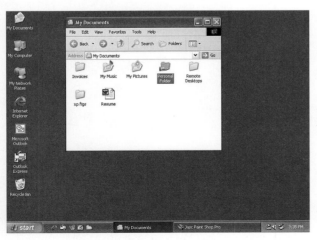

❷ Lock Your Computer

From the **Windows Security** dialog box, click the **Lock Computer** button. The **Computer Locked** window appears. Now, no one but you (and the network's system administrator) can unlock the computer to use it.

❸ Unlock Your Computer

When your computer is locked, you unlock it in much the same way that you log on to Windows. First, press the **Ctrl**, **Alt**, and **Delete** keys all at once. The **Unlock Computer** dialog box opens.

❹ Enter Your Password

Type your logon password in the Password box and then click the **OK** button.

Locking Is Quicker

Many people find that locking their computers when leaving their desks is quicker than logging off, mainly because logging off requires that you save your work, stop and shut down programs, and then log on and relaunch programs again when you get back. This is normally fine, especially if you won't be away for long, but your network administrator might prefer that you log off when you leave for long periods, such as overnight or over weekends.

❺ Return to Work

After you unlock your workstation, you'll find it in exactly the same state in which you left it—running programs and all.

How to Assign a Screen Saver Password

⬤ften, people forget to log off or lock their workstations every time they leave their desks. One way to create a kind of security safety net is to use a screen saver that is password protected. With such a system in place, once the screen saver activates, you or someone using an account with administrator permissions (such as the special **Administrator** account) must enter your password to get back into the computer. If you are the administrator of your own computer (as is the case on a home network), there is no real way to recover from a forgotten password.

➊ Open the Control Panel

Click **Start** and then click **Control Panel** to open the **Windows Control Panel** window.

➋ Open the Display Applet

The **Control Panel** features a number of applets that let you change various settings for your computer. The screen saver options are controlled by the **Display** applet. Double-click the **Display** applet to open the **Display Properties** dialog box.

➌ Switch to the Screen Saver Tab

Switch to the **Screen Saver** tab by clicking it once.

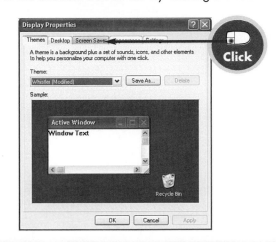

④ Choose the Password Protected Option

Click the **Password protected** option to require that a password be entered when returning to the desktop from a screen saver. If no screen saver is selected, this option is not available. For more on how to set up a screen saver, see Chapter 5, "Changing Windows XP Settings." When password protection is enabled and you come back to your computer from the screen saver (by moving the mouse or touching a key), you must enter the same username and password you use to log on to Windows.

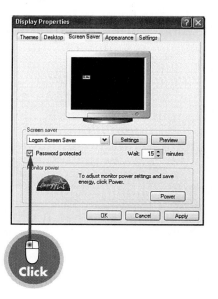

How-to Hint

Remembering to Log Off

Although a screen saver password can help you protect your system, it is not a good substitute for logging off or locking your workstation. Even though the screen saver is up, you are still logged on to Windows, and any programs you left open are still running. Both situations can present security problems. In fact, many network administrators don't allow users to use screen saver passwords at all for fear that they will grow reliant on them.

How to Change Your Logon Password

It is a good idea to change your logon password periodically in case someone has gained access to it. On more secure networks, it is often company policy that users must change their passwords every month or two. On some even more secure networks, administrators change and distribute new passwords and do not allow users to select passwords themselves. Check with your network administrator to find out the policy for your network. If you're on a home network, it's up to you how often your passwords change, or whether you use them at all.

1 Open the User Accounts Window

Open the **Control Panel** window and double-click the **User Accounts** icon to open the **User Accounts** window.

2 Choose an Account to Change

Click the account for which you want to change the password.

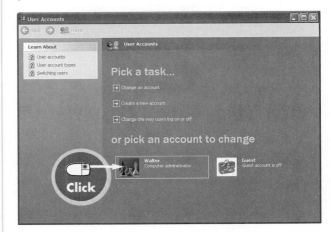

3 Click Change My Password

On the list of options for managing the selected user account, click the **Change my password** link.

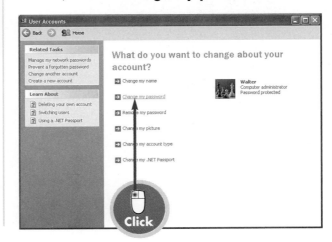

4 · Type Your Current Password

You must enter your current password to ensure that you have the right to change the password. Type the current password into the **Type your current password** text box.

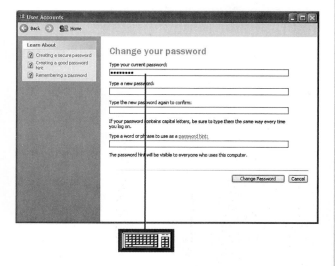

5 · Type and Confirm the New Password

Type your new password in the **Type a new password** box and then type it again in the **Type the new password** again to confirm box. Click the **Change Password** button to change to the new password. You are returned to the screen that lists the maintenance choices for the account (shown in Step 3).

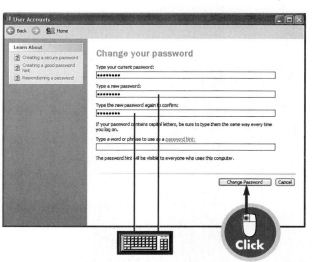

How-to Hint

Password Security

For the best possible security, don't write your password down anywhere and never tell it to anyone. You should change your password every so often just in case it has been discovered. If your administrator supplies you with a password, memorize it and destroy the paper it came on.

Password Hints

Never create passwords with names, dates, or words that might appear in the dictionary. If you find it hard to remember cryptic passwords full of uppercase and lowercase characters and numbers, you can create a password that is both secure and easy to remember. One way is to think of two four-letter words and join them with a two-digit number. For example, **lion72dunk** is pretty easy to remember and almost impossible to guess. You can also think of an easy-to-remember seven- or eight-letter word. Then, instead of typing the word itself, type the characters that are to the upper-left of the real characters on the keyboard. This way, an easy-to-guess word such as **astronomy** becomes **qw549h9j6**. Remember to check with your administrator about the password policies used on your network.

10

Protecting Yourself on the Web

Part of the World Wide Web's appeal is its wide-open nature. Anyone can put a site on the Web and reach people all over the world.

This has its advantages—free speech is exercised on the Internet with great success. This also has its disadvantages—content that some people find objectionable is available in great quantity.

Another disadvantage of the Internet is that Web pages can contain interactive programs that can sometimes expose security holes that put your own computer at risk.

When you run a program in a Web browser, the program runs on *your* computer just like any other software you use. For this reason, browsers such as Internet Explorer 6 have security settings that restrict the ways a page can interact with your system.

Another way to reduce your risk is to install an antivirus program such as Norton AntiVirus 2002 and use it to scan all files you receive.

How to Choose a Security Setting

Although security risks are extremely small on the World Wide Web, you may encounter sites that try to damage files on your computer or steal confidential data. Internet Explorer 6's security settings can restrict or disable browser features that are most susceptible to abuse, such as JavaScript, Active Scripting, Java, and cookies. Restricting these features can limit your enjoyment of the Web because many popular sites rely on them, but you may feel it's a fair trade-off for a more secure computer system.

❶ Configure Your Browser

Pull down the Internet Explorer **Tools** menu and select the **Internet Options** command. The **Internet Options** dialog box opens.

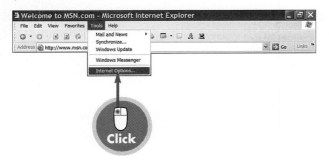

❷ View Security Settings

Click the **Security** tab to view your current security settings and to make changes to those settings.

❸ Set Your Internet Security

Internet Explorer enables different levels of security for sites on the Internet as well as sites on a local *intranet*— a private network of documents shared by people in a company, school, or organization. To change your Internet settings, click the **Internet** icon from the **Select a Web content zone to specify its security settings** list box.

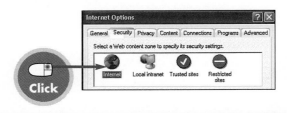

④ Pick a Security Level

There are four basic security levels: **High**, **Medium**, **Medium-Low**, and **Low**. These levels determine the kind of content Internet Explorer will load and the tasks it will restrict. To choose a security level, click the **Default Level** button and drag the slider toward the **High**, **Medium**, or **Low** setting, and release it. (The How-To Hints box at the end of this task provides some guidelines for setting a security level.)

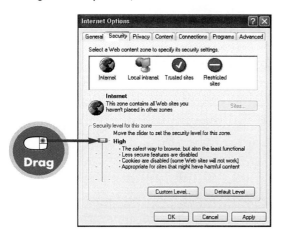

⑤ Oppose a Recommendation

Microsoft recommends that you use **High** or **Medium** security level while browsing the Internet. If you choose lower security level, a dialog box appears, asking you to confirm this choice. Click **Yes** if you want to disregard Microsoft's recommendation and choose a lower security level.

⑥ Restore the Default Level

If you want to restore your browser security to the level recommended by Microsoft, click the **Default Level** button.

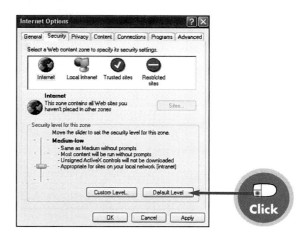

Deciding on a Security Level

Unless you're a Web-site developer, you probably won't have much to go on when choosing a security level. To help guide your decision, we suggest you try **High** security first. Afterward, as you're visiting Web sites, your browser and some sites will often tell you what you're missing out on because of your chosen security level. You can repeat the steps in this task to select a slightly lower security level if you want to access some of the features you've been missing.

How to Customize Your Security Setting

For most people, Internet Explorer 6's basic security levels should be sufficient. If you want more control over your browser's security, however, you can customize each of its security settings. This enables you to turn on and off specific features such as cookies, Java, JavaScript, file downloading, and some browser security warnings. Doing this can increase security risks, so you should be cautious about making drastic changes.

1 Change Your Settings

Pull down the **Tools** menu and select the **Internet Options** command to open the **Internet Options** dialog box and view your Internet Explorer settings.

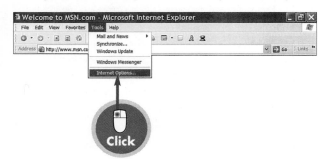

2 Choose a Custom Level

Click to see your current security settings. To change how your browser handles specific security issues, click the **Custom Level** button.

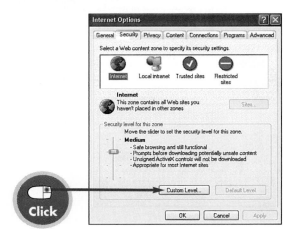

3 Set Up a Custom Level

By default, custom settings are identical to those specified by the **Medium** security level. To make them identical to a different level, click the down arrow next to the **Reset to** box and select the level you want to use as a starting point.

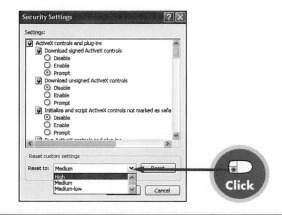

4   Reset All Settings

Click the **Reset** button to make all the custom settings the same as the level shown in the **Reset to** box.

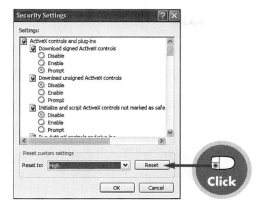

6   Undo Customization

To remove a custom security level and undo all the changes you have made since opening the **Internet Options** dialog box, return to the **Security** tab of the **Internet Options** dialog box and click the **Default Level** button.

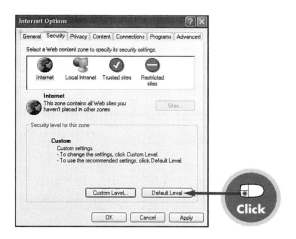

5   Customize Your Settings

Scroll through the **Settings** list box to see the various settings you can affect. To change a specific setting, click the appropriate radio button. Click **Disable** to turn off a feature, **Enable** to turn on a feature, and **Prompt** if you want the browser to ask whether a feature should be used each time it is encountered on a Web page. Click **OK** to save all your changes.

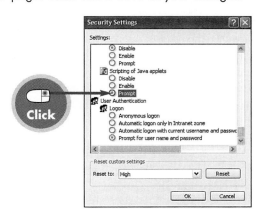

How-to Hint

Turning Off Form Warnings

By default, Internet Explorer warns you before it sends data you've entered on a form that's located on an unencrypted Web server. This feature keeps you from sending private information (such as your credit-card number) without *encryption*—a way to encode data so that it remains confidential. This warning is cumbersome if you're one of those people who never reveals personal data on the Web. To turn off this warning, find the **Submit nonencrypted form data** setting in your custom settings (see step 5) and click the **Disable** radio button.

How to Block Objectionable Content from Being Viewed

To place restrictions on the material that can be viewed with Internet Explorer 6, use the browser's *Content Advisor*. The Advisor relies on RSACi ratings—an industry standard adopted voluntarily by some Web publishers to indicate their site's level of objectionable language, nudity, sex, and violence. Although the Content Advisor is far from foolproof—it relies on Web sites to honestly assess their own content—you may find it useful in conjunction with other methods of filtering the Web.

1 View Content Settings

The Content Advisor is configured with all other browser settings. Choose **Tools**, **Internet Options** from the menu bar to open the **Internet Options** dialog box. Then click the **Content** tab to view the browser's content settings. To set up the Content Advisor, first click the **Enable** button.

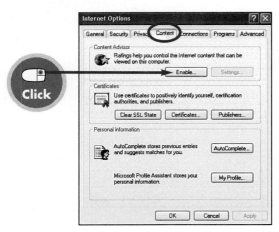

2 Set Your Content Ratings

The **Content Advisor** dialog box opens to the **Ratings** tab, ready for you to set your browser's acceptable RSACi rating. Click the RSACi category you want to set, then drag the slider to a content setting. A site must have content rated at or below all four settings to pass the Content Advisor. Pages that don't pass are not displayed.

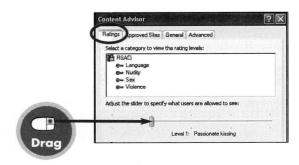

3 View Unrated Sites

By default, Web pages without RSACi ratings cannot be viewed. This keeps out unrated sites that contain objectionable material, along with thousands of sites that don't participate in RSACi. To allow unrated sites to be viewed, click the **General** tab of the **Content Advisor** dialog box and enable the **Users can see sites that have no rating** check box.

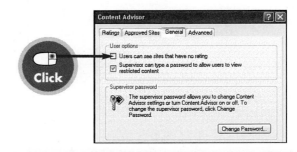

④ Approve Individual Sites

To allow individual sites to bypass the Content Advisor, click the **Approved Sites** tab, type the site's main address in the **Allow this Web site** text box, and click the **Always** button. Alternatively, you can completely restrict access to the specified site by clicking the **Never** button instead.

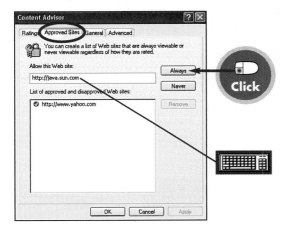

⑤ Save Your Changes

Click the **OK** button to save your new settings and close the **Content Advisor** dialog box. If you have imposed content restrictions, you should close Internet Explorer and launch it again. This action keeps recently visited sites from being reloaded without first being checked by the Content Advisor.

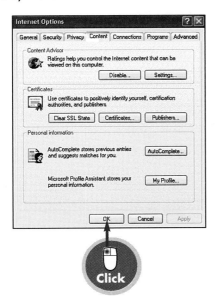

⑥ Choose a Password

When you save your content settings for the first time, you will be asked to select a supervisor password. This password can be used to change Content Advisor settings or turn it off completely. After you set one up, you can't modify the Content Advisor without it. Enter your password in both text boxes and click **OK** to return to the **Internet Options** dialog box.

⑦ Turn Off the Content Advisor

To turn off the Content Advisor completely, choose **Tools**, **Internet Options** to open the **Internet Options** dialog box. Click the **Content** tab, and then click the **Disable** button. You must type the supervisor password in order to disable the Content Advisor feature.

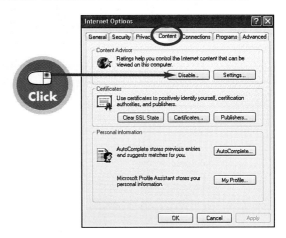

How to Use Security Certificates

As you are visiting Web sites, you may come across pages that contain interactive programs. These small programs are downloaded to your computer and run as if you installed them from a CD-ROM, but they must be approved before your Web browser runs them. Internet Explorer 6 presents a *security certificate*—a window vouching for the authenticity of the program's author. Examine this certificate and decide whether to let the program run.

① Inspect a Certificate

When you load a page that contains an interactive program, Internet Explorer presents a dialog box asking whether the control should be installed. The author of the program is presented as a hyperlink. Click this hyperlink to find out more about the author.

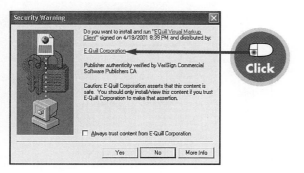

② Determine Authenticity

The link opens a security certificate associated with the program's author. Companies such as VeriSign and Thawte create these certificates after verifying the program's authorship. Click the tabs to find out more about the certificate and the author. Click **OK** to close the window.

③ Always Trust an Author

If you are comfortable with the program's author, you can automatically approve the download of any programs that author creates in the future. To do so, enable the **Always trust content** check box. (You should note, however, that it's safer to approve programs individually than to issue blanket approval with this check box.)

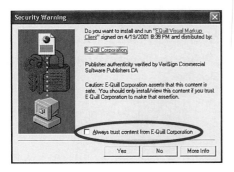

④ Reject an Author

To prevent a program from being installed, click the **No** button in the **Security Warning** dialog box. You can still use anything on the current Web page that doesn't rely on the program.

⑤ Approve an Author

To approve a program and run it in your browser, click the **Yes** button. The program will be saved on your system in the `Windows/Downloaded Program Files` folder so that it doesn't have to be installed again every time you visit the page.

Restricting Programs on Your Browser

How-to Hint

If you are never asked whether a program should be installed before it starts running on a Web page, your browser may be configured with a low security level. To check your security settings, select **Tools**, **Internet Options** to open the **Internet Options** dialog box and click the **Security** tab. Refer to Tasks 1 and 2 in this chapter of the book for instructions on setting and customizing a security level in Internet Explorer.

How to Disable Cookies in a Web Browser

Web sites can keep track of visitors by using *cookies*—small files that contain information collected by a site. Internet Explorer 6 saves cookie files for Web sites on your computer; when you revisit a site for which you have a cookie, Internet Explorer 6 sends the cookie file back to the site. The cookie can be used to store personal information such as your name, billing information, and similar data. By design, Internet Explorer sends a cookie file that exists on your computer only to the site that created it. Some Web sites require cookie files, but you can turn them off entirely by adjusting the browser's privacy settings.

❶ Change Your Settings

Select **Tools**, **Internet Options**. The **Internet Options** dialog box opens to the **General** tab, displaying how your browser is configured.

❷ View Privacy Settings

Click the **Privacy** tab to bring its settings to the front of the dialog box.

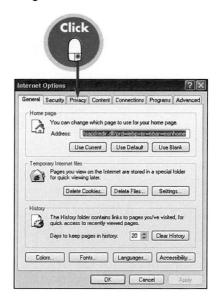

❸ Block All Cookies

To block all cookies from being stored on your computer, drag the slider up to the **Block All Cookies** setting. You should note, however, that this is the strictest setting and may prevent you from using some popular sites.

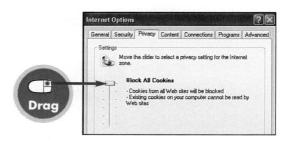

4 Block Most Cookies

To block most cookies (except for those already on your computer), drag the slider to the **High** setting. Cookies that store information related to your identity will not be stored without your consent.

6 Save Your New Settings

To make your privacy changes take effect, click the **OK** button. Your cookie privacy settings will be in force until you change them or return to the **Privacy** tab and click the **Default Level** button.

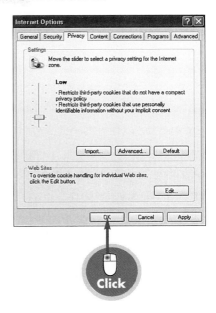

5 Block Advertiser Cookies

To block most cookies from advertisers and some others, drag the slider to the **Medium** setting. Ad cookies and cookies that identify you will not be stored unless you consent.

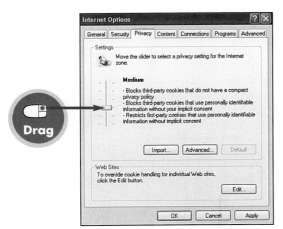

How-to Hint

Approving Cookies on a Case-by-Case Basis

As you will discover after changing your privacy settings to block cookies, many of the sites you use will no longer be fully functional—especially if they offer features that are personalized specifically for you. To allow a specific site to store cookies on your computer, return to the **Privacy** tab and click the **Edit** button. The **Per Site Privacy Actions** dialog box opens. Type the main URL of the site in the **Address of Web Site** text box and click the **Allow** button. When you have finished adding sites, click the **OK** button to close the dialog box.

How to Make Your Internet Connection More Secure

When you are connected to the Internet, the Internet is also connected to you. Malicious people can use that Internet connection to look for ways to access your computer's files, programs, and devices such as printers. Although problems of this kind are relatively rare, several software developers now offer *firewalls*—programs that restrict the kind of information that can be exchanged over an Internet connection. Windows XP comes with its own protection against unwelcome intruders: the Internet Connection Firewall.

1 View Your Connections

In order to work, an Internet Connection Firewall must be associated with a network connection on your computer. (Note that the Internet Connection Firewall is available only with Windows XP.) To view your network connections, click the **Start** button, choose **Connect To**, and choose **Network Connections**.

2 Choose a Connection

The **Network Connections** folder lists the connections you have set up to the Internet and other networks. To begin adding a firewall to an Internet connection, right-click the desired connection icon and choose **Properties** from the shortcut menu that opens.

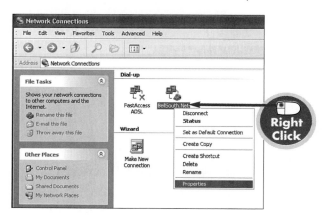

3 View Advanced Settings

The **Properties** dialog box includes five tabs that can be used to modify its settings. Click the **Advanced** tab to bring it to the front.

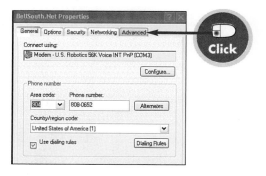

④ Turn On the Firewall

To turn on a firewall, enable the **Protect my computer and network by limiting or preventing access to this computer from the Internet** check box. To learn more about the Internet Connection Firewall, click the link of the same name.

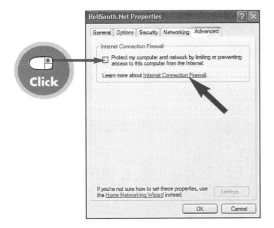

⑤ Save Your Settings

Click the **OK** button to save the changes you have made to your Internet connection. If you are connected to the Internet when the firewall is set up, the current connection is not protected by the firewall. Disconnect and reconnect to the Internet so that the new connection will be protected by the firewall.

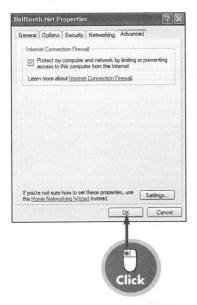

⑥ Connect Through the Firewall

After you have turned on the firewall, your Internet connection icon will change to show that a firewall is in place. Nothing else changes; double-click the connection icon to connect to the Internet as you normally would.

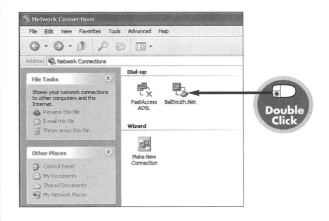

How-to Hint

Choosing a Different Internet Firewall

The Internet Connection Firewall is available only on Windows XP and does not protect against some security risks. If you don't use Windows XP or want a more full-featured firewall, you might be interested in the ZoneAlarm firewall. ZoneAlarm is available in free and pay versions from Zone Labs for Windows 95, 98, Me, XP, NT, and 2000. To find out more, type the URL http://www.zonealarm.com in your Web browser and press **Enter**; you can then download the free version of the software if desired.

How to Install Antivirus Software

It's only a matter of time before your computer is exposed to its first *virus*—a harmful program that runs without permission, tries to spread itself to other computers, and may damage or delete your files. Viruses infect millions of computers each day on the Internet. To avoid them, you should buy an antivirus program that can check files for viruses before you open them, even as they arrive in email. One of the best is Norton AntiVirus 2002, which sells for $39 at many software retailers. Most computer and office superstores sell the software, including Office Max, Staples, and CompUSA.

1 Load the Wizard

When you place the Norton AntiVirus 2002 CD in your CD drive, it loads automatically. To begin installing the program, click the **Install Norton AntiVirus** link. An installation wizard starts.

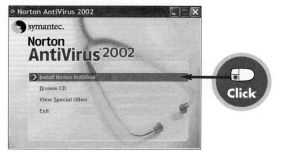

2 Run the Wizard

If possible, you should close all other programs before installing Norton AntiVirus 2002. After you have done so, click **Next** to run the installation wizard.

3 Review the License

The wizard presents the software's license agreement. If you agree to its terms, select the **I accept the license agreement** radio button and click **Next**.

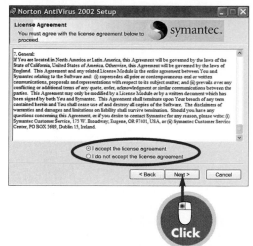

④ Choose a Folder

The wizard recommends a folder for the software: **\Program Files\Norton AntiVirus**. Click **Next** to accept this. (To pick a different folder, click the **Browse** button, use the **File** dialog box to choose a folder, and click **OK**, then click **Next**.)

⑥ Begin Registration

The software will be installed. Click **Finish**. An information wizard opens; use it to register your name, email address, and mailing address with Norton, and then click **Next**.

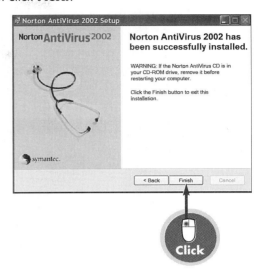

⑤ Confirm Your Choice

The wizard displays the folders where Norton AntiVirus 2002 and related files will be installed. Click **Next**. Some last-minute information is displayed. After reading it, click **Next**.

Avoiding Virus Infection on Your Computer

How-to Hint

If you install antivirus software such as Norton AntiVirus 2002 or McAfee VirusScan 6.0 and keep its virus database current, you should be able to avoid any problems with viruses on your computer. That said, you always should be careful about the programs you install and the files you open while using the Internet. Don't open files sent to you via email by people you don't know—even if the files appear to be something innocuous such as a digital photograph. Also, if an email from someone you know contains a file and seems a little suspicious, don't open it until checking with the person. If that person's computer is infected with an email virus, it may have sent the mail to you. Virus programmers count on tricks like this to spread viruses around the world.

7 Use LiveUpdate

Norton AntiVirus 2002 includes a free one-year subscription to LiveUpdate, a service that keeps your computer up-to-date on new virus threats and keeps the program current. After reviewing the dates of your subscription, click **Next**.

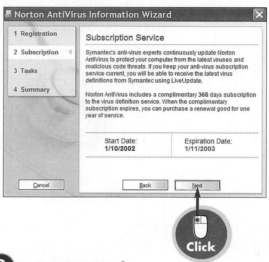

8 Set Up Tasks

Enable the check boxes for tasks you want Norton AntiVirus 2002 to undertake. (Choosing all three is a good idea.) When you're finished, click **Next**.

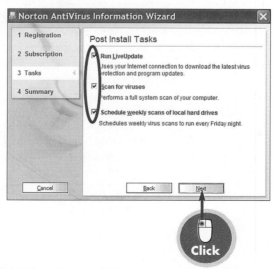

9 Review the Tasks

Review the tasks you have enabled and click **Finish**. Norton AntiVirus 2002 does a lot of the work automatically, including a Friday-evening scan of your entire computer.

10 Look for Updates

If you chose to run LiveUpdate, it begins immediately. Connect to the Internet (if you aren't already online) and click **Next**.

⑪ Select Updates

LiveUpdate connects to Symantec's Internet site and lists the things that need to be updated on your computer, with check marks next to each one. To install them, click **Next**.

⑫ Close LiveUpdate

LiveUpdate downloads and installs each selected update and presents a status report. (You may also see a dialog box telling you to run LiveUpdate several times, as discussed in the next step.) Click **Finish** to close the program.

⑬ Run LiveUpdate Again

You are encouraged to run LiveUpdate several times when you first install Norton AntiVirus, just to make sure you get everything up to date (including LiveUpdate itself). To run the program, click **Start**, choose **All Programs**, choose **Norton AntiVirus**, and click **LiveUpdate—Norton AntiVirus**.

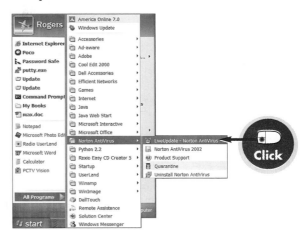

⑭ Look for Updates

The process of running LiveUpdate is the same as before; connect to the Internet and click **Next** to begin. Keep running LiveUpdate until you are told that no more updates are available. After that, LiveUpdate will run automatically while you are subscribed.

How to Check Your Computer for Viruses

After you install antivirus software such as Norton AntiVirus 2002 (described in Task 7), you should immediately use the software to look for viruses on your computer. This is called a *scan*. Norton AntiVirus 2002 conducts its own scan automatically every Friday evening if your computer is on during that time. The software also scans all incoming email, reporting immediately if any file that arrives is infected with a virus.

❶ Run the Program

Click the **Start** button, choose **All Programs**, choose **Norton AntiVirus**, then click **Norton AntiVirus 2002**.

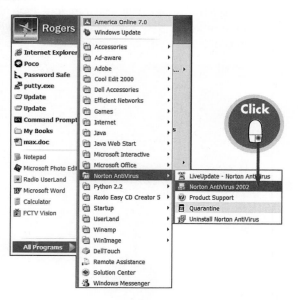

❷ Begin a Scan

Norton AntiVirus 2002 presents a status report, which may contain items you need to handle. To scan your computer, click the **Scan for Viruses** link.

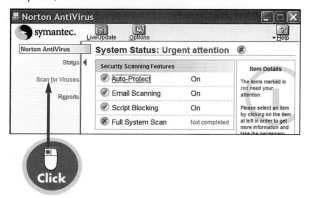

❸ Choose What to Scan

You can scan your entire computer, or scan specific parts of it such as a drive, folder, or file. For a full scan of your entire computer, click the **Scan my computer** link.

④ View the Summary

A complete scan can take an hour or more. If any viruses are found, a dialog box opens, advising you to either delete the file or put it in quarantine—a special folder with files that can't be opened. Click **Finished** to close the program.

⑤ Deal with a Virus

If a virus is emailed to you in a file, Norton AntiVirus 2002 opens automatically and asks you to deal with it immediately. Click **Quarantine** to put the file in the quarantine folder (or **Delete**, if that option is offered).

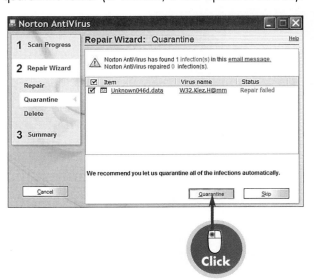

⑥ Close the Program

After Norton AntiVirus 2002 deals with the virus according to your instructions, click **Finished** to close the program.

How-to Hint

Scan a File for a Virus

Because a full scan of your computer can take an hour or longer, you will probably be reluctant to do one when you are concerned about an individual file and want to check it out before opening it. To scan a single file quickly, open the folder that contains the file, right-click its icon, and select **Scan with Norton AntiVirus** from the pop-up menu that appears. A quick scan will be performed of only that file.

Task

11

Back Up and Restore Your System

Computers are pretty complicated. A lot of things can happen during the course of normal use that can slow a computer down or keep certain things from working as they should. In this chapter, you'll learn to back up your system to safeguard your data and restore it to the way it should be.

After you have your system backed up, you might need to install or reinstall Windows. Even though the product itself is far more complex than previous versions of Windows, the installation of Windows XP is much simpler than the installation of previous versions of the program. This is, in part, because the setup routine is smarter and can detect and configure more types of hardware for you. It is also because Microsoft has taken a lot of the decisions out of the setup process.

The installation of the Home and Professional versions of Windows XP do not differ significantly, except that the Professional version offers a few more networking choices. The tasks in this chapter focus on the Professional version, but are virtually identical for the Home version. There are several ways to install Windows XP. The simplest method is to upgrade from another operating system, such as Windows 98/Me, Windows NT, or Windows 2000. In this case, Windows XP takes the place of the old operating system. You can also install Windows XP while keeping an old operating system, such as Windows 98. This is known as a *dual-boot configuration*. When you turn on your computer, you are given the choice of booting to Windows XP or booting to your old operating system. Yet another way to install Windows XP is to install it on a *clean system*—one that has no operating system at all. This is the method you should choose if you build your own computer or if you decide to clear off or format your hard drive before installation. You might also use this method if you put a new hard drive in your computer.

In this chapter, you are introduced to each of these methods of installing Windows XP. You are also shown how to create a set of setup floppy disks to use when installing Windows XP on a clean system. Finally, you are shown how to activate Windows XP and register the software after it is installed.

How to Back Up Your Files

The single most important thing you can do to prevent loss of work should your computer fail is back up your files. Many companies have automated routines for backing up users' files, and you should check with your administrator to see what the policy is at your company. Windows XP comes with a program named Backup, which lets you back up files on your computer to floppy disks, a Zip drive, a recordable CD-ROM drive, or even another computer on your network. Even if your network has backup routines in place, you might also want to use the Backup program on your more important files.

❶ Start Backup

Click the **Start** button and select **All Programs**, **Accessories**, **System Tools**, and **Backup**.

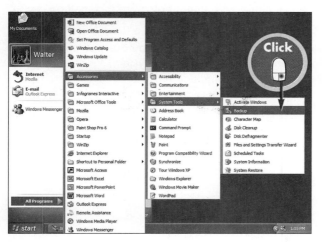

❷ Start the Backup Wizard

Click the **Backup Wizard** button to start the Backup Wizard. The first page of the wizard is a welcome page. Just click the **Next** button when you see the welcome page.

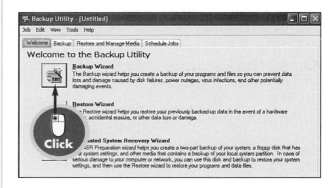

❸ Choose What to Back Up

Choose what you want to back up on your computer. Unless your backup media (floppy, tape drive, and so on) is very fast, it is usually best to back up only selected files.

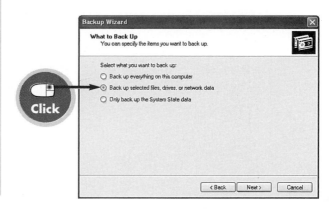

④ Choose the Files to Back Up

This page of the Backup Wizard works just like Windows Explorer. In the left pane, select a folder you want to browse. Files in that folder appear in the right pane. Click the boxes next to the files to indicate that you want to include those files in the backup. You can also select whole folders. When you have selected all the files you want to back up, click the **Next** button to go on.

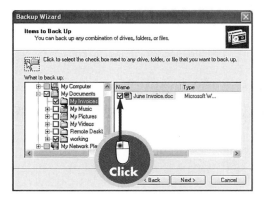

⑤ Choose Where to Back It Up

No matter how many files you back up, the whole backup is saved as a single file with a .bkf extension. Type the path for the drive and folder where you want to save the backup. If you don't know the exact path, click the **Browse** button to locate it. Using the Browse button also lets you locate drives on other computers on the network. Click the **Next** button to go on.

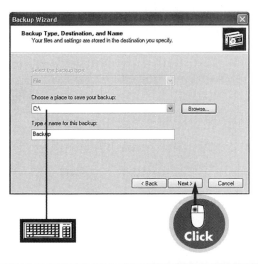

⑥ Finish

The last page of the Backup Wizard gives you a second look at all the settings you've made. Click the **Back** button to go back and change settings. Make sure that your backup media (floppy disk, CD-ROM, tape, Zip disk, and so on) are inserted in the appropriate drive. Click the **Finish** button to go on with the backup.

⑦ View the Report

While the backup is in progress, a dialog box appears that shows you how things are going. When the backup is finished, Windows lets you know that it was completed successfully. Click the **Report** button to view a detailed report on the backup. Click **Close** to finish up.

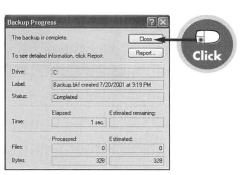

How to Restore Files from a Backup

Whether you are restoring files from a backup following a computer failure or you just want to dig up an old file you deleted, Windows makes the process pretty easy. Before you get started, make sure that the disk you backed up to (Zip disk, CD-ROM, or whatever) is inserted in your drive.

① Start Backup

Click the **Start** button and choose **All Programs**, **Accessories**, **System Tools**, and **Backup**.

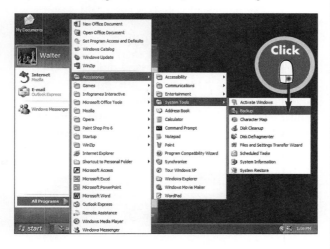

② Start the Restore Wizard

Click the **Restore Wizard** button to start the Restore Wizard. The first page of the wizard is a welcome page. To continue, just click the **Next** button when you see the welcome page.

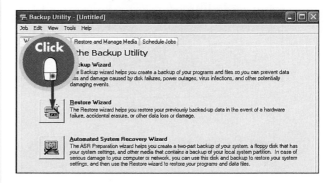

③ Choose What to Restore

A list of backup sessions on your backup media is displayed. Choose the backup session you want to restore by clicking the check box next to it. Sessions are listed by date. If you want to know exactly what is in a session, right-click it and choose **Catalog** from the shortcut menu. When you're done, click the **Next** button.

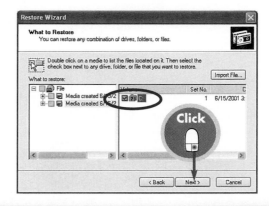

4 Finish

The last page of the Restore Wizard gives you a second look at all the selections you've made. Click the **Back** button to go back and change settings. Click the **Finish** button to go on with the restore process.

5 Enter the Backup Filename

Type the path and name of the backup file you want to restore from. If you don't know the exact path or name, click the **Browse** button to locate the file. When you're ready to start, click the **OK** button.

6 View the Report

While the restore is in progress, a dialog box appears, showing you how things are going. When the restore is finished, Windows lets you know that it was completed successfully. Click the **Report** button to view a detailed report on the backup. Click **Close** to finish up.

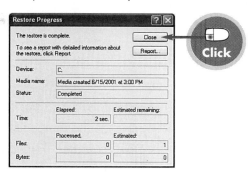

Choosing a Backup Session

If you are using a large backup media, such as CD-ROM, you might have a number of backup sessions available from which to restore. Sessions are listed by date and by the name you gave them during the backup. This is why it is important to give your backup sessions names that mean something to you. You can also right-click any session and choose Catalog from the shortcut menu to browse the actual files contained in the backup.

How to Use Automated System Recovery

Automated System Recovery is a two-part backup process. First, a snapshot of your vital system settings and files is taken and backed up to the backup media of your choice. Second, an Emergency Recovery Disk is created that you can use to boot your system and recover the saved system settings in the event of failure.

1 Start Backup

Click the **Start** button and choose **All Programs**, **Accessories**, **System Tools**, and **Backup**.

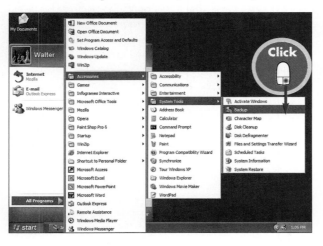

2 Start the Automated System Recovery Wizard

Click the **Automated System Recovery Wizard** button to start the Automated System Recovery Wizard. On the welcome page of the wizard that opens, click **Next** to go on.

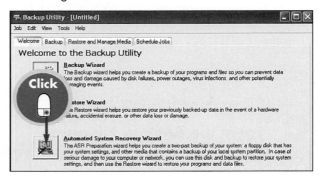

3 Enter a Backup Destination

Type the path for the location where selected files should be backed up. The files will probably consume a good amount of disk space, so you will need to select a location on your hard disk or use a large backup medium, such as a tape, a Zip drive, or a CD-RW. Click **Next** to go on.

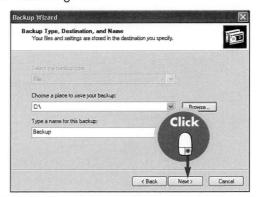

④ Click Finish

Click the **Finish** button to begin the backup.

⑤ Insert a Disk

After Windows backs up certain vital system information to the location you specified, it will prompt you to insert a floppy disk in the A: drive. This floppy disk will become your Automated System Recovery disk (also known as the Emergency Repair Disk). Insert a blank, formatted floppy disk into your A: drive and click the **OK** button.

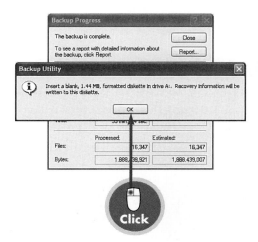

⑥ Finish and Label the Disk

When the Automated System Recovery disk has been created, a dialog box lets you know the process was successful. Click the **OK** button to finish. Be sure to label the disk and keep it in a safe place.

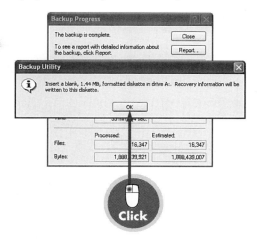

How-to Hint

Using the ASR Disk

If your computer experiences a major system failure (for example, it cannot finish booting), you will have to repair the operating system. If you suffer a hardware failure (such as a crashed hard disk), you can run this process after repairing the hardware to restore your system. To start the emergency repair process, start your computer using the original Windows XP setup disks or CD-ROM. During the setup process, you are given the option of performing setup or performing a repair. Choose to repair the system; the setup program prompts you to insert the ASR disk.

How to Upgrade to Windows XP

Upgrading is the easiest way to install Windows XP. You can upgrade to Windows XP from Windows 95, Windows 98, Windows Me, Windows NT Workstation 3.5 or 4.0, and Windows 2000 Professional. To get started with the upgrade, all you have to do is insert the Windows XP CD-ROM in your computer's CD-ROM drive.

① Upgrade

When you insert the Windows XP CD-ROM into your drive, a splash screen automatically appears along with a dialog box that asks what you want to do. Click the **Install Windows XP** button to start the upgrade. If the splash screen does not appear, you must open the CD-ROM and run the **Setup** program yourself.

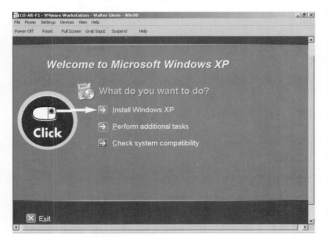

② Upgrade or Clean Install

From the **Installation Type** drop-down list, choose the type of installation you want to perform. If you choose **Upgrade**, your old operating system (such as Windows 98) is overwritten by Windows XP. Settings you have made in the previous version of Windows and all your software are preserved. If you choose **Clean installation**, Windows XP is installed in addition to your old operating system. After you decide which type of installation you would like to perform, click the **Next** button to go on.

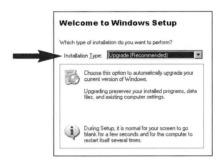

③ Accept the License Agreement

You must accept Microsoft's licensing agreement by clicking the **I accept this agreement** option before you can click the **Next** button to proceed with the installation.

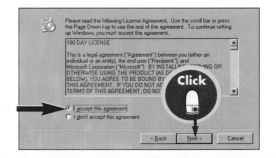

④ Enter the Product Key

Type the 25-digit product identification key from the back of your CD-ROM case and click **Next** to go on.

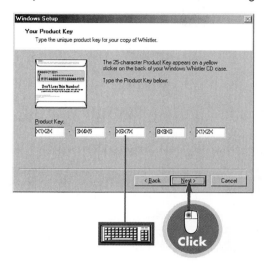

⑤ Perform Dynamic Update

Microsoft often updates the setup files used to install Windows XP. If your computer has Internet access, the Setup program can download any available updates. Make sure that the **Yes, download the latest Setup files** option is selected and click **Next**.

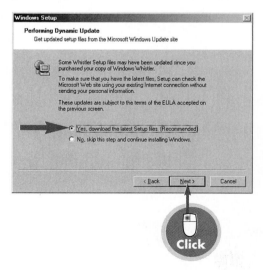

⑥ Download Updates

From this point on, the upgrade is mostly an automatic process. After the updated files are downloaded, the Setup program will begin examining your system and copying files. During this process, your computer might restart once or twice.

⑦ Finish the Upgrade

You can watch the progress of the upgrade. Depending on the speed of your computer, the process could take a good bit of time. If it ever seems that nothing is happening, you can verify that the upgrade is still working by watching the progress indicator in the lower-right corner of the screen. If this indicator stops flashing for a long period of time, you should turn your computer off and turn it back on to resume the upgrade process.

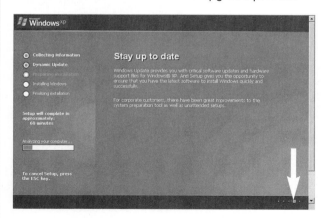

How to Install Windows XP on a Blank Hard Drive

Installing Windows XP on a blank hard drive is a bit more complicated than upgrading from an existing version of Windows. It requires that you have a bootable CD-ROM drive or a set of five setup floppy disks. The procedure for creating the floppy disks is discussed in Task 7, "How to Create Setup Floppy Disks." To begin, insert the CD-ROM or the first of the five floppy disks into your floppy drive and start your computer. If you are using floppy disks, setup asks you for the second, third, fourth, and fifth disks before you can make any other setup decisions.

① Choose Setup or Repair

The first decision you are asked to make is whether you want to set up Windows XP or whether you want to repair an existing installation. For more on repairing, see Task 3. To continue with setup, press the **Enter** key.

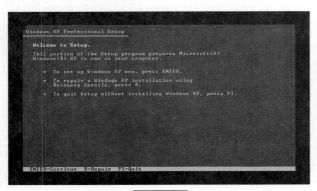

↵Enter

② Agree to Licensing

To continue setup, you must agree to Microsoft's licensing agreement. Press the **F8** key to continue.

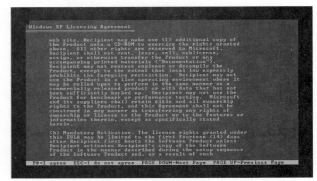

F8

③ Choose a Partition

You must choose the disk partition on which to install Windows XP. Highlight a partition using the up and down arrow keys (in this example, only one disk partition is available). Select the highlighted drive by pressing the **Enter** key. You can also create and delete drive partitions.

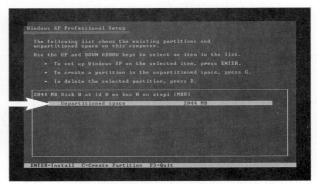

↵Enter

4 Format Your Drive

Use the arrow keys to choose whether to format your drive with the NTFS or FAT32 file system. NTFS is more secure, but only Windows XP, Windows 2000, and Windows NT recognize it. Windows 95 and 98 can recognize the FAT system. If your computer will only run Windows XP, you should use NTFS. If your computer will dual-boot Windows XP and Windows 95/98/Me, you should choose FAT32. Other users on the network will be able to access shared files no matter what file system you choose. If your drive is already formatted, you also have the option of saving the existing format or doing a quick format. Press **Enter** when you have made your selection. On the next setup screen, you'll be asked to confirm the format option. Depending on the size of your drive, formatting can take a few minutes.

5 Copy Files to Your Disk

The Setup program then copies files to your hard drive. This process can take several minutes.

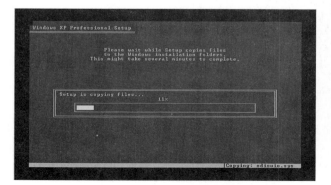

6 Restart Your Computer

After all files are copied to your disk, your computer must restart. This happens automatically after 15 seconds, but you can also press the **Enter** key as soon as you see this screen. Make sure that you remove any floppy disks before you restart the computer. When the computer starts back up, the Setup program continues in a more familiar graphical interface.

⏎Enter

7 Look for Hardware Devices

After your computer restarts, the Setup program initially spends several minutes looking for hardware devices attached to your computer and preparing the installation. It is normal for your screen to flicker during this process. It is also possible that the Setup program might have to restart your computer a few times. All this happens automatically. You can watch the progress indicator in the lower-right corner of the screen to make sure that the installation is proceeding.

8 Customize Your Locale

When all the hardware devices on your system have been identified, you are given the chance to customize your locale and keyboard input. The default is for the English language. Click the **Customize** button to change this locale. When you're done, click the **Next** button to go on.

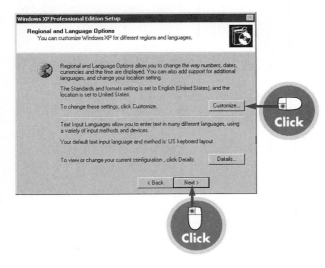

9 Enter Your Name and Organization

Type your name and the name of your company. If you want, you can leave the company name blank. When you're done, click the **Next** button to go on.

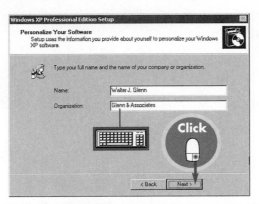

10 Enter Your Product Key

Type the 25-digit product identification number from the back of your CD-ROM case and click **Next** to go on.

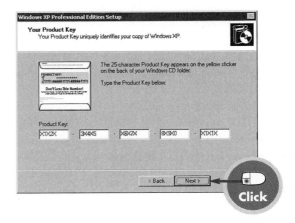

11 Enter a Computer Name and Password

When you install Windows XP on any computer, that computer must be given a name. If you are going to be on a network, this name distinguishes your computer from other computers. Even if you're not planning to put your computer on a network, you must still give the computer a name. A primary user account for your computer is created during installation. This account is given the name **Administrator**. This account is used to change basic computer settings. You can also create additional accounts that other people can use to log in (see Part 9, "Protecting Your Files"). On this screen, you should create and confirm a password for the **Administrator** account.

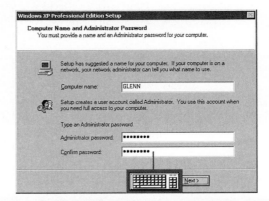

⑫ Enter the Date and Time

Enter the correct date and time if the Setup program is not reporting it correctly. Select the correct time zone from the drop-down list box. If you want Windows to automatically adjust the system time for daylight savings time, enable that option. Click the **Next** button to go on.

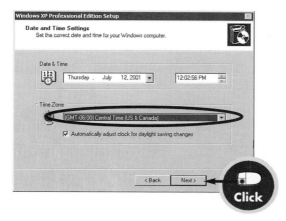

⑬ Choose Network Settings

The Setup program then installs networking components for your computer. When it's done, you must choose your network settings. Unless you know that custom settings are required for your computer (such as a specific IP address or the names of specific servers on your network), choose the **Typical** option. When you're setting up a home network, you should choose the **Typical** option. You can always change the settings after installation if needed. Click the **Next** button to go on.

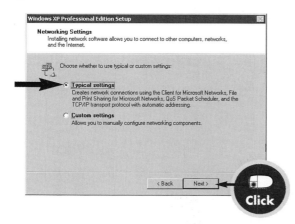

⑭ Join a Workgroup or Domain

If your computer will be part of a Windows networking domain, choose the **Yes** option. If instead your computer will be part of a workgroup (or will be a stand-alone computer), choose **No**. Either way, type the name of the domain or workgroup with which this computer is to be associated into the appropriate text box. After you enter this information, the setup program will copy the needed files to your computer, finalize the installation, and restart one more time. You'll then be ready to start using Windows.

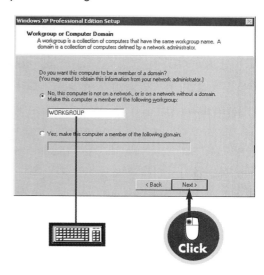

How to Activate Windows XP

Windows XP is the first version of Windows that requires *activation*. You must register your copy of Windows over the Internet or by phone if you want to use it for more than about 14 days. The Activation Wizard will start immediately the first time you start Windows if you upgraded from a previous version of Windows that had Internet access. Otherwise, you might have to run the **Activate Windows** shortcut located on the **Start** menu to launch the wizard.

1 Welcome to Windows

The welcome page of the wizard presents an opportunity to run a short tutorial on using the mouse. After you watch it (or if you choose not to watch it), click **Next** to continue.

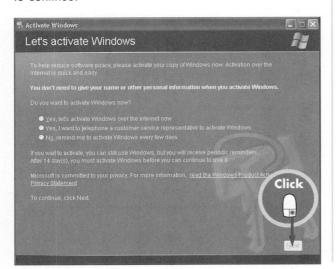

2 Choose to Activate Windows

Make sure that the **Yes**, **activate Windows over the Internet now** option is selected and click **Next**.

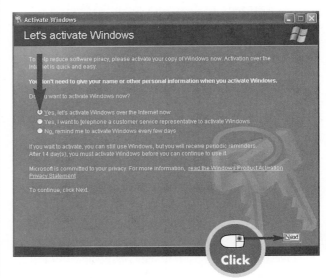

③ Register Windows

During the activation process, you also have the option of *registering* Windows with Microsoft. When you register, you are registering for a warranty; Microsoft will email or mail you information about its products. If you want to do so, choose **Yes, I'd like to register with Microsoft now** and click **Next**.

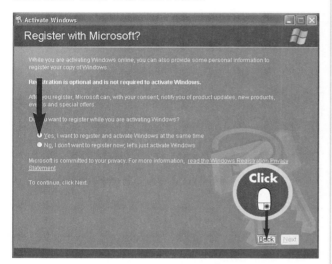

④ Enter Registration Information

If you chose to register, enter the appropriate information in the text boxes. Disable the two check boxes near the bottom of the screen if you don't want to receive advertisements from Microsoft or its partners. Click **Next** to continue.

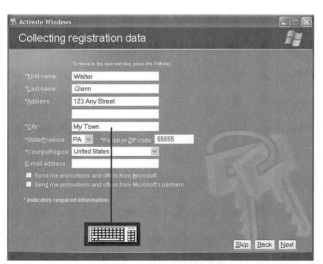

⑤ Finish

When the activation process is finished, click **OK**. You'll be returned to the Windows desktop.

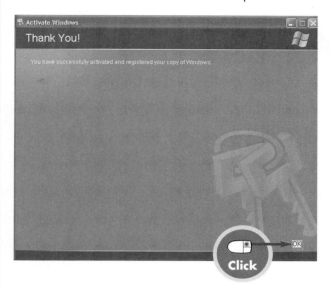

How to Create Setup Floppy Disks

If you plan to install Windows XP on a clean system (one without an operating system on it already), you first must create a set of five setup floppy disks. These disks are used to start your computer so that it can recognize your CD-ROM drive and other hardware and install Windows XP. To make these disks, you must perform this task on a computer that has some version of Windows already installed. Insert the Windows XP CD-ROM into that computer's CD-ROM drive and follow these steps.

① Browse This CD

When you insert the Windows XP CD-ROM, a splash screen should appear automatically, presenting you with several choices. Click the **Browse This CD** link.

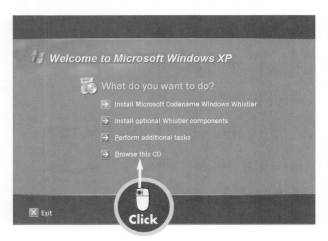

② Open the BOOTDISK Folder

Double-click the **BOOTDISK** folder to open it.

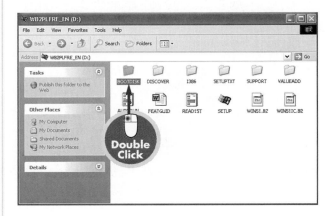

③ Start MAKEBT32

From the list of files in the **BOOTDISK** folder, double-click the **MAKEBT32** program icon to start it. A DOS window from which the boot disks will be created opens.

4 Type the Floppy Drive Letter

Type the letter of the floppy drive you want to use to make the setup floppies. This is usually drive **A**.

[A]

5 Insert Floppy and Press Enter

Insert a blank, formatted floppy disk into the selected drive and press the **Enter** key. The program begins copying files to the disk, which becomes the first disk in the set. When finished copying, the program prompts you for the next disk and then the next. When the last disk is done, the DOS program window closes automatically.

[↵Enter]

6 Label the Disks

It is important that you label the disks in the order in which they were made. When you use these disks to perform a clean installation as described in Task 5, you must insert the disks in proper order. Use a felt-tip marker to write the disk numbers on the disk labels.

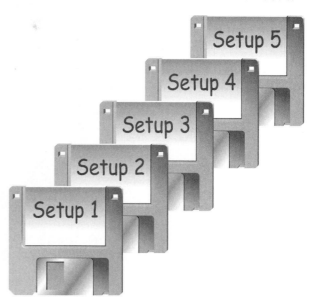

Task

12

Troubleshooting Your Computer

Every so often, believe it or not, Windows XP will act up. You will see error messages and programs may close down unexpectedly. Or, software and hardware you have installed will malfunction. Sometimes this is a matter of incompatibility—you should make sure that anything you install in Windows XP is supposed to run under this operating system.

Sometimes the manufacturer will tell you that although a product is not *certified* it has been tested and will still run. Go ahead and use such a product, but take precautions which we cover here.

How to Clean Up the System Tray

Your System Tray is at the bottom right of your Task Bar. It consists of icons representing programs that are loaded into memory automatically on startup. Sometimes you have given permission to an item to inhabit the System Tray—and sometimes it has taken it upon itself to set itself up there. In any case, closing down a System Tray item can free up memory, and also eliminate a conflict between itself and another program. For example, let's temporarily close down our antivirus program.

① Expand the System Tray

If you don't immediately see the icon representing the offending program, click the **left double arrow** to expand the System Tray

② Locate the Icon

Moving your mouse over the icons should give a clue as to which program each represents. For example, if your virus checker has automatic scheduling, it may be enabled.

③ Open the Option Panel

A System Tray program should open an options panel when right-clicked.

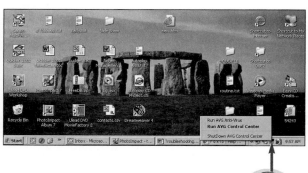

④ Disable the Program

Click the **Disable** option if it appears. If you don't see it, you might have to actually open the program itself, and look under **Tools**, **Options** for a System Tray disabling option. (It might say something like Run on Startup, with a checkbox you need to clear.) Many System Tray programs will ask you again if you *really* want to disable them.

⑤ Check the System Tray

Expand your System Tray again and make sure the program is really gone.

⑥ Reload the Program

After you have checked whether this was a problem, by running another set of tests or programs, you can generally restart the removed application from the Start menu. (In many cases it will reload again automatically if you restart Windows.)

<table>
<tr><td>

How-to Hint

</td><td>

Permanently Stop Programs from Loading

Remember that most System Tray items are only temporarily disabled with this method. To permanently stop them from appearing, you need to go into the actual program options (usually Tools, Options) or, as we'll see in the next step, troubleshoot the startup routine of Windows.

</td></tr>
</table>

How to Boot Selectively

Many problems begin at startup, when all of your system device drivers and *services* are loaded together. A lot of these are Windows programs, but others represent the software choices you have made in your various installations. If a later installation is causing problems, it can be helpful to boot up selectively, either with no other programs or only those you know you want.

1 Open MSCONFIG

On the Start menu, click on **Run**, and type in `msconfig`. Then click **OK**.

2 Choose Selective Startup

Your Normal startup is automatic. Click **Selective Startup** to make some modifications.

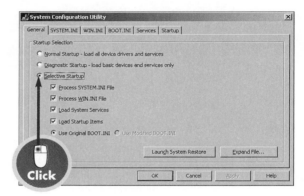

3 Open the Services Panel

The Services Panel shows all the services that begin each time Windows loads. Click the tab to reveal its contents.

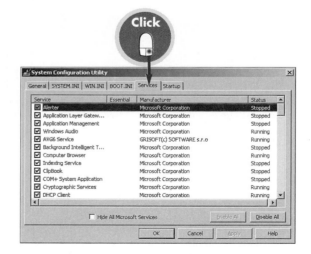

④ Hide the Microsoft Services

Because we don't want to mess with anything that actually affects Windows itself, we'll click **Hide All Microsoft Services**.

⑤ Select and Disable Services

Now you can *uncheck* services that you suspect might be in conflict, or in potential conflict with an impending installation. Then click **Apply** and **OK**.

⑥ Reboot the Computer

To implement the changes you made, you must accept the prompt to reboot. When Windows restarts, click **OK** on the default windows (informing you that you have loaded selectively). Now try an offending program, or do an installation that previously failed. If things work smoothly, return to **MSCONFIG** and reselect a **Normal** startup.

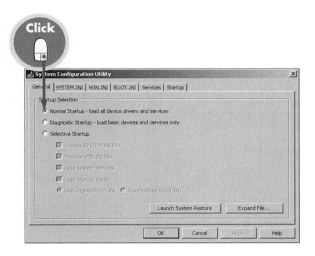

How to Stop a Service

Now that we've seen how Windows services load on startup, let's see how we could close one any time we want (or dare). We'll also see how we can shut down any program that is giving us trouble or is showing an error.

① Open the Windows Task Manager

On your keyboard press **Ctrl+Alt+Del**. This used to reboot your system, but now it gives you more options.

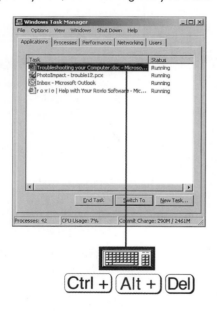

② Look at What's Running

Sometimes you can be surprised that programs are running which you thought were shut down. If a program is showing an error message, you can shut it down by clicking **End Task**. (Sometimes this takes one or two attempts.)

③ Open the Processes Panel

The **Processes** panel shows everything that is running—all services and programs. Click the tab to reveal its contents.

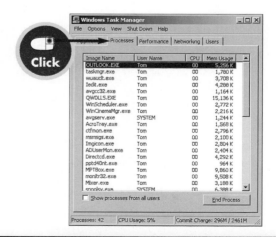

④ Scroll Through the Processes

Scroll through to review and locate any processes that might be interfering with something you are trying to do, or causing trouble. Some are identified by the User name that is currently logged in; others are System or Network processes.

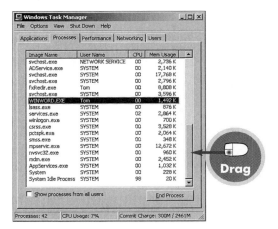

⑤ Shut Down a Process

Now you can click to select a process that you suspect might be in conflict, or potential conflict with another process or task. Then click **End Process**.

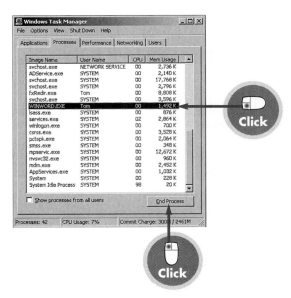

⑥ Check the Other Options

Clicking **Performance** can show you how efficiently your CPU is handling all your tasks. The other tabs relate to networking and user functions.

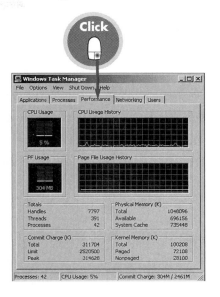

How-to Hint

Be Careful When Ending Processes

Needless to say, *you don't want to end a process that is critical to your entire system*. Only attempt to shut down a process or task that you know is operating in error, or in potential error, with another program or task.

You can also *carefully* monitor and adjust services in the Control Panel, by clicking **Administrative Tools** and then **Services**. You can click on a service to learn more about it, and start or stop it from the controller at the top of the panel.

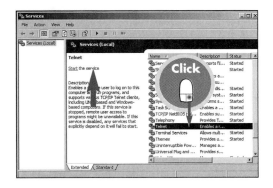

How to Uninstall a Program

Sometimes you don't just want to stop a program, you want to get rid of it altogether. While some programs will provide an Uninstall program in their folders, you can get rid of most programs in Control Panel.

① Open the Control Panel

Click **Start**, and click the **Control Panel**.

② Go to the Programs Category

Click **Add or Remove Programs**—if you're in Category view.

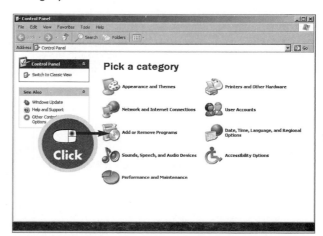

③ Look at What's Loaded

All the programs that you have installed will momentarily appear. Drag through the list.

④ Sort by Frequency

To find programs that you rarely even use, click the drop-down arrow by **Sort by**, and select **Frequency of Use**.

⑤ Uninstall a Program

Now you can click to select a program that is causing trouble or that you no longer need. Then click **Change/Remove**.

⑥ Clean Out the Program Folder

To free up disk space, you sometimes still need to go to the actual program folder under Program Files with the C drive to locate subfolders that have not been deleted. Click to select them and press **Del** on your keyboard to get rid of these.

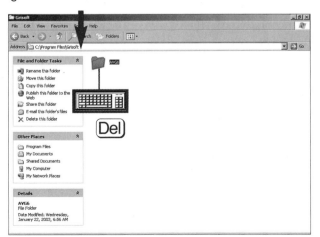

Close the Program First

You can't uninstall a program that is currently running, and in some cases you need to reboot to complete an uninstallation.

Modify Your View

If the Category View confuses you, you can modify the look of Control Panel to what you were used to in the past by clicking **Switch to Classic View**.

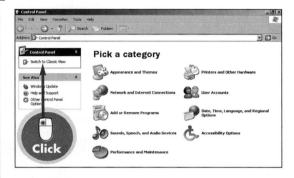

How to Use the Event Viewer

Windows XP lets you dig way down and find out a lot about what might have gone wrong with your system. You can do this with the *Event Viewer*.

1 Open the Control Panel

Click **Start**, and click the **Control Panel**.

2 Go to Administrative Tools

If you're in Category view, click **Performance and Maintenance**, and then click **Administrative Tools**. If you've switched to Classic view, you can go directly there.

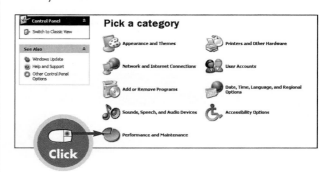

3 Open the Event Viewer

The Event Viewer is now available—double-click its icon.

④ Look at What's Available

The Event Viewer can tell you about errors with regard to applications, security, or the system itself. Double-click **Application**.

⑥ Get Help

While this information may be gibberish to you, note that it does reference a specific DLL file, and you have a link to go online to find out more. With the events sorted by time and other parameters, you should be able to eventually get to the root of problems in your system.

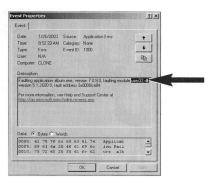

⑤ Analyze the Results

Notice the icons for errors, warnings, and general information. Double-click the latest error.

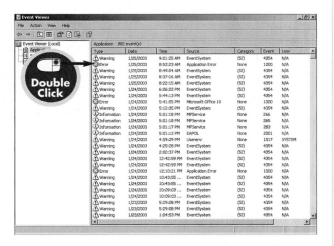

Saving Event Properties

To save the information in the *Event Properties* window, hold down the **Alt** key and press **PrtScn** on your keyboard. Then open Microsoft Word and hit **Ctrl+V** to paste it into a Word document that you can fax to your IT department or other tech support resource.

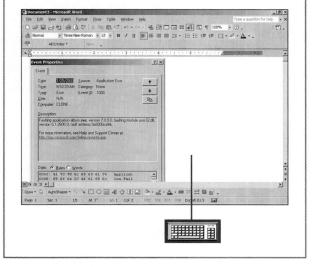

Maintenance, Optimization and Upgrading

13

Performing Computer Maintenance

When it comes to taking care of your computer, the old adage, "An ounce of prevention is worth a pound of cure," couldn't be more true. The best way to help ensure that you won't need to needlessly repair your PC is to perform basic computer maintenance—doing things such as scanning your hard disk for errors, using antivirus software, and cleaning out the inside of your PC.

In this chapter, we look at the basic computer maintenance you should perform regularly—everything from backing up your hard disk, to defragmenting your hard disk, to making sure you always have the latest drivers for your hardware, to blowing dust out of the inside of your computer. If you follow this advice every several weeks, your computer will be more likely to keep running at tip-top shape.

And we also look at basic troubleshooting tips, should something go wrong with your PC. Before calling in a technician, or deciding to replace a computer part, there are a variety of steps you can take that can save you time and money. Doing basic things such as checking whether your add-in boards are properly secured, whether the cables are all tight, and even whether everything is plugged in means less hours of computing frustration—and less money spent on needless repairs.

Software Maintenance You Should Perform

The best way to ensure that nothing goes wrong with your computer is to perform computer maintenance on your software and hard disk regularly. Take the following steps, and you'll help ensure that you fix problems with your computer—before they happen.

❶ Create a Windows Startup Disk

A Windows Startup disk lets you start your computer from its floppy drive, if something goes wrong with your computer or hard disk and it won't start. To create a Windows Startup disk, select **Settings** from the Start menu, and then select **Control Panel**. After Control Panel opens, double-click **Add/Remove Programs**. From the window that appears, click the **Startup Disk** tab and follow the instructions for creating a Startup disk. Use a blank floppy disk or one with data you don't mind losing.

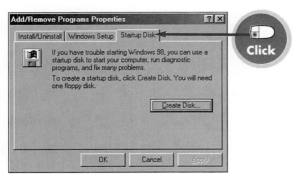

❷ Scan Your Hard Disk

As you use your computer, you can get disk "errors," which can result in the loss of data, programs not running, and even worse. To be sure that you've cleaned up any disk errors, run the ScanDisk program in Windows. To use it, click the **Start** menu and select **Programs**, **Accessories**. From the Accessories menu, select **System Tools**, **ScanDisk**.

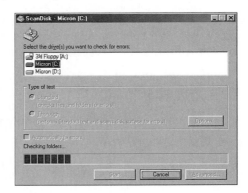

❸ Defragment Your Hard Drive

As you use your hard disk, the files on it become fragmented and spread out over your entire hard disk. So, your hard disk has to work harder. Most versions of Windows have defragmentation software. To use it, click the **Start** menu and select **Programs**, **Accessories**. From the Accessories menu, select **System Tools**, **Disk Defragmenter**.

④ Run Antivirus Software

You can get a computer virus from anywhere. To ensure that your computer doesn't get infected, buy and run antivirus software, such as Norton's AntiVirus. Most antivirus software has an "auto-protect" feature in which the antivirus runs all the time. To be safe, use the auto-protect feature.

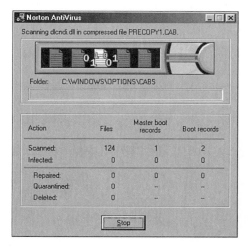

⑤ Back Up Your Hard Disk

To ensure that you don't lose any vital information, back up your hard disk to a removable drive, your company's network, or even the Internet. Windows includes backup software. To use it, click the **Start** menu and select **Programs**, **Accessories**. From the Accessories menu, select **System Tools**, **Backup**. You also can buy special backup software.

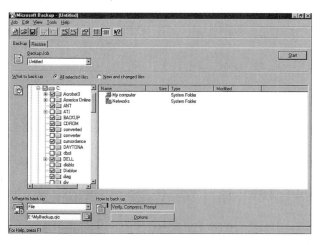

⑥ Check the Web Sites

Drivers are required for hardware such as printers, modems, graphics cards, and other devices to work with Windows. Sometimes the drivers have small bugs in them or become outdated. To ensure that you don't run into hardware problems, you should regularly check manufacturers' Web sites to see whether they have new versions of drivers that you can download and install. Video and sound drivers are often updated every three to six months.

Physical Maintenance of Your PC

Physical problems with your PC are a frequent cause of computer problems—and there's a lot you can do to ensure those problems never occur. Dirt and dust can damage your components by acting as a blanket and trapping heat, which can overheat the components. Additionally, dirt and dust can cause electrical shorts inside the components of your computer. Canned air, which you can buy in many computer stores, is invaluable in cleaning out dust.

Other physical things can go wrong as well. Connectors and boards can come loose, and grime can disturb the contacts between devices.

❶ Swab Any Heavy Dust Areas

Debris and grime, in addition to dust, might have accumulated on the motherboard and any expansion boards. To loosen and clean it, use foam rubber swabs. Don't use any kind of cleaning solution, unless the solution has been specifically designed for electronic components. Be careful not to use brushes, cotton swabs, or pieces of cloth because they can leave a residue and produce static charges.

❷ Blow Out Accumulated Dust

Using the nozzle of the canned air, blow out any dust that might have accumulated on the motherboard and the sides of the expansion cards. Be sure to blow the dust out from a variety of angles to ensure you clean out the hidden areas. Also remove backplates from where you screw in add-in cards so you can blow dust out of them.

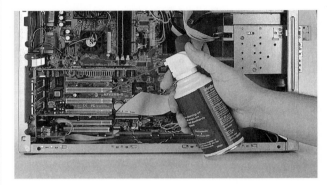

❸ Spray the Power Supply

Dust and grime accumulating in your power supply can freeze it. So clear it by spraying air through all the supply's vent openings. Be careful not to open the power supply because it retains a powerful electric charge even when turned off. Also spray inside your floppy drives, and spray their cable connections as well.

④ Clean the Keyboard

A great deal of dust, hair, grime, grit, and paper accumulate inside your keyboard by falling through the cracks. Spray between the cracks of the keyboard and hold it upside down to enable the particles to fall out. A swab will also enable you to clean between the keys.

⑤ Clean the Mouse

Clean the mouse by taking off the twist-lock on the bottom, taking out the ball, and cleaning the ball as well as the hole into which the ball is normally seated. This will prevent grime and dust from causing erratic mouse movements.

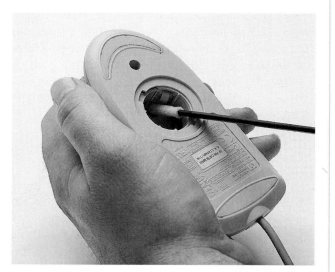

⑥ Clean Connectors

If connectors and contacts get grimy, your computer might not work properly. Using a foam rubber swab and special electronics cleaning solution, clean all the connections and contacts.

Watch Out!

- Only use special electronics cleaning fluid, which you can buy at computer stores and electronics outlets. Any other kind of fluid or liquid can seriously harm your computer.
- Don't smoke or allow anyone to smoke near your computer. The smoke contains chemicals that can damage your computer and corrode its parts.

What to Check for When You Run into Problems

Computers are such complex pieces of equipment that literally thousands of unique problems can occur—and it often can be almost impossible to track down the source of the problem. Here, however, are things you should do when you run into a problem on your PC.

❶ Restart Your Computer

Problems might occur for unexplained reasons and then never happen again. Often the simplest way to fix them is to restart your computer. Shut the computer down by clicking the **Start** menu and selecting **Shut Down**. If that doesn't work, try pressing **Ctrl+Alt+Delete** twice. If neither of those works, try pressing the **Reset** switch on your computer. If that doesn't work, or if your computer doesn't have a reset switch, press the **Power** button to turn it off, and then press it again to turn it back on.

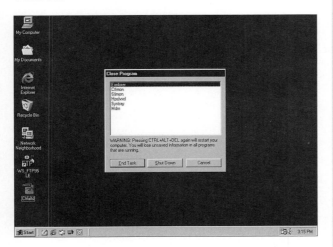

❷ Ensure Things Are Plugged In

You'd be surprised how frequently the cause of a computing problem is simply that not all the hardware has been plugged in and turned on. As technical support personnel will tell you, many printer "problems" are caused by the printer not being plugged in.

❸ Check Your Cables

Often, the cause of the problem is loose cables, switches, or connections. Check external connections and cables to see that they're tight. If that doesn't solve the problem, check the internal connections, such as between controller cards and cables, or drives and cables, to ensure they're tight. Pay particular attention to the connections of your power supply cable.

4 Use the Device Manager

The Windows Device Manager checks your hardware to see whether everything is working properly, so it's a good place to troubleshoot problems. To get to it, right-click **My Computer** and select **Properties**. Then, click the **Device Manager** tab. If Windows detects problems with a device, you'll see an exclamation mark.

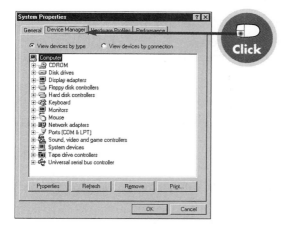

5 Look for Signs of Overheating

Turn off your PC and let it cool down for an hour. Then, turn it back on again. If the problem goes away but then returns after your PC has been on for a while, the problem might be caused by overheating. If your microprocessor chip has a cooling fan, make sure it's connected and working. Check any other fans inside your case as well, including any on chips. Use canned air to blow away dust—dust can lead to overheating. You will need to replace any fans that aren't working properly.

6 Reseat Add-In Boards and Chips

The problem could be caused by an add-in card that was loose. You won't be able to tell that they're loose by looking at them, so you'll have to reseat each of them. Make sure each is firmly seated into the slot on the motherboard. Also check the chips on your motherboard, such as the CPU, to see whether they've come loose. Reseat each of them to ensure that they're firmly in position. And make sure your RAM is connected tightly as well.

How-to Hint

- If you have a PC with many drives, add-in cards, and other devices, your power supply might not provide enough electricity to power them. Consider buying a new power supply that has a higher rating than your current one. Make sure you buy it from a well-known manufacturer.

Watch Out!

- Make sure that your home's or office's power outlets are grounded properly. Improperly grounded outlets can cause problems, as can unreliable PC power supplies.

The Tools You Need

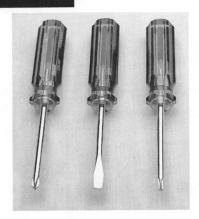

Screwdriver

You'll need some type of screwdriver to open the cases of most PCs and to add or remove expansion cards inside the PC. Get both a Phillips screwdriver and a medium-sized flathead screwdriver (left). Some computers also use special star-headed screws called Torx screws, so if your computer uses these special screws, you'll need a Torx screwdriver (right). Screwdrivers that are 3/8" are best.

Nutdriver

Many screws used in a PC also have hexagonal heads, so a hexagonal-head nutdriver will work on them; in fact, they often work better because they surround the head of the screw, making it less likely that a slip will strip the screw head. A 1/4" nutdriver is your best bet because it's a standard size for computer equipment, and is can be used when adding some heatsinks.

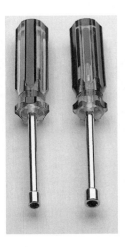

Small flathead screwdriver

You'll need a small, flathead screwdriver about 1/8" across. You'll mainly use it to tighten cables attached to serial, parallel, and other ports. It is also helpful for setting various switches.

Grounding wrist strap

Static electricity you pick up can seriously damage some components of your computer. To ensure you don't zap an electronic part, wear this. Wrap it tightly around your wrist, and then attach the other end to a grounded piece of metal, such as a metal table leg, or clipped to the metal case of the PC. You can also use an antistatic mat.

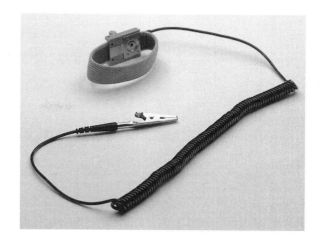

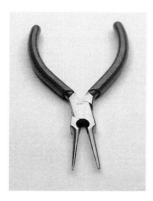

Needle-nose pliers

A good, all-around tool for holding screws, getting objects that are too heavy for the pickup tool, or a hundred other things.

Chip puller

Good for extracting chips that otherwise would be difficult to remove. You won't need this tool for newer memory or processors.

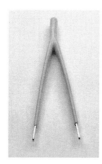

Tweezers

These are good for holding small objects and changing settings on an expansion board. Get the cross-locked kind, pictured here.

How to Prepare for Your Upgrade

Task 4

Anytime you upgrade your computer, you need to take certain basic steps to ensure that you can recover your system information if things go bad and to ensure that your PC can handle your upgrade. Shown here are the steps you should take particularly when installing critical components such as new drives, cards, or a new motherboard in your computer.

1 Back Up Using Windows

You should always have a copy of your hard disk, so that you can restore everything if something goes wrong. You might want to back up only your data (the data files you want to keep, such as word processing documents), or you might want to copy the operating system and your programs. Back up your hard drive to a CD-R or CD-RW, tape drive, Zip drive, or similar removable media. Backup software is built into Windows. To use it, click the **Start** menu and select **Programs**, **Accessories**. From the Accessories menu, select **System Tools**, **Backup**.

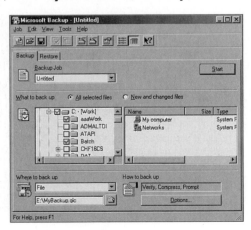

2 Back Up Your Hard Drive

You can buy special software that offers more options than the software built into Windows to back up your hard disk. NTI Backup Now Deluxe is specially designed for backing up to CD-R and CD-RW drives, while Backup Plus can back up to any device.

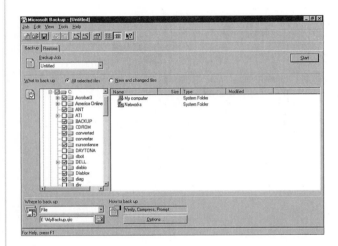

3 Put Backup in a Safe Place

Make sure that your backup is secure and in a safe place where it won't be damaged. That way, you can be sure you can restore your hard disk. Consider buying a small fireproof safe and putting CD backups in the safe.

④ Create a Bootable Floppy

Make a bootable floppy disk so that you can start (also known as *boot*) your computer even if something goes wrong with your hard disk during an upgrade. To do that, put a disk in your floppy drive. Open the Control Panel by double-clicking **My Computer** and double-clicking **Control Panel**. Next, double-click **Add/Remove Programs** and click the **Startup Disk** tab. From the tab, click **Create Disk** and follow the instructions.

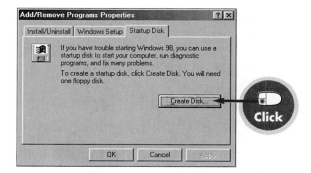

How-to Hint

- Remember to record your BIOS information before taking out your old hard drive or installing a new one.
- Always make a boot disk before installing a new hard drive or adding a second one.

⑤ Check Your BIOS Settings

In many types of upgrades, particularly when you're upgrading a drive, you need to know your BIOS settings. And it's generally a good idea to have these handy, in case something goes wrong with the installation and you must reinstall an old hard drive. Go to the CMOS screen and write down all the information it contains about your hard drive.

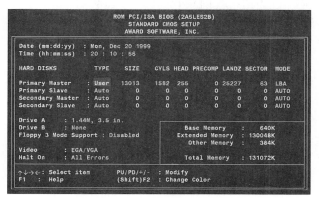

How to Open the Case

To expand or upgrade almost anything, you have to get inside the case of your PC. Although there are variations in how you do this, you'll be able to safely open the case of just about every computer by following these steps.

1 Turn Off Your PC

Before doing anything, you have to turn off your PC. If you try to upgrade or repair the computer while it's on, you can do damage to the computer as well as to yourself. Be sure to turn off anything attached to your computer, such as a printer or monitor.

2 Unplug the Power Cord

If you open the case of your PC while it's plugged in, you could hurt yourself or your computer, so unplug it first. The power cord usually plugs into the back of your PC. Unplug it from there, not from the wall or the power strip. If you unplug it from the wall or power strip, you could accidentally unplug the wrong device and end up opening your PC with the power cord still attached. You might find your monitor plugged into your power supply, so remove that as well.

3 Get Rid of Static Electricity

You often build up a static charge simply by walking on carpets and upholstery, especially during the winter months when the air is dry. You can destroy some PC components if you accidentally discharge static electricity onto them. Because of that, always get rid of any static charge you might carry before opening the case. One way is to use a grounding wrist strap. You can also touch a grounded object, such as the power supply of your PC.

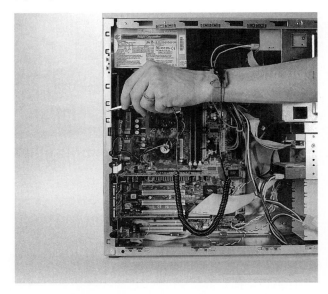

④ Find the Screws on the Case

If you have a desktop model, usually three to five screws hold it in place. A minitower usually has two or more screws, and a full tower might have as many as eight or ten. In some instances, instead of screws, there are thumbscrews you can unscrew by hand. Many cases now have snap-on front covers that, when removed, reveal the screws that hold on the cases. Some cases forgo these kinds of screws altogether and instead use one or more thumbscrews to hold them in place.

⑤ Remove the Screws

You might need a Phillips screwdriver, flathead screwdriver, or Torx screwdriver, depending on the type of screw. Better yet would be to use a hexagonal nutdriver if your screws have hexagonal heads, because that way you'll be less likely to strip the screws. Be sure to place the screws in a safe place, such as a paper cup. You also might want to tape them to the case until you need them again.

⑥ Remove the Case

You usually remove the case by sliding the cover toward the front or rear of the computer and then lifting it off its rails. After you've removed the case, you should ground yourself again before reaching inside to do whatever work you're planning, if you are not using a wrist strap.

Watch Out!

- Remember to turn off any devices attached to your PC, as well as the PC itself, before opening the case.
- Be sure that you're grounded so that you don't damage any delicate internal components.

How-to Hint

- When you remove the screws, put them nearby in a safe place, or tape them to the case after it's opened—you'll need them when you reattach the case.

How to Remove an Existing Card

In many cases, such as when installing a sound card or graphics card, you might have to remove an existing card from your system before installing a new one. Follow these steps to remove a card from your system.

1 Remove the Drivers and Software

Before installing a new sound card, uninstall drivers and other software for your existing card. To do this, right-click the **My Computer** icon in Windows and select **Properties**, the **Device Manager** tab. Click on the hardware you're planning to remove and select your sound card. Click **Remove** and follow the instructions. To remove any special software that works specifically with the card, double-click **Add/Remove Programs** from the Control Panel, select the program you want to remove, and click **Add/Remove, Yes**.

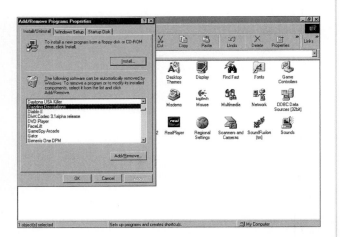

2 Turn Off and Remove Case

Follow the steps outlined earlier in this chapter in the section "How to Open the Case" to turn off your computer and remove its case.

3 Detach Devices and Cables

If you look on the back of your card (the side that faces the outside of your computer) you will most likely see one or more connectors and plugs. A variety of devices might be connected to the card. Unplug the devices. Cables and devices might be attached internally to your card as well. Disconnect them.

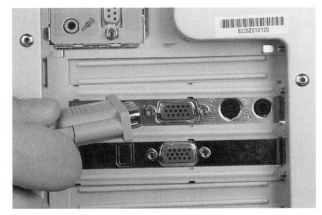

④ Remove Backplate and Card

The card is secured to your system by a screw connecting it to the backplate. Remove that screw, probably with a Phillips screwdriver. Then lift the card free from the system. Hold the card by its top edge with two hands and lift straight up. If the card doesn't move, pull up one edge slightly first and then lift the other.

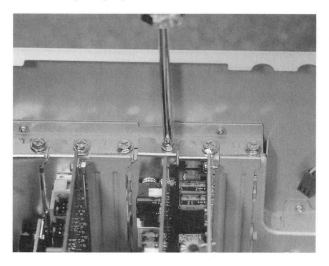

⑤ Attach Case and Turn On PC

Put the case back on, and once it's secure, turn on your computer. If you're going to be installing a new card in place of your old one, don't do this step yet. Instead, install your new card first.

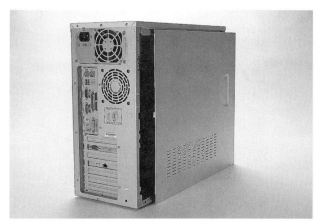

⑥ Double-Check Software

You want to be absolutely sure that all the old software and drivers for the old card are gone from your system. Run the **Add/Remove Wizard** from the Control Panel. In most cases, the wizard won't find any software associated with the old card, but if it does, tell it to remove the software.

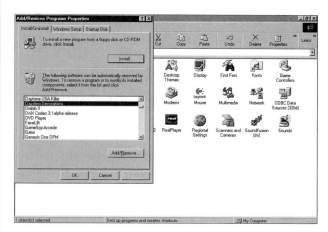

How-to Hint

- When you remove the screw for the slot, put it nearby in a safe place—you'll need it when you install your new card.

How to Install a Basic Card

7

You could need to install a new card on your system for many reasons: You might be adding a sound card or graphics card, or you might need to add a card to attach a device to it, such as a removable drive or SCSI device. Before you install a card, turn off your PC and remove its case, following the instructions earlier in this chapter in the section "How to Open the Case." Then follow these steps.

1 Find and Verify a Free Slot

After you remove your computer's case, look on the motherboard and locate an empty slot. Ensure that the free slot matches the type of card you're installing. For example, if installing a graphics card, you might require a free AGP slot, while many other types of cards require a free PCI slot. Check your computer's or motherboard's documentation for information. When checking the documentation, ensure the free slot is not an Audio Modem Riser (AMR) or Communications and Networking Riser (CNR) slot, since these can't be used by general-purpose cards.

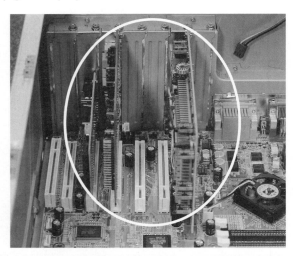

2 Remove the Slot's Backplate

To install the card, you have to remove the small metal flap protecting the slot, called a *backplate*. The flap is held in place by a small screw. Remove the screw (usually a Phillips screw), and then remove the flap. Put the screw in a safe place. (You'll need it to secure the card you're inserting.) In some instances, you must punch out a blank instead of unscrewing the backplate.

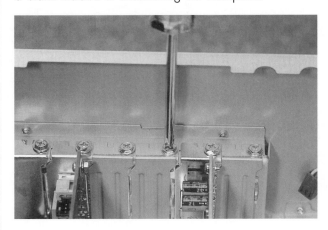

3 Set Jumpers

In some instances, before you install the card, you must set its jumpers. Check the card documentation to see whether you need to set jumpers.

④ Install the Card

Align the card in the free slot, making sure the connectors on the card line up properly with the slot into which you're inserting the card. Then, using two hands, apply gentle, even pressure to push the card down into the slot. After the card is in place, press down firmly to ensure that it's all the way into the slot.

⑤ Screw the Card into Place

To ensure that the card doesn't come loose, you need to screw it into the backplate. Using a Phillips screwdriver, screw in the sound card, but be careful not to overtighten it so that you don't strip the screw.

⑥ Attach Devices and Cables and Restart

Some cards have devices and cables attached to them internally and externally. Attach them, then put the case back on, plug in your PC, and restart the computer. A wizard for installing hardware might appear. If so, follow the instructions. In many cases, you'll now have to install drivers for your new card to work. To learn how to install drivers, see "How to Install Hardware Drivers," later in this chapter.

Watch Out!

- Be sure that the card is seated firmly—if it isn't, the card won't work.
- Don't press too hard when inserting the card or you could damage the card or motherboard.

How to Remove an Old Drive

When installing certain kinds of drives such as a floppy drive, you first should remove your old drive. You take the same basic steps for removing most drives, so follow these steps when you need to remove an old drive. Before you remove a drive, turn off your PC and remove its case, following the instructions earlier in this chapter in "How to Open the Case." Then follow these steps.

① Locate the Drive You Want to Remove

Your PC will have several drives in it, so after you open the case, be sure to find the drive you want to remove—you don't want to accidentally remove the wrong drive.

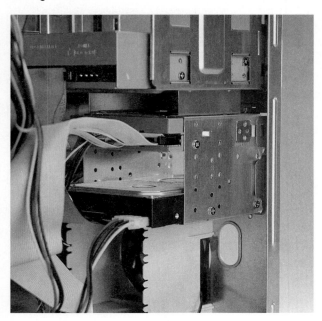

② Remove the Ribbon Cable

A flat ribbon cable runs from the motherboard or a controller card to a drive. Data runs back and forth along this cable. A plug connects the cable to the drive. Remove the cable from the drive by pulling it straight off. It should come off easily.

③ Remove the Power Cables

Power cables run from the power supply to the drive, supplying it with power. These cables are attached to the drive by connectors. Pull the connectors off the drive. It might take more force to pull these off than it did to take off the ribbon connectors.

Take Off Mounting Screws

Some drives are held onto the computer by small rails that slide into your computer, along with the floppy drive. If your drive uses rails, look for the mounting screws and remove them. If it doesn't use rails, the mounting screws will be along the sides. Unscrew the mounting screws and keep them in a safe place.

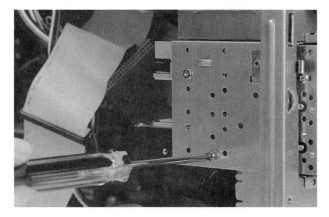

 Slide the Drive Out

Now that all the cables are off and the mounting screws are taken out, the drive can easily be taken out of the computer. Simply slide it out of the computer. It should come out easily.

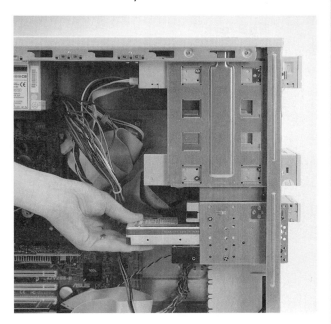

How to Install a Basic Drive

Many of the devices you'll install in your PC are drives of some sort: floppy drives, hard drives, CD drives, and DVD drives. The instructions for how to install each varies, so turn to the specific chapter on how to install that particular drive. Here are instructions for installing a basic drive. Before you remove a drive, turn off your PC and remove its case, following the instructions earlier in this chapter in "How to Open the Case." Then follow these steps.

❶ Find a Free Bay

If you're going to install a drive of any type, you need a free drive bay. After you remove your computer's case, look inside to see which drive bay you have free. Drives come in 3 1/2" and 5 1/4" sizes, so be sure your bay accommodates the drive you buy. You can fit a 3 1/2" hard drive into a 5 1/4" bay by getting a special adapter kit, but a 5 1/4" hard drive won't fit into a 3 1/2" bay. Additionally, some hard drives are mounted inside bays via mounting rails or adapter kits. Look at how your current hard drive is mounted to see whether you need a kit or rails.

❷ Remove the Faceplate for the Drive

A faceplate will cover the front or back of your computer, in front of the empty bay. Remove the faceplate. It might be a blank that you need to punch out, or it might need to be unscrewed.

❸ Attach Mounting Rails or Spacers

Many drives need to be mounted using special rails or spacers. Follow the instructions for installing them.

4 Set Jumpers

In some instances, before installing the drive, you must set its jumpers. Check the drive documentation to see whether to set jumpers.

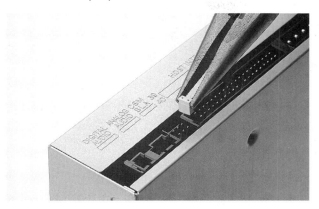

5 Slide in and Secure the Drive

Slide the drive into the drive bay, and screw it into the drive bay or railings. Connect all the screws so that the drive is held firmly in place, but don't overtighten or strip the screws.

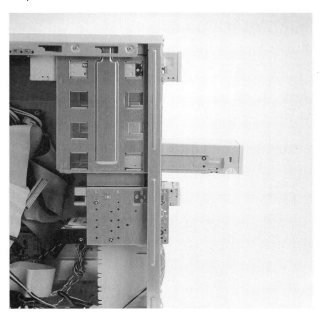

6 Attach the Cables and Restart

Depending on the type of drive you're installing, you must attach a cable or variety of cables, such as controller cables or power cables. Turn to the relevant chapter about the kind of drive you're installing for more information about which cables to attach.

Watch Out!
- Ensure that all the cable connectors are tight before putting the case back on your PC.

How to Install Hardware Drivers

Whenever you install a new piece of hardware, you also have to install drivers. *Drivers* are software that mediate between your hardware and your operating system—they're what enable your hardware to work with the software in your computer.

You install drivers after you install the hardware. With Windows, installing drivers is relatively easy. Be aware that Windows will automatically install its own drivers for your hardware if you don't provide them on disc or downloaded from the Internet.

❶ Turn Your Computer Back On

Turn on the computer if you've had to turn it off during installation of the hardware. That way, the operating system should recognize that you've installed new hardware, if what you've added supports plug-and-play. If you didn't have to turn off the computer, or if the operating system didn't recognize that you added new hardware, tell the operating system to find your new hardware. Click the **Start** menu and select **Control Panel** from the **Settings** menu. Then, double-click the **Add New Hardware** icon and follow the onscreen instructions.

❷ Identify the New Hardware

Your computer will now search for the new hardware you've installed. This could take several minutes. At some point it might ask whether it should search for the hardware itself or whether you want to specify the hardware you've added. Tell it to find it itself.

❸ Insert the Driver Disc

After several minutes, the computer will identify the hardware you've installed. It will ask you whether you have a disc from the manufacturer that contains the driver. If you have that disc, insert it into your drive and then indicate the drive and subdirectory where it should look. If you've downloaded the driver from the Internet, indicate in which drive and subdirectory the driver is located. If you don't have the disc or haven't downloaded a driver from the Internet, insert your Windows CD and tell it to find the driver on that disc.

4 Finish Installing the Driver

The operating system will find the driver and start to install it. Follow the directions onscreen to finish the installation. At each step, you'll click the **Next** button, until at the end, when you'll click **Finish**. At this point, your new hardware should be ready to use.

5 Confirm the Driver Works

To confirm that the hardware has been installed properly, go back to the **Control Panel** and double-click **System**. Then, click the **Device Manager** tab. Click the small cross next to the type of device you've installed, such as a modem. If the driver has been installed properly, you'll see its name there—if it hasn't, you'll see an error message of some sort. Try installing the driver again by turning off your computer and then turning it back on.

6 Check the Web for Newer Drivers

After you've installed a piece of hardware, you should go to the hardware manufacturer's Web site, download any newer versions of the driver, and then install them.

Maximizing System Performance

We saw earlier how we can graphically see the efficiency of our CPU in the Performance tab of the System Task Manager (press Ctrl+Alt+Del). Overall performance is a combination of hardware, software (especially Windows itself), and the device drivers that you load to make your peripheral devices function properly.

Let's take a look at some things we can do to make a system work up to its potential.

How to Check Hardware Settings

If a particular device, such as a printer, CD/RW drive, or scanner, isn't working properly, the best place to start looking is in the Hardware Device Manager. And, even if things are working fine, sometimes a trip inside the Hardware Device Manager can help make everything run more smoothly.

① Open the Control Panel

Click **Start**, and click the **Control Panel**.

② Find the System Icon

If you're in Category view, click **Performance and Maintenance**, and then double-click **System**. If you've switched to Classic view, you can go directly there by double-clicking.

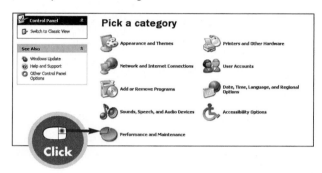

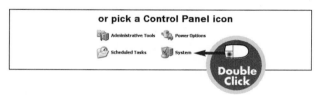

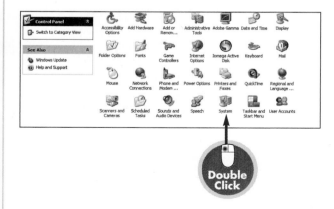

③ Open the System Properties

The System Properties panel is now available.

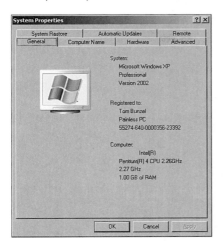

④ Open Hardware

Almost there! Click the **Hardware** tab to reveal **Device Manager**, and click it.

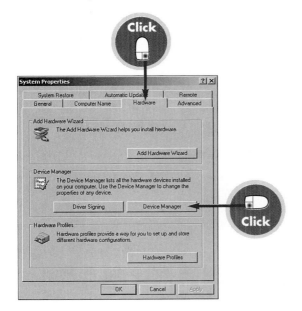

⑤ Check the Device Manager

Yellow exclamation points and question marks indicate an improperly configured piece of hardware. Here we see that we will need to reload something for the Universal Serial Bus.

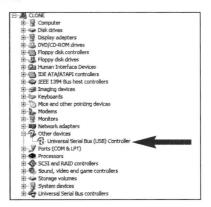

⑥ Expand the Categories

Click the **+** sign next to any device category to reveal the peripherals in your system. This is how you can begin to maximize their performance and get them working properly.

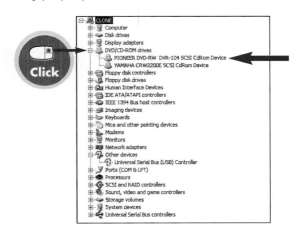

How-to Hint

Shortcut

If you have a Windows key on your keyboard, you can open the System Properties panel in one step by holding it down while pressing the **Pause/Break** key.

How to Check DMA Status

If your DVD or CD recorder is not working at peak performance, it might be your DMA (Direct Memory Access) setting. To check this option, you'll need to return to the Hardware Device Manager.

1 Open the System Properties

Follow the steps in the previous task to get to the System Properties panel, or open the **Start** menu and right-click on **My Computer** (not the shortcut on your desktop) and click **Properties**.

2 Open Device Manager

Click the **Hardware** tab, and click **Device Manager**.

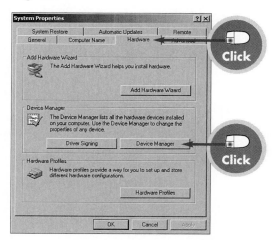

3 Select IDE ATA/ATAPI Controllers

Click the **+** sign next to **IDE ATA/ATAPI controllers** to reveal your two channels.

④ Choose the Right Controller

Usually a DVD- or CD-RW is attached to a secondary controller, so right-click it and select **Properties**.

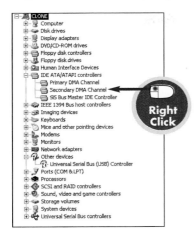

⑤ Enable or Disable DMA

Now on the **Advanced Settings** tab, you can either enable or disable DMA for the devices attached to that controller.

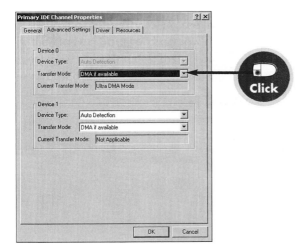

⑥ Alternative Scenario

If you cannot find the **Advanced Settings** tab, you can try to disable the DMA controller under **System Devices**.

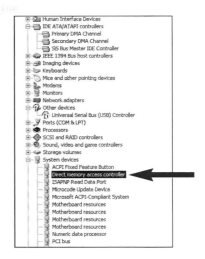

How-to Hint

Be Careful with Settings

Your Device Manager is a strange beast, especially with respect to the controllers attached to your hard drive. Make sure you don't change the settings for your primary controller and your PCI bus unless you really know what you're doing.

How to Use Advanced System Properties

The daring ones among you will want to go further into System Properties to enhance your performance. You will find some goodies in the Advanced area—so let's take a look.

① Open the System Properties

Follow the steps in the previous tasks to get to the System Properties panel, or open the **Start** menu and right-click on **My Computer** (not the shortcut on your desktop) and click **Properties**.

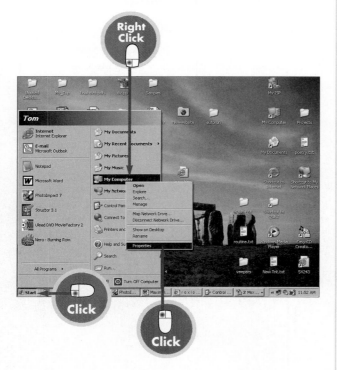

② Open the Advanced Panel

Click the **Advanced** tab to open more options for performance. Then click **Settings**.

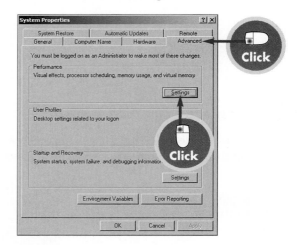

③ Adjust Visual Effects

Under **Visual Effects**, click **Adjust for Best Performance** (or customize the settings with some experimentation).

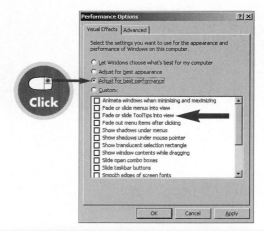

④ Adjust the Advanced Options

Under the **Advanced** tab, click to try to maximize background services or system cache.

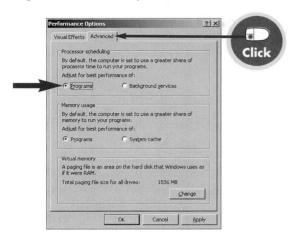

⑤ Adjust Memory Settings

Click **Change** under **Virtual Memory** to try to allocate a bigger portion of your hard disk as a memory sector. When you're done "tweaking," click **OK** and **Apply**.

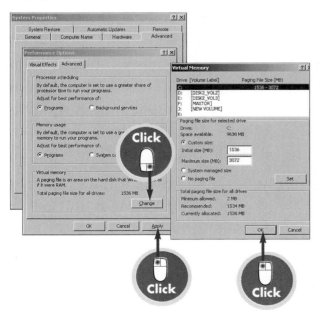

⑥ Check the Results

You will need to experiment with these tweaks to see if they enhance performance or lead to unexpected results you don't want.

How to Set a Restore Point

Now that we've discussed some of the hardware settings in your computer and we've installed some software, it's not a bad idea to set what is called a *restore point*. This is basically a snapshot of how your computer is configured to which you can presumably return at a later date.

The word *presumably* is used here because if you restore to a point that conflicts with stuff you've installed later on, you could have a problem. But it's a way to "go back in time" to when your system worked using a former set of drivers and options.

1 Open the System Restore Area

From the **Start** button, click **Accessories**, **System Tools**, **System Restore**.

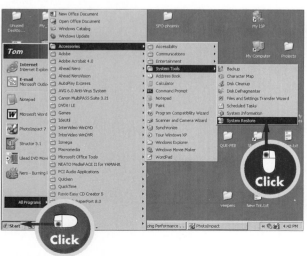

2 Create a Restore Point

Click **Create a Restore Point**, and then click **Next**.

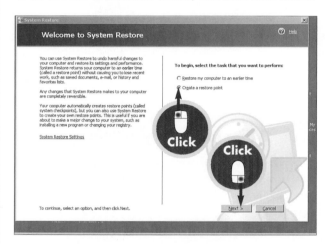

3 Enter a Description

Type in the reason for this restore point, or what you are about to do next. You might also use an event—like before a business trip. Then click **Create**.

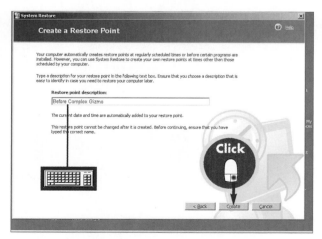

④ Check the Results

Your restore point is set with a time and date. Click **Home**.

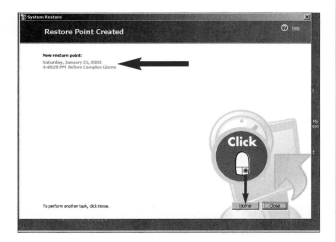

⑤ Restore your System

To see how to "go back in time," click **Restore my computer to an earlier time**, then click **Next**.

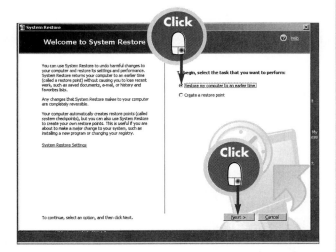

⑥ Pick a Restore Point

Your newly named point is ready to be restored. In addition, you can go to an earlier date when restore points were created automatically. To restore, just click **Next** to continue through the wizard.

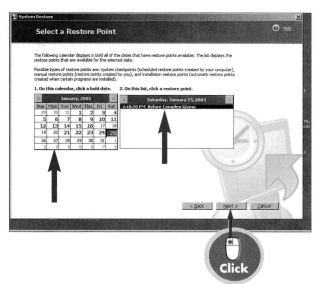

Setting Restore Points

A great time to set a restore point is just before you are about to install a potentially tricky peripheral, such as a graphics card or video capture device.

How to Use Windows Update

Sometimes when you're online, Windows will let you know that an updated driver or software program is available, and you can click a link to get right to it. But you can update your system regularly to ensure peak performance.

❶ Open the Windows Help Panel

From the **Start** button click **Help and Support**.

❷ Pick the Update Task

Under Pick a Task, click **Keep your computer up-to-date with Windows Update**. (*Make sure you are connected to the Internet.*)

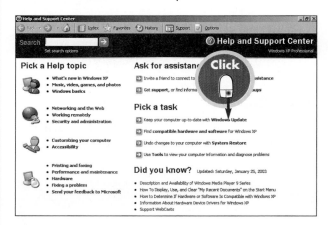

❸ Wait for the System Check

Read the instructions as Windows scans your system for possible updates.

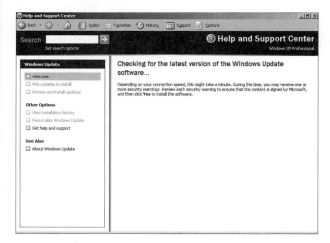

④ Install the Updates

When you see an update with a Security Warning from Microsoft, click **Yes** to install the update. (Click **Always trust content from Microsoft Corporation** to bypass this box in the future.)

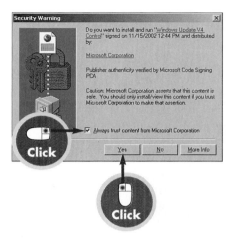

⑤ Continue Updating

You can also choose to update your version of Windows Update, or get help with Windows Update.

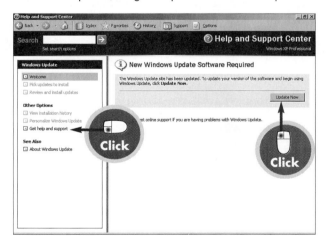

⑥ Let the Software be Installed

Wait while Windows installs its new software.

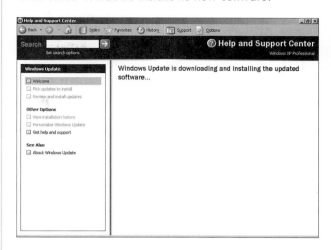

<table>
<tr><td rowspan="10" style="writing-mode: vertical-lr">How-to Hint</td><td>

Close Programs Before Updating

In general, during Windows Update or any software installation, close all other software programs. If possible, also disable your virus protection software, especially for software that requires a reboot. (See Chapter 12, "Troubleshooting Your Computer," for information on closing software in the System Tray.)
</td></tr>
</table>

How to Monitor Your System

One important aspect of keeping your system working at its best is knowing exactly what is going on in Windows XP. There are a number of diagnostic tools you can use, but Windows System Information is as good as any.

① Open System Information

From the **Start** button, click **All Programs**, **Accessories**, **System Tools**, **System Information**.

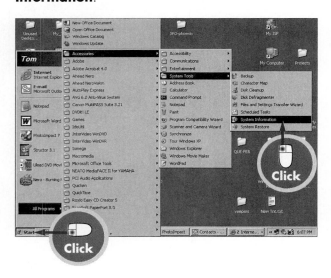

② Check Hardware Resources

Click the **+** sign next to **Hardware Resources** to expand the category. Note the various system parameters you can check, many of them mentioned elsewhere in the book.

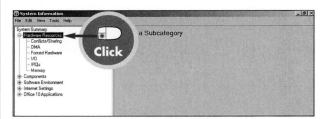

③ Check for Hardware Conflicts

Windows allows peripherals to share resources, and the PCI components can get along. But conflicts can show up in this panel. Click **Conflicts/Sharing** to check.

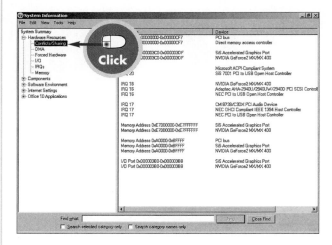

④ Check Hard Drive Capacity

While it's easy to check an individual hard drive for free space, here you can look through all your fixed drives at once. Just click **Components**, **Storage and Drives**.

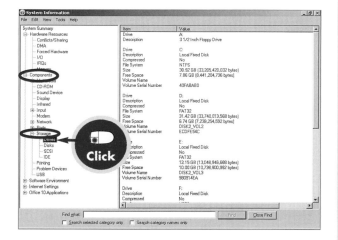

⑤ Check DirectX

DirectX is the Windows accelerator driver system for your graphics card. The latest DirectX drive should be installed. Click **Tools** and click **DirectX Diagnostic Tool** to see which version is installed.

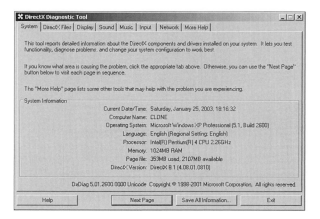

⑥ Check for Acceleration

Click the **Sound** and **Display** tabs to make sure that video and audio are fully accelerated by your hardware.

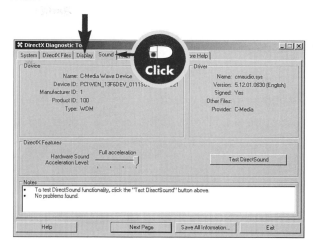

<table>
<tr><td>How-to Hint</td><td>

Get a User-Friendly View

If you click to expand the Software Environment, you can get a much more user-friendly view of the programs that load each time you start your system by clicking **Startup Programs**. To learn how you can shut some of them off, see Chapter 12, "Troubleshooting Your Computer."

If you can't find what you're looking for, use the search panel at the bottom of the System Information screen.

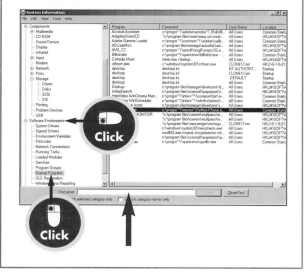
</td></tr>
</table>

How to Clean Up Your Hard Drive

Another useful Windows tool lets you quickly recapture lost hard drive space taken up by obsolete or orphan files.

① Open Disk Cleanup

Click **Start**, **All Programs**, **Accessories**, **System Tools**, and **Disk Cleanup**.

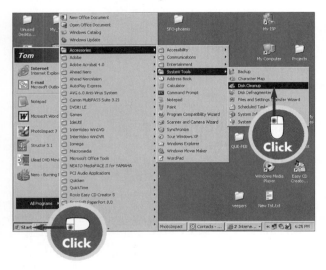

② Select Your Drive

Click the drop-down arrow to select the disk you want to clean. Click **OK**.

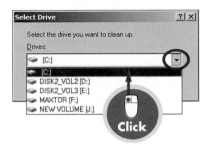

③ Wait for Compression

Windows will take a few minutes to analyze and compress your disk.

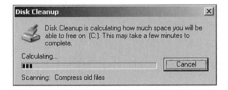

④ Select Your Categories

You can see some areas where you can save space—**Temporary Files** and the **Recycle Bin**. Click to clean them.

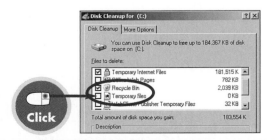

5️⃣ Dig Deeper

Click **Clean up** under **More Options** to find Windows components you don't use, such as games or communication tools. (You can reinstall them later if necessary.) Clicking the button starts a wizard.

6️⃣ Clear Restore Points

Cleaning up all but the latest restore points and some seldom-used installed programs will also free up space. Click **Clean up** under **More Options**.

7️⃣ Begin Cleanup

Click **OK** to clear the items you selected.

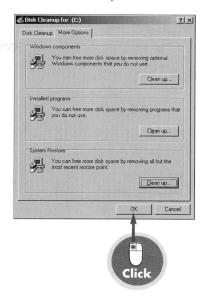

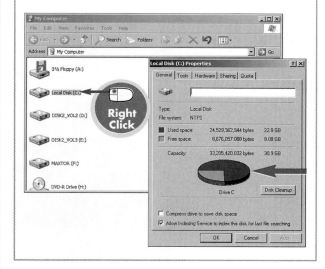

8

How to Download and Set Up a Driver

As we saw earlier, some settings and programs in Windows can be updated automatically using the Windows Update feature. Frequently, however, the manufacturer of a peripheral device (graphics card, scanner, printer) will post a new updated driver on its Web site. If you are having problems with the device or want better performance, you can go to the site and download the later version.

1 Locate the Right Version

Go to the manufacturer's Web site and find the proper version in Support or Drivers. Click the link to download.

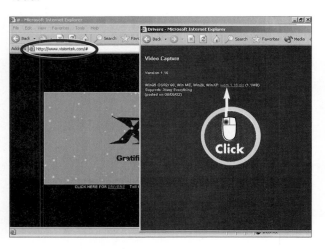

2 Choose Save the File

Click **Save** to save the file to your hard drive.

3 Choose a Folder/Location

Direct the download to a specific folder, and note the filename. Click **Save**.

4 Wait for the File

Depending on the file size, the download can take minutes or hours.

5 Locate the Files

When download is complete, click **Open Folder**, or browse to the file location you selected. Double-click to open the downloaded *zipped* folder.

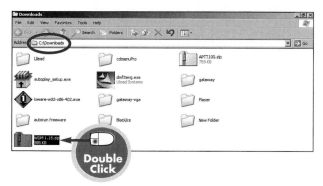

6 Look for a Setup File

If the folder contains an automatic setup file, you can update the driver using this program by double-clicking it. If not, read the How to Hint.

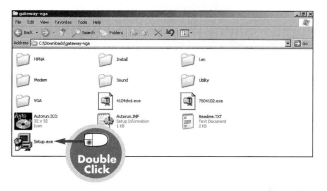

How-to Hint

No Setup File?

If there is no setup file in the zipped folder, create a new folder by right-clicking in the same or another folder and giving it a name. Then open the downloaded folder and copy its files to the newly created and named folder. (Press **Ctrl+A** to select all the files and drag and drop them to the new folder.) Now you're ready to update the driver through Windows.

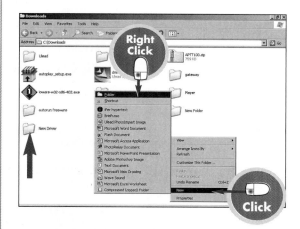

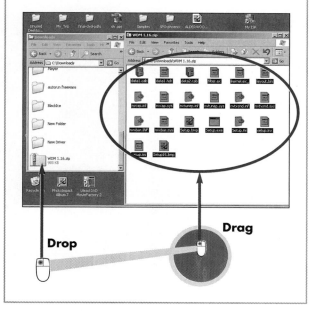

9

How to Update a Driver

Once the new driver files are downloaded to a local folder, if they don't have an automatic setup program, you can use Windows Device Manager to begin the update.

① Open System Properties

From the **Start** button, right-click **My Computer** and select **Properties**.

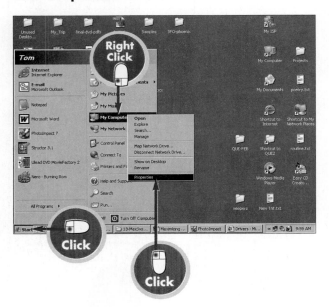

② Open Device Manager

Click the **Hardware** tab and click **Device Manager**.

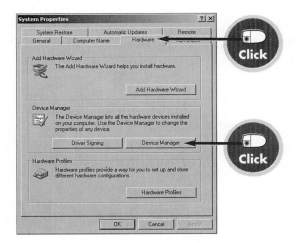

③ Find Your Peripheral

Click the **+** sign next to the appropriate category and click to select the peripheral whose driver you will update.

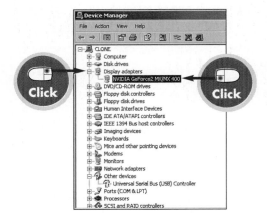

4 Start the Update

Right-click the peripheral and select **Update Driver**.

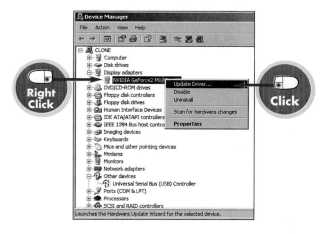

5 Install from Location

Click to have Windows install the driver from a specific location (your downloaded files). Click **Next**.

6 Locate the Folder

Click **Include the location in the search** and browse to the folder with the downloaded files (see previous task for how to download a driver file). Then click **OK** and follow the wizard through the rest of the installation.

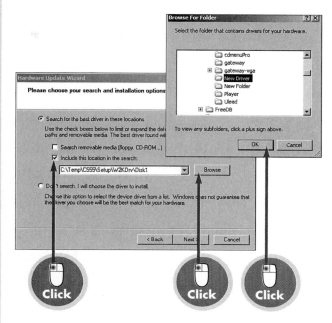

Don't Let Windows Search for the Best Driver!

You can use the same procedure to update a driver that you receive on a CD or other media. Just browse to the media itself after telling Windows to load from a specific location.

Having Windows search for *the best driver* rarely works because it will simply list and reinstall the drivers that were previously installed, and not find the new driver in your system.

Task 10

How to Roll Back a Driver

If your new driver is misbehaving, you might want "roll it back" to a previous version.

① Open Device Manager

Use the steps shown previously to open System Properties (or press the **Windows** key and **Pause/Break** on your keyboard) and click **Device Manager** under the **Hardware** tab.

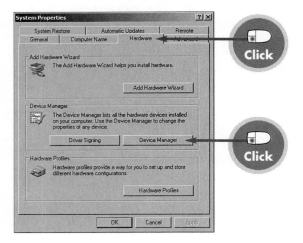

② Find Your Peripheral

Click the **+** sign next to the appropriate category and click to select the peripheral whose driver you will update.

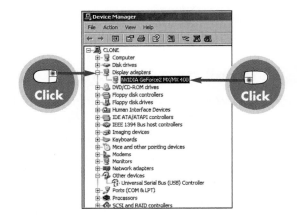

③ Go to Properties

Right-click the peripheral and select **Properties** or click the **Properties** icon.

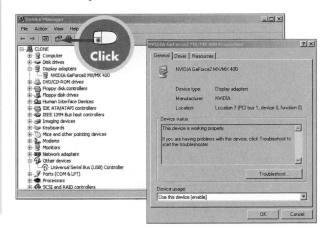

Start the Rollback

Click the **Driver** tab and click **Roll Back driver**.

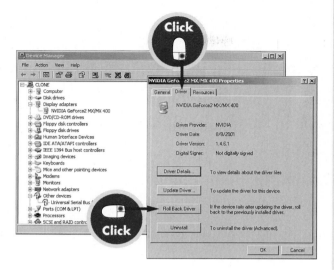

Uninstall Drivers Before Updating

You can sometimes (and should in some cases) *uninstall* a driver before updating it using Add and Remove Programs within Control Panel. Always check the FAQ and directions from the manufacturer before loading and updating new drivers.

If rolling back a driver doesn't work, you can sometimes revert to an old driver set successfully by using a system restore point before the new driver was installed. (See Chapter 12, "Troubleshooting Your Computer.")

5 **Proceed with the Rollback**

Click **OK** to *return to the previous driver*. Check the driver details to determine which driver version you are currently using.

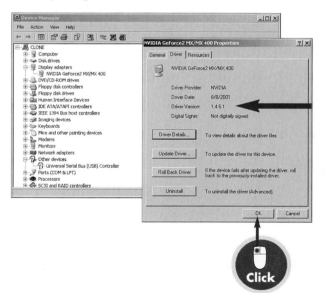

Task

15

Installing a Printer

Printers change as quickly as do computers these days. Laser printers, once the exclusive province of the office because they were so expensive, have dropped in price enough so that they're affordable for the home. And some color inkjet printers now sell for under $100, although if you want higher-quality color and faster speed, you have to pay more than that—often in the $150–$500 range. But even in that range, buying a new printer is cheaper than ever.

Printers typically connect to the computer via printer ports or USB ports. For more information on installing USB hardware, turn to Chapter 21, "Installing USB and FireWire Devices."

Upgrade Advisor

The most basic decision you need to make when buying a new printer is whether to get an inkjet or a laser printer. As a rule, laser printers print faster and have a higher quality output. But if you buy a laser, you'll be limited to black-and-white printing because color laser printers aren't affordable. They also tend to cost more than inkjets. But if you need only black-and-white printing and are willing to pay more than for inkjets, they're a great choice. If you want to do color printing, or want a less expensive printer than a laser, choose an inkjet.

There are a features you should know about before buying a new printer. The most important are the quality of its output and its speed. The quality of output is measured in dots per inch (dpi)—how many dots of ink per inch is put on the page. As a general rule, the higher the dpi, the higher the quality of the output. Lasers these days usually have 600dpi, although you might be able to find less-expensive lasers with 300dpi resolutions.

Buy as high a resolution as possible. You also should get the fastest printer you can afford, measured in pages printed per minute. If you're buying an inkjet printer, keep in mind that black-and-white pages print faster than color pages, so when buying, take into account which types of pages you expect to print more and buy according to that.

If you are primarily going to print out photographs, consider buying a special photo printer. These printers turn out very high-quality photographs compared to other types of printers, but they tend to be more expensive than inkjets, and have a higher cost of materials, so are more expensive to operate.

Printing speed is rated in pages per minute (ppm). As you would expect, the higher the rating, the faster the printing—and the more expensive the printer.

Aside from those two specs, you should also consider whether you want a printer that attaches via the parallel port or USB port, or both. There's no great difference between them. If you have other USB devices you're planning to attach to your PC, you might want to choose a parallel port printer because that way, you'll leave your PC's USB ports free for those other devices.

How a Printer Works

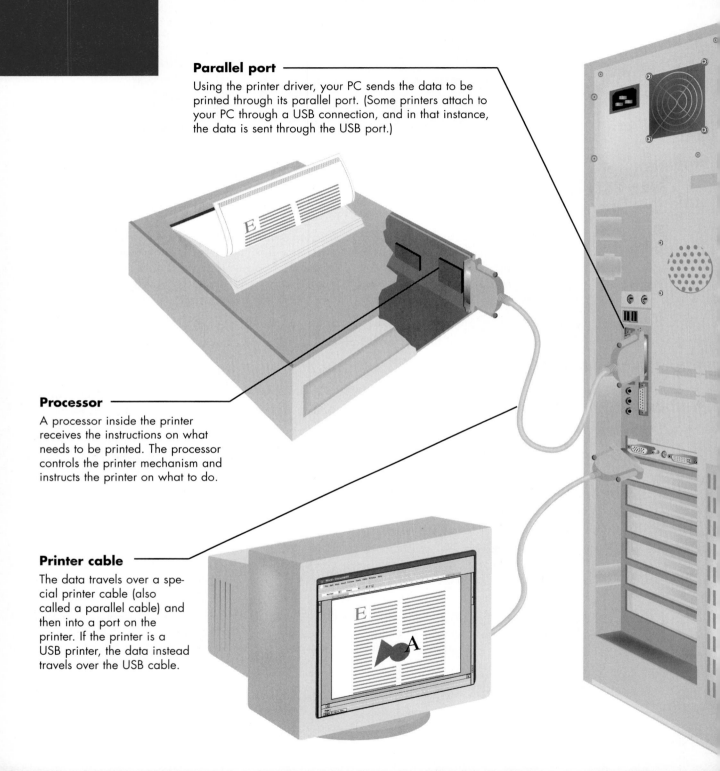

Parallel port

Using the printer driver, your PC sends the data to be printed through its parallel port. (Some printers attach to your PC through a USB connection, and in that instance, the data is sent through the USB port.)

Processor

A processor inside the printer receives the instructions on what needs to be printed. The processor controls the printer mechanism and instructs the printer on what to do.

Printer cable

The data travels over a special printer cable (also called a parallel cable) and then into a port on the printer. If the printer is a USB printer, the data instead travels over the USB cable.

Page description language

When your PC is ready to print something, it needs to tell the printer how to print it, so it must include information about fonts, where to print text, how to print pictures, and so on. It does this by using the printer's page description language. The most common page description language is PCL, used by Hewlett-Packard printers. PostScript is a common page description language as well.

Printer driver

To translate what's on your PC into the printer description language, your PC needs to use a piece of software called a printer driver. This driver takes the information from your file and formats it in such a way that the printer can understand it, using the printer's page description language. Each printer has its own unique printer driver.

Print head

Different kinds of printers, such as laser printers and inkjet printers, use different technologies to do their actual printing. An inkjet printer, for example, uses a print cartridge that moves sideways across a piece of paper, which fires colored ink through tiny nozzles onto the paper. If you are having problems with your current printer, the problem might be as simple as a bad head or an empty cartridge, so to fix the problem, you will only need to buy a new cartridge.

How to Install a New Printer

After you buy a printer, you'll find it's easy to install. You need the proper printer cable—and in almost all cases, a cable won't come with the printer, so if you don't have one, buy it when you buy the printer. In addition to a printer cable, you need a printer driver. In most cases, this driver is on a CD or floppy disk provided by the manufacturer, but if it's not, you can use the drivers built into Windows.

❶ Get the Correct Printer Cable

A printer attaches to a PC via the PC's parallel port, a female 25-pin connection, or a USB port. Your printer cable should match the printer and PC ports. If your printer has extra features, such as bidirectional printing, enhanced parallel port (EPP), or extended capability port (ECP), be sure you have a cable that has IEEE-1284 printed on it. You often can use CMOS to set your parallel port to use ECP or EPP.

```
                ROM PCI/ISA BIOS (2A5LES2B)
                    STANDARD CMOS SETUP
                    AWARD SOFTWARE, INC.

Date (mm:dd:yy)  : Mon, Dec 20 1999
Time (hh:mm:ss)  : 20 : 10 : 56

HARD DISKS         TYPE   SIZE   CYLS HEAD PRECOMP LANDZ SECTOR  MODE

Primary Master   : User   13013  1582 255      0  25227    63  LBA
Primary Slave    : Auto       0     0   0      0      0     0  AUTO
Secondary Master : Auto       0     0   0      0      0     0  AUTO
Secondary Slave  : Auto       0     0   0      0      0     0  AUTO

Drive A     : 1.44M, 3.5 in.
Drive B     : None
Floppy 3 Mode Support : Disabled        Base Memory     :    640K
                                    Extended Memory : 130048K
                                        Other Memory    :    384K
Video       : EGA/VGA
Halt On     : All Errors             Total Memory    : 131072K

↑↓→←: Select item      PU/PD/+/-  : Modify
F1  :  Help            (Shift)F2  : Change Color
```

❷ Plug In the Cable

After turning off your printer and computer, take off the computer's power cable. Next, plug the printer cable into the proper port on your PC. Some PCs have 25-pin female serial ports, as well as 25-pin parallel ports, so be sure to plug the cable into the parallel port. The parallel port on your computer is a female connection. After you plug each cable in, secure the cable. Sometimes you do this by tightening tiny screws, and other times you do so by simply snapping wire connectors on each side of the connector.

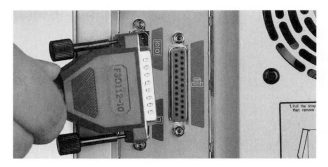

❸ Install the Ink

The printer you've bought might or might not already have an ink cartridge (for inkjet printers) or a toner cartridge (for laser printers) in it. Turn on the computer and printer, and then follow the manufacturer's instructions for installing the cartridges. Inkjet printers might require more than one cartridge—they might require two or even three.

④ Install the Printer Drivers

In Windows, select **My Computer** from the Desktop, and then select **Printers**. Double-click the **Add Printer** icon to launch an Add Printer Wizard. You'll be asked for the model of your printer and the location of your printer driver, if you have one. Type in its location on your floppy disk or CD-ROM drive. If you don't have a disk, use the Windows drivers. In some cases, to install a printer driver, you have to run the setup program from the printer-supplied CD to install the driver.

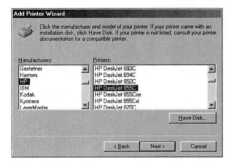

⑤ Print Out a Test Sheet of Paper

To ensure your printer is working properly, print out a test sheet of paper. The Installation Wizard asks you whether you want to do this, so be sure to answer Yes. After it prints out, you'll be asked whether it printed properly. Allow enough time for the printer to print the test page before answering Yes or No. You also can print out a test page by going through the **Control Panel**, selecting the **Printers** folder, right-clicking the correct printer, and selecting **Print Test Page** from the **General** tab.

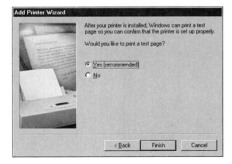

Watch Out!

- Be sure that you have the proper printer cable—if you have a bidirectional printer, be sure the cable has IEEE 1284 printed on it.
- Plug the printer cable into the parallel port on your computer. Some serial ports might look like parallel ports because they have a 25-pin connection like a parallel port.

How-to Hint

- If a printer driver didn't come with your printer, check the manufacturer's Web site or use a driver that comes in Windows. Use the most up-to-date driver you can find, either on a disk supplied with the printer or from the manufacturer's Web site.
- If you are considering buying a new printer because you are unhappy with the quality of its output, first consider buying more expensive paper and seeing whether using the new paper produces the quality you are looking for.

Task

16

Printing

Printing is one the basic functions you will perform with your computer. Windows XP makes printing as easy as it has ever been, coordinating all the mechanics in the background so that you can focus on your work.

In the tasks in this chapter, you learn how to print a document from within the program that created it and also from the Windows XP desktop. You also learn how to manage various printer settings, such as how to set your default printer, paper source, and paper size. You learn how to install a printer attached to your own computer and how to set up your computer to use a shared printer—one that's available on the network. Finally, you learn how to share your own printer with others on the network.

How to Print a Document from a Program

Most of the time, you print documents directly from the program you used to create them. Because most programs designed for Windows follow similar guidelines, you will find that the process of printing from any Windows program is very similar to the following steps. Many Windows programs also offer a **Print** button on the main toolbar. This button usually prints one copy of the document using all the default printer settings. If you print this way, you bypass the **Print** dialog box described in this task altogether.

1 Open the File

Open the file you want to print using the **File**, **Open** command of the program used to create the file. In the program's **Open** dialog box, navigate to the folder where the file is stored, select the file, and click **Open**.

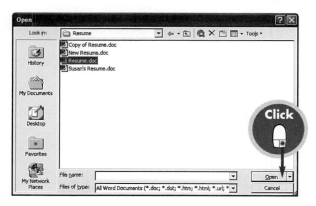

2 Choose the Print Command

When you are ready to print the open document, choose **File**, **Print** from the program's menu bar. The **Print** dialog box opens, which allows you to specify which pages of the document as well as how many copies you want to print.

3 Choose the Printer to Use

If you have access to more than one printer, use the **Printer** drop-down menu to select a printer.

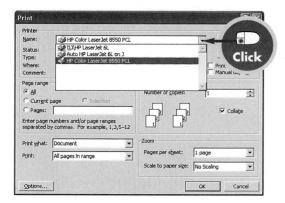

4 Choose Printing Options

Some programs let you set special printing options that are specific to that program. This is usually done by clicking an **Options** button in the **Print** dialog box. For example, some programs allow you to print a document in draft mode, which can save a lot of time and printer ink because it prints characters in a lighter text.

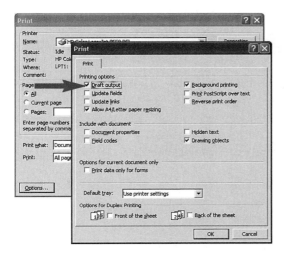

5 Choose Pages and Number of Copies

Almost every Windows program lets you specify the range of pages you want to print. You can use the program's **File**, **Print Preview** command to see a preview of what the document will look like when printed so that you can determine which pages of a lengthy document you want to print. In the **Number of copies** box, type the number of copies of the document you want to print.

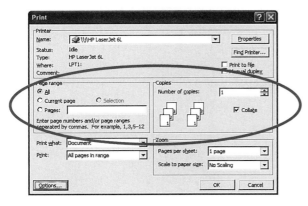

6 Print the Document

After you have selected your printer, specified the pages and number of copies you want to print, set any extra options, and click **OK** to print. Most programs allow you to continue working while your document is being printed.

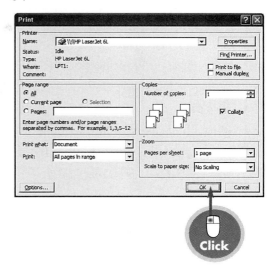

How-to Hint

Setting Printer Properties

The Print dialog boxes for most programs include a **Properties** button. This button gives you quick access to system-wide properties for your printer— the same properties you can set from within Windows, as described in Task 4, "How to Change Printer Settings."

Previewing Before You Print

Some programs offer a feature named **Print Preview**, usually available from the **File** menu, that lets you see your document onscreen as it will look when it is printed. This can be a handy way of making sure that your document looks the way you think it should before using up paper and ink to print it.

How to Print a Document from Windows

Most of the time, you print documents from within programs. However, Windows offers a few ways to print documents straight from the desktop without first opening the document's program. This is a great way to dash off quick copies of documents, or even to print multiple documents at once.

① Find the Document You Print

The first step to printing a document in Windows is to find the document. You can use the **My Computer** folder, the **My Documents** folder, or **Windows Explorer**—whichever you prefer. Here, a document named **Resume** is selected in a folder named **Personal Folder**. You learn more about navigating in Windows in Chapter 4, "Working with Files and Folders."

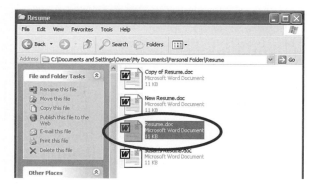

② Right-Click and Choose Print

To quickly print the document using your default printer and the default settings of the document's program, right-click the document (or select multiple documents and right-click any one of them) and choose **Print** from the shortcut menu. Windows prints one copy of each document. Windows opens the associated program just long enough to print the document and then closes the program again. Note that this trick does not work with all programs—just with programs that have included this feature.

③ Open Your Printers Folder

Another way to print a document in Windows is to drag the document onto a printer icon. To perform this action, both the folder holding the document you want to print and your **Printers** folder must be open. To open the Printers folder, click **Start** and select **Printers and Faxes**.

④ Select Documents to Print

Using **My Computer** or **Windows Explorer**, find the folder with the document or documents you want to print and select those document icons.

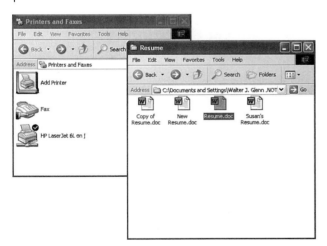

⑤ Drag a Document to a Printer Icon

Drag any document (or group of documents) from the folder and release it on the icon for the printer you want to use. Windows prints the documents using the default settings for the program that created the documents. This method is the same as using the **Print** toolbar button mentioned in Task 1, but lets you choose the printer you want to use.

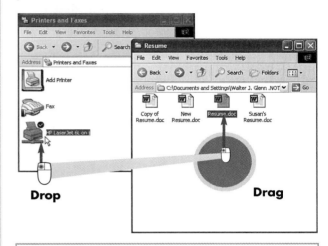

Drop   **Drag**

How-to Hint

Don't See Printers and Faxes on the Start Menu?

If you don't see the Printers and Faxes shortcut on the **Start** menu, open the **Control Panel** instead. You'll find the Printers and Faxes folder inside. You can add the Printer and Fax shortcut to your **Start** menu by right-clicking the taskbar and choosing **Properties**.

Dragging Multiple Files

You can drag multiple documents to a printer icon in one step: Hold down the **Ctrl** key while you left-click documents in the **My Computer** window.

Creating a Printer Shortcut on Your Desktop

If you frequently drag files to a printer icon and don't want to keep your **Printers** folder open all the time, drag the desired printer icon to your desktop and release it. When Windows offers to create a shortcut for you, click **OK**.

How to Manage Documents Waiting to Print

Whenever you print a document, that document enters a print queue, a line of documents waiting for their turn at the printer. A printer icon appears in your system tray next to the clock to let you know that the queue is active. You can open the print queue and do some document management. Some of the things you can do in the print queue depend on whether you are using a printer hooked up directly to your computer or a network printer. Network printers are usually shared by many users; you can manage only the documents that belong to you. You cannot affect other user's documents or the print queue itself, unless you are the administrator of the printer.

❶ Open the Print Queue

To open the print queue, double-click the printer icon in the notification area when it appears. Right-clicking the printer icon opens a shortcut menu that lets you open the print queue for any printer on your system, not just the actively printing one.

❷ View Documents Waiting to Print

The print queue shows a list of documents waiting to print in the order in which they are to be printed. For each document, details such as owner, number of pages, document size, and time of submission are also shown.

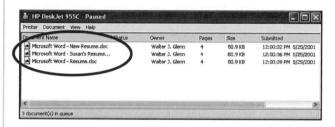

❸ Cancel the Printing of a Document

To remove a document from the print queue—that is, to stop it from being printed—right-click the document and choose **Cancel** from the shortcut menu. Be sure that you choose the correct document because Windows does not ask whether you are sure that you want to remove the document.

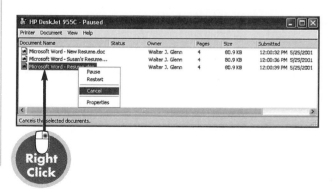

4 Pause the Printing of a Document

If you pause a document, it remains in the print queue but does not print until you choose to resume printing. Other documents waiting in the queue continue to print. To pause a document, right-click the document and choose **Pause** from the shortcut menu; the status of the document in the print queue window changes to **Paused**. Choose **Resume** from the document's shortcut menu when you are ready for the document to continue printing.

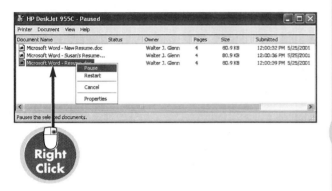

5 Restart the Printing of a Document

When you *restart* a paused document, it begins printing again from the beginning. This can be useful if, for example, you start to print a document and then realize the wrong paper is loaded in the printer. You can pause the document, change the paper, and then restart the document. To restart a document, right-click the document and choose **Restart** from the context menu.

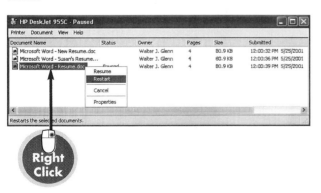

6 Change a Document's Priority

A document's *priority* governs when it prints in relation to other documents in the print queue. By default, all documents are given a priority of 1, the lowest priority available. The highest priority is 99. Increasing a document's priority causes it to print before other waiting documents. Double-click the document to open its **Properties** dialog box. Then drag the **Priority** slider to set a higher priority.

7 Pause the Whole Print Queue

Pausing the entire print queue keeps *all* documents from printing. This can be useful if you suspect a problem with your printer (perhaps it's low on toner). You can pause the queue, fix the problem, and then restart the queue. To pause the queue, open the **Printer** menu and choose **Pause Printing**. The title bar for the print queue window changes to indicate that the printer is paused. To resume printing, choose the **Pause Printing** command again.

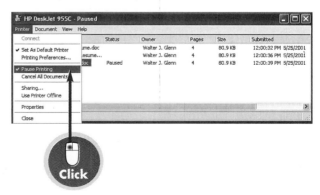

How to Change Printer Settings

When you first install a printer in Windows XP, common settings are configured for you. The settings include which printer is used by default, whether pages are printed vertically or horizontally, what kind of paper is being used, and where that paper comes from. After you use your printer for a while, you might find that you need to change those printer settings.

1 Open the Printers Folder

Click the **Start** button and select **Printers and Faxes**. The **Printer and Faxes** window opens.

2 Set the Default Printer

In the **Printers and Faxes** window, the default printer has a small check by it. To set a different printer as the default, right-click its icon and choose **Set as Default Printer** from the shortcut menu.

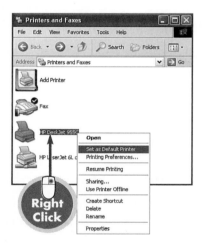

3 Open Printer Preferences

To specify your preferences for the printing options that a particular printer uses, open its **Printing Preferences** dialog box. Right-click a printer and choose **Printing Preferences** from the shortcut menu.

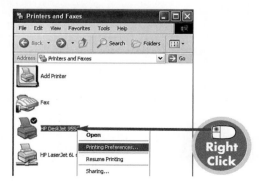

④ Change the Page Layout

Select the orientation of the pages to be printed. You can choose to print the pages in **Portrait** format (normal vertical orientation) or **Landscape** (horizontal orientation).

⑤ Change the Paper Source

Click the **Paper/Quality** tab to see more preferences. Click the **Paper Source** drop-down list to choose a different tray on your printer. The options you see in this list vary based on the printer you are configuring.

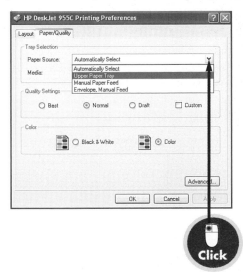

⑥ Change the Media Type

Click the **Media** drop-down list to choose the type of paper you want to print to. Some printers can use special kinds of paper (such as glossy paper for photos or presentation graphics, transparencies, and even slides). Those printers print differently depending on the kind of paper being used.

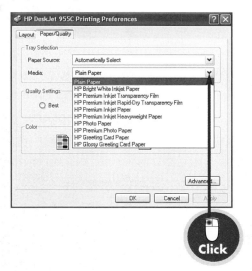

⑦ Change the Print Quality

Choose the quality of print you want. Better quality uses up more ink and takes more time. Draft quality prints quickly and uses less ink. When you're done setting preferences for this printer, click **OK** to close the dialog box and put these options into effect.

How to Share a Printer with Others

When you share a printer, it becomes accessible to other users on your network. By default, all users on the network can see and print to your printer. You can change this so that only particular users or groups of users can use your printer. To share your printer, your computer must be properly configured on a network.

❶ Open the Sharing Dialog Box

In the **Printers and Faxes** window, right-click the printer you want to share and choose **Sharing** from the shortcut menu. The **Properties** dialog box for the selected printer opens.

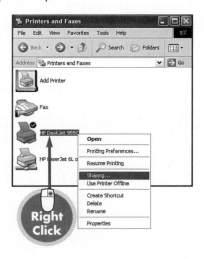

❷ Share the Printer

On the **Sharing** tab, enable the **Share Name** option and type a name for the shared printer. This is the name others will see when they look for a printer.

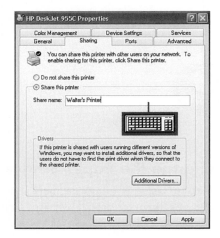

❸ Click the Security Tab

If you are using Windows XP Professional on a domain-based network, Windows also provides a **Security** tab that lets you limit the users who can access your printer. You will only be able to access this tab if you have administrative privileges.

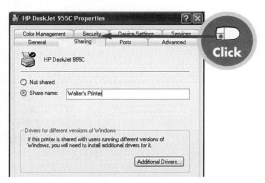

4 Remove the Everyone Group

Select the group named **Everyone** and click **Remove**. This action removes the permissions for all users to access the printer.

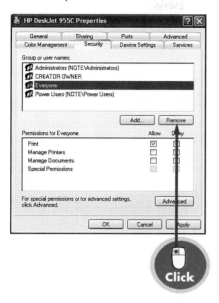

5 Add New Users

Click **Add** to give a new user or group of users permission to access the printer. The **Select Users or Groups** dialog box opens.

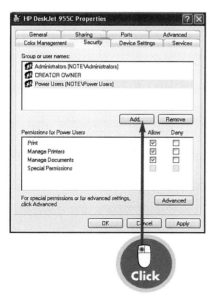

6 Select a User to Add

Select a user from the list at the bottom of the dialog box and click **OK** to add that person or group to the list of users who can use the printer. You return to the printer's **Properties** dialog box.

7 Apply the New Permissions

Select the exact permissions each user should have using the check boxes. The **Print** permission allows the user to print to the printer. **Manage Printers** allows the user to change printer settings. **Manage Documents** allows the user to move, pause, and delete documents waiting to print. Click **OK** to grant the new users you have added access to your printer.

How to Install a Local Printer

In Windows lingo, the actual piece of hardware you usually think of as the printer is called the *print device*. The *printer* is the icon you install in the **Printers and Faxes** folder that represents the print device. After you have attached the print device to a computer, it is relatively easy to install the printer to the **Printers and Faxes** folder. In fact, Windows will normally find the print device automatically and configure a printer icon for you. If Windows doesn't find it, use the steps in this task to add the printer yourself.

❶ Run the Add Printer Wizard

In the **Printers and Faxes** folder, click the **Add a Printer** link to launch the **Add Printer Wizard**. When you see the Welcome screen, click **Next**.

❷ Choose Local Printer

On the first page of the wizard, enable the **Local printer** option. A *local printer* is attached directly to your computer.

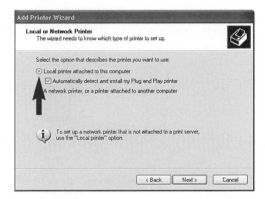

❸ Don't Detect the Printer Automatically

Disable the option to automatically detect the printer. If Windows didn't find it automatically already, it probably won't now. If you leave this option selected, Windows will attempt to find the printer itself and figure out what kind it is. If Windows does not find the printer, the wizard will continue as described in this task. If Windows does find the printer, it will set it up for you.

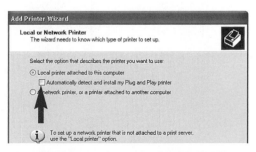

④ Go to the Next Page

Whenever you finish with the options on one wizard page, just click **Next** to go to the next page.

⑤ Choose a Port

Choose the port on your computer to which the print device is attached. The first print device on a computer is usually on the LPT1 port (the first parallel port). The second print device is usually on the LPT2 port (the second parallel port). Newer printers may be installed on a USB port. When you've selected the port, click **Next** to go on.

⑥ Choose a Manufacturer

On the left side of this page is a list of common printer manufacturers. Choose the manufacturer for the print device you are installing.

⑦ Choose a Model

After you choose a manufacturer from the left side of the page, the list on the right changes to display printer models made by the selected manufacturer. Choose the model of the print device you are installing. Click **Next** to go on.

8 Name the Printer

By default, Windows creates a name for your printer based on its manufacturer and model number (for example, **HP DeskJet 855C**). If you want the printer icon to have a different name, type a new name in the **Printer name** text box.

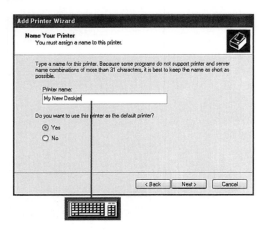

9 Make It the Default Printer

If you want your new printer to be the default printer used by programs on your computer, click **Yes**. If you prefer to preserve an existing default printer, click **No**. Click **Next** to go on.

10 Share the Printer

To share the new printer with other users on the network, select the **Share name** option. Windows creates a share name for you based on the printer name you selected in Step 8 of this task, although you can type a different share name. For more on sharing a printer, see Task 5, "How to Share a Printer with Others." Click **Next** to go on.

11 Enter a Location and Description

Optionally, you can enter a location and description for the printer to help identify it to others who may use it. You won't see this screen if you did not choose to share the printer in Step 10. Whether you fill in these fields or not, click **Next** to go on.

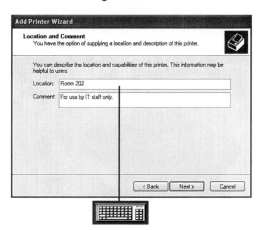

Print a Test Page

Click **Yes** if you want Windows to print a test page to ensure that your new printer is working properly. If the test doesn't work, you are shown how to troubleshoot the installation. Click **Next** to go on.

13 **Finish the Installation**

Review the configuration of your new printer. If you discover any problems or errors in this information, click **Back** to go back through the steps of the installation. If you are satisfied with the information displayed here, click **Finish**.

Creating a Share Name

When you create a share name for your printer, it is best to keep the name under eight characters in length. Older programs (those created for use with pre-Windows 95) can recognize only eight-character names. If you are at all unsure whether any users of older programs will print to your printer, keep the name short.

Installing a Printer More Than Once

Each icon in the **Printers and Faxes** folder represents a real printer. You can install more than one icon for a single printer by running the **Add Printer Wizard** again, choosing the same printer and port during setup, and giving the new icon a new name. You may want to do this to configure each icon with different settings. For example, your printer may have two paper trays: one for letter-size paper and one for legal-size paper. You could name one icon **Letter Printer** and configure it to use paper from the letter-size paper tray. You could name the other icon **Legal Printer** and configure it to use the legal-size paper tray. You can also set up additional printer icons to use different print quality, paper types, or whatever other configurations you desire.

How to Set Up Your Computer to Use a Network Printer

A *network printer* is often one that is attached to another computer on the network; that computer's user has shared the printer with other users on the network. Some network printers are attached directly to the network and are not on a computer. Either way, setting up your computer to print to a network printer requires that you know where on your network the printer is located. This means knowing the name of the computer the printer is attached to (if it is attached to a computer) or the name of the printer itself (if it is attached directly to a network) and maybe the workgroup that the computer or printer is part of.

① Run the Add Printer Wizard

In the **Printers and Faxes** window, click the **Add a Printer** link to launch the Add Printer Wizard. Click **Next** to skip the Welcome page.

② Choose Network Printer

On the first page of the wizard, enable the **A network printer, or a printer attached to another computer** option.

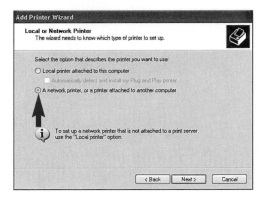

③ Go to the Next Page

When you finish with the options on one wizard page, just click **Next** to go to the next page.

4 Find the Printer

If you know the exact name of the printer you want to connect to (including the network path to that printer), you can enter it in the **Name** text box. You can also connect to an Internet-based printer by entering its address in the **URL** box. If you don't know the name or address (which is usually the case), leave the **Find a printer in the directory** option selected and click **Next** to browse the network for the computer.

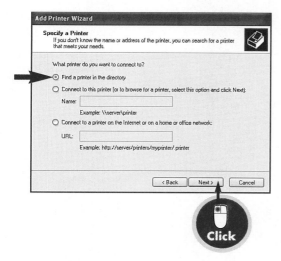

5 Choose the Printer

The **Browse for Printer** page of the wizard shows a hierarchical view of the workgroups and computers on your network. All shared printers are listed at the top. Choose the printer you want to set up and click **Next**.

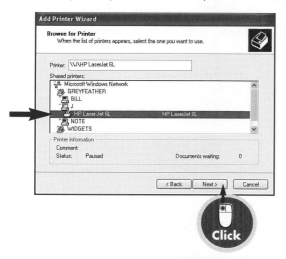

6 Make It the Default Printer

If you want this new printer to be the default printer used by programs on your computer, click **Yes**. If you prefer to preserve an existing default printer, click **No**. Click **Next** to go on.

7 Finish the Installation

Review the configuration of your new printer. If you discover any problems or errors in the information shown here, click **Back** to go back through the steps of the installation. If you are satisfied with the information displayed, click **Finish**.

Task

Installing a Keyboard and Mouse

Upgrading your keyboard and mouse or other pointing device is one of the easiest and least expensive ways to make your computing life more productive. For example, there are enhanced keyboards for Windows that have extra keys to give you fast access to features such as the Start menu or enable you to run specific programs. Similarly, a well-designed mouse makes pointing and clicking easier. And new mice, such as those with wheels on them, make scrolling through programs and documents easier. Some keyboards, such as the Microsoft Natural Keyboard, are even shaped to help minimize disorders related to typing such as carpal tunnel syndrome.

Upgrade Advisor

If you have problems with a keyboard or mouse and can't fix it yourself, it's never worthwhile to try to get it repaired. Instead, buy a new one, and install it yourself, as detailed in this chapter.

Keyboards are particularly important—after all, you spend most of the time on your computer typing on them. Consider buying the Microsoft Natural Keyboard or a similar ergonomic keyboard that splits the rows of keys and angles them. At first, using a keyboard like this is uncomfortable, but it ensures that your arms, hands, and elbows are in the proper position for typing, so you'll be less likely to suffer an injury. Also consider buying a keyboard with special, programmable keys. That way, you can visit your favorite Web sites, check your email, and do similar tasks by simply pushing a button on your keyboard—a big time-saver.

You have an even wider selection of mice. Some mice are ergonomically shaped, and some include a middle "wheel" and extra programmable keys. If you're considering an upgrade to a new mouse because the pointer doesn't seem to respond anymore or responds erratically, first wipe the bottom of the mouse clean. You also can take out the little ball inside and clean that, as well as the contacts inside the mouse. Rubbing alcohol works well. Finally, use a new mouse pad. You can eliminate these problems entirely if you buy an optical mouse because those mice don't use balls or other mechanical devices.

You also might want to buy a wireless keyboard or mouse, or keyboard/mouse combination. This eliminates the clutter of wires on your desktop. When buying, though, be sure that the mouse or keyboard uses RF (radio frequency), technology, such as those made by Logitech, rather than infrared technology. You can also buy USB keyboards and mice.

How a Keyboard and Mouse Work

Ergonomic design

If you have a medical condition such as carpal tunnel syndrome or are worried that you might develop one, you should invest in upgrading to a new ergonomic keyboard. They are shaped so that when you type, you are less likely to develop a condition.

Programmable keys

Some keyboards contain extra keys that do things such as launch an email program or visit a certain Web site. Often, these keys are programmable, so you can customize them to perform whatever task you want. You might want to buy a new keyboard just to take advantage of these keys.

Keys

If the contact between a key and the underlying electronics becomes damaged, you will need to buy a new keyboard. Keys can also become sticky, but you can often fix that by cleaning them and using compressed air to blow out dirt, dust, and grime that has accumulated between the keys.

Wireless connection

A transmitter can be attached to one of the computer's ports that will allow a mouse or keyboard to communicate with the PC wirelessly.

Mouse Connector

The mouse connects to a PC via a special connector. Mice can have one of three different types of connectors—a PS/2 connector, a serial port connector, and a USB connector. Sometimes the small pins in the serial or PS/2 connector can bend or break, which would require that you buy a new mouse.

Keyboard Connector

The keyboard connects to a PC via keyboard connector or a USB connector. Sometimes the small pins in the keyboard connector can bend or break, which would require that you buy a new keyboard.

Buttons

Mice have two and sometimes more buttons, and some even have a wheel that can be used to scroll through documents. The functions the mouse buttons and wheel perform can often be programmed. The extra buttons and wheel add enough extra functionality that you might want to upgrade to a newer mouse simply to get the buttons and wheel.

Optical mouse

The movements of regular mice can be erratic and sometimes imprecise. In that case, buying an optical mouse is a good solution. It doesn't use moving parts and works by the use of a light on its bottom shining onto a desktop or other surface. If reliability and precision are important, consider upgrading to one.

Ball and rollers

As you move most mice, a ball protruding slightly in the bottom turns in the direction in which you move the mouse. Two rollers inside the mouse rotate as the mouse moves. This ultimately translates into mouse movement on your screen. Dirt, dust, and grime sometimes build up on the ball and rollers, so if your mouse has erratic movements, try cleaning it before buying a new one. The rollers can also become damaged, which would require that you buy a new mouse.

How to Install a Keyboard and Mouse

Installing a keyboard or a mouse is one of the simplest and most straightforward things you do when upgrading or enhancing a PC. As you see here, the main thing to look for is that you have the correct type of connector. If you have a damaged keyboard, don't bother to get it repaired. Buying a new one and installing it yourself is cheaper. If you're installing a wireless mouse or keyboard, or mouse/keyboard combination, you do things only slightly differently than pictured on these pages. After you determine the connector type, plug a small transmitter into the mouse or keyboard port on your PC.

1 Look at the Connector

There are several ways you can plug a mouse or keyboard into your PC. The mouse can go into a PS/2, serial, or USB port, whereas a keyboard can go into a keyboard or USB port. In general, use a PS/2 port for your mouse because you won't use up a serial port, which is often used for other devices such as modems. There's also less of a chance of software conflicts if you use a PS/2 mouse. You also might want to keep the USB port open for installing other devices, such as a NetCam or scanner. The keyboard can plug into a keyboard port or USB port.

2 Turn Off Your PC

Don't unplug the old mouse or keyboard until the PC is turned off. When you unplug the mouse or keyboard, don't force it; it should slide off relatively easily. If you have a serial mouse, you must unscrew it before you can slide it off. Sometimes you won't need a screwdriver for this. However, you might need a small flathead or Phillips screwdriver to unscrew it. After you unscrew the serial mouse, slide it off.

3 Plug In Your New Keyboard or Mouse

Be sure that you're plugging your mouse into the mouse connector and not the keyboard connector—they often look identical, but the keyboard connector has a picture of a keyboard, whereas the mouse connector has a picture of a mouse. Many computers color code the connectors green for the mouse and purple for the keyboard. Don't force the connector; that could damage it.

④ Turn On Your PC

Your PC should automatically recognize the mouse or keyboard when you turn it on.

⑤ Install Any Special Drivers

Some mice or keyboards can require special drivers—for example, if you're upgrading from a normal mouse to a mouse with a wheel in the middle of it. In that case, install the drivers after your PC turns on.

⑥ Customize Your Keyboard or Mouse

Windows lets you adjust many of the mouse and keyboard settings. You can adjust things such as the sensitivity, what the mouse cursor looks like, whether there should be animations, and similar features. Click the **Start** button, and then select **Control Panel**. From the Control Panel, double-click **Mouse** to customize how your mouse works and double-click **Keyboard** to customize how your keyboard works.

Watch Out!

- Make sure you plug the mouse into the mouse connector and the keyboard into the keyboard connector.

- Be sure the mouse or keyboard is plugged in all the way before turning your PC back on.

- Be sure to turn off and unplug your computer before disconnecting the keyboard—otherwise, you could blow a small inline fuse on the motherboard.

- Check that nothing on the keyboard is holding down a key when you turn on your computer. If there is, the computer might refuse to boot.

Task

Installing a Joystick or Other Gaming Devices

Joysticks and other gaming devices enable you to easily play games, in particular controlling the direction of your movement, especially in 3D and driving games. With a mouse or keyboard, it's awkward to control these kinds of games, but joysticks and other gaming devices make playing the games with more natural movements easy. Plus, gaming devices include a variety of programmable buttons that enable you to control features of games, such as accelerating or braking in driving games or shooting weapons in action games.

Many joysticks and gaming devices include a "force-feedback" feature, making for much more realistic game play. With force feedback, the joystick responds much as it would in real-life situations. For example, if you crash in the game, you'll feel the crash through a jolt in the joystick; if you're making a tight turn with a car at a high speed, you'll feel the same type of pressure on the joystick as you would on a car's steering wheel in the same situation.

Upgrade Advisor

If you're buying a new joystick or other gaming device, here's one no-brainer decision: Buy one that works with your USB port rather than a game port. Game ports are analog in nature and slower than USB ports. Gaming devices attach via game ports and can't keep up with today's sophisticated hardware and games. They're slower and lack adequate support for features such as force feedback, in which the game controller shakes, rattles, rolls, and responds to game action.

Look for a gaming device that's programmable and that will allow you to change how the buttons and movements of the device function. Check to ensure that you can set up a variety of profiles—that way, you can create separate profiles for how the device will work with specific games. If sophisticated game play is important to you, look for a joystick that tracks rotational movement.

A number of different kinds of gaming devices are available. The following table lists the different types and for which games each is best suited:

Gaming Device	Used for
Joystick	Action games, flight games, shooting games
Steering wheel	Driving games
Game pad	Driving games, sports games, arcade games
Strategy controller	Strategy games

How a Joystick Works

Position sensors

Attached to the yoke are sensors that respond to the movements of the joystick in the x- and y-axes. The sensors interpret the precise x,y coordinate of each movement of the joystick and send signals describing the movement to the PC. Software then interprets those signals and controls game play. In force-feedback joysticks, signals are sent back from the computer that tell the joystick when to make a "jolt," to apply force to your hand, or similar motions.

Yoke

The joystick's handle is connected at its base to a yoke inside the joystick. This yoke enables the joystick to move freely in any direction.

Ports

The joystick attaches to a USB port or game port on a PC. (Game ports are often found on a sound card, although they can also be found on a separate game card.) If you're using a game port, in many cases, you can connect more than one joystick or gaming device to your PC through the use of a *Y-adapter*.

x,y coordinate

Your computer responds to the motion of your joystick by interpreting the position of the x,y coordinate of the joystick handle. The joystick's x-axis controls the side-to-side motion in games; the y-axis, shifted 90° from the x-axis, controls forward and backward movements.

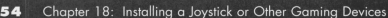

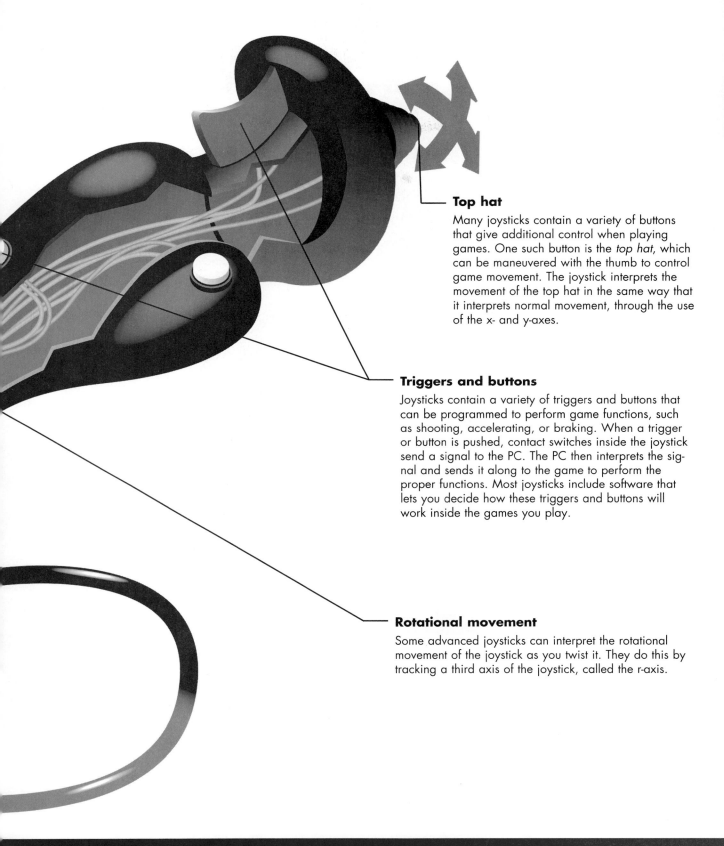

Top hat

Many joysticks contain a variety of buttons that give additional control when playing games. One such button is the *top hat*, which can be maneuvered with the thumb to control game movement. The joystick interprets the movement of the top hat in the same way that it interprets normal movement, through the use of the x- and y-axes.

Triggers and buttons

Joysticks contain a variety of triggers and buttons that can be programmed to perform game functions, such as shooting, accelerating, or braking. When a trigger or button is pushed, contact switches inside the joystick send a signal to the PC. The PC then interprets the signal and sends it along to the game to perform the proper functions. Most joysticks include software that lets you decide how these triggers and buttons will work inside the games you play.

Rotational movement

Some advanced joysticks can interpret the rotational movement of the joystick as you twist it. They do this by tracking a third axis of the joystick, called the r-axis.

How to Install a Joystick or Gaming Device

Whether you install a joystick or other gaming device, you follow the same steps: Plug in the device, run the installation software or add drivers, and then calibrate it.

❶ Plug In the Device

If you're installing a device onto the game port, the port (sometimes called a MIDI port) is generally attached to your PC's sound card or a special gaming card. It usually is a 15-pin female connector. Turn off your PC before plugging in the joystick.

❷ Attach a USB Device

If you are installing a USB joystick, attach the USB cable to your joystick and to the USB port on your computer. You don't have to turn off your PC before installing a USB joystick. If your USB ports are full with other devices, you can buy a USB hub that allows you to plug multiple USB devices into a single unit. For more information about USB devices, turn to Chapter 21, "Installing USB and FireWire Devices."

❸ Install Vendor Software

If the joystick comes with installation software, run it. Joysticks often come with installation software that sets up your joystick for you. If yours comes with installation software, run it now. The software might be necessary for properly calibrating the joystick, properly assigning buttons, or using any of the joystick's special features.

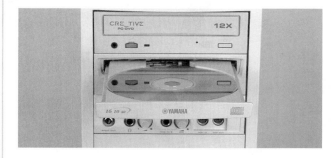

④ Install Windows Software

If no installation software is included, tell Windows to recognize your joystick by using the Add New Hardware feature. To do this, first go to the Windows Control Panel by clicking the **Start** button and selecting **Settings**, **Control Panel**. Double-click **Add New Hardware**. A wizard launches that guides you through installation. For some joysticks, you should instead use the "add" feature under Game Controllers in Control Panel. Check your documentation.

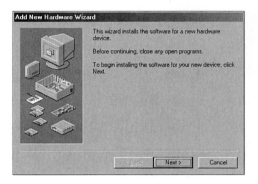

⑤ Insert Manufacturer's Disk

At some point, the wizard will ask whether you have a disk for your new joystick. If you have one, insert it at the right time; then select the device's .inf file from the disk. If no disks are supplied by the manufacturer, select the type of joystick you have from the list supplied by the wizard. If your joystick isn't on the list, select one from the list that most closely matches your joystick, which very often is CH Flightstick Pro.

⑥ Calibrate Your Joystick

For best gaming results, calibrate your joystick so that it responds in the best possible way. Check your joystick's documentation for details on how to do that. After you calibrate your joystick, you can program how it works for different games by selecting a "profile" for each game. Check your documentation to see how.

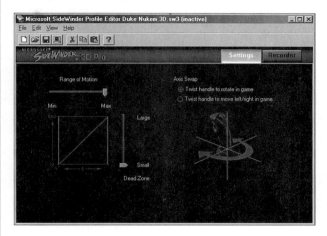

Watch Out!

- Before installing your joystick, check Windows' Device Manager to ensure that your game port or USB port is working properly.

How-to Hint

- Don't throw away your old non-USB gaming device. Some older games might require them.

- Be sure that the connections you make are tight before using the joystick.

- After installing the joystick, check for updated drivers and other profile software from the manufacturer's Web site.

- If your PC has more than one game port, connect the joystick to the game port on your sound card.

Task

Installing a Modem, Cable Modem, or DSL Modem

To communicate with the world, you need a modem. Modems enable your computer to send and receive information from other computers. In doing so, modems enable you to do things such as hook up to the Internet, browse the World Wide Web, and send and receive email. Modems also include fax capabilities so you can send and receive faxes.

Traditional modems come in two types: internal modems and external modems. *Internal* modems are less expensive but more difficult to install. Generally, an external modem is worth the extra money.

In addition to traditional modems that use phone lines, you can get a high-speed connection to the Internet with a cable or DSL modem. These aren't true modems, and they work differently from traditional modems. But they enable you to connect to the Internet at speeds significantly faster than modems that use regular telephone lines.

Upgrade Advisor

If you have a modem slower than 56K, you should buy a new one. Its higher speeds will make life online much more pleasurable. When buying a new modem, be wary of buying one that calls itself a *WinModem* or a *software modem*. Depending on the software modem you buy, your system might take a performance hit when you use it.

Some software modems don't include a processing chip, relying instead on your PC's main processor to do their work. That means that you'll slow your PC down whenever you use the modem. Modems with chips don't cost much more than those without chips, and it's worth paying the extra money.

If you're going to instead install a cable modem or a DSL modem, you'll often have a choice of whether to buy one yourself or to pay a monthly rental fee to your Internet access provider. As a general rule, you'll save money buying the modem yourself. The only benefit to renting it from your access provider is that the company will give you a new modem if your old one goes bad.

How a Modem Works

External modem

An external modem plugs into a serial port on the back of the computer. It gets power from an AC adapter plugged into an electrical outlet and will attach to either a 25-pin or 9-pin serial port. Adapters/gender changers are available if your modem cable does not match the PC connection.

Serial port

Data is sent via the serial port to and from the computer, through the modem, and then through the phone lines.

Modem

The analog signals travel over the phone system and are received by another modem, where they are changed (demodulated) by the receiving modem from analog data back to digital data and then sent into the computer via the serial port. This modulating and demodulating of data gives the modem its name: modulating/demodulating.

Data

Your computer works with *digital data*, binary bits of information that are either on or off. The telephone system, on the other hand, works with *analog information*, streams of continuous electric current that vary in frequency and strength. When you send information from your modem to another modem, as on the Internet, the digital data in your computer must be changed to analog information so it can be sent via the telephone system. The computer sends digital information to the modem, which changes (modulates) it into analog signals.

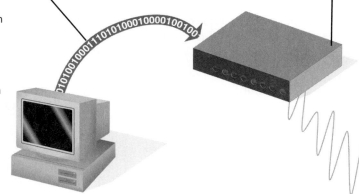

Internal modem

An internal modem is installed in an empty slot on a computer's motherboard. It does not need to be connected to the PC's serial port. It draws power from the motherboard.

Phone jack

The phone jack is a second connector on the back of the modem. By plugging a telephone into this jack and then plugging the line jack into the phone jack on your wall, you are able to use your telephone when not using your modem.

Phone line

The phone line plugs into the jack on the back of the modem and connects the modem to the phone system. You can connect the modem directly to the phone system without a telephone by connecting the line directly to the line jack.

How to Install an Internal Modem

If both of your serial ports are in use, such as by a mouse and other devices, you must install an internal modem. Follow these steps to do it.

1 Find a Free COM Port

To communicate with the outside world, your computer uses a *communications port*, also called a *serial port* or *COM port*. You cannot configure your internal modem to use a COM port already in use. To find out which COM ports are in use in your computer, in Windows, right-click the **My Computer** icon and select **Properties** and the **Device Manager** tab. Click the **+** sign next to the Ports item. You will see a list of the COM ports in use. You might also need to assign an IRQ to the modem by using your CMOS setup screen. Check your system documentation for details.

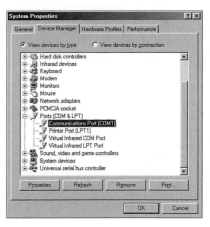

2 Set the Jumpers

Some internal modems require jumpers configured for certain COM ports. Set them now by following the modem's documentation. Sometimes you can set the jumpers to Plug and Play (PnP) mode, which enables Windows to set up your modem for you.

3 Install Modem in Free Slot

Plug your modem into a free slot. Either use the slot your existing internal modem uses or, if you don't yet have an internal modem, plug it into an empty slot. Find a free slot and remove the bracket in front of it. If you already have an internal modem, remove it and use that slot.

4 Connect the Phone Cord

If you're dedicating a phone line to your modem, plug one end of the phone cord into the phone jack and the other end into the modem's connector. If your modem is sharing a phone line with your telephone, use two jacks on the modem. One jack is labeled *phone* or *telco* and the other is labeled *line*. Attach a phone cord from the *phone* jack on the back of the modem to the telephone, and a phone cord from the *line* jack on the back of the modem to the wall jack. Then, close the case and turn on your PC.

5 Install the Modem Drivers

After you turn on your computer, Windows should launch an installation wizard. If not, go to the **Control Panel**, double-click the **Modems** icon, and then double-click the **Add** button. Windows will probably detect your model of modem and which port you're using. If not, add them manually. When prompted for a driver, use the driver disk or CD that came with the modem. In some cases, you must run an installation program from the CD to install the drivers.

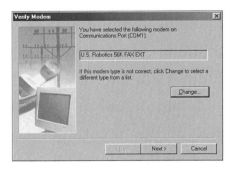

6 Install Special Software

Sometimes special software comes with an internal modem. If yours comes with special software, install it after installing the modem drivers.

How to Install an External Modem

External modems are more expensive than internal modems because they include chips, a power supply, and housing for the modem. But they are easier to install. They also have the added benefit of lights that blink to tell you what's happening during your communications session, as well as easier control over how loud the modem speaker is. Additionally, if something goes wrong, you can reset the modem in the flick a switch. Here's what you need to know about installing an external modem.

❶ Plug In Your Modem

Look on the back of your computer to find a free serial port. Most PCs have two serial ports, usually 9-pin male connectors. However, in some instances, one might be a 9-pin connector and the other a 25-pin connector. After turning off your computer, plug one end of a serial cable into your modem and the other into a free serial port on the back of your computer.

❷ Connect the Power Cord

Your modem comes with an AC adapter, which might have a large transformer at the end where it plugs into a wall outlet. Plug one end of the adapter into your modem and the other into the wall outlet or power strip.

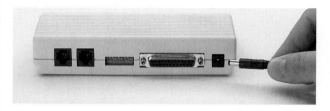

❸ Plug In the Phone Cord

If you're dedicating a phone line to your modem, plug one end of the phone line into the phone jack and the other end into the connector on the back of the modem. If your modem is going to share a phone line with your telephone, use two jacks on the back of the modem. One should be labeled *phone* or *telco*, and the other should be labeled *line*. Attach a phone cord from the *phone* jack on the back of the modem to the telephone and a phone cord from the *line* jack on the back of the modem to the wall jack.

4 Turn On Your Modem

You now can turn on your modem using its power switch. When you turn it on, an LED or light indicator should turn on. Next, turn on your computer.

5 Install the Modem Drivers

After you turn on your computer, Windows should launch an installation wizard. If not, go to the **Control Panel**, double-click the **Modems** icon, and then double-click the **Add** button. As you're walked through the setup, tell your computer the make and model of your modem and which COM port to use. Windows will probably detect your model of modem and which port you're using, but if not, add them manually.

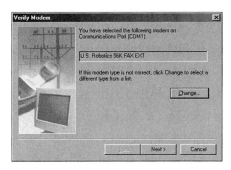

6 Install Extra Software

During installation, you might be asked whether you want to use modem driver software from a disk or use a driver from Windows. It's always best to use the driver software supplied with your modem, so insert that disk into your computer and tell the installation wizard to use the software from that disk. In some cases, you must run an installation program from the CD to install the drivers.

How-to Hint

- Check the manufacturer's Web site to see if newer drivers are available or if a patch is available to download to your modem's BIOS to improve its performance.
- Verify that the phone jack you're connecting to has a dial tone; otherwise, your modem won't work.

How to Install a Cable or DSL Modem

Cable modems and DSL modems connect at high speeds to the Internet. Although they're called modems, they don't actually work like modems—they use a different technology. Both need to be connected to your PC via a network card, so you first must install a network card before installing either of these modems. In this task, I give instructions for installing a cable modem, but installing a DSL modem is similar. Check with your DSL provider for precise details on how to do it.

❶ Install a Network Card

Your computer connects to a cable or DSL modem via a network card (often called a NIC), so before you can install a cable or DSL modem, you first must install the card. Turn to the section "How to Install a Network Card," in Chapter 35, "Installing a Home Network," to learn how to install one.

❷ Find the Card's MAC Address

Every network card has a specific number that identifies it to the network and Internet. The number is called a *MAC address* or an *adapter address*. To find your card's MAC address, click the **Start** menu, click **Run**, type in **WINIPCFG**, and press **Enter**. (In Windows NT/2000, open a command-prompt window, type **Ipconfig/all**, and press **Enter**.) Click the down arrow until you see your network card listed. The MAC address is the long number listed next to **Adapter Address**. It will read something like this: 00-20-B4-E0-3C-4D.

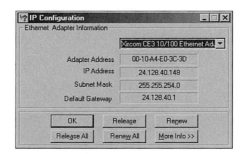

❸ Connect the Modem to Your Cable System

Connect the coaxial cable to the coaxial port on your cable modem. The cable company first must come out to run cable to a spot near your computer.

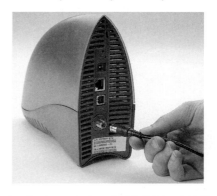

④ Connect the Modem to Your NIC

Use Ethernet cabling to connect your modem to your network card. Ethernet cabling is typically thicker than telephone wire but has a connector that looks and works much like phone wire—you connect it the same way you plug a telephone into a telephone jack. Connect the other end of the cable to your network card (NIC). Both ends of Ethernet cabling are the same, so it doesn't matter which end you plug into the modem and network card.

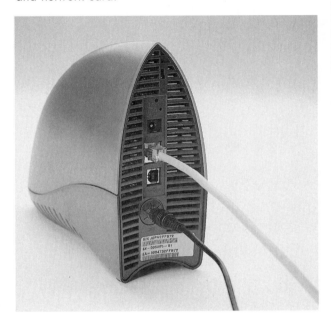

⑤ Turn On the Cable Modem

Connect the AC adapter to a power outlet. Then find the on/off switch and turn it on. (The cable modem may not have a switch and may automatically turn on once you connect the AC adapter to a power outlet.)

⑥ Call Your Cable Company

To start using your cable modem, call your cable company and give them your network card's MAC address. If you've bought the cable modem yourself instead of renting it, you'll also have to give them the cable modem's MAC address. Frequently, it can be found printed on a label underneath the modem. Check the documentation to see how to find it. After you call and give them the information, you should be able to begin using the Internet at high speed with your cable modem.

How-to Hint

• When finding your MAC address, scroll down to the name of your network card. If you give the PPP adapter address, for example, your cable modem won't work.

• You must have something called TCP/IP installed and configured properly, and the IP address field must be set to **Obtain IP Address Automatically**. Check your system documentation or network card documentation, or with your cable company to learn to do it properly.

Task

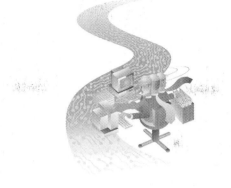

20

Installing a SCSI Device

Hard drives, CD-ROM drives, scanners, and other devices need some way to connect to your computer's motherboard. One of the ways to provide that connection is with a small computer system interface (SCSI). SCSI provides very high throughput, so the equipment you connect will run quite fast. A SCSI drive can transfer data faster than IDE drives You can also connect up to 15 devices to a single SCSI controller in a daisy-chain, depending on your controller; each device is connected in an unbroken chain to the next. That's the good news. The bad news is that it's more difficult to install SCSI devices than to install other kinds of devices.

You'll install SCSI devices by first installing a SCSI controller and then connecting each device in turn. This chapter shows you everything you need to know about it.

Upgrade Advisor

SCSI is not as popular an upgrade technology as it had been years ago. It has been favored in high-end systems, and for upgraders it has the added benefit of allowing devices to be daisy-chained. But because newer technologies such as USB and FireWire allow multiple devices to be connected in daisy-chain fashion to a PC, SCSI has lost some of its allure.

Unless you have a need for very high-speed peripherals like hard drives and scanners, it's a better idea to stay with FireWire and USB devices because they're simpler to install. But if you want the utmost in speed then SCSI is the way to go. There are several SCSI standards, including SCSI, SCSI-2, and SCSI-3, so double-check to make sure that the devices you buy are compatible with the kind of SCSI interface on your system.

How SCSI Works

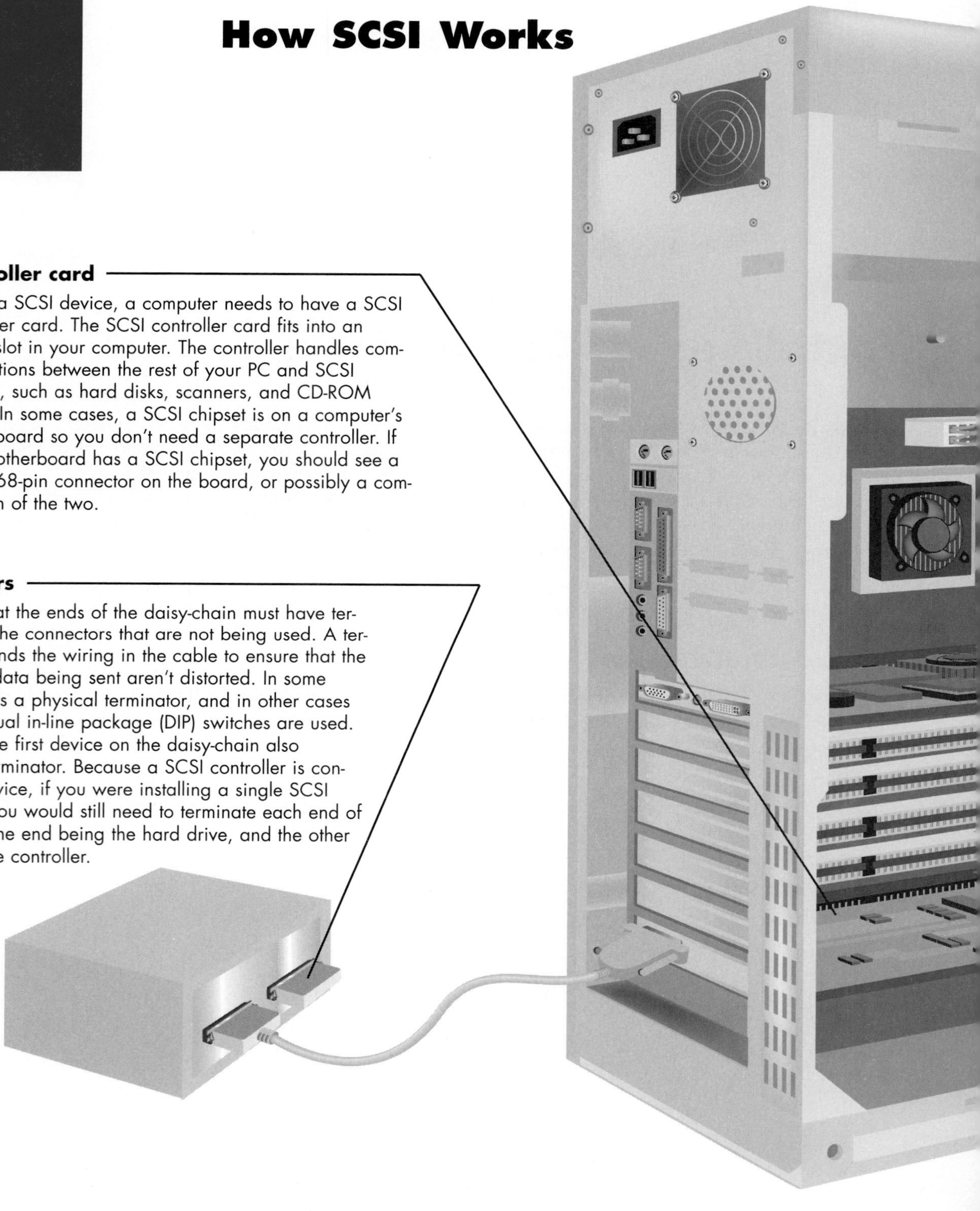

Controller card

To use a SCSI device, a computer needs to have a SCSI controller card. The SCSI controller card fits into an empty slot in your computer. The controller handles communications between the rest of your PC and SCSI devices, such as hard disks, scanners, and CD-ROM drives. In some cases, a SCSI chipset is on a computer's motherboard so you don't need a separate controller. If your motherboard has a SCSI chipset, you should see a 50- or 68-pin connector on the board, or possibly a combination of the two.

Terminators

The devices at the ends of the daisy-chain must have terminators on the connectors that are not being used. A terminator grounds the wiring in the cable to ensure that the signals and data being sent aren't distorted. In some cases, there is a physical terminator, and in other cases jumpers or dual in-line package (DIP) switches are used. Sometimes the first device on the daisy-chain also requires a terminator. Because a SCSI controller is considered a device, if you were installing a single SCSI hard drive, you would still need to terminate each end of the chain—one end being the hard drive, and the other end being the controller.

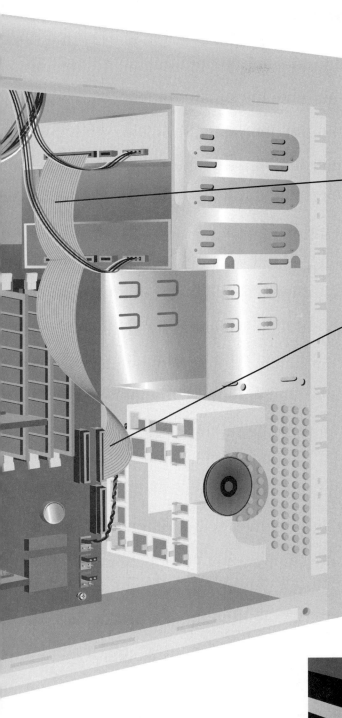

Daisy-chain

A single SCSI controller can handle up to 15 devices. The devices are attached in a daisy-chain via a series of cables that start from the controller and go to each device in turn.

SCSI cable

SCSI devices are attached by sets of SCSI cables. A SCSI cable from the outgoing port of one device in the daisy-chain attaches to the incoming port of another SCSI device. Another SCSI cable attaches to the outgoing port on that device, which connects to the next SCSI device on the daisy-chain. Daisy-chains use 50-pin (for normal SCSI) and 68-pin (for wide SCSI) connectors.

SCSI ID number

Each device on the daisy-chain needs a unique SCSI ID number. This SCSI ID number labels the device so that the controller and computer can recognize and use it properly. Some devices require certain ID numbers. You assign SCSI ID numbers in different ways for different devices. Often, jumpers are used to set the ID numbers, or the ID number is set by using the CMOS setup screen to change the BIOS. In the case of a SCSI controller, the ID number, termination, and other features are usually set through an onboard BIOS.

How to Install a SCSI Controller Card

Before you can install a SCSI device in your computer, you need to install a SCSI controller card. In some ways, it's like installing any other card—you open your PC, find an empty slot, and install the card in it. But in other ways, it's more difficult because you must set SCSI IDs and attach a terminator. Before installing a SCSI controller card, open your case and ground yourself. For details on how to do it, turn to "How to Open the Case" in Chapter 13, "Performing Computer Maintenance."

① Set Jumpers or BIOS

Check the documentation for your SCSI controller and motherboard and see whether you must set any jumpers or alter your computer's BIOS. If you need to set jumpers, set them now. Often, though, controllers are changed via the onboard BIOS. Check your system's documentation and SCSI card's documentation for details on how to do it.

② Remove Backplate

Your SCSI controller card goes in an empty slot on the motherboard. As a general rule, it needs to fit into a peripheral component interface (PCI) slot. To install the card, remove the small metal flap protecting the slot, called a *backplate*. The flap is held in place by a small screw. Remove the screw (it's usually a Phillips screw), and then remove the flap. In some instances, you might need to punch out a blank instead of unscrewing the backplate.

③ Install the Card

Align the card in the free slot, making sure the connectors on the card line up properly with the slot into which you're inserting the card. Then, using two hands, apply gentle, even pressure to push the card down into the slot. After the card is in place, press down firmly to ensure that it's all the way in the slot.

4 Screw the Card into the Backplate

To ensure that the card doesn't come loose, screw it into the backplate using a Phillips screwdriver. Be careful not to overtighten it and strip the screw.

5 Verify SCSI ID Numbers

SCSI devices have unique ID numbers, from 0 through 7 (or 0–15 in the case of wide SCSI). Most SCSI controller cards are set by default to 7, or in the case of wide SCSI, to 15. It's generally good to keep the default, but if you want to change it, you can by setting jumpers, DIP switches, or some other kind of control. Check the card's documentation for how to do it. Write down on a slip of paper the SCSI ID that you've assigned to the controller card, even if you've accepted the default of 7.

6 Put a Terminator on the Card

Most SCSI controllers allow seven devices to be attached to one another in a daisy-chain. The device at the end of the chain needs to have a terminator on it, and the device at the beginning needs one as well. A terminator will come with your SCSI card, or you might set it via a jumper, DIP switch, or some other means.

Watch Out!

- Don't press too hard when inserting the card; you could damage the card or motherboard.

How-to Hint

- Be sure the card is seated firmly—if it isn't, the card won't work.

How to Install a SCSI Device

After you put the SCSI controller in, install your first SCSI device. Installing any SCSI device is relatively the same. In this example, we look at installing a SCSI hard drive—your primary hard drive, the one you boot from. I'll assume you've already taken out your hard drive. Before you begin, open the case as outlined in "How to Open the Case" in Chapter 13. For more information about removing a hard drive, turn to "How to Remove an Old Drive" in Chapter 13.

❶ Find a Free Bay

You need a free drive bay into which to install your drive. After you remove your computer's case, take a look inside and see which drive bay you have free. Drives come in 3 1/2" and 5 1/4" sizes, so be sure your bay accommodates the drive you buy. You can fit a 3 1/2" drive into a 5 1/4" bay by getting a special adapter kit, but a 5 1/4" drive won't fit into a 3 1/2" bay.

❷ Set the SCSI ID

Each SCSI device must have a unique ID number, from 0 through 7 (or 0–15 in the case of wide SCSI). The usual ID for a boot drive is 0, so set it there. In a few cases, the number might be different, so check your documentation. You'll often set the number via jumpers or DIP switches. Check your documentation. Write down the ID number on a slip of paper, along with the SCSI ID for your controller card, to refer to when you install other SCSI devices.

❸ Terminate the Device

The device at the end of the chain needs to be terminated. You terminate a device by plugging a terminator into it; the terminator goes onto the device itself, not into its cable or connector. Sometimes, you don't physically plug in a terminator but instead set a special jumper. You might have what's called a pass-through terminator. Your documentation will show you exactly how to terminate the device. In some cases, the device at the beginning of the daisy-chain needs to be terminated as well.

④ Slide In and Secure the Drive

Slide the drive into the drive bay. If you're installing a 3 1/2 '' drive into a 5 1/4 '' bay, you might need to use rails. Screw the drive into the drive bay or the rails. Secure all the screws so that the drive is held firmly in place, but don't overtighten or strip the screws.

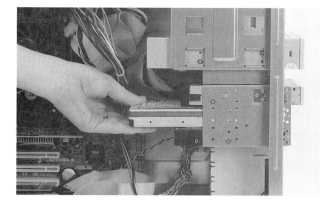

⑤ Connect the Cables

For your new SCSI hard disk to work, it needs to connect to your SCSI controller. Using the cables supplied with the card or the hard disk, attach the cables to the hard disk and to the connector. You also need to connect the power cable to the drive. The power supply cable has a connector on the end of it, which is usually four sockets encased in a small sheath of white plastic. Plug the cable into the connector on your hard disk. Use the larger 4-pin connector that is notched so it will connect only one way.

⑥ Format the Hard Disk

Turn on your PC with the boot disk in the floppy drive so you can boot from it. Before you can use your hard disk, you must format it so that your computer can use it. For information about formatting your hard disk, refer to the section "How to Format and Partition a Hard Drive" in Chapter 30, "Adding or Replacing a Hard Drive." If you've removed an IDE drive, you may have to tell the CMOS that the IDE drive has been removed.

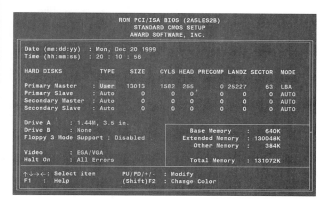

How-to Hint

- If installing a bootable SCSI hard drive, its ID should be set to 0 in almost all cases. Check the drive's documentation.

How to Install Multiple SCSI Devices

SCSI controllers are useful not just because SCSI devices are fast—SCSI also allows you to daisy-chain multiple devices on a single controller. Here's how to do it. This section assumes you've already installed a SCSI controller and another SCSI device, as outlined in the previous sections. If you'll be installing an internal device, open the case as outlined in "How to Open the Case" in Chapter 13.

❶ Check Existing SCSI ID Numbers

SCSI devices are daisy-chained from one to another. They each need to be identified with a unique SCSI ID, 0–7 (or 0–15 in the case of wide SCSI). Before you install an existing device, know what IDs your other SCSI devices use. The best way to accurately determine the ID number is to physically look at the device itself. By using software and other diagnostic methods, you will not necessarily know whether two devices are conflicting over the same ID number.

❷ Set the New Device's SCSI ID

The SCSI ID can be set in different ways, such as via jumpers, DIP switches, or some other kind of control (such as an onboard BIOS for a controller). Check the device's documentation to see how to set the ID. Make sure you choose an ID that isn't in use yet. Some devices require a particular SCSI ID. Check to see whether your device has that requirement; if so, use that ID. If another device already has that ID, change the ID of the other device and then set the SCSI ID of the device you're adding.

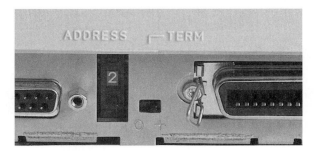

❸ Physically Install the Device

If it's an internal device, unplug the computer, take off the case, ground yourself or wear an antistatic wrist strap, and install the device following the manual's instructions or instructions elsewhere in this book. If it's an external device, unplug the computer and install the device following the manual's instructions or by following the device's installation instructions found elsewhere in this book.

④ Attach It to the Daisy-Chain

After you've installed the SCSI device, connect it to an existing SCSI device. Attach a device to the daisy-chain via SCSI cables. Verify that the cables you use match the connector's pin width of your existing devices. If the external device will be in the middle of the daisy-chain, it will connect to two SCSI devices. You must connect one SCSI cable to the incoming port of the device you're adding and connect one SCSI cable to the outgoing port of the device. The ports should be labeled. Then connect the SCSI cables to the other devices. If you're putting a new device into the middle of the chain, make sure it's not terminated—many devices come terminated by default.

⑤ Terminate External Devices

SCSI requires that devices at each end of the SCSI daisy-chain have terminators on them. If you're installing an external device at the end of the daisy-chain, put a terminator on it. Most external SCSI devices have two ports on the back. Put a terminator on one of those ports and the SCSI cable connected to another SCSI device on the other port. In some cases, you won't have a physical terminator but instead will set your device to be a terminator by using a jumper or DIP switch. You might have what's called a *pass-through terminator*. Check your documentation to see which termination method yours uses.

⑥ Set Internal Terminators

If installing an internal device, at the end of the chain, use a terminator. Internal devices set terminators by using a jumper, a pass-through terminator, or a DIP switch.

Watch Out!

- If installing a device in the middle of a SCSI chain, make sure it's not terminated because most new devices are terminated by default.

How-to Hint

- Ensure that each SCSI device gets its own unique ID to avoid conflicts.

- Verify that the controller termination is set correctly for internal and external chains.

- Be sure to get the same type of connector for your devices and controller (50- or 68-pin); although there are converters/gender changers, they are expensive.

Task

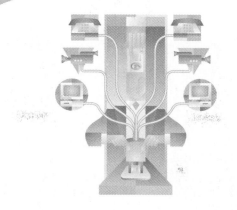

21

Installing USB and FireWire Devices

Perhaps the best news in the last several years for those who want to expand and upgrade their computers is the advent of the Universal Serial Bus (USB) and FireWire, sometimes known by its formal name IEEE-1394, or simply 1394. They provide the easiest way yet to attach devices such as scanners, joysticks, keyboards, mouse devices, modems, removable drives, CD and DVD drives, MP3 players, digital cameras, digital camcorders, and more to your computer.

Another plus of USB is that you can daisy-chain up to 127 devices to your computer using its USB. Sometimes, devices let you plug other USB devices into them. For example, if you install a scanner, it might have a second USB port, into which you can plug another USB device. You won't have to plug that device into your computer's USB port; instead, plug it into the extra port on another USB device. However, not all USB devices have these extra ports, and a solution is to buy a USB hub, a device that plugs into your computer's USB port, and into which you can plug several USB devices. It is by using many hubs that you can connect up to 127 devices to your USB port. FireWire devices can also be connected in a daisy-chain or by using a FireWire hub or hubs.

If you bought a computer in the past several years, odds are that it comes with one or more USB ports. FireWire ports are rarer, but do come on some PCs.

Note the two speeds of USB: the older USB 1.1, which allows devices to communicate with your PC at 12Mbps, and the newer USB 2.0 standard, which allows devices to communicate at 40 times that speed, or 480Mbps. Many computers use the 1.1 standard, because the USB 2.0 standard only came into use in 2002. FireWire allows for communications at 400Mbps, although a faster FireWire standard that would communicate at 1,600Mbps has been proposed.

In this chapter, you'll see how to install USB and FireWire devices. You'll learn how to install a USB hub to make it easy to daisy-chain many USB devices. FireWire devices and hubs install much like their USB cousins, so follow the same directions for both.

How the Universal Serial Bus Works

Daisy-chained devices

The USB enables up to 127 devices to be attached in a daisy chain to your computer via the USB port. A USB controller in your PC is the brains of USB. If you don't have a USB port and controller, you can add them by installing a USB card on your PC, but only if you have Windows 98 or above.

USB ports

Computers have one or more USB ports. Whether you have one or more ports, however, up to 127 devices can be daisy-chained via USB to a computer. Plugs from USB devices attach to USB ports. In this way, you can connect USB devices to your computer without opening the case. USB ports are marked with the special symbol in this illustration.

USB hubs

You can connect up to 127 devices to your USB port by using USB hubs. A hub attaches to a USB port or to another USB hub. These hubs have USB ports on them, enabling numerous USB devices to be plugged into them.

Power

D+

D-

Ground

USB cables

Inside USB cables are four wires. Two provide electricity to the USB devices attached to your computer: One provides the electricity, while the other is a ground. (Some USB devices, such as scanners, require more electricity than the USB cables can provide and still need to be plugged into a power outlet.) The other two wires, D+ and D-, transmit data and commands.

USB device as a hub

Some USB devices include extra USB ports so that they can function like a hub. For example, a monitor could have USB speakers, a microphone, and a keyboard plugged into it.

Extra hub

Devices and hubs can be daisy-chained, enabling devices to be attached to one another. As pictured here, a keyboard that has been plugged into a monitor can in turn have a mouse, a digitizing pen, and other devices plugged into it.

Automatic configuration

After you install a new USB device, the USB controller communicates with the device, in essence asking it to identify itself. This helps the controller decide whether the device is a high-speed device such as a monitor, scanner, or printer, that can communicate at 6Mbps–12Mbps, or a slower device, such as a keyboard or mouse, that transfers data at 15Mbps. In the newer USB 2.0 standard, devices can communicate at 480Mbps. (By way of comparison, a serial port communicates at 100Kbps, whereas a parallel port communicates at about 1.5Mbps.) The USB controller also assigns the device an identification number.

Data transfer priorities

The USB controller assigns three different levels of priority to devices attached to it, in this order:

Highest priority

This is assigned to an *isochronous* or real-time device such as a video camera or a sound device. In these devices, the data is not allowed to be interrupted.

Medium priority

This is assigned to devices such as keyboards, mice, and joysticks, which don't always need to use USB to communicate with the computer because they're not in constant use. However, when they are in use, the data must be transferred immediately.

Lowest priority

This is assigned to devices such as printers, scanners, and digital cameras, in which a great deal of data must be sent at once, but in which slight delays in transfer won't be a problem.

How to Install Universal Serial Bus and FireWire Devices

Because you don't need to remove the case of your PC to install USB or FireWire devices, they are among the easiest devices to install. Almost all USB and FireWire devices are *hot swappable*, meaning you can connect and disconnect them while your machine is running; digital cameras and joysticks are good examples of this. Here's how to install a USB or FireWire device. For more information on how to install specific devices, refer to the chapters that cover them more directly.

❶ Make Sure You Have a Port

You can install a USB or FireWire device only if you have a USB or FireWire port on your PC. Look for one or two rectangular ports on the front, side, or rear of your PC. USB ports have the USB symbol next to them, whereas FireWire ports will generally have 1394 printed next to them.

❷ Check Device Manager

Most versions of Windows support USB and FireWire, although Windows 95 support is erratic. To ensure that your computer properly supports USB or FireWire, check the Device Manager and look for the USB setting or the IEEE-1394 setting. To do that, right-click the **My Compute**r icon and select **Properties**. Then, click the **Device Manager** tab and scroll down. You should see a USB controller entry or an IEEE-1394 entry. It shouldn't be expanded to show any exclamation points next to any of the entries within it.

❸ Install Device Software

Some devices, such as scanners, require special software to work. If your device requires special software, install it now.

④ Turn On the Device

First, connect the device's power cable. Some devices need to be plugged into a wall outlet. If the device needs to be plugged in, plug it in and turn it on.

⑤ Connect the Cable

The device comes with a USB or FireWire cable. USB cables have a rectangular connector, called *Series A*, and a square connector, called *Series B*. Plug the square, Series A end into the device and the rectangular, Series B end into the computer. The USB cable connects only one way, so don't force it. If you don't have a free USB port on your PC, you can buy a USB hub to give you extra USB ports to plug devices into. FireWire cables have four-pin (for self-powered devices) or small six-pin connectors.

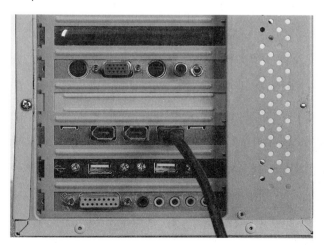

⑥ Restart Your Computer

With some devices, you'll have to restart your computer. When you do, Windows recognizes that you've added new hardware and an Add New Hardware Wizard launches. Follow the directions for installing your new hardware. If you have a disk from the manufacturer, insert it when asked to, so Windows will use the manufacturer's drivers. You can install most USB and FireWire devices while the computer is still running. In that case, wait a few seconds after you install it, and the Add New Hardware Wizard will appear. (Note that many USB and FireWire devices don't require restarting your computer when you install them.)

Watch Out!

- Check the Device Manager to ensure that your system properly recognizes your USB or FireWire port.
- Check your CMOS to ensure that USB is enabled in it.
- Be sure that all the USB or FireWire connectors are tight.
- Use the manufacturer's disk when the Add New Hardware Wizard asks if you have a disk from the manufacturer.

How to Install a Universal Serial Bus or FireWire Hub

In theory, USB and FireWire allow you to daisy-chain up to 127 devices from a single USB. But most PCs come with only one or two USB or FireWire ports, and most devices don't have any extra ports into which you can attach other devices. So in practice, it appears that you can attach only one or two USB or FireWire devices to your PC at one time. The way around the problem is to buy a USB or FireWire hub. These inexpensive devices plug into your USB or FireWire port and give you four or more ports into which you can plug other devices. And you can daisy-chain hubs by plugging them into one another, so they're an easy way to connect as many devices as you need. This section shows how to install a USB hub, but a FireWire hub installs in the same way.

❶ Attach the AC Adapter

Most hubs come with an AC adapter so they can receive electricity from a power outlet. Although a hub can get its electricity from your computer, some devices are power-hungry, so you should use the AC adapter, especially when first installing the hub. Plug the AC adapter into the hub, and then plug the adapter into a power outlet.

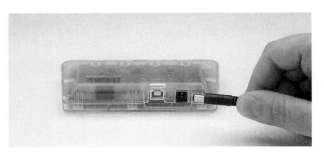

❷ Connect the Cable to Your PC

The USB hub comes with a cable that has a rectangular plug and a square plug. (The rectangular plug is called the *USB-A connector*, whereas the square plug is called the *USB-B connector*.) Plug the rectangular end (the USB-A connector) into the matching USB port on your computer. The USB cable connects only one way, so don't force it.

❸ Connect the USB Cable to the Hub

Connect the square plug on the USB cable to the matching port on your USB hub. (This port will be the USB-B connector type.) Usually, the port on the hub will be set away from the other USB ports, all of which are the rectangular, USB-A connector type. Sometimes this port will be called the *root port*. The USB cable connects only one way, so don't force it.

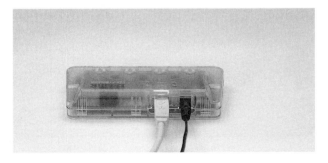

4 Connect the USB Devices to the Hub

Following the instructions in the previous task, connect USB devices to your hub the same way you would connect them to your PC. Remember that the rectangular plug connects to the USB hub, and the square plug connects to the USB device.

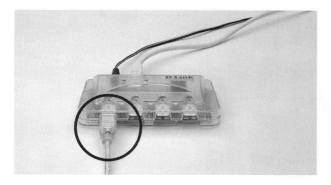

5 Try Out the Devices

Try using each of the devices to verify that they work. If one or more doesn't work, check that the connectors are seated firmly in their ports.

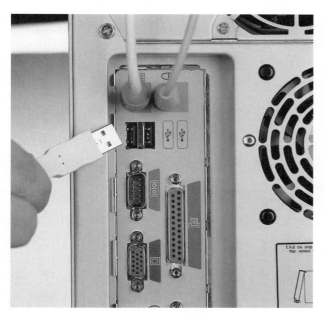

6 Test the Devices Without AC Power

If you want to run the hub without AC power, unplug the AC adapter and test each device in turn. If they all work properly, you can run the hub without the external AC power. However, if you have problems running any of them, you need to use the AC power. Also, some hubs require AC power, so check the documentation before trying to run the hub without external power.

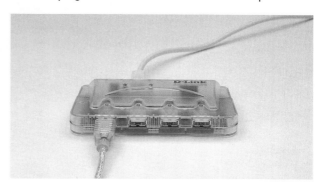

Watch Out!

- Some USB devices, such as some USB CD-RW drives, require connection directly to the computer, not to a hub. Read the devices' documentation to see if they can be connected to a hub.
- Double-check that you connect your PC to the hub via the hub's root port; otherwise, the hub won't work.

How-to Hint

- Some motherboards have a connector that will let you add a backplate that contains USB ports. If you want more USB ports on your computer, you can do that instead of adding a hub, although it will take much more work.
- Some portable devices, such as MP3 players and digital cameras, have a smaller-than-normal USB B connector (called a *mini-B connector*). If a cable that fits it didn't come with the device, you can buy one at a computer store.

Task

22

Installing a Digital Camera

Digital cameras are quickly replacing the more traditional kind. They enable you to preview pictures before taking them, and after you take the photos, no film is required—all you need is your computer. And if you take a photo you don't like, you don't waste any film—just delete it from your camera and try again.

Your pictures are stored on a memory card of some type in the camera. You can buy more than one card so that you can take more pictures and also a card reader that connects to your PC. If you do that, you'll never have to connect the camera to your computer—you'll only need to put the card into the reader; then you'll be able to transfer pictures to your computer that way.

Upgrade Advisor

All digital cameras are not created alike, and it's very important before buying one that you carefully check its specifications. Unlike hard disks and CD drives, they're not commodity items, so you'll need to do a bit of homework before buying.

The first thing to consider is the resolution of your camera. Camera resolutions are measured in pixels. In general, the more pixels, the better the resolution. And the more pixels, the more expensive the camera and the larger the print you'll be able to make on your printer at a reasonable image quality.

Resolution is measured in megapixels, or one million pixels. There's no reason to buy a camera under 1-megapixel—the quality of images taken with cameras with lower resolutions simply isn't acceptable. If you can afford it, consider cameras with resolutions of 2- or 3-megapixels and above.

Also consider whether you want zoom, and if so, how much zoom you want. But be sure you read the fine print and understand what type of zoom the camera has. You want a true, optical zoom—in other words, the camera lens itself can zoom in. In some instances, a camera does digital zoom, merely by using software, and in that case, you're not getting a true zoom. All you're doing is taking the same picture at the same resolution, so the quality isn't there.

Buy a camera with a USB or FireWire connection. These are faster and easier to install and use than those that connect via a serial cable.

How a Digital Camera Works

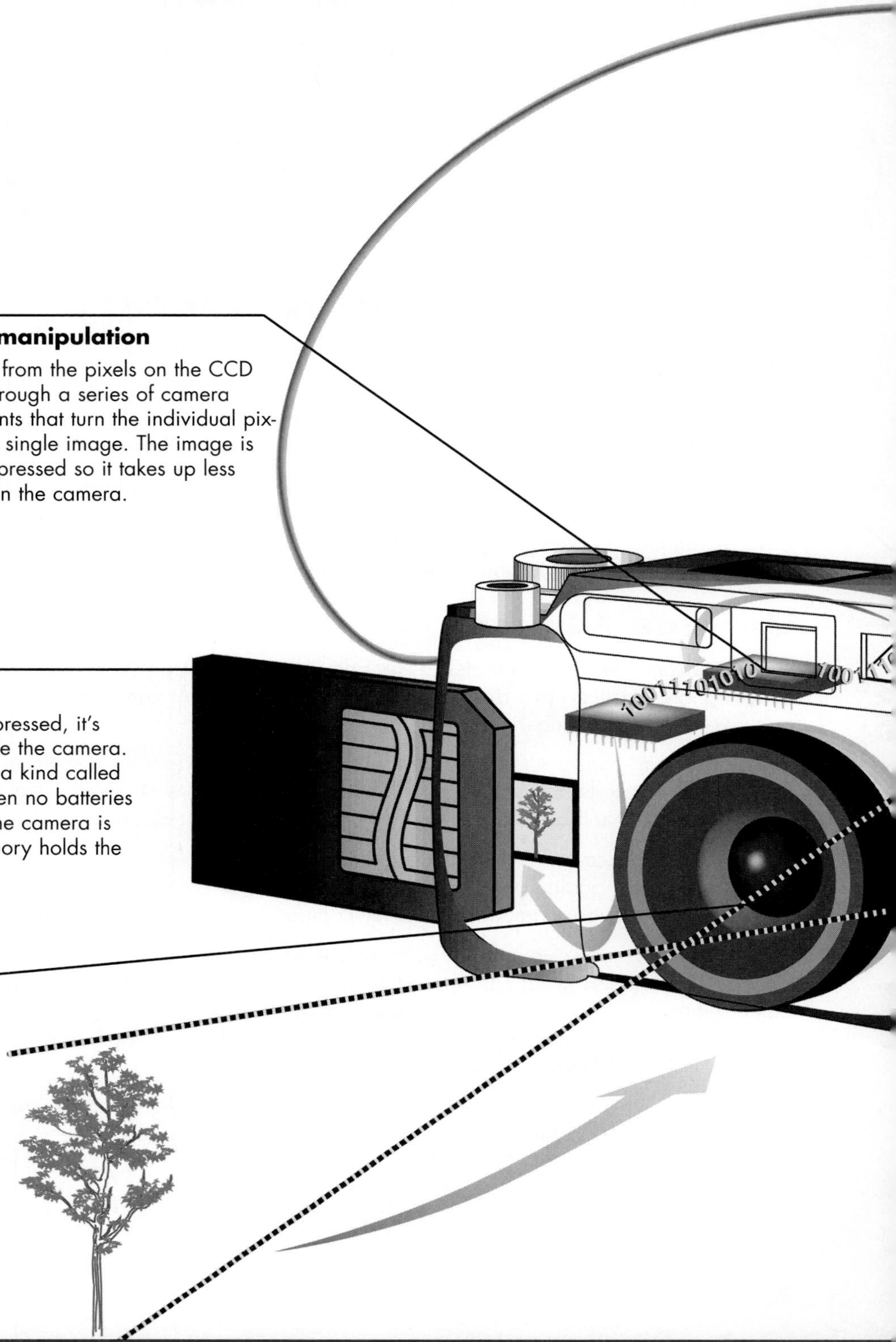

5 **Image manipulation**

The data from the pixels on the CCD passes through a series of camera components that turn the individual pixels into a single image. The image is also compressed so it takes up less memory in the camera.

6 **Flash memory**

After the image is compressed, it's stored on memory inside the camera. Usually, this memory is a kind called flash memory. Even when no batteries are in the camera, or the camera is powered off, flash memory holds the images safely.

1 **Shutter and lens**

When you hold down the shutter button to take a picture, a metering cell takes a light reading and determines how much light is required for the exposure. It then instructs the shutter to stay open for a specific amount of time. The lens focuses the image, as it does in a traditional camera.

7 **PC transfer**

To manipulate and print the pictures, you must transfer them to a computer. The digital camera attaches to the computer via a cable of some sort, often a USB or serial connection. Even after you transfer the pictures to your computer, they stay on the digital camera until you delete them either using the PC software or using the camera itself. Some printers let you attach camera memory cards to them and print from the cards. In those instances, you don't need to first transfer the pictures to your PC.

4 **Digital conversion**

After the exposure, each pixel's charge is converted into a digital number, corresponding to the amount of light that fell on that particular pixel.

View screen

Digital cameras generally include a view screen that lets you preview your pictures before you take them, and they also let you view the pictures stored on your camera.

2 **Image sensor**

Instead of hitting film, as in a traditional camera, the light hits an image sensor, called a charged-coupling device (CCD). The image sensor is a silicon chip about the size of a fingernail and contains a grid made up of millions of photosensitive pixels.

3 **Pixels**

Each site on the CCD captures a single pixel—either red, blue, or green. Where that color light falls on the pixel, it records the color; if the color doesn't fall on the pixel, it remains dark. Each pixel can record only a single, specific color. So, if red light falls on a blue-recording pixel, for example, that pixel doesn't record any data. Each pixel retains a charge that corresponds to the brightness of the light falling on it. So, when a great deal of light falls on a pixel, it has a high charge, and if little light falls on it, it has a low charge.

How to Install a Digital Camera

Two major things must be done to install a digital camera. First, you must prepare the camera so it can be used on its own. Second, you must connect the camera to your PC and install software so the camera can transfer pictures to your PC. To prepare the camera, you must install batteries and a storage card, which holds the camera's pictures. Then, you connect the camera to your PC with a cable and install the camera software.

❶ Install the Batteries

Open the battery compartment and insert the batteries, taking care to line up the positive and negative terminals properly.

❷ Insert the Memory Card

Most digital cameras require you to install a small memory card called flash memory or a smart card. This memory card is what holds your pictures. You can even buy additional memory cards and swap them to store more images. Next, insert the memory card into the camera. Some cameras also require that you format the memory card after you've installed it. Follow the camera's directions for how to format the card—each camera does it differently.

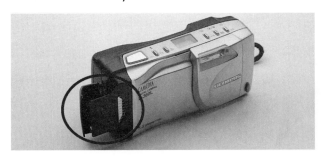

❸ Turn On the Power

For many digital cameras, to turn on the power, all you need to do is slide open the lens protector on the front of the camera. If your memory card needs to be formatted, you'll usually get an error message telling you a problem exists with the card, so now is the time to format.

④ Connect the Camera

Some cameras connect via a USB cable, whereas others connect via a serial port. Either way, the cables will connect only one way, so don't force them. If you don't have a free USB port on your PC, you can buy a USB hub to give you four USB ports into which you can plug devices. If you don't have a USB port, you can install one in your computer. (To learn how to install USB hubs and ports, turn to Chapter 21, "Installing USB and FireWire Devices.")

⑤ Run the Software

If you're connecting via a USB cable, your computer will recognize that you're adding a digital camera. The Add New Hardware Wizard will appear, or an installation routine will automatically start. Follow the onscreen directions for completing the installation. For serial connections, your computer might not recognize the camera, so you must install the software that came with your camera. Even if you install via USB, however, be sure you install the software for your camera after you follow the installation instructions. In either case, you might have to go through two installation routines: one to install drivers for the camera and one to install software to work with the camera.

⑥ Take Pictures and Transfer Them

After you've installed the camera, unplug it and take pictures, following the camera's instructions. Then, use the camera software you installed to view the pictures on your camera and transfer them to your PC.

Watch Out!

- Be sure you install the correct type of memory card into your camera. There is more than one standard for memory, so match the proper card to your camera's specifications.

- Keep memory cards away from extreme heat and magnets—both can destroy data.

- Use only the type of batteries specified by the camera manufacturer. Some cameras can be damaged by overheating if you use manganese batteries.

Task

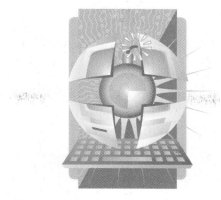

23

Installing a WebCam

One of the more amazing devices you can add to your computer is a WebCam—a small video camera that can send video to your PC and that often sells for about $100, or even less. You can use WebCams for many things. One of the more popular uses is for videoconferencing, in which you can not only talk to other people over the Internet, but also see video of them. And they can see you and hear you.

WebCams can be used for more than videoconferencing, though. You also can use them to send live pictures to a Web site. In addition, you can capture videos into a computer file that you can view, listen to, and send to others. As you'll see in this chapter, installing a WebCam is surprisingly easy. WebCams attach to your PC via a USB port or a FireWire port.

Upgrade Advisor

Most WebCams sold today connect to your computer via USB. That makes for simple installation, but there's a problem—the data transfer rate of USB is slow, so the resulting video images can be of a low quality. However, the USB 2.0 standard allows for much higher transfer rates, and at some point the standard will become popular enough to be commonplace on PCs and WebCams.

An increasing number of cameras connect to your PC via a FireWire connection. This is a higher-speed connection than USB (although lower speed than USB 2.0). So if you have a FireWire connection on your PC, a FireWire camera is a better bet.

If you've used the Internet, you've probably noticed ads for wireless video cameras. These are primarily designed to work with a TV or VCR rather than a PC. You can get USB adapter kits to make them work with PCs, but they're designed for security purposes rather than for videoconferencing and similar applications, so you'd be better off with a traditional WebCam if you're interested in those applications.

Increasingly popular are WebCams that do double duty as digital cameras. These nifty devices let you use them as regular digital cameras, so they come with enough memory for taking still pictures. They're a way to save money and get a digital camera and WebCam in one device. However, they're generally inferior to regular digital cameras, so if still pictures are important to you, you'll be better off choosing a separate digital camera and WebCam.

How WebCams Work

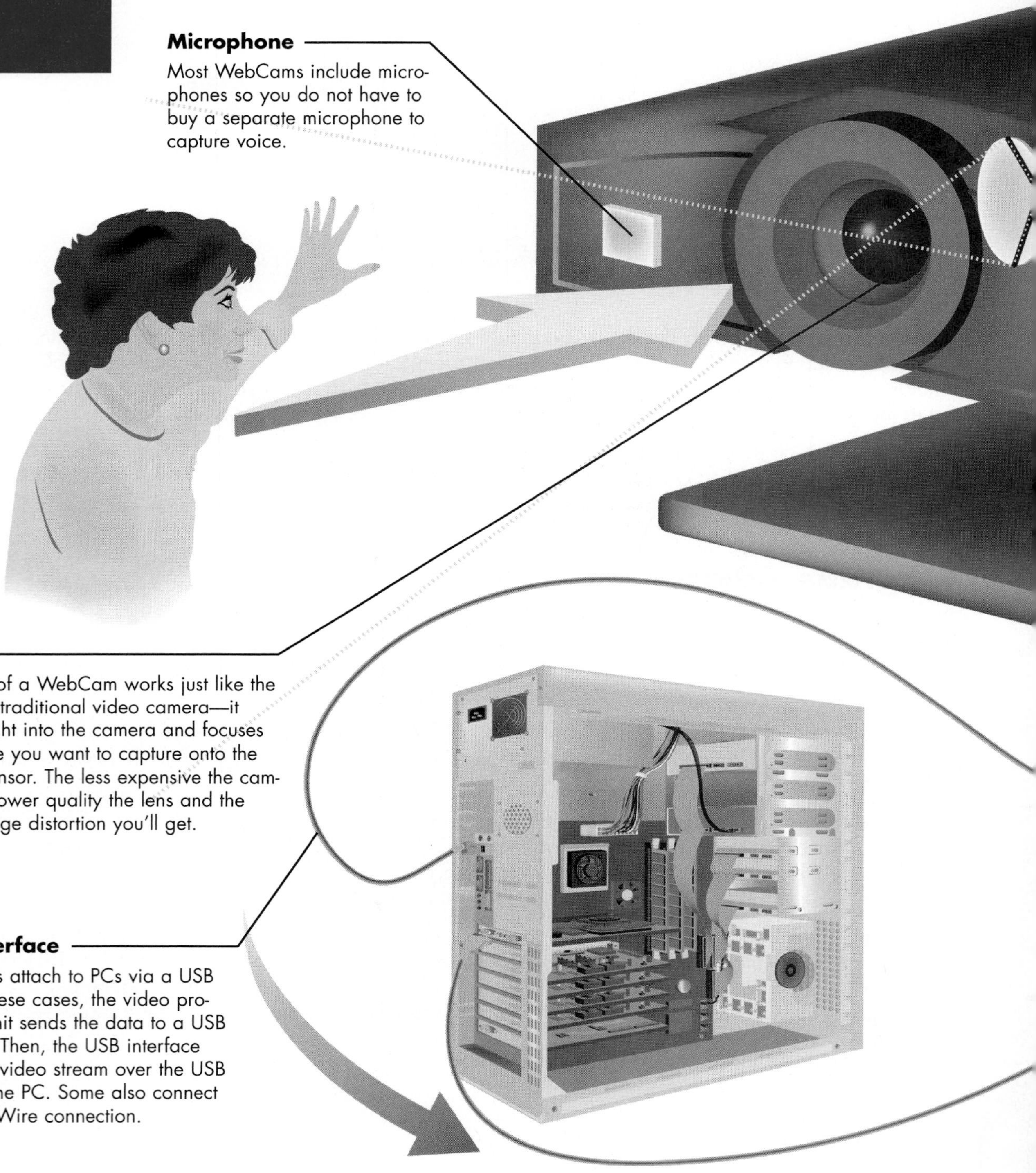

Microphone

Most WebCams include microphones so you do not have to buy a separate microphone to capture voice.

Lens

The lens of a WebCam works just like the lens of a traditional video camera—it allows light into the camera and focuses the image you want to capture onto the image sensor. The less expensive the camera, the lower quality the lens and the more image distortion you'll get.

USB interface

WebCams attach to PCs via a USB port. In these cases, the video processing unit sends the data to a USB interface. Then, the USB interface sends the video stream over the USB cable to the PC. Some also connect via a FireWire connection.

Video processing unit

After the CCD converts the images into pixels, the video processing unit converts the pixels back into images. It compresses the images and sends them as a data stream in the JPEG file format so that they appear as a moving image.

Image sensor

The image falls on the image sensor, which collects the light and digitizes it into small dots called pixels. Several kinds of image sensors are available. Inexpensive WebCams use complementary metal-oxide semiconductor (CMOS) sensors, whereas more expensive cameras use the higher-quality charged-coupled device (CCD) sensors. CCDs offer better quality images, and in particular, they enable a higher frame rate. The frame rate is a measurement of the number of times per second a video image is captured, so the higher the frame rate, the higher the quality of the video image. Low frame rates can cause a jerky-looking image.

Video driver

The video stream is sent to a video driver, the PC's graphics unit. In some cases, the video driver manipulates the video stream so that it displays better on a PC. In other cases, though, it simply passes the video stream to a piece of the video.

Video software

Many types of software can use the video images. For example, software such as NetMeeting can let you videoconference with other people over the Internet by sending your video image to them and by them sending their video image to you. Other kinds of video software include video capture software, which enables you to turn video into computer files you can play on your PC or send to others.

How to Install a WebCam

WebCams can do many things for you: let you videoconference with other people, enable you to put live images on your own Web site, and let you capture video and then send that video to friends and family. To work, WebCams must connect to your PC in some way. Most WebCams attach via a USB port, although an increasing number connect via Firewire.

❶ Install the Software

To use your WebCam, you must install the software that came with it. Depending on your brand of WebCam, it might have several pieces of software—for example, to enable videoconferencing and videocapture. You're not limited to the software that came with the WebCam; you can use many other types of software, such as NetMeeting, Microsoft's free videoconferencing software. After installing the software, shutdown your computer.

❷ Plug In the USB Cable

If you're installing a WebCam that uses a USB port rather than an add-in card, plug the USB cable into the USB port on your computer.

❸ Connect the WebCam

Using the cable that came with the WebCam, attach one end to the card you just installed and the other end to your WebCam. Many WebCams come with built-in microphones so you can talk to others while you see them. To use the microphone, you might need to connect a cable from the WebCam to a port on your sound card. Check your documentation to see whether that is required. If you have a USB WebCam, plug the USB port into the WebCam. If you have a USB-connected WebCam, you generally won't need to install the extra sound cable.

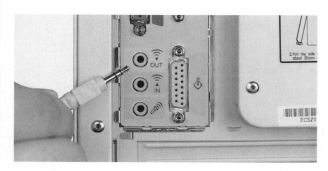

4 Turn On Your Computer

When you turn on your computer, Windows will detect that you've install a WebCam and an Add New Hardware Wizard will appear. Follow the directions for installation, including adding the manufacturer's disk if you're prompted. If the Add New Hardware Wizard doesn't launch, run it manually by clicking the **Start** button, selecting **Settings**, selecting **Control Panel**, and then double-clicking **Add New Hardware**.

5 Focus the WebCam

Run the software and test and focus the WebCam. Some, but not all, WebCams come with a lens that can focus, so use it until you get a sharp image. If your WebCam doesn't come with a lens, try moving the camera closer to or farther away from the image you want to display until the image is as sharp as possible.

6 Calibrate the Sound

Use the built-in software or videoconferencing software to calibrate the sound to the proper level for transmitting.

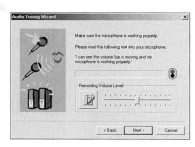

Watch Out!

- If installing a card, be sure the WebCam card is seated firmly—if it isn't, your WebCam won't work.
- Go to the WebCam manufacturer's site and download the latest drivers and software.
- If can see video but not hear sound after you install your WebCam, make sure you have properly connected your WebCam to your sound card.

Task

24

Installing a Scanner

Scanners enable you to take images and text from pictures, photographs, paper printouts, books, or other sources and transfer them to your computer. To get the text and images into your computer, you first place the image source, such as paper, on a flatbed scanner, which then scans the image or text from the paper into your PC. This chapter shows you how to install a flatbed scanner; you can install other types of scanners, including handheld and page-fed scanners, the same way as you install flatbed scanners.

In general, scanners attach to a PC via the parallel port, a USB port, a FireWire connection, or a SCSI connection. The SCSI connection transfers text and images to your PC from the scanner at the highest rate of speed, although it is also the most difficult to install. The easiest scanner to install is via the USB port, which transfers data faster than a parallel port scanner.

Upgrade Advisor

A flatbed is the most common type of scanner—with it you lay a photo or sheet of paper on the scanner's surface and scan a single page at a time. If you're using the scanner for text-scanning instead, get a sheetfed scanner or a flatbed scanner with an automatic document feeder. This will let you place many pages at a time into the scanner, and it will scan one page after another automatically.

For scanning in pictures, of primary importance is the quality of the scan. Generally, the more money you pay, the better the quality of the scanned image. The way to compare scanners' quality is by comparing their resolutions and bit depths. Resolution is measured in dots per inch (dpi); all other things being equal, the higher the dpi, the better the image quality. Be careful when comparing dpi between scanners that you compare what's called the *optical* dpi. The optical dpi tells you the actual resolution of what the scanner can see. You might instead be given an interpolated resolution. An *interpolated* resolution is the result of a scanner using software to increase the dpi. But interpolated resolution is not as high quality as optical resolution.

Most scanners you buy will have at least a 600 dpi rating, and it's best not to buy a scanner rated at less than that. For many purposes a 600 dpi rating is adequate. But if you're planning to scan photographs or slides and want very high-quality output, choose a 1200 dpi scanner or better.

The bit depth of a scanner tells you the number of gradients of color the scanner can recognize. A 24-bit depth scanner is more than adequate for most purposes, although if you are scanning photographs or slides and want very high-quality output, you'd be better off with a 36-bit scanner.

How a Scanner Works

Image

The process begins by placing an image face down on a glass window in the scanner. Beneath the glass window is a light source and a scanning mechanism—the scan head.

PC connection

The pixels are sent to the PC via one of a variety of physical connections. Some scanners are connected via the parallel port, others via a USB port, and still others via a SCSI connection. No matter which connection is used, the data is stored on the PC in a digital format. Parallel port scanners have the slowest transfer rates. USB transfer rates are higher than the parallel port but slower than SCSI.

Scan head

As light bounces off the page from the light source, the scan head moves by means of a small motor beneath the glass. As the scan head moves, it captures the light that bounces off the page. The head can read very small portions of the page—less than 1/90,000 of a square inch. If a scanner head goes bad, you must either have it repaired or buy a new scanner. Scanners are generally inexpensive devices, so unless you have an expensive scanner, it's often a good idea to simply buy a new one.

Analog-to-digital converter

A device called an *analog-to-digital converter (ADC)* reads this constantly changing stream of electrical voltage. It converts this analog stream into a series of thousands of digital pixels. Depending on the resolution of the scanner, it creates from 300 to 1,200 pixels per inch. In a color scanner, light is first directed through red, green, or blue filters before hitting the image being scanned. The quality of the ADC is one element in determining the ultimate quality of the scan.

How to Install a Scanner

Scanners attach to your PC in a variety of ways, including via the parallel port, the USB port, and a SCSI connection. Although the actual attachment can vary, the basics of how you install a scanner remain the same. So follow these steps for installing a scanner. For more details on how to install a USB device, turn to Chapter 21, "Installing USB and FireWire Devices," and for how to install a SCSI device, turn to Chapter 20, "Installing a SCSI Device." If you want to install a USB scanner but don't have a USB port on your PC, you can add one in. Turn to Chapter 21 to see how.

① Place the Scanner on a Flat Surface

Before doing anything, turn off your PC. Next, put the scanner on a level, flat nearby surface, and make sure it's close enough to your PC so that its cable can reach your computer. If the surface is not level, the quality of the scan can be affected.

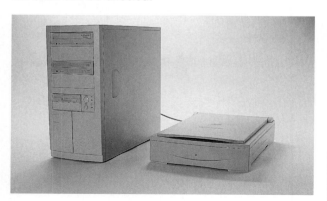

② Plug In the Cable

What you do now depends on how you'll connect the scanner to your PC. If you have a parallel port scanner, unplug the printer's parallel cable from your PC and plug the scanner's parallel cable into your computer, into the port where the printer's cable was attached. If you want to use your printer as well as your scanner, connect the printer to your scanner with cable, and then connect your scanner to your computer. For USB and SCSI scanners, attach them as you would any USB or SCSI device

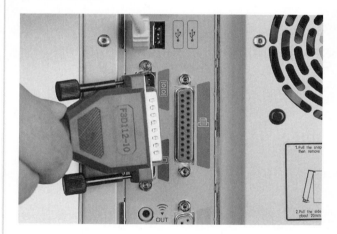

③ Turn On the Scanner

Plug the scanner's power cord into an outlet. When you plug it in, the scanner might turn on by itself. Some scanners need you to turn them on; others don't need to be turned on. If yours has an on/off switch, turn the switch on after you plug in the cord.

④ Turn On Your PC

When you turn on your computer, Windows will know new hardware has been added. If, when you turn on your PC, it doesn't automatically recognize that new hardware has been added, you can tell your computer that new hardware is present. To add the new hardware, first go to the Windows Control Panel by clicking the **Start** button and then selecting **Settings, Control Panel**. Double-click **Add New Hardware**. A wizard launches that will guide you through the installation process.

⑤ Insert the Driver Disk

At some point, the wizard will ask whether you have a disk for your new scanner. If you have one, insert it at the correct time; then select the device's INF file from the disk.

⑥ Calibrate the Scanner

Most scanners come with extra software you can use for scanning and using scanned images. Check the documentation to see whether yours does. If it does, install the software. For best scanning results, calibrate your scanner before you begin to use it. Check your scanner's documentation for details on how to do that.

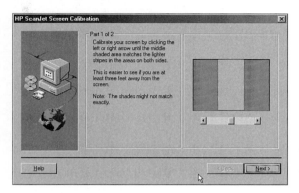

Watch Out!

- Before adding a parallel port scanner to a machine with an existing printer, you should go to the printer vendor's site and update to the latest drivers.

- Check the scanner's documentation to see whether the scanner requires an Enhanced (EPP, SPP, ECP) Parallel Port. If so, you might need to change this option under your CMOS.

- If this is the first USB device you install, be sure your USB ports are enabled in your CMOS.

- If you installed a SCSI controller with your scanner, when you turn on your computer, Windows will first have to install the SCSI controller before installing the scanner.

- If the SCSCI connection doesn't match your existing SCSI connector, buy a SCSI converter that will let you attach it.

Task

Installing a Palmtop Device

It's now possible to carry the power of a PC with you wherever you go, tucked safely into your pocket. So-called palmtop devices are portable, miniature computers that hold your schedule, your appointments and deadlines, your contacts, a notepad, and increasingly applications like word processors and access to the Internet as well.

You can buy many different types of palmtop devices, but most are based on one of two operating systems: the Palm operating system or the Pocket PC operating system. The devices can cost from just over $100 to $600 and up. Their primary purpose is a personal information manager, and they synchronize their information with information on your PC.

For those who are always on the go and need access to their schedules and similar information, palmtops have become a must-have item. Increasingly, they are offering wireless access to email and the Internet as well, although that makes the devices significantly more expensive.

Upgrade Advisor

The majority of palmtop devices sold are based on the Palm operating system, but attributes of each system can help you decide which to buy.

Devices based on the Palm operating system tend to be easier to set up and install and less expensive than those based on the Pocket PC operating system. They also tend to be easier to operate and are much easier to synchronize with your PC.

Devices based on the Pocket PC operating system, however, often add extra capabilities such as the ability to listen to music in MP3 format. And they frequently have Word and Excel applications, so that you can more easily transfer Word and Excel files between the desktop and palmtop. They're more expensive, though.

You also must decide whether to buy a palmtop that has built-in wireless capabilities, and if not, whether you want to buy an attachment that gives it wireless capabilities. Palmtops with built-in wireless access usually cost hundreds of dollars more than those without the access. And access fees usually cost at least $30 a month or more. If you need instant access to email and always-on access to the Internet, consider spending the extra money. And if email is your main concern, consider buying a Blackberry-type device. These are small, pager-like devices primarily designed for wireless access.

How a Palmtop Works

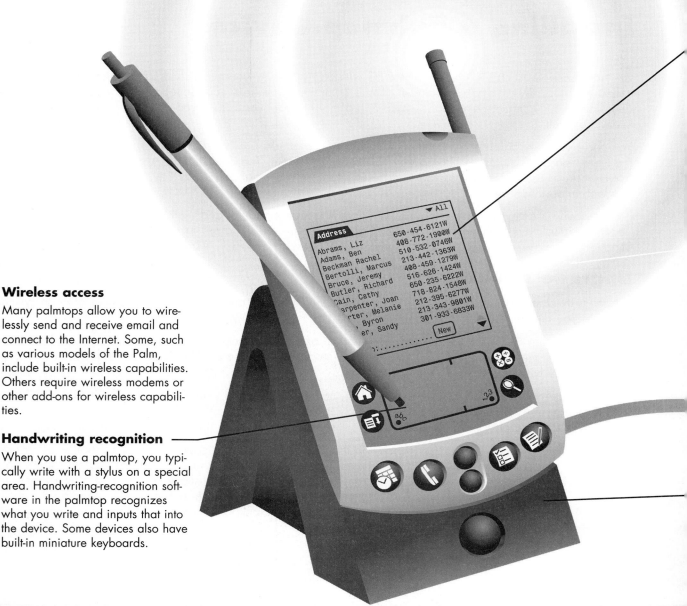

Wireless access

Many palmtops allow you to wirelessly send and receive email and connect to the Internet. Some, such as various models of the Palm, include built-in wireless capabilities. Others require wireless modems or other add-ons for wireless capabilities.

Handwriting recognition

When you use a palmtop, you typically write with a stylus on a special area. Handwriting-recognition software in the palmtop recognizes what you write and inputs that into the device. Some devices also have built-in miniature keyboards.

Data

Palmtops have many uses but are primarily personal information managers, so most of the data stored in them is information such as contacts, to-do lists, and calendar information. However, increasingly, palmtops are also used to browse the Web and to send and receive email.

PC connection

The palmtop's cradle attaches to the PC. It can be connected via a number of ways, including the serial port or the USB port. USB port connections are faster and more error-free than serial port connections.

Data synchronization

You can enter personal information, such as contacts, to-do's and calendar information in either your palmtop or PC, and when you press a button, data will be synchronized in both directions. Software checks both the palmtop and the PC, sends data in both directions, and ensures that the same up-to-date information can be found on both.

Cradle

Palmtops typically are used in conjunction with PCs and send and receive data to and from the PC. The most common way to send and receive data is through the palmtop's cradle. The palmtop has a connector at the bottom that fits into the cradle. Data flows through this connector into the cradle and to the PC.

How to Install a Palmtop Device

The precise steps to install a palmtop device will depend on the exact device, manufacturer, and model. But for most palmtops, you'll follow these steps.

❶ Install the Batteries

In most devices you'll turn the palmtop on its back to find the battery cover. Remove the cover, install the batteries, and put the cover back on. Then turn on the device. Some devices have special batteries that recharge when the device is in the cradle.

❷ Calibrate the Screen

When you turn on the device, you may be prompted to calibrate the screen by tapping on onscreen targets with your stylus. Even if you aren't prompted to do this, you should calibrate the screen at some point before you start using the device. If the screen isn't calibrated, it might be difficult to use the device properly.

❸ Connect the Device's Cradle to Your PC

Turn your PC on and attach the cradle. The cradle of many palmtops attaches to the PC through the USB port, though some connect via a serial port.

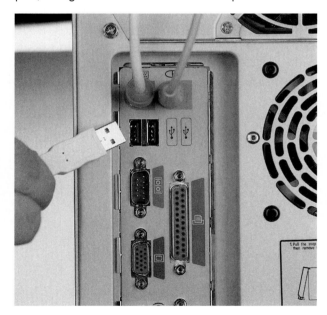

④ Install the Software

Insert the CD-ROM and follow the installation instructions. Don't put the palmtop device in the cradle before or during installation; do that after installing the software. During the software installation, pay particular attention if you're asked whether you use a personal information manager like Outlook because the palmtop can automatically synchronize information with whatever personal information manager you use.

⑤ Run the Software

After installing the software, run it. You generally need to do this before synchronizing your device.

⑥ Put the Device in the Cradle and Synchronize

One of the great benefits of a palmtop device is the ability to synchronize its data with data on your PC. So before you begin using the palmtop, synchronize it by placing it in the cradle and pressing the synchronize button. From now on, at least once a day synchronize the device with your PC to keep information on the device and the PC up-to-date.

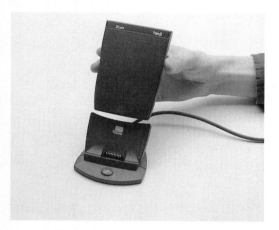

Watch Out!

- When installing batteries, make sure that all are the same model and make—you shouldn't mix different types of batteries. When replacing batteries, replace all at once. Some devices use rechargeable types of batteries, such as NiMH. Read the documentation for details.

- Before attaching a cradle to your COM port, ensure that the port isn't being used by another device, such as a modem.

- When you synchronize, be careful about the settings you use. If you use the improper synchronization settings, you can overwrite all the data on your palmtop, or your PC, with old information. Check your documentation to see which settings to use.

- Buying backup software for your palmtop device is worth it. This software will always keep a fresh copy of all your data and applications so in the event of a system crash or an error in synchronization, you'll always have a backup.

Task

Installing a Portable MP3 Player

MP3 players are small, portable devices that can play music recorded in a variety of digital formats, notably in the MP3 format. Although the devices are typically called MP3 players, they often can play music recorded in other formats, such as the Windows Media format (WMA).

You get music to place in an MP3 player in several ways. Digital music can be downloaded from the Internet, or you can insert an audio CD into your computer and convert that music into the MP3 format (or another music format). Converting music to MP3 format from a CD is called *ripping* music from a CD. Many portable MP3 players come with software that will rip music in this way. Ripping software is also widely available on the Internet. Once the music is on your PC, you transfer it to an MP3 player via a USB cable and software that comes with the MP3 player.

The music is commonly stored in flash memory on the MP3 player, although other types of storage are available as well. MP3 players usually come with at least 64MB, and sometimes more memory, and can be expanded by adding flash memory cards to a special slot in the MP3 player. And some MP3 players now come with hard disks of several gigabytes so that hundreds of songs can be stored on them.

Upgrade Advisor

One of the most important features of an MP3 player is rarely, if ever, advertised, yet it's the entire point of the device: The quality of the sound. It's not true that all MP3 players sound alike; some feature a better sound than others. So when buying an MP3 player, test the sounds of several before buying.

Sometimes, the difference in the quality of the sound is because of the headphones. Better headphones can add to the cost of an MP3 player, and considering that most manufacturers try to advertise a lower price, you'll find that sometimes they skimp on the quality of the headphones.

Another excellent upgrade to your MP3 player is an addition that lets you play it through your car's stereo system. Typically, one end of these is shaped like an audio cassette and slips into your car's cassette system, and the other end fits into the headphone jack. For those who travel often by car and always want their customized music, it's a great, inexpensive upgrade.

How an MP3 Player Works

CD ripping

Music has to be in a digital music format such as MP3 for it to be transferred to a portable MP3 player and played. One way of getting music into MP3 format is to *rip* it from a CD—use software to convert it to an MP3 format. This kind of software generally comes with the MP3 player, or can be downloaded from the Internet.

Playlists

To transfer music from your PC to the MP3 player, you use software that comes with the MP3 player to create playlists. A playlist is a group of MP3 files, put in the order in which you want to listen to them.

Downloading music

Another way to transfer music to an MP3 player is by downloading MP3 files from the Internet. File-sharing software such as Kazaa can be used to locate and download MP3 files.

USB cable

To transfer files from a PC to an MP3 player, MP3 players use a USB connection. A USB cable connects the USB port on the PC to the USB port on the MP3 player. MP3 files are sent over the cable from the PC to the MP3 player, using software that comes with the MP3 player or software downloaded from the Internet.

Music processing

Inside the MP3 player, a variety of processors, controllers, and other devices converts the digital data in the MP3 file into analog data—music the human ear can understand.

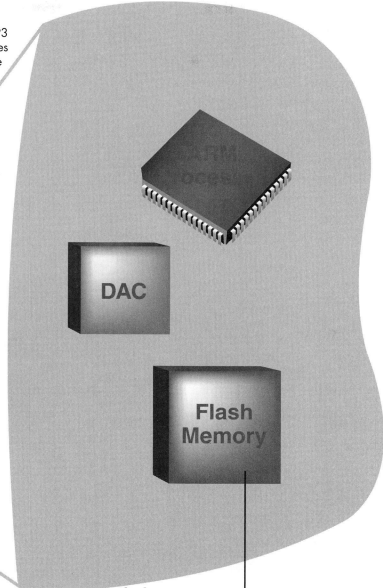

Flash memory

MP3 files are stored in flash memory chips in the MP3 player. Anything stored in flash memory chips stays stored on them, even when the MP3 player is off—similar to a computer's hard drive. Many MP3 players have an empty slot into which a flash memory card can be installed, as a way to increase the amount of music that can be stored and played from the MP3 player.

How to Install an MP3 Player

Installing an MP3 player is easy. Whereas older players sometimes require you to connect them to your computer via a serial port to copy MP3 files to them, the newer ones all connect via a USB port. To install the player, you install software, connect the USB cables, and then install drivers. After the player is installed, you transfer files to the player via the USB port and delete files from the player that way, as well.

❶ Install the Software

You transfer files to your MP3 player and delete files from the player by using software you install on your PC. Before connecting the MP3 player, install the software that came with the MP3 player. You also can use jukebox software to do this, such as Real JukeBox or MusicMatch JukeBox. Both are available for free from download sites on the Internet.

❷ Turn On the MP3 Player

Look for the switch—sometimes it's a very small one. And remember to first install a battery. MP3 players typically run on batteries—usually AA batteries. They often need only one.

❸ Connect the MP3 USB Cable

The MP3 player comes with a USB cable that may look different than most common USB cables. It's called a mini-B. One end is small and designed to fit into a special port on the MP3 player. Find the port and plug in the cable.

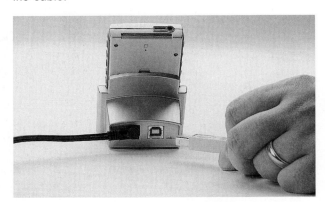

④ Connect the USB Cable to the PC

The other end of the USB cable is rectangular and designed to plug into a PC. The USB cable connects only one way, so don't force it. If you don't have a free USB port on your PC, you can buy a USB hub that will give you four USB ports into which you can plug devices. If you don't have a USB port, you can install one in your computer. (To learn how to install USB hubs and ports, turn to Chapter 21, "Installing USB and FireWire Devices.")

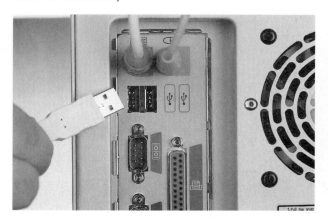

⑤ Follow Any Installation Instructions

When you plug in the USB cables, your computer will recognize that you're adding an MP3 player. The Add New Hardware Wizard will appear, or an installation routine will automatically start. Follow the onscreen directions for completing the installation.

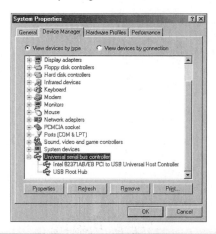

⑥ Run the Jukebox Software

Now that your MP3 player is installed, you should transfer MP3 files to it so you can listen to them. To transfer the MP3 files, when your MP3 player is connected to your PC, run the software that came with the player—or use other software you can download from the Internet—and transfer music files to the MP3 player. JukeBox software also can be used to convert music from audio CDs into MP3 files.

Watch Out!

- Some tof the MP3 files you can get from the Internet might violate copyright laws because the recording artists haven't agreed to have those files posted online.

How-to Hint

- If you notice that MP3 files "skip" or are in some other way distorted, it might be that the CDs from which you're recording have small scratches or dirt on their undersides. Wipe the bottom sides of CDs with a soft cloth before converting them—that might solve the problem.

Adding Memory to Your PC

One of the easiest and cheapest ways to make your computer run faster is to upgrade it by adding more memory, called random access memory (RAM). If your PC seems sluggish, especially when you run several applications at once, you might be in need of a memory upgrade. When your computer doesn't have enough memory, it can't hold all your programs and data in RAM, so it has to take some of those programs and data and put them temporarily on your hard disk. Your hard disk is much slower than RAM, causing your computer to work sluggishly. If your computer is constantly reading from your hard disk, you might be in line for a RAM upgrade. RAM doesn't cost very much these days and is getting less expensive all the time. It's one of the least expensive and most effective ways to upgrade your PC.

Upgrade Advisor

How much memory do you need to buy for your PC? The short answer is as much as you can afford. However, there are certain basic RAM requirements to keep in mind when upgrading your system. In general, newer versions of Windows need more RAM than older versions. So if you have Windows 95, for example, you can get by with 16MB of RAM, but with Windows 98, you'd be better off with at least 64MB. If you run many programs simultaneously or use RAM-hungry applications such as graphics and multimedia programs, you might need even more. So to be as safe as possible, buy more RAM than you think you need. Given the low prices of RAM, it'll still be a bargain, even if you buy more than you really need.

How Memory Works

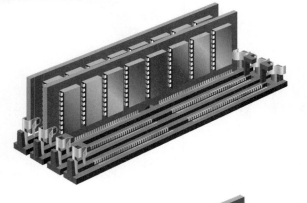

RAM (random access memory)

Memory is put on your computer using RAM chips placed into special slots or sockets. When your computer is turned off, RAM is empty—unlike a hard disk, it can't store data unless the RAM is powered by electricity. Generally, the more RAM you have, the faster your computer runs because RAM is much faster than a hard disk. If you don't have enough RAM, your computer has to read data from your hard disk frequently, slowing things down. But if you have enough RAM, the data you need is often stored in RAM, which can be accessed much faster than a hard disk can, so your computer is speeded up.

Single inline memory modules

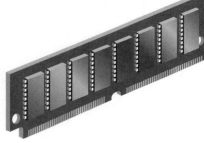

SIMMs (Single inline memory modules) plug into long, matching sockets on your motherboard. They're an older form of memory and work only with older computers. Typically, a motherboard has several banks of SIMM sockets into which you plug SIMMs. SIMMs come in 30-pin and 72-pin formats. Generally, 30-pin SIMMs are outdated because they have little memory capacity, often 256K, 1MB, 2MB, and 4MB. 72-pin SIMMs have more capacity and come in 1MB, 2MB, 4MB, 8MB, 16MB, and 32MB.

DIMMs

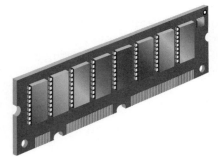

DIMMs (dual inline memory modules) look much like SIMMs, but they come in 168-pin and 184-pin formats. They are a faster and higher-performance memory than SIMMs. They have much higher capacities than do SIMMs.

RIMMs

Rambus inline memory modules (RIMMs) look like DIMMs and SIMMs but are even larger and come in a 184-pin format. They are a higher-speed memory than SIMMs and DIMMs.

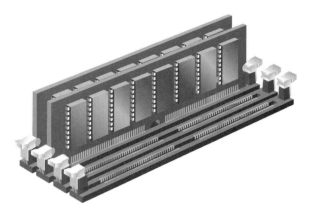

Socket

RAM modules connect to the motherboard via a socket. The socket will be different according to the type of RAM the motherboard requires. The most common type of socket is a DIMM socket, which has a locking tab at either end to secure the module into the socket.

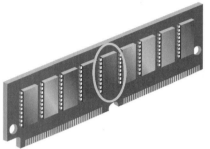

ECC Versus Non-ECC

A SIMM or DIMM may use techniques called parity or error-correcting code (ECC) to make sure that there are no memory errors. In the vast majority of instances, your memory will not use parity or ECC—those techniques are usually reserved for expensive, high-end computers called *servers*. However, to make sure, check your PC or motherboard's manual to see which kind of memory your PC requires.

Speed

The faster the memory, the faster data can be shuttled between RAM and the CPU, and the faster a computer operates. Memory comes rated at different speeds, and the faster the memory, the more it costs. Memory speed is often measured in nanoseconds, and the lower the nanosecond rating, the faster the memory. For example, a 2.5-nanosecond chip is faster than an 8-nanosecond chip. Be sure that the memory you buy is as fast as the memory you're replacing.

How to Determine What Memory You Need

The most difficult parts of upgrading your computer's memory are figuring out the specific kind of memory you need and knowing how much memory you can add in what configuration. The best way to answer these questions will be in your owner's manual. Here's what you need to know.

① Determine How Much Memory You Have

You can see how much memory you have in several ways. When you first start your computer, you see information flash by on the bootup screen, including how much memory you have. In Windows, however, there's an even easier way. Right-click the **My Computer** icon and select **Properties**. The screen shows how much memory you have. In some cases, however, this screen might not accurately report your memory, so it's safer to look at the information in the bootup screen.

② ECC Versus Non-ECC

Some computers require parity memory or ECC memory. Check your system's documentation or motherboard manual (or head to the manufacturer's Web site or call technical support) to see whether yours requires parity memory, nonparity memory, ECC memory, or non-ECC memory.

③ Determine the Connector Type

Check your system documentation to see how your memory connects to the motherboard. Alternatively, open the computer case and look. Look inside at the memory chips and see what kind of memory is in the bank. SIMMs have either 30 or 72 pins. DIMMs are larger and usually have 168 pins. RIMMs are also larger and have 184 pins, as do DDR DIMMs. If you're adding memory to a notebook computer, you might have SO-DIMMs, which have 72 pins or 144 pins, or SO-RIMMs, which have 160 pins. To be absolutely sure about what kind of memory you need, check your computer or motherboard documentation.

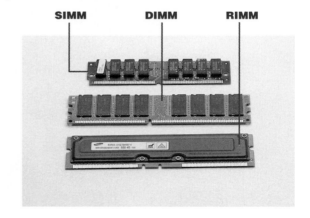

SIMM   DIMM   RIMM

④ Determine the Memory Type

Several different standards for memory exist. Newer systems can have Rambus Dynamic RAM (RDRAM) or Double Data RAM (DDR), while older systems might use Extended Data Out RAM (EDO RAM) or Synchronous Data RAM (SDRAM). Check your computer or motherboard documentation to see what kind you need.

RD RAM   DDR RAM   EDO RAM   SD RAM

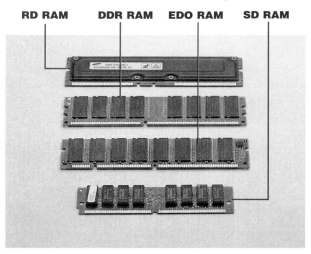

⑤ Determine the Memory Speed

Get memory at least as fast as the memory in your PC. Check your system documentation or call technical support to find out how fast the memory in your PC is.

⑥ Determine the Configuration

Your computer has a set of memory slots, and the motherboard can handle a maximum amount of memory. To find out the maximum amount, check the manual or the manufacturer's Web site, or call technical support. Some computers can handle memory modules only in certain configurations, so you might have to throw away your existing memory and buy all new memory. Also, some memory requires that you add memory modules in pairs rather than singly. Check your computer or motherboard documentation for details.

⑦ Determine If You Need Proprietary Memory

Although many computers accept memory chips from a variety of manufacturers, some computers accept memory only from the manufacturer of the computer. If that's the case, you have to buy the memory from the manufacturer. Proprietary memory typically costs more than other types of memory.

Watch Out!

- You can use memory with parity chips on a computer that doesn't require parity chips. Memory without parity chips, however, won't work on a computer that requires them.

- Combining different types of memory modules on the same motherboard will not work, so make sure to buy all of the same type.

How to Add or Replace Memory

After you've figured out the type of memory and the configuration of RAM chips you need to put in your computer, the hardest work is done. But you still have to open the case, take out the old memory, and put in the new. Here's how to do the final steps in a memory upgrade. Before you begin, turn off your PC and open the case as outlined in the section "How to Open the Case" in Chapter 13, "Before You Begin." You won't need any special tools to add or replace memory. It should take you under an hour to do the job.

❶ Locate the Memory Sockets

Memory sockets are long sockets with some or all the sockets occupied by memory modules.

❷ Remove Existing SIMMs

To upgrade SIMM memory, you might have to remove existing modules. SIMMs hold on to the memory slots by metal holders or plastic tabs on each side of the SIMM. A good way to remove the SIMM is to use two small flathead screwdrivers to press the tabs outward until the SIMM is released. If instead metal tabs are holding the SIMM, you can still use the small screwdrivers, although it is often easier to use your thumbnails.

❸ Install the SIMM Modules

Locate the notch on the SIMM; it enables memory to be installed in only one way. Match up the notch to the module. You usually tilt the SIMM at a 45° angle, push gently until it goes into the slot, and then tilt it upward to an upright position. Often you hear a small click as it fits into place. For other SIMMs, press them straight in first, and then down at an angle. The bottom of the SIMM should completely fit into the slot and should be perfectly level before pulling or pushing the SIMM upward from the 45° angle.

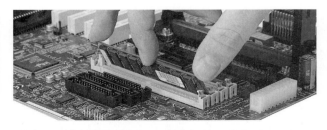

④ Remove the DIMMs or RIMMs

To upgrade DIMM memory or RIMM memory, you might have to remove existing modules. DIMMs generally are easier to remove than SIMMs. DIMMs have tabs on each side, often made of plastic. Push down on these tabs at thesame time, and the tabs push the DIMM out of its socket. RIMM modules are removed similarly, except in some instances, in which a RIMM module might have a terminator that attaches to the motherboard to fill empty RIMM slots. If it does, remove the terminator (also known as a continuity module).

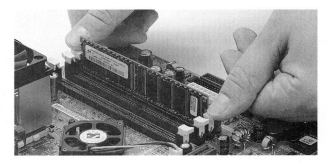

⑤ Install the DIMMs and RIMMs

DIMMs have two notches on the bottom that match the DIMM socket. Align the slots properly with the socket. Press down evenly across the top of the DIMM until the tabs on each side of the DIMM slip up into place. DIMM memory is removed similarly, except that in some instances with RIMMs you will have to attach a terminator to the motherboard. Check your documentation.

⑥ Turn On the Computer

Your computer might automatically boot into the CMOS screen, and the BIOS will automatically recognize the new memory. You have to exit the CMOS screen for the settings to take effect, and your computer might then reboot. If, when you first turn on your PC, you get an error message, bring up the CMOS screen, and the BIOS will automatically recognize the new memory. Exit the screen and save the CMOS settings for them to take effect.

Task

28

Installing and Upgrading a Graphics Card and Monitor

One of the most important upgrades you can make to your computer is to add a new graphics card or monitor. You'll see the following improvements: a far richer and more detailed display on your computer; more of the screen display because you'll be able to run it at higher resolutions; and, particularly if you play games, a huge difference in the quality of how you run your software. The newest generation of graphics cards features 3D technology, which enables you to play the most realistic-looking three-dimensional games. In fact, without a 3D graphics card, there are many games you won't even be able to play. Many graphics and computer-aided design programs use 3D graphics cards as well.

This chapter shows you how to install a new graphics card and monitor, and it also shows you how you can use two monitors on a single PC if you use Windows 98.

Upgrade Advisor

If you're buying a new monitor, the most basic decision you'll need to make is how large it should be. Monitors are measured in inches, diagonally. The most common monitor size sold today is 17", and it's the best size to get. It offers the best value for your money, although 19" monitors have come down in price. Smaller monitors display too little information to be useful, and larger monitors tend to be pricey. Additionally, larger monitors can be uncomfortable to use because you generally need to sit farther back from them. The most common larger monitor sizes are 19" and 21".

Increasingly popular are flat-panel monitors. They offer bright, vivid colors and take up very little space when compared to traditional monitors. They also, however, tend to be more expensive than traditional monitors. And they can be more difficult to install because they generally work only with special, digital graphic cards. However, they are worth it if your desk space is at a premium and you want vivid color.

If you're buying a new video card, you'll find a wide price range. They can cost less than $100 or more than $1,000. The more expensive cards are for those who do professional design or photo editing. The least expensive won't accelerate your PC for playing games. For most purposes, buy a card with 3D capabilities and with 8MB or more of RAM. The more RAM on the card, the higher the resolution and the more colors it will run. If you plan to play 3D games, get 16MB or 32MB. If you're going to play games, be sure the card has 3D acceleration and as much memory as possible. Also, if you're going to install a flat-panel monitor, you'll have to buy a digital graphics card. When buying a card, be sure to buy one that will do what you want tomorrow, not just today. It's worth spending a little extra just to be sure.

How a Graphics Card and Monitor Work

Video port

The graphics card sends its signals to the monitor through a port on the back of the card. The monitor cable plugs into this port. It is typically a 15-pin female connector. One way to tell whether your PC has an embedded graphics chip or video card is to check how the monitor connects to a video port. If the monitor connects to a port that is on a card on your computer, you have a separate graphics card, and if it connects to a port not attached to a card, you likely have an embedded chip.

Monitor

The signals are sent to the monitor, where they're displayed. Monitors come in many sizes, such as 15", 17", 19", and 21". If you want to use higher resolutions, you should use a large monitor. If you use high resolutions on a small monitor, it will be very hard to see anything. The *dot pitch* of a monitor refers to the distance between the phosphors that display an image; the smaller the dot pitch, the sharper the image. A monitor's frequency is related to its refresh rate. The refresh rate is the rate at which the screen image is rewritten, and it is measured in hertz (Hz). Too low a refresh rate cases screen flicker; in general, the refresh rate should be at least 72Hz. The frequency rate of a monitor must match that of the video card in the system.

Two monitors

In Windows 98 and above, two monitors can be run off the same computer. To do that, you must have two separate graphics cards, so that each monitor plugs into its own card. This works best if both graphics cards are the same make and model, although it's not required that they be. Additionally, some graphics cards offer support for two or more monitors.

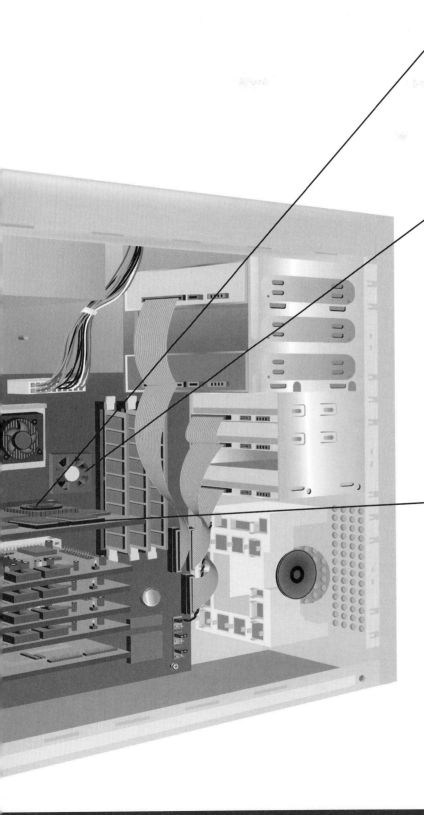

AGP slot

Newer motherboards include the an Accelerated Graphics Port (AGP) slot. The AGP standard enables 3D graphics to display quickly on a computer. The AGP bus is dedicated solely to graphics and offers more bandwidth than the PCI bus. If your computer has an AGP bus, make sure you buy an AGP card.

Embedded graphics chip

Some graphics processors aren't on a separate card but instead are on a chip on the motherboard itself. If you want to upgrade a PC that has an embedded graphics processor, you first have to disable the graphics processor on the motherboard. Normally, this is done either via a jumper on the motherboard or by changing a BIOS setting. Check the documentation that came with your computer to see how to do it. Often, embedded graphics chips lead to lower graphics performance than dedicated graphics cards because they sometimes share RAM with the computer itself rather than having their own RAM.

Graphics card

To display graphics on your PC, you need a graphics card. The card is attached to the motherboard via a slot. (There are many different kinds of cards with differing capabilities, such as 3D cards that accelerate the display of 3D graphics.) As a way to speed up graphics processing, graphics cards have special graphics coprocessors that perform graphics tasks so that the main CPU doesn't have to. Graphics cards also have memory devoted solely to graphics. The more memory on a card, the higher the resolution and the greater the number of colors that can be displayed.

How to Install a Graphics Card

Before installing a graphics card, find out what kind of slot you have. If you have a Pentium II PC or better, you might have an AGP slot with a graphics card in it. If you do, buy an AGP graphics card because that's the fastest type. Otherwise, use a PCI slot, which is second only to AGP in terms of speed. Make sure that the graphics card you buy will work properly with your monitor. Check your system documentation to see what type of capabilities your monitor has.

① Change Your Video Driver

Before installing a new video card, change the driver to a standard VGA driver. Right-click **My Computer**, select **Properties**, click the **Device Manager** tab, click the **+** sign next to Display Adapters, and click your video card. Next, click the **Properties** button and then the **Driver** tab. Click **Update Driver**. When a screen appears asking, `What do you want Windows to do?` click the bottom button to display a list of all the drivers available on your computer. On the next screen that appears, select **Show All Hardware**. Scroll to the top of the screen on the left and select **Standard Display Types**. Then, from the right side, select **Standard Display Adapter**.

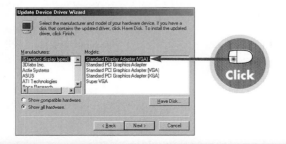

② Remove Old Video Source

If you have an existing graphics card, remove it after first turning off your computer, disconnecting the monitor, and removing the PC's case. For information on removing the case and taking out an existing card, turn to Chapter 13, "Performing Computer Maintenance." Some computers don't have graphics cards but instead use a graphics chip embedded on the motherboard. If you have one like this, you must disable the graphics chip before you can install a graphics card. You might have to disable it with DIP switches or jumpers, or it might be in the BIOS (in which case you'd have to disable the chip before you turn off your computer). Check your system documentation on how to do it.

③ Install the Graphics Card

Carefully position the card over the slot and push it down with even force. Press it down all the way. When the card is fully in the slot, screw it into the backplate using a Phillips screwdriver. If you're installing a board into a PCI slot, always install the graphics card in one of the first two slots. The slots are numbered on the motherboard.

4 Put on the Case and Reattach Monitor

To find out how to attach a monitor and its cable to a PC, turn to "How to Install a Monitor" on the next spread in the book.

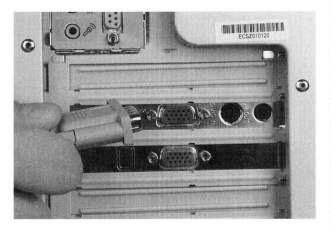

5 Install Drivers and Software

Turn on your computer. When you turn it back on, a dialog box should appear, walking you through installing drivers for your new graphics card. If Windows doesn't detect the card, go to the Windows Control Panel and double-click **Add New Hardware**. A wizard guides you through the installation process. If you have a disk from the manufacturer with drivers on it, insert it when prompted and select the driver from there. Restart Windows. If your graphics cards came with custom utilities and software, install them after you restart your computer.

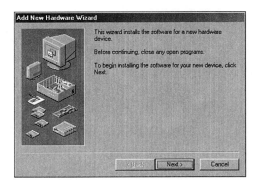

6 Change Your Video to New Settings

With a new video card, you might want different settings than you had in the past—for example, a higher resolution or more colors. Change those new settings by right-clicking your desktop, selecting **Properties**, clicking **Settings**, and then selecting the screen resolution and color quality you want.

Watch Out!

Check Your Slot Type

If you're installing an AGP card, be aware that some of them require what is called an AGP2x or AGP4x slot and will not work in earlier AGP slots.

How-to Hint

No Video?

If, when you turn your computer back on after installing a graphics card, no image appears on your screen and you hear a beeping from the computer's speakers, you probably didn't seat the card properly in its slot. Open the case and reseat the card.

After installing the card, go to the manufacturer's Web site to download the newest drivers for your card because video drivers are updated all the time.

How to Install a Monitor

Installing a new monitor is one of the easiest ways to upgrade your PC. All you need to do is plug it in and install new drivers. Installing a flat-panel monitor takes a little more work because you also might have to install a matching graphics card, which you'll install before installing a monitor. You might need to do this because not all digital flat-panel monitors work with all digital graphics cards. Be sure that the card and monitor will work together.

❶ Unplug Your Old Monitor

Turn off your computer before installing a new monitor. And then, unplug your old monitor. You need to unplug its connection from your PC and also unplug its power cord.

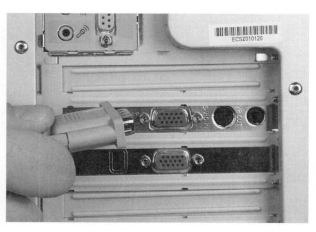

❷ Install the Graphics Card

If you're installing a flat-panel monitor and have to add a digital graphics card, add it now. Install a digital graphics card as you would any other graphics card, according to the instructions earlier in this chapter.

❸ Plug In New Monitor's Cables

You need to plug cables into the PC's video port and into a power outlet. Plug your new monitor into the same video port where you unplugged your old monitor. Most monitors plug into a 15-hole port. If you're installing a digital flat-panel monitor, plug it into the DVI port on the graphics card. Plug your monitor's power supply cable into an outlet.

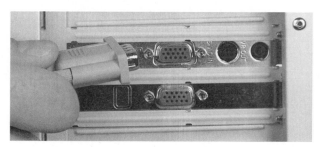

④ Turn On Your Computer and Monitor

When you turn your computer back on, it should detect your new hardware. Follow the directions for installing the drivers for your monitor. At some point the wizard asks whether you have a disk for your new monitor. If you have one, insert it at the right time, and then select the driver from there. In many cases, you won't need to install drivers because many monitors work with generic Windows plug-and-play monitor drivers.

⑤ Troubleshoot Installation Problems

If Windows doesn't detect your monitor, you have to manually tell Windows to find it. Go to the Control Panel and double-click **Add New Hardware**. An installation wizard will launch. At some point the wizard asks whether you have a disk for your new monitor. If you have one, insert it at the correct time and then select the driver from there. If your monitor comes with special software or utilities, install them after you've installed the drivers.

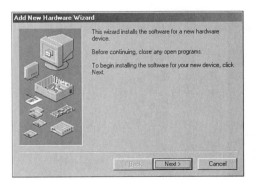

⑥ Adjust the Settings

Find the controls on your monitor, often on the front, that let you adjust settings such as brightness and contrast. These settings also let you resize and center the image onscreen. Check the manual to find out how to adjust the settings.

Check for New Drivers

After you've installed your monitor, check the manufacturer's Web site to see whether newer drivers are available.

Use Plug-and-Play

Your computer's capability to detect plug-and-play monitors might be disabled. To ensure that it isn't, double-click the **Display** icon in Control Panel, click the **Settings** tab, click the **Advanced** button, click the **Monitor** tab, and make sure the check box next to **Automatically Detect Plug-and-Play Monitors** is checked.

Check Monitor Settings

Some monitors are limited in the way they can display information. If some settings are set improperly, such as the refresh rate, the monitor can be damaged. Check the documentation for more information

---

How to Install a Second Monitor Under Windows XP

If you have Windows XP, you can take advantage of one of the more intriguing features of Windows—the capability to use two monitors simultaneously. Using two monitors gives you much more screen real estate because you are able to work on both screens. Those who create graphics or use desktop publishing software will be most interested in installing two monitors. Here's how to do it.

❶ Install a Second Graphics Card

For Windows XP to use two monitors, you need to have a second graphics card. You can also buy multimonitor cards that support two monitors. First, install a graphics card and its drivers as outlined earlier in this chapter, while keeping your existing graphics card and monitor. When using two cards, it works best if both video cards are the same make, although it's not required.

❷ Plug In Your New Monitor's Cables

Attach your new monitor to the graphics card that you just installed. To do that, plug cables into the card's video port. Most monitors plug into a 15-hole port. After you do that, plug your monitor's power supply cable into an outlet.

❸ Turn On Your Computer

When you turn your computer back on, a dialog box should appear telling you that new hardware has been detected. Follow the directions for installing the drivers for your monitor. At some point the wizard asks whether you have a disk for your new monitor. If you have one, insert it at the correct time, and then select the driver from there. In many cases, you won't need to install drivers because many monitors work with generic Windows plug-and-play monitor drivers.

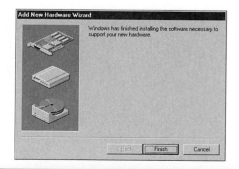

④ Troubleshoot Installation Problems

If Windows doesn't detect your monitor, you have to manually tell Windows to find it. Go to the **Control Panel** and double-click **Add New Hardware**. An installation wizard will launch. At some point the wizard asks whether you have a disk for your new monitor. If you have one, insert it at the correct time, and then select the driver from there.

⑤ Install Software

If your monitor comes with special software or utilities, install them after you've installed the drivers.

⑥ Determine Your Primary Monitor

When you install a second monitor, you need to tell Windows which graphics card and monitor should be the primary one. To do this, right-click the **Desktop**, click **Properties**, and select the **Settings** tab. Select which display adapter you want to use as your primary adapter, and check the box labeled **Extend My Windows Desktop onto This Monitor**.

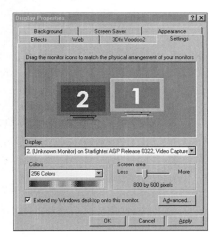

⑦ Arrange Your Monitors

If you want to move items from one monitor to the other by dragging left and right, arrange the icons side-by-side. Drag the numbered icons beside one another, or beneath one another, to change the orientation you use for multiple monitors.

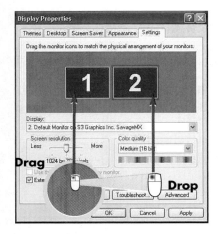

How to Calibrate a Monitor

Monitor calibration, or color matching, means synchronizing how an image looks on your screen with an image that was scanned into your computer or printed from it. Part of the issue is what makes you comfortable, and part of it is how faithfully your printer will reproduce an image that you are viewing in a graphics program.

❶ Use the Digital Controls

Most monitors today have digital controls to adjust brightness, gamma, saturation, and the color values of RGB—Red, Green, and Blue. With a scanned image on your screen, hold up the original photo as you use the digital controls to adjust these values.

❷ Print the Image

Once you have set the color calibration and made some adjustments to the scanned image, print it on your color printer and see how the result compares to the work you did.

❸ Use Your Graphics Program

Many graphics programs have a Color Management or Calibration option to help you adjust the software to the monitor image. In Ulead PhotoImpact you would click **File**, **Preferences**, **Color Management**.

④ Use Photoshop

If you have Adobe Photoshop, the Color Management options are found under the Edit menu.

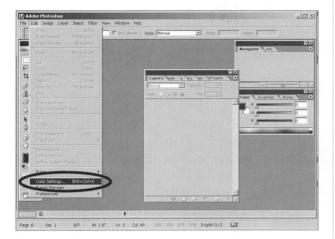

⑤ Advanced Mode

If you click **Advanced Mode**, you can roll your cursor over the settings to see what they will accomplish if selected. You can also use preset modes (such as NTSC or Web for television or Internet graphics) by clicking **Load**.

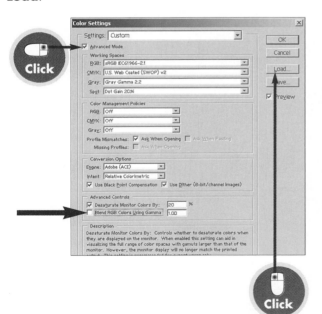

⑥ Check Your Printer

Before printing, you can change the settings for your specific printer. Here you can see the suddenly washed-out results. If you want the same looks as Normal (above), you would need to adjust the brightness and color saturation of this picture accordingly (to match its original look—see next image).

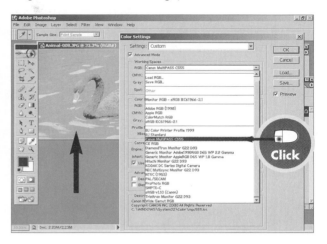

Monitor Calibration

Monitor calibration is a matter of trial and error. If you find an Advanced mode in Photoshop, and calibration is important, be sure you save the setting file, and back up your Photoshop settings (including your Actions [macros]).

Click **Save** to name and safeguard your current Photoshop settings before beginning to experiment. Then you can load them back in or try the other settings.

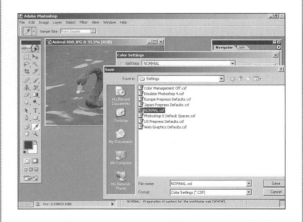

Task

29

Installing a Sound Card

To play music, listen to voices, hear game sound effects, hear system sounds, and hear other kinds of sounds on your PC, you need a sound card. A sound card plugs into your motherboard on an empty slot, connects to your CD or DVD drive via an audio cable, and plays sounds through speakers that you plug into the back of the sound card.

These days, almost any program you run includes sounds, so any properly equipped PC should include a sound card, or onboard sound in which the sound capabilities are on the motherboard itself. If you already have an older sound card, you might want to upgrade it to improve the quality of the sound it can play, particularly sounds that are an integral part of games, entertainment programs, or other multimedia software.

This chapter shows how to take out your old sound card and how to install a new one.

Upgrade Advisor

Sound cards offer an extremely wide range of capabilities, so take care to buy the right one. The main things to check when buying are the quality of the sound it can produce, the number of different devices it can support, and any extra features such as support for surround sound.

The mix you want will be determined by what you intend to use your PC for. Are you a hard-core gamer who needs realistic 3D and surround sound? Are you planning to watch DVD movies on your PC, and so need to support Dolby sound? Or do you just want good, basic sound and don't want to pay extra for those features? First, determine what you'll use the sound in your PC for. Then use the table below to help determine which features your card should have.

Use	Features and Ports
Gaming	3D sound, audio acceleration, game port, surround sound
Watching DVD movies	Dolby decoding
Creating music in MIDI format	MIDI port
Recording music from external sources such as CD players	Audio-in port
General computing	At least 16-bit sound

How a Sound Card Works

Sound card

A sound card plugs into an empty slot on a PC. All communications between the PC and sound card happen through the connections between the sound card and the motherboard on the slot. The card converts the digital signals used by computers to analog signals used by speakers. Many motherboards include onboard sound so the PC has no separate sound card. However, if you need to upgrade your onboard sound, you can often disable it through jumper settings and then install your card. (To find out whether your system has onboard sound, check the documentation.)

Electromagnet

The weak electrical current is amplified by an amplifier and sent to power an electromagnet inside a speaker. The electromagnet makes speaker cones vibrate, and these vibrations create sound.

MIDI sound

Most sound cards also can play musical instrument digital interface (MIDI) sound. MIDI is a special computer music format developed to conserve disk space. MIDI technology doesn't record actual sounds. Instead, it saves a set of instructions describing how music sounds on electronic versions of musical instruments. These MIDI instructions are sent to the DSP. The DSP is capable of interpreting the instructions to know which instruments should play the music and how it should be played.

Wavetable synthesis

Some sound cards use *wavetable synthesis* to reproduce music. In this technology, a sound card ROM chip stores sound samples from musical instruments. The more memory a sound card has, the more sounds it can play and the more realistic and vivid the sounds are. To play the sound, the DSP looks in the ROM's table. If the sound is there, the sound card plays it. If, though, the sound is supposed to be a clarinet's B-flat, but the ROM has only a sample of the note B for the clarinet, the DSP processes the B note sound sample and lowers it to a B-flat pitch.

DSP chip

When the sound card needs to play a recorded sound found on a WAV file, the central processing unit (CPU) fetches the WAV file containing the compressed digital information from the hard drive or CD-ROM and sends that file to a chip called a *digital signal processor (DSP)* on the sound card.

DAC chip

The DSP takes the file and decompresses the data. Then it transfers the data to a digital-to-analog converter (DAC) chip. The DAC chip converts the digital data to an analog electrical current that constantly changes. Many sound cards also include an analog-to-digital converter (ADC) that changes incoming sound from the microphone into digital data that the computer can understand.

How to Remove an Existing Sound Card

If you already have a sound card in your system, you need to remove it before installing a new sound card. Here's how to remove your existing sound card. You can also turn to "How to Install a Basic Card" in Chapter 13, "Performing Computer Maintenance," for more information about removing a card. Then follow these instructions.

① Remove the Sound Card Drivers

Before installing a new sound card, you should uninstall drivers and other software for your existing card. Right-click the **My Computer** icon in Windows, select **Properties**, and then select the **Device Manager** tab. Click **Sound Video and Game Controllers** and select your existing sound card. Click **Remove** and follow the instructions.

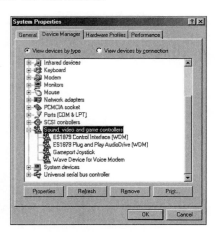

② Remove Special Software

Remove any special software installed specifically for the sound card because it probably won't work with your new card. To remove the software, double-click **Add/Remove Programs** from the Control Panel, select the program you want to remove, click **Add/Remove**, and click the **Yes** button on the screen that appears.

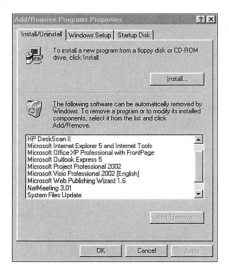

③ Detach Devices

A variety of devices might be connected to the sound card, such as speakers, headphones, a microphone, a joystick, or other gaming devices. Unplug all these devices after turning off your PC.

4 Disconnect Cables

Now open your case as explained in Chapter 3 and find your sound card. Cables and devices might be attached internally to your sound card. Disconnect the CD or DVD audio cable. Note all the various connections so that when you put in a new sound card, you make those same connections again. There are two types of CD audio cables. Be sure your new sound card either comes with an audio cable that fits your CD or that your existing cable fits into the new sound card.

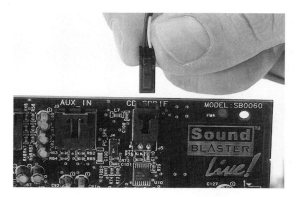

5 Remove the Backplate and Lift Out Card

A screw on the backplate secures the sound card to your system. Remove that screw, probably with a Phillips screwdriver. Then you can lift the card free from the system: Hold the card by its top edge with two hands and lift straight up. If the card doesn't move, pull up one edge slightly first, and then lift the other.

6 Double-Check Software

You want to be absolutely sure that all the old software and drivers for the old sound card are gone from your system. After removing the sound card, reboot your computer and run the Add/Remove Wizard from the Control Panel. In most cases, the wizard won't find any software associated with the card, but if it does, tell it to remove the software.

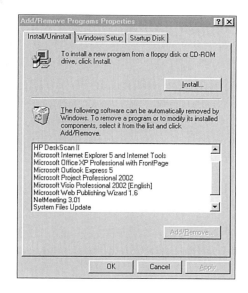

How-to Hint

- Keep the screw from your old sound card; you can use it when you install the new one.

How to Install a Sound Card

Before installing a new sound card, you need to either remove your existing sound card or disable your motherboard's onboard sound. To disable the onboard sound, check your motherboard's documentation or visit the manufacturer's Web site to find out how. This is normally done via a jumper on the motherboard or by altering a BIOS setting. To remove the card, refer to the previous illustration.

❶ Connect the CD or DVD Audio Cable

After installing your card as outlined in "How to Install a Basic Card" in Chapter 13, you will need to attach the card to the internal drives. Locate the audio cable running from the drives, and attach it to the sound card. Connecting this audio cable enables you to listen to audio CDs on your computer.

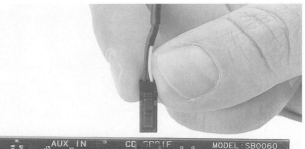

❷ Connect Other Internal Cables

Sound cards can come with a variety of connectors for different devices. Many of the connectors are on the outside of the card, but some require internal connections. If you have an internal modem with a telephone answer device (TAD) capability, for example, connect the TAD cable from the modem to the sound card. If you have other devices with internal connections, connect them now as well. Finally, close the case.

❸ Turn On Your PC

After you turn your PC back on, it should automatically recognize that you've installed new hardware. An **Add New Hardware Wizard** dialog box appears. Follow the directions for installing your sound card. If Windows doesn't recognize that you've added a sound card, run the Add New Hardware Wizard. First go to the **Control Panel** by clicking the **Start** button, and then select **Control Panel** from **Settings**. Double-click **Add New Hardware**. You have the option of using drivers supplied with your sound card or using the ones supplied by Windows. Use the ones supplied by the manufacturer, and insert the manufacturer's CD or disk.

④ Install Special Software

Some sound cards come with special software to help you take full advantage of their capabilities. Using the manufacturer's disk, install the software.

⑤ Attach External Devices

Attach the speakers to the proper external port on your card. If you have a microphone, attach it as well. If you have other devices, such as for Dolby Surround and MIDI, plug those in as well.

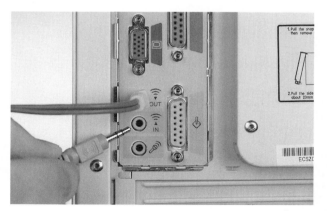

⑥ Troubleshoot Conflicts

Test the card to ensure that it is working properly. If not, you might have an interrupt request (IRQ) conflict. To troubleshoot IRQ conflicts, use the Device Manager. To get to it, right-click **My Computer** and select **Properties**. Then, click the **Device Manager** tab. If Windows detects problems with a device, you'll see an exclamation mark next to it. To change the IRQ of the sound card, check the card's documentation and follow directions. Note that some sound cards can use two IRQs. Also, sometimes you can fix IRQ problems by disabling DOS support in the card. Check the sound card's documentation on how to do that.

Watch Out!

- When you put in the sound card, be sure it is seated tightly into the slot, so the card will work.
- When hooking up speakers, be careful to put the speaker plug into the proper connector on the back of the sound card—not into the microphone jack.

How-to Hint

- To play music CDs with your CD drive and sound card, you need a software CD player installed. You can use the one included with Windows.
- If you can hear sound but not music or vice versa from data disks, check your DMA settings for a conflict. If you cannot hear music or audio CDs, check that the CD-ROM audio cable has been connected properly.

30

Adding or Replacing a Hard Drive

To a certain extent, your hard drive *is* your computer. It's where you store all your data, all your files, and all your programs.

You might need to add or replace a hard drive for many reasons. You might be running out of hard drive space, or the hard drive might be continually reporting errors, which might mean it's time for a replacement. Or you might simply want a new hard drive that's faster and holds more data than your current one. You have the option of either replacing your existing hard drive or adding a second one. The main hard disk on your system, from which your system boots, is called the *master*. A second hard drive is called a *slave*.

A hard drive can connect to the rest of your computer in several ways, notably via an ATA connection (also known as an IDE or IDE/EIDE connection) or a SCSI connection. The most common kind of connection is via ATA, and that's what this chapter covers. To install a SCSI drive, turn to Chapter 20, "Installing a SCSI Device."

Upgrade Advisor

When getting a new hard drive, a simple rule to follow is that bigger and faster is better. It's not uncommon for hard disks today to be 40GB, 60GB, 80GB, and up. Buy as large as you can afford because another rule about hard disk storage is that you fill up hard disks faster than you think you will. If you use graphics or video or store MP3s on your hard disk, you'll find that space goes very quickly, and you should consider getting an 80GB drive or more. If you use primarily word processing and similar files, you can get by with a 40GB or 60GB drive.

When measuring speed, manufacturers might tout two specs: average seek time and transfer rate. The average seek time measures the average time it takes to move the heads on a hard disk cylinder from one spot to another. It's measured in milliseconds (ms), and the smaller the number, the better. A very fast hard drive will have an average seek time of 4ms–5ms. Transfer rate measures how much data can be transferred from a hard disk in a second. The problem with this measurement is that for a single hard drive, depending on what you are measuring, there can be many different transfer rates. For a single drive, for example, these can range from 30MB per second to 100MB per second.

How a Hard Drive Works

Ribbon cable —————————————————

The controller sends and receives information to and from the hard drive via a 40-pin, 40-wire ribbon cable, or a 40-pin, 80-wire cable. (In an 80-wire cable, 40 of the wires are ground wires.) A connector at each end of the cable plugs into the hard drive and into the controller. Some ribbons are marked with a different color to indicate the first pin. Knowing this makes connecting them easier. The connectors are also keyed so that improper connections can't be made.

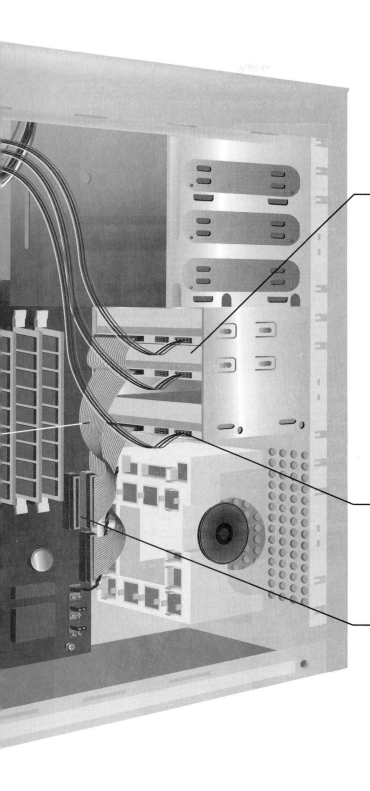

Hard drive

The hard drive, inside its sealed metal housing, fits into a drive bay on a computer. Magnetized platters in the hard drive store the data and spin at high speeds—up to 15,000 revolutions per minute. As a general rule, the faster the rotation speeds, the faster the hard disk. Read/write heads move across the spinning platter to retrieve and store information. The space between the read/write heads and the spinning platters is minute so that data can be read accurately—typically less than the width of a human hair, at 2/100,000 of an inch. Several standards exist for ATA drives, including ATA/33, ATA/66, and ATA/100. The higher the number, the faster the hard disk, so an ATA/100 hard disk is faster than an ATA/33 hard disk.

Power connection

The hard drive gets its power from the power supply. It connects to the power supply by a cable and a universal connector that plugs into the hard drive.

Controller

A controller sends instructions back and forth between your PC and the hard drive, sending information to be stored or asking for information to be retrieved. Sometimes the controller is on a separate board, although usually it is on the motherboard itself. Several kinds of controllers exist, most notably ATA (also known as IDE) and SCSI. A hard drive with a SCSI controller is usually faster than one with an ATA controller, although SCSI controllers and hard drives are more difficult to install.

How to Install a Hard Drive

In most cases, when you put a new hard drive in your PC, you're going to keep your existing hard drive. If you're replacing a hard drive, first remove your hard drive. Turn to the section "How to Remove an Old Drive" in Chapter 13 and follow the instructions on how to remove an existing drive. Because you'll be copying data from your old hard drive to your new one, turn to the section "How to Prepare for Your Upgrade" (also in Chapter 13) to learn how to back up a hard drive. To begin, you will need to turn off your PC and remove the case. See "How to Open the Case" in Chapter 13 and follow the instructions for removing the case.

1 Find a Free Bay

To install a hard drive, you need a free drive bay. After you remove your computer's case, take a look inside and see which drive bay you have free. Drives come in 3 1/2" and 5 1/4" sizes, so be sure your bay accommodates the drive you buy. Most often, you'll have a 3 1/2" drive. You can fit a 3 1/2" hard drive into a 5 1/4" bay by getting a special adapter kit, but a 5 1/4" hard drive won't fit into a 3 1/2" bay.

2 Set Jumpers

In some instances, before you install the drive you will have to set its jumpers. You can make your new hard drive either a master or slave. Check the drive documentation to see whether you need to set jumpers, and if so, how to set them.

3 Slide In and Secure the Drive

Slide the drive into the drive bay, and screw it into the drive bay or railings. Secure all the screws so that the drive is held firmly in place, but don't overtighten or strip the screws. Some hard drives are mounted inside bays via mounting rails or adapter kits. Install the mounting rails or adapter kit before sliding in the drive. Also, make sure a free data cable and power cable to which you'll attach the drive are present.

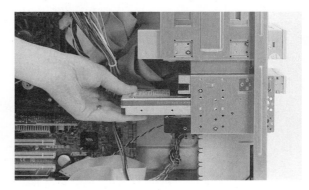

④ Connect the Data Cable

The data cable, a wide ribbon cable, runs from your motherboard to your hard drive. If there is no free connector on the cable, you have to buy a new one. In either event, connect the ribbon cable connector to the slot on the hard drive. The ribbon cable has a stripe on one side of it, indicating that that side of the cable plugs into pin 1 on the hard drive connector—the pin closest to the power supply connector.

⑤ Connect the Power Supply

Your hard drive needs power to work, so you must connect it to your power supply. The power supply cable has a connector on the end of it, which is usually four sockets encased in a small sheath of white plastic. Plug that into the connector on your hard drive. Then, close the case and restart your PC.

⑥ Set CMOS and Format the Disk

Before you can use your hard drive, you have to tell your computer about it by using the CMOS setup screen to change the BIOS settings. You must also format the hard drive so your computer can use it. For information about changing BIOS settings and formatting your hard drive, turn to the section "How to Format and Partition a Hard Drive" later in this chapter.

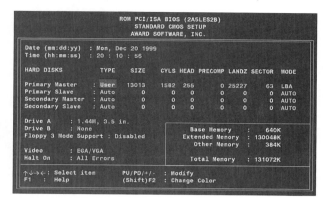

Watch Out!

- You won't be able to use your new hard drive until you change the CMOS settings, partition it, and format it, as seen in the next spread.
- If you're installing a second hard drive and both are attached to the same interface, double-check that you've set the jumper settings on the drives properly so that one is the master and the other is the slave.

How-to Hint

- Be sure to have a spare connector on your ribbon cable to attach to the new hard drive.
- If you have more than four devices attached to your controller, you might need to get a new one.
- Make sure to use rails or an adapter kit if your new hard drive doesn't fit in your drive bay.

How to Format and Partition a Hard Drive

Physically installing your hard drive is only the first part of the process of installing a hard drive. After you've made the proper physical connections, you have to tell your computer to recognize the hard drive, partition it (divide it into pieces), and finally format it so that it can be used.

If your computer or new hard disk comes with special software, use it and skip this section. Check the documentation closely for details.

❶ Run CMOS Setup

Press whatever key you need to for entering CMOS information. Often, your new hard drive will be automatically recognized and you won't have to do anything more to the BIOS. If it is not recognized, you have to select the hard drive in the CMOS setup screen and then enter information about the hard drive's cylinder, heads, and sectors.

```
              ROM PCI/ISA BIOS (2A5LES2B)
                  STANDARD CMOS SETUP
                  AWARD SOFTWARE, INC.

Date (mm:dd:yy)  : Mon, Dec 20 1999
Time (hh:mm:ss)  : 20 : 10 : 56

HARD DISKS          TYPE   SIZE   CYLS HEAD PRECOMP LANDZ SECTOR  MODE

Primary Master   : User   13013  1582  255      0 25227     63   LBA
Primary Slave    : Auto       0     0    0      0     0      0  AUTO
Secondary Master : Auto       0     0    0      0     0      0  AUTO
Secondary Slave  : Auto       0     0    0      0     0      0  AUTO

Drive A    : 1.44M, 3.5 in.
Drive B    : None                    Base Memory    :   640K
Floppy 3 Mode Support : Disabled     Extended Memory : 130048K
                                     Other Memory   :   384K
Video      : EGA/VGA
Halt On    : All Errors              Total Memory   : 131072K

↑↓→←: Select item     PU/PD/+/-  : Modify
F1  : Help            (Shift)F2  : Change Color
```

❷ Boot from a Boot Disk

When you exit the CMOS setup screen, the computer should restart if you're replacing your hard drive. Put in a boot disk (it can be a floppy or a CD) that you've prepared before it restarts. If you are using Windows 95, you see a prompt that looks like this: A:\>. If you're using a later version of Windows, you get a startup menu asking you if you want to start the computer with or without CD-ROM support. Select **CD-ROM Support**. In Windows 98, a RAM drive will be created. Write down the letter of the RAM drive; you'll need it later.

❸ Partition Your Hard Drive

You can have a single partition, or you can divide your disk into separate drives. To partition your hard drive, type **FDISK** at the DOS prompt and follow the instructions. If you're replacing your old hard drive with a new one, be sure to select **Create DOS Partition** and then **Create Primary DOS Partition**. If you're adding a second hard drive instead of replacing your old one, you see the option **Change Current Fixed Disk Drive**. Select that, and then choose to create a Logical DOS partition to make your new drive D: (or E:, if you already have a D: drive). If you're partitioning your C: drive into several partitions, you *must* set the primary partition to **Active**.

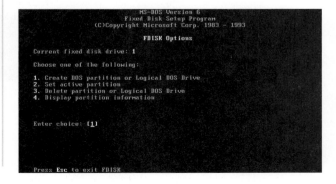

```
                MS-DOS Version 6
             Fixed Disk Setup Program
       (C)Copyright Microsoft Corp. 1983 - 1993

                   FDISK Options

Current fixed disk drive: 1

Choose one of the following:

1. Create DOS partition or Logical DOS Drive
2. Set active partition
3. Delete partition or Logical DOS Drive
4. Display partition information


Enter choice: [1]



Press Esc to exit FDISK
```

④ Format Your Hard Drive

If you're replacing an old hard drive with a new one, you need to restart your computer, so leave in your boot floppy. After it reboots, type `Format C: /S` at the DOS prompt to format your new hard drive and put the DOS operating system onto it. With Windows 98, the operating system files copy to your new hard drive from the RAM drive that Windows 98 previously created. Assuming that the RAM drive was letter *D*, type the following to format your hard drive and put basic operating system files onto it: `D:\Format C: /S`. If you're not replacing your old hard drive from the DOS prompt, type `Format D:` (or whatever letter your new drive will be). If you've created separate partitions instead of just one, format each of them in turn.

⑤ Reinstall Your Operating System

If you're replacing an old hard drive with a new one, you have to reinstall your operating system. To do that, use your Windows disks or CD to reinstall Windows onto your new hard drive. If you're not replacing your old hard drive and are only adding a second one, you won't need to put the operating system on it.

⑥ Copy Backed-Up Data and Files

After you've confirmed that the hard drive is working properly, copy all the data and files you've previously backed up to your new hard drive. Make sure you've first backed up your hard disk. For information about how to back up your hard disk, turn to the section "How to Prepare for Your Upgrade" in Chapter 13.

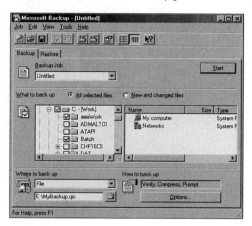

Watch Out!

- If you're replacing your old hard drive, when you format your new hard drive, be sure to use the `/S` parameter, which will add system files to the new hard drive so that it's bootable.

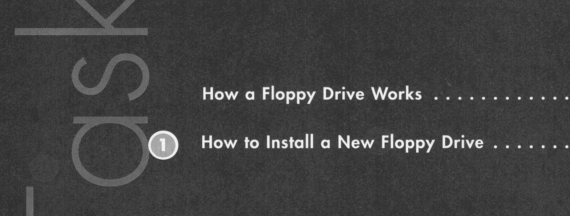

Task

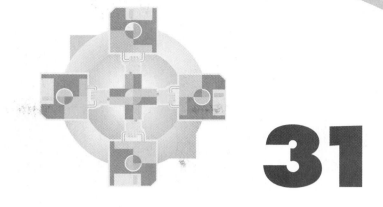

31

Installing a Floppy Drive

Floppy drives aren't as important today as they used to be, considering that much software is distributed on CD-ROMs and other software is available via the Internet. However, they're still useful, especially when you're exchanging data with someone.

Upgrade Advisor

There are only two reasons you'll need to replace a floppy drive: Your old one breaks, or you want one that can store much more data than traditional drives. If you want a floppy drive that stores a great deal of data on a floppy, you can install what's called a SuperDisk floppy drive (sometimes called an LS-120 drive). It works like a floppy drive in all ways, except that it can accept disks that have the capacity for storing 120MB of data and it reads and writes data at a much higher speed than standard floppy drives. The SuperDisk also reads normal 1.44MB floppies as well as the high-capacity 120MB disks. The only drawbacks are that it's more expensive than a regular floppy drive and the disks are more expensive than standard disks. But if you want high-capacity storage in a floppy drive, it's worth the cost.

How a Floppy Drive Works

Power supply

The floppy drive is powered by the computer's power supply. Cables attach the floppy drive to the power supply and bring power to the drive.

Indicator light

A light on the front of some floppy drives lights up when data is being accessed from the drive.

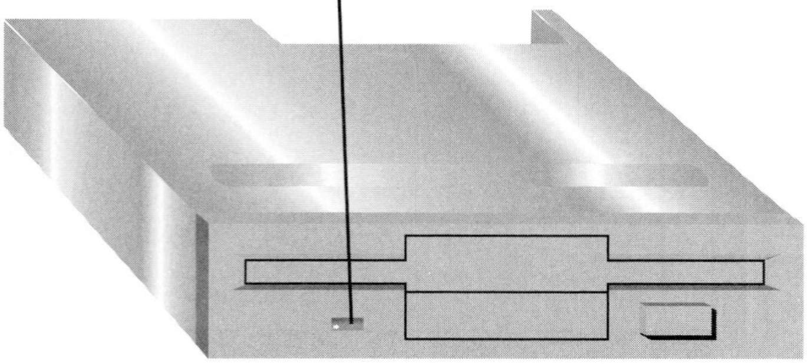

Ribbon cables

The motherboard communicates with the floppy drive by sending and receiving information along a ribbon cable that runs from the motherboard or an add-in card plugged into the motherboard to the floppy drive. The cable has a twist in it, with a connector before and after the twist. If the connector after the twist is used, the drive is designated as the A drive, and if the connector before the twist is used, the drive is designated as the B drive.

Read/write heads

When floppy drives store data, read/write heads move along the surface of the disk until they find an empty spot to place the data. When the drives are looking for data, the read/write heads move along the surface of the disk until they find the data being looked for and then read the data. When a floppy drive goes bad, it is often because these heads stop working properly, so the drive must be replaced.

Mounting screws

Floppy drives sit in a computer's drive bay and are secured by mounting screws on the front or sides of the drive. Mounting rails sometimes are used if the floppy is a much smaller size than the bay. Sometimes the 3 1/2" drive cages hold the floppy and hard disks in one removable unit.

Controller

When data is read from or written to the disk, the floppy drive's controller receives information from the motherboard and sends signals to the drive's circuit board. The controller then controls the movement of the floppy disk and of the read/write heads located inside the floppy drive. Most systems have this controller built into the motherboard itself in the form of an input/output chip that also controls other input/output devices or ports. Settings are controlled by the CMOS setup screen, which alters the BIOS.

How to Install a New Floppy Drive

To install a floppy drive, first take out your old drive; then install a new one by simply sliding it into the spot where the old one was and re-attaching the cables. After you install the drive, you'll use the CMOS setup screen to tell your computer's BIOS to recognize the new floppy. To install a new floppy, you need a new floppy drive, a free drive bay (usually the bay that held your old floppy drive), and a screwdriver.

❶ Remove the Old Drive

You install a floppy drive only if your old one doesn't work, so first remove the old drive. For instructions on how to remove a drive, turn to "How to Remove an Old Drive" in Chapter 13, "Performing Computer Maintenance." Match the size of the drive you're installing to the empty bay. Drive bays and floppy drives generally come in three sizes: 3'', 5'', and bays that require mounting rails. In some instances, you can use a floppy drive cage that mounts into the case. In all instances, make sure the drive is accessible from the front of the case so you can slide floppy disks in and out.

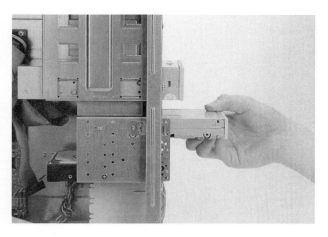

❷ Set Jumpers

In some instances, you might have to set the drive's jumpers before installing the drive. Check the drive documentation to see whether you need to set jumpers.

❸ Slide In and Secure the Floppy

Slide the drive into the drive bay. If you're installing a 3'' floppy into a 5'' bay, you might need to use rails. Screw the drive into the drive bay or rails. Connect all the screws so that the drive is held firmly in place, but don't overtighten or strip the screws.

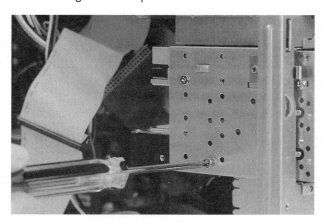

4 Attach Cables and Restart

Attach the ribbon and power cables to the drive. The ribbon cable has a twist, with a connector before the twist and another after. If you're installing drive A, use the connector after the twisted section; for drive B, use the connector before the twist. Ribbon connectors usually can be plugged in only one way. If yours can go in both ways, be sure that the colored edge of the ribbon cable attaches to the number 1 on the drive connector. When installing the power supply cable, be aware that it will fit into the drive in only one direction. Be careful not to force it. After the cables are attached, close the case and restart the PC.

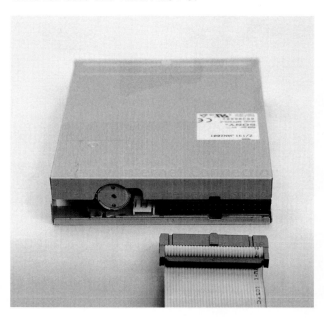

5 Test the New Drive

Before putting your case back on, you should make sure the new drive works. Your computer should start with no problem. If you've added a new drive, you'll have to use your computer's CMOS setup screen to get the BIOS to recognize it. How you do this varies from BIOS to BIOS, but in general, look under the Advanced Menu for the Diskette Configuration Submenu and make sure the new device is recognized. If it's not, use the setup to recognize it. After it is recognized, put a floppy disk into the drive and try saving and reading data to it. If the drive doesn't work, check that the cables are all plugged in properly and the connections are tight. When everything checks out, screw the computer's case back on.

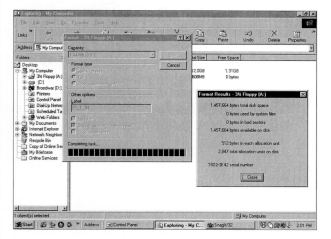

<table>
<tr><td>Watch Out!</td><td>• If the floppy's drive lights continuously, the connector on the ribbon cable is attached backwards.</td></tr>
</table>

<table>
<tr><td>How-to Hint</td><td>• If your old floppy was attached using mounting rails, either use those when sliding in your new drive or buy a set of new rails.
• When attaching ribbon cables to the new drive, be sure that the ribbon connectors are attached to the correct ends of the drive connector.</td></tr>
</table>

Task

32

Installing a CD-ROM or CD-RW

No PC is complete without a CD-ROM. These drives read data, run software, and play music CDs. CD-RW drives can also write data, which means you can save your personal files or even burn your own music CD!

A CD drive needs an interface to connect to your PC. The most common type is an IDE/EIDE, which can be found on an IDE/EIDE card, directly on the motherboard, or on a sound card installed on your system. However, you can also connect a CD drive to your PC with a SCSI interface. For information on installing a SCSI device, see Chapter 20, "Installing a SCSI Device." You can also connect CD drives to your PC via both the USB and FireWire ports. For information on installing USB and FireWire devices, see Chapter 21, "Installing USB and FireWire Devices."

You'll often notice a number or series of numbers next to a CD drive—for example, 32X/16X/40X. These numbers refer to the speed of the drive—in general, the higher the number, the faster the drive. The X refers to how many times the transfer rate of the drive is faster than the original CD standard. The first number tells you how fast you can write to the drive, and the second number tells you how fast you can rewrite to the drive. The final number tells you how fast you can read from the drive.

How a CD Drive Works

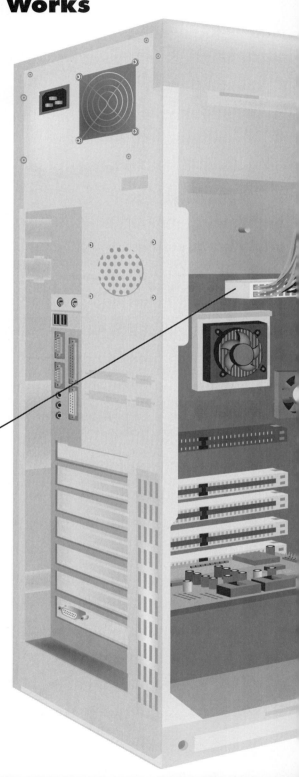

Disk speed

The faster the disk spins, the faster data can be copied to it and read from it. The first ordinary CD ROMs, with a 1x speed, had access times of 400 milliseconds. New CD-RWs, rated 32x or greater, have access times of 85 milliseconds and less. A good reason to upgrade a CD drive is to get a faster speed for both playback and recording.

Controller

A controller inside the computer sends instructions back and forth between your PC and the CD drive, instructing the drive to send data to the PC. Some older drives use a proprietary card, but these days it's best to stick with an IDE/EIDE or a SCSI controller for ease and compatibility.

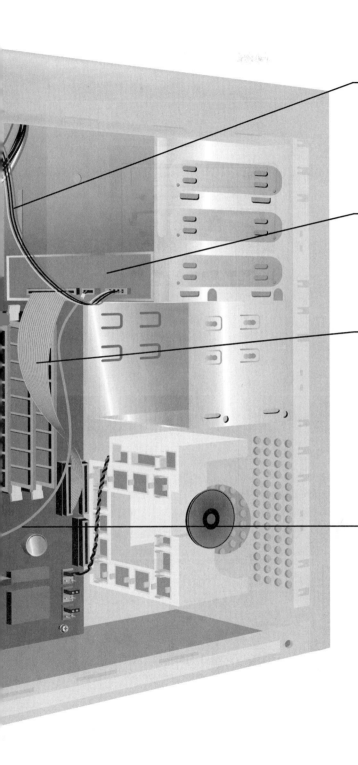

Power connector

The CD drive gets its power from the power supply. It connects to the power supply by a cable and 4-pin connector that plugs into the drive, similar to the ones that plug into your hard drive.

CD-RW

An Internal CD drive fits into a drive bay on a computer. CD-RWs fit into 5 1/4" bays. Screws hold the drive in place inside the bay.

Ribbon cable

The controller sends and receives information to and from the drive via a 40-pin or 80-pin ribbon cable, if you're using an IDE/EIDE controller. A connector at each end of the cable plugs into the drive and into the controller. A SCSI or some type of proprietary controller might use a 32-, 50-, 68-, or 72-pin cable.

Audio cable

Because CDs include sound and music as well as other types of data, they need to send sounds to the PC's sound card. They send data over an audio cable that attaches to the sound card. The sound card, in turn, sends the sound and music to the PC's speakers. The audio cable is required if you want digital output from the CD, as well as the ability to listen to music CDs on your computer.

How to Install or Replace a CD Drive

If you don't have a writeable CD-RW, a decision about whether to upgrade is very simple: You should upgrade. These rewriteable drives are ideal for backing up data and storing MP3 files and other music files, and can even be used to make your own audio CDs. It's one of the least-expensive upgrades you can make—and one that you'll probably use more than almost any other. To install a new CD-RW, you'll need a free drive bay (it can be the bay that held your old CD-RW if you're replacing one), and a screwdriver.

① Find a Free Bay

To install a CD drive, you need a free drive bay, a cable connector, and a power connector. Verify that you have the right-size bay to match your CD and that you have a free ribbon cable and power connector. You might need to install railings to fit the drive to your PC. Check your drive documentation for details.

② Set Jumpers

A CD drive can be either a "master" or a "slave." The only time you should set it as a slave is if you're connecting the drive to the same cable attached to your boot hard drive—but, generally, you don't want to do that because it can affect hard drive performance. So, you'll typically set it as a master. Check your CD documentation to see how the jumpers should be set. You also might need to set the jumpers to "cable select," in which case the CD-RW would automatically configure itself as a master or slave.

③ Slide In and Secure the Drive

Slide the drive into the drive bay, and screw it into the drive bay or railings. Connect all the screws so that the drive is held firmly in place, but don't overtighten or strip the screws.

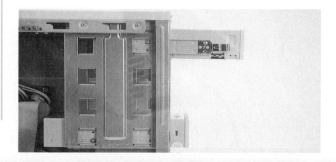

④ Connect the Cables

Connect the data cable—the wide, 40-pin ribbon cable that runs from an IDE/EIDE card, a motherboard, or a sound card—to your CD drive. The ribbon cable has a stripe on one side of it, indicating that it connects to pin 1 on the CD drive. Pin 1 is usually nearest to the power connector. Next, connect a power cable from your power supply to your drive. The power connector will be notched, as will the space on the CD for it, meaning it can be plugged in only one way.

⑤ Attach the Audio Cable

For your computer to play sound, it generally needs to connect to the sound card. You connect a cable from your sound card to a port on your CD drive. Two types of connectors can be used between a CD drive and a sound card. One is a large connector with a clip; the other is a small white connector with no clip. Be sure that you get the proper connector for your sound card and drive. If you don't connect the CD to the sound card, you generally won't be able to play audio CDs.

⑥ Close the Case and Install Software

After checking that everything is secure, close up your PC, plug the power cable back in, and turn it on. Your drive should be recognized automatically when you start it up. If you installed a CD-RW drive, install the software that came with it, for doing things such as copying files to a CD.

Watch Out!

Don't Crimp the Cables!

When closing your case, be careful that no ribbon or power cables are hanging out the side. Most of the time you won't notice them until after you have jammed or crimped the cable.

How-to Hint

Trouble with Sound?

If you can't play an audio CD in the drive, double-check that the audio cable is attached securely.

You might need to change your BIOS settings using the CMOS setup screen to install or replace a CD drive. Check your system's documentation for details.

Task

33

Installing a DVD Drive

Digital versatile discs (DVDs) have become the next revolution in multimedia computing. These discs can hold the equivalent of many CDs, and their multimedia capacities far outstrip anything available on CD. The quality of the animation and the music they can play is much more advanced than what you can get on a CD.

With a DVD drive, you not only can run DVDs made for computers, but can also watch movies recorded on DVDs on your PC, or on a TV by hooking a TV up to your computer. And DVD drives can run CD-ROMs as well as DVDs.

Installing a DVD drive is similar to installing a CD-ROM drive. You put it in an empty drive bay, and then attach it to your PC via an Integrated Development Environment (IDE) interface, which can be found on an IDE card or directly on the motherboard. Some DVD drives can also be hooked up via a SCSI interface. When installing a DVD drive, you must also install a DVD decoder card and hook the drive up to that. In some cases, you might have a graphics card that has a decoder already, so you won't need to install a separate decoder card. Check your graphic card's documentation to see whether yours has a DVD decoder on it. You can install a DVD without a decoder, but then you wouldn't be able to watch DVD movies on your PC, and you might not be able to see some movie scenes in DVD games. So, it's best to install a decoder.

If you have an older PC, ensure before buying a DVD drive that your computer has enough horsepower and other system capabilities to play DVD titles or to install a DVD drive. Check with the DVD manufacturer for system requirements.

Upgrade Advisor

The major issue you'll face when buying a DVD drive is whether to buy a recordable one that will let you record data, music, and movies onto DVDs. Unfortunately, no single standard exists for recordable DVDs. Instead, there's an alphabet soup of competing standards, which are not all compatible with one another. If you record a DVD using your DVD drive, you might not be able to use or play it on another system's DVD drive. The upshot is this: If you do decide to buy a recordable DVD drive, don't assume anyone except you will be able to use the DVD you record.

That having been said, the standard that currently seems to be gaining the most momentum is *DVD+RW*, which lets you record onto a DVD disk and then rerecord onto the disk as well. So, if you do opt to get a recordable DVD drive, your best bet is to buy one that adheres to that standard. Still, you can't ensure that others will be able to read the DVD you record.

How a DVD Drive Works

Graphics card —————————

Some decoder cards attach to your existing graphics card, whereas others don't. You have to check your drive's documentation to see whether yours needs to attach to your graphics card. Some graphics cards have DVD decoders built into them. And for a number of graphics cards, you can buy a special DVD decoder daughterboard to plug into the card.

Decoder card —————————

A DVD drive can play DVD movies and computer DVDs. For the drive to play movies, it requires a decoder, or decoder card, which also makes the video display smoothly. This decoder is a separate device from the SCSI or EIDE controller and requires a separate connection to your computer. It doesn't replace your normal graphics card, so if you have a graphics card, use it along with the decoder. Your monitor plugs directly into the decoder card. If your graphics card includes a DVD decoder, however, keep the monitor attached to the graphics card because no separate decoder is needed.

Typically, if no decoder is present, a software DVD player will have to be used. On systems with only a software player/decoder, you will require at least a 400MHz CPU, and a 700MHz CPU or better would provide more-desirable playback.

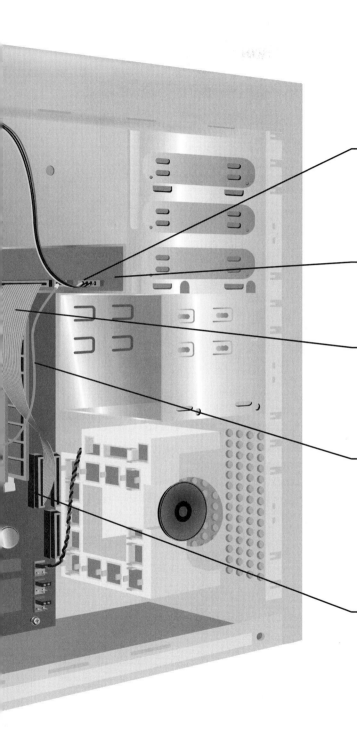

Power connector

The DVD drive gets its power from the power supply, to which it connects via a cable and a connector that plugs into the drive. The power connector is notched so that it can be connected only one way. Use the larger 4-pin connector for power.

DVD drive

The DVD drive fits into a 5 1/2" drive bay on a computer.

Ribbon cable

The controller sends and receives information to and from the DVD drive via a 40-pin ribbon cable. A connector at each end of the cable plugs into the DVD drive and into the controller.

Decoder cable

The DVD drive often connects to a DVD decoder card via a cable. The decoder card makes the video display smoothly, among other features, and allows you to play DVD movies on your computer. The decoder cable looks different from a normal ribbon cable that connects to the SCSI or EIDE controller. It might look like a standard CD audio cable or like a small ribbon cable.

Controller

IDE/EIDE or SCSI controllers inside the computer send instructions back and forth between the components of your PC and the DVD drive, instructing the DVD to send data to the PC and receive instructions from it.

How to Install a DVD Drive

Installing a DVD drive is a bit more complicated than installing other drives because you need to install a DVD decoder card as well.

To install a new DVD drive, you'll need the new drive, the decoder card, a free drive bay, and a screwdriver. Before you begin, turn off your PC and open the case as outlined in "How to Open the Case" in Chapter 13, "Performing Computer Maintenance."

① Find an Empty Slot

First, you'll install the decoder card. To do that, you need an empty PCI slot on your PC. Check your system's documentation if you're not sure whether you have one.

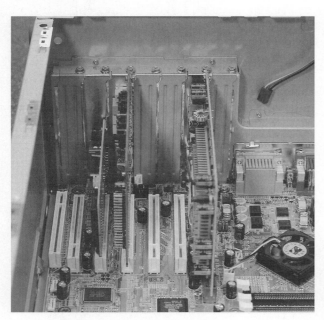

② Install the DVD Decoder Card

Install the DVD decoder card into the empty PCI slot inside your PC. The slot should be a PCI slot. For details on how to install a card, turn to "How to Install a Basic Card" in Chapter 13.

③ Connect the Sound Card

Each DVD kit and decoder card is different. Yours might or might not need to be attached to a sound board. Check your documentation, and if it needs to be, attach the cable from the DVD decoder card to your sound card.

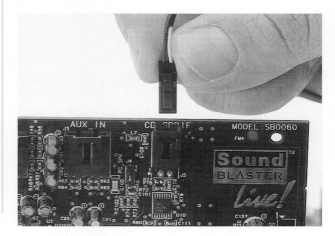

④ Connect Your Monitor

Some DVD decoder cards must be connected to your existing graphics card. Check your DVD drive's documentation. If required, disconnect the monitor cable from your graphics card. Next, connect one end of a cable provided with the kit to the **VGA In** port on the DVD board, and connect the other end to your graphics card (in the spot the monitor was formerly plugged in). Then, connect the monitor to the DVD's **VGA Out** port. If your DVD decoder board doesn't require a connection to your graphics card, don't do anything.

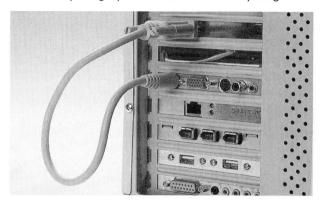

⑤ Find a Free Bay

To install a DVD drive, you need a free drive bay, cable connector, and power connector. Verify that you have the right sized bay to match your DVD drive and that you have a free ribbon cable and power connector. You might need to install railings to fit the drive to your PC. Check your drive documentation for details.

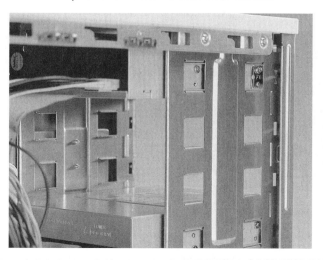

⑥ Set Jumpers

A DVD drive can be either a master or a slave. As a general rule, the drive should be the slave. Set the jumpers to the proper setting. Check your DVD documentation to see how.

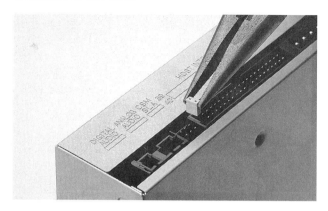

⑦ Slide In and Secure the Drive

Slide the drive into the drive bay and secure it via screws in the drive bay or railings. Secure all the screws so that the drive is held firmly in place, but don't overtighten or strip the screws.

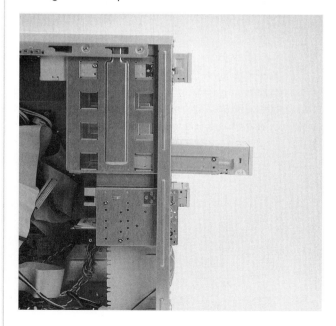

❽ Connect the Cables

Connect the data cable (the wide, 40-pin ribbon cable that runs from an IDE card, a motherboard, or a sound card) to your DVD drive. The ribbon cable has a stripe on one side, indicating that that side connects to pin 1 on the DVD drive. Pin 1 is usually nearest to the power connector.

❾ Connect the Power Cable

Connect a power cable from your power supply to your DVD drive. The power connector on the cable will be notched, as will the space on the DVD drive, meaning it can be plugged in only one way.

❿ Connect the Decoder Card

Connect the DVD drive to the DVD decoder card by using the cable supplied in the DVD drive kit. It's possible to have more than one cable, depending on your kit. Check the documentation.

⓫ Attach Speaker and TV-Out Cables

You can use surround sound speakers with your DVD drive, and you can also play DVDs on your computer and route them through your TV to watch DVD movies. To do this, attach the speaker cables and TV-out cables to the DVD decoder drive via the connections on the back of the card. Depending on your drive, you might instead run a cable from the drive to the video card (if it has an onboard decoder) and then from the video card to the sound card.

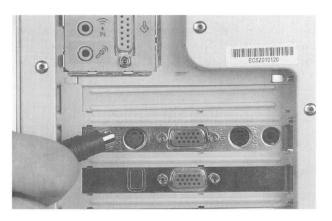

Close the Case and Install Software

After ensuring that everything is secure, close your PC, plug the power cable back in, and turn on the computer. Your DVD drive should be recognized automatically when you start it up, but you may need to install drivers for your decoder card. If you don't know how to install drivers, turn to "How to Install Hardware Drivers" in Chapter 13. You might also need to install DVD software from the manufacturer's disk. Do that after installing any drivers.

Watch Out!

- Ensure your cables reach from your power supply and controller to your DVD drive's future location.
- If you have playback problems when trying to play a DVD, try using different DVD software than that shipped with your drive. You can find DVD software at download sites on the Internet or in retail stores.

How-to Hint

- Ensure that all the cable connectors are tight before putting the case back on your PC.
- When plugging the ribbon cable into your DVD drive, ensure that the side with the stripe lines up with pin 1 on the DVD drive. The pin should be labeled.
- Make sure that you know whether you need to attach your DVD decoder card to your graphics card. If you do, follow the directions carefully when hooking it up.
- If you want to play DVD movies, make sure your DVD player comes with software for doing that.

Task

34

Installing a Removable Drive

To back up your hard disk or to share large amounts of data with other people or computers, the best thing you can do is to install a removable drive. Removable drives enable you to store hundreds of megabytes (MB) of data—even a gigabyte (GB) or more—onto a single floppy-size disk or other medium.

Of the several popular kinds of removable drives, the most popular are made by Iomega. Iomega's best-known drive is the Zip drive, which can hold up to 250MB of data, depending on the model. The Jaz drive can hold even more data: up to 2GB.

This chapter shows how to install Zip drives. Jaz drives install similarly, so if you need to install one of those, this chapter is still a good starting point.

Upgrade Advisor

Deciding which removable drive to buy is not a difficult matter. Base your decision on how much removable storage you need and how much you're willing to pay.

If you're only storing and backing up data, and that data doesn't include many multimedia files, MP3 and other music files, and large graphics, your best economic bet will be a relatively small capacity drive, such as Iomega's Zip drive. It holds 250MB, but generally you'll compress the files before storing them, so you can probably get 400MB of data or more onto the disk after you compress the data. Not only are the Zip drives themselves less expensive than larger capacity drives, but the disks on which you store data are less expensive than those that hold more data. For example, you can often buy 250MB Zip disks for between $15 and $20, whereas a 2GB Jaz disk can cost $125.

If you're interested in a money-saving option for backing up your PC, you can use a CD-RW drive because rewriteable CDs cost approximately $2 each and hold 650 MB of data.

Because of the price difference, you should buy a more expensive Jaz drive only if you need the greater capacity—for example, backing up a PC, including its operating system and applications.

How a Removable
Drive Works

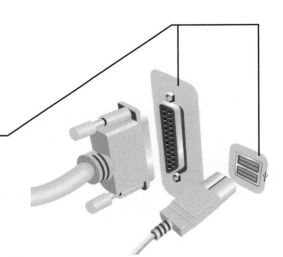

Connectors

Zip drives attach to your computer in a number of ways. Some attach to the parallel port of your PC; others attach via USB ports; and others attach via SCSI and EIDE connectors.

Zip disk

A disk for an Iomega Zip drive looks similar to a floppy disk. It's about the same size, although slightly thicker. But the Zip drive has many times the capacity of a normal floppy disk—up to 250MB. Other removable drives, such as Jaz, hold more data, up to 2GB.

Cookie

Inside the disk is a magnetic-coated Mylar disk called a *cookie*. It's protected by a hard plastic shell with a metal plate that slides open to give read/write heads access to the cookie. Special magnetic particles that allow the cookie to hold more data than a normal floppy drive coat it. The heads on a Zip drive are much smaller than those on a floppy drive, allowing more data tracks to be used per inch and increasing the disk's storage capacity.

Metal shield

When you insert a Zip disk, a metal shield in the drive slides to one side to expose a small opening along the edge of the plastic case. A motor, spinning at 3,000rpm, engages a metal hub in the cookie. The hole in the disk's casing matches up with a hole in the housing that surrounds the read/write heads, which reduces the damage done to the cookie by dust and other airborne contaminants.

Read/write heads

Two read/write heads, one for each side of the cookie, read and write data to the Zip drive. The heads touch the cookie, but very lightly as compared to a floppy drive (and unlike hard drive heads, which never touch the surface of the disk). Because the heads touch the Zip disk lightly, the cookie experiences less wear and tear, and a higher spin rate can occur.

How to Install an External Zip Drive

One of the least complicated ways to install a Zip drive is to install one on your parallel port. Then, when you want to transfer data to or from the drive, data is sent over your parallel port. If you want to use a printer, you'll also have to install a special pass-through cable provided with the drive. You can also install a USB Zip drive. To learn how to install USB devices, see Chapter 21, "Installing USB and FireWire Devices."

When installing a parallel port Zip drive, it's a good idea to first turn off all power to your computer and its peripherals, including the printer and the monitor. You won't need any special tools for installing an external Zip drive, just the drive itself.

1 Connect Cable to the Zip Drive

A cable will come with your Zip drive. Look for the proper end and connect it to the Zip connector on the back of your Zip drive.

2 Connect the Other End to PC

The parallel port is what your printer plugs in to and is usually larger than the serial port on your PC. It is often labeled with a picture of a printer.

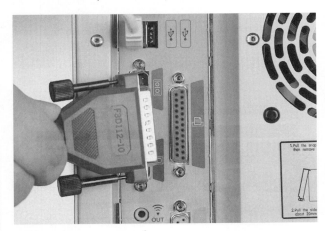

3 Attach Your Printer

To use your printer as well as your Zip drive, attach the cable provided to the pass-through connector. Attach one end of the supplied cable to your Zip drive, and the other end to your printer. You can now use your Zip drive as well as your printer.

4 Connect the Power Supply

The Zip drive connects to a normal wall outlet or a power strip. After you've connected it, turn it on.

5 Turn On Your PC

When you turn on your computer, Windows will know new hardware has been added. If, when you turn on your PC, it doesn't automatically recognize that new hardware has been added, tell your computer that new hardware is present. To add the new hardware, first go to the Windows Control Panel by clicking the **Start** button and selecting **Settings**, **Control Panel**. Double-click **Add New Hardware**. A wizard will launch and guide you through the installation process.

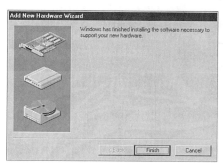

6 Install Software

You still need software to use your new drive. Put the Zip CD-ROM in your CD drive. The installation software should automatically start. If it doesn't, run `Setup.exe` from the disks or CD-ROM supplied with the Zip drive. When you install the software, you install everything you need to use the Zip drive, and your computer will automatically recognize the Zip drive.

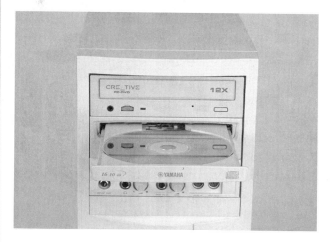

Watch Out!

- If you are having difficulty printing after installing the external Zip drive, your printer might not be compatible with the pass-through port. Refer to the owner's manual.

How-to Hint

- Keep the Zip drive power on when you use your printer. It must be powered for the pass-through connector to work.
- Ensure that the power supply connector is plugged tightly into the Zip drive.
- It's a good idea to use the latest drivers and software for your Zip drive. Go to the Iomega Web site at **www.iomega.com** for the latest drivers and software.

How to Install an Internal Zip Drive

If you prefer, you can install an internal Zip drive instead of installing it externally via your parallel port. How you install it varies slightly depending on how your hard disk and CD drive are installed in your computer (and depending on whether you have a CD drive). In this instance, we'll assume that you're installing a Zip drive into a computer that has a hard drive and a CD drive and that each of those drives are attached to their own channel on the controller. If your setup is different, check your Zip drive's documentation on how to install it. Before you begin, turn off your PC and open the case as outlined in the section "How to Open the Case" in Chapter 13, "Performing Computer Maintenance."

❶ Find a Free Bay

To install an internal Zip drive, you need a free drive bay, cable connector, and power connector. Verify that you have the right sized bay to match your drive and that you have a free ribbon cable and power connector. You might need to install railings to fit the drive to your PC. Check your drive documentation for details.

❷ Set Jumpers

You install the Zip drive as a slave to the existing CD drive, which is a master. The Zip drive should come from the factory set as a slave, but to be sure, check the jumper settings. To be set as a slave, the drive should have no jumper blocks on the back. In some cases, the jumpers will be across the two middle pins. Check the documentation to verify which way it should be to be set as a slave.

❸ Slide In and Secure the Drive

Slide the drive into the drive bay, and secure it with screws in the drive bay or railings. Secure the screws so that the drive is held firmly in place, but don't over-tighten or strip the screws.

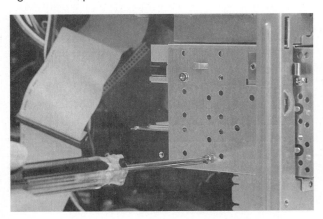

④ Remove Cable from CD Drive

Your CD drive connects to the IDE controller on the motherboard via a wide, 40-pin ribbon cable. Disconnect that cable from the CD drive, and then disconnect the cable from the IDE controller on the motherboard. Put the cable aside; you won't need it.

⑤ Connect the Cables

Now connect both your Zip drive and your CD drive to the controller on the motherboard with the 40-pin ribbon cable that came with your Zip drive. Look for the end of the cable farthest from the middle connector, and plug that end into the controller. Plug the ribbon's middle connector into the CD drive and the final connector into the Zip drive. In all cases, make sure that pin 1 on the connector, indicated by a stripe on the cable, connects to pin 1 on the drive or controller. Also connect the power supply cable.

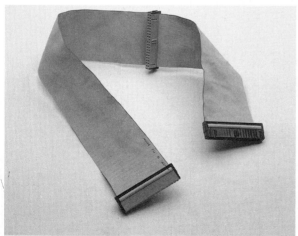

⑥ Close the Case and Install Software

After checking that everything is secure, close your PC, plug the power cable back in, and turn it on. When you turn on your computer, Windows will know new hardware has been added. If, when you turn on your PC, it doesn't automatically recognize that new hardware has been added, you can tell your computer that new hardware is present. To add the new hardware, first go to the Windows Control Panel by clicking the **Start** button and selecting **Settings**, **Control Panel**. Double-click **Add New Hardware**. A wizard will launch and guide you through the installation process. You still need software to use your new drive. Put the Zip CD-ROM in your CD drive. It should automatically start the installation software. If it doesn't, run `Setup.exe` from the disks or CD-ROM supplied with the Zip drive. When you install the software, you install everything you need to use the Zip drive, and your computer will automatically recognize it.

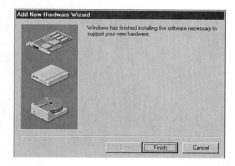

Watch Out!

- Your CD drive should be set as a master. Check its documentation to be sure.

How-to Hint

- It's best to install your Zip drive to the secondary IDE channel—not the same one your hard drive is on.
- Make sure all the cables are connected tightly.

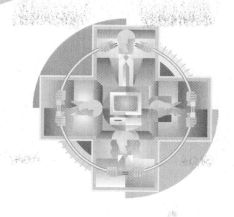

35

Installing a Home Network

These days, many homes have not just one computer in them, but two, three, and sometimes even more. The problem with having multiple computers in a home is that they can't communicate with one another or share devices such as printers if they are not connected by a network. An even bigger problem is that the computers can't share a high-speed Internet connection, such as a cable modem or DSL modem, because those devices allow only one computer to plug into them.

A home network can enable several computers to share a single high-speed Internet connection, as well as enable them to share devices such as printers. Many types of home networks can be set up, but the most common and most useful one—especially for sharing a high-speed Internet connection—is one that uses a hub/router that all the computers plug into. To set up a home network, as you'll see in this chapter, you must install network cards in each computer and then connect the computers to a hub/router using special cabling called Ethernet cable.

Upgrade Advisor

A home network requires that you install a central hub/router and a network card in each of the computers that you will network. These hub/routers are available inexpensively in any computer store or over the Internet. If you don't yet have network cards for your computers, you might be able to save money by buying a home networking kit, which contains both the hub/router as well as network cards. You don't have to buy a kit, however. You can also buy the hub/router and the network cards separately.

If you buy the cards separately, buy a PCI network card instead of an ISA network card because PCI cards are much easier to set up. Also, the most common network cards—and network hub/routers—are sold in 10Mb and 100Mb speeds. Match the speed of the card you buy to the hub/router you buy.

One of the biggest hurdles in setting up a home network isn't in installing the hub/router or the network cards—it's in the cables connecting them all. If your computers are all in a single room, it's simple to run cables between them and the hub/router. But if you have computers in separate rooms, or on separate floors of your house, running the cables can become problematic. You might have to drill through walls or floors. If so, you should consider hiring an electrician to run cables for you. Or, you might instead prefer to buy and install a wireless network, as outlined later in this chapter.

How Home Networks Work

Internet

Cable modem

Firewall

When a network is connected to the Internet via a high-speed connection such as a cable modem or DSL modem, it's vulnerable to hackers. To keep hackers out, a firewall is used. The firewall stops any unauthorized access to the network or any computers on the network. A firewall can be software or a combination of hardware and software.

Firewall

Hub/router

TCP/IP address sharing

A network hub/router can enable several computers to share an Internet connection, such as a high-speed cable modem or DSL modem. One way it does this is by allowing several computers to share a TCP/IP address, sometimes called an Internet address. To the rest of the Internet, every computer on the network looks as if it has the same Internet address—which is why the computers can all share the connection. But inside the network, the hub/router gives each computer a different internal address.

Network hub/router

The heart of a home network is the network hub/router—a device that connects PCs with one another and lets them communicate and share resources, such as a high-speed connection to the Internet via a cable modem. The hub physically connects all the PCs to one another, whereas the router connects the network to the Internet. Although hubs and routers can be sold separately, for many home networks, they are both contained in the same device, often combined with similar devices known as switches and gateways. Typically, the hub/router connects to PCs via Ethernet cable.

Printer sharing

One reason for setting up a home network is to enable several computers to share a single printer. The printer is attached to a single PC. Other PCs on the network can send a request to use the printer. The request goes through the hub/router and is then routed to the PC attached to the printer. The printer then prints out what was requested, just as if the local PC were printing it.

Network card

To be on a network, a computer needs a network card (sometimes called a NIC for "network interface card"). The computer sends and receives requests for data and other services through the network card. The network card is connected to the Ethernet cable.

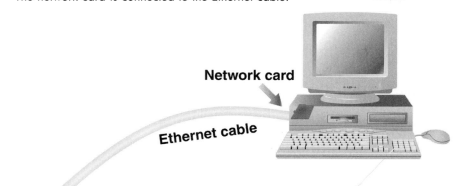

Network card

Ethernet cable

Ethernet cable

Connecting the computers to the hub is special Ethernet cable, made up of a type of wiring that enables computers to communicate with each other over high speeds.

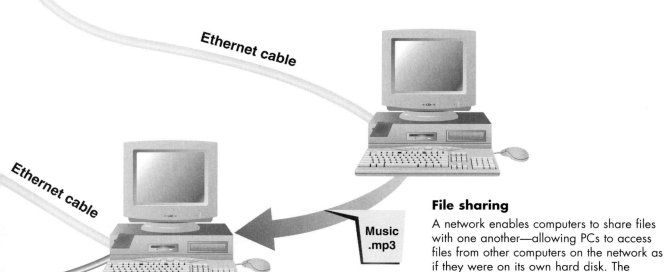

Ethernet cable

Ethernet cable

Music .mp3

File sharing

A network enables computers to share files with one another—allowing PCs to access files from other computers on the network as if they were on its own hard disk. The request goes through the hub/router and is then routed to the PC whose files the first computer wants to share. The first computer can then access those files just as if they were on its own hard disk.

How to Install a Network Card

For you to be able to set up a home network, each of the computers you want to connect must have a network card installed in it. You connect the network cards to your home network hub/router with an Ethernet cable. Before you can do that, though, you first must install a network card in each computer. (In some instances your PC might already have a network connection. In that case you won't need to install a network card. Check your system's documentation for details.) You can buy a variety of network cards and cabling for a home network. The most reliable and highest speed are Ethernet cards and cables, so that's what you'll learn to install in this task.

1 Consider a USB Device

USB network devices, sometimes called USB cards, have become affordable and can be easier to install than internal PCI cards because you don't have to take off the computer's case to install them. If you don't want to take off your computer's case, consider buying a USB network device. But be aware that there could be problems if you're using the network at the same time as you use some USB devices that require high-speed data transfers, such as a USB CD-RW drive. By the way, the USB "card" isn't a card in the sense that it installs inside your PC; it installs externally like other USB devices.

2 Install the Card

If you're installing a PCI card instead of a USB network device, follow the steps outlined in "How to Install a Basic Card," in Chapter 13, "Performing Computer Maintenance," to take off the case, install the card, and then restart you computer.

3 Check the Card Configuration

To ensure that your network card has been installed properly, check the Device Manager. Right-click **My Computer**, select **Properties**, and click the **Device Manager** tab. Scroll down until you see **Network Adapters** and make sure no yellow ! or red X is next to your network card.

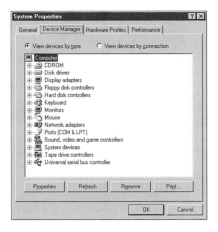

④ Make Sure TCP/IP Is Enabled

To use the Internet, and even to use many networks, your computer needs to use a networking protocol called TCP/IP. To ensure it's enabled, right-click the **Network Neighborhood** icon and select **Properties**. Then, scroll through the list and find your network card. When you find it, highlight it, click **Properties**, click the **Bindings** tab, and make sure there is a check next to the TCP/IP entry. If there isn't, check the entry and follow the instructions for enabling TCP/IP.

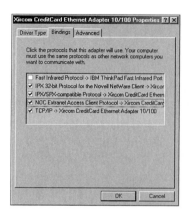

⑤ Configure TCP/IP Properly

After TCP/IP is enabled, you need to ensure that it's properly configured. To do that, right-click the **Network Neighborhood** icon and select **Properties**. Then, scroll through the list and find an entry that reads **TCP/IP ->** followed by the name of your network card. When you find it, highlight it, click **Properties**, and then click the **IP Address** tab. Make sure the **Obtain an IP Address Automatically** radio button is selected.

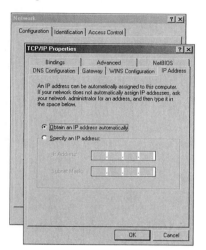

Watch Out!

- Be sure the network card is seated firmly—if it isn't, you won't be able to connect your PC to your home network.

- Don't press too hard when inserting the network card because you could damage the card or motherboard.

- Go to the network card manufacturer's Web site and download the latest drivers for the card.

How to Connect the Network

You can install many types of home networks, but the best one for most homes that plan to use a network for sharing a cable modem or DSL modem is one that uses a combination hub and router. Each PC can then connect to the Internet through a cable modem or DSL modem by way of the hub/router. First, you must set up the hub/router and connect PCs to it. That's what we'll cover in this section. In the next section, you'll learn how to connect your network to the Internet so your computers can share an Internet connection.

❶ Plan Your Network

Before installing any hardware, decide where you want to place the hub/router and measure the distance between each computer and the hub/router. Make sure you have enough cable to reach between them. If your computers will be in different rooms, determine how you will run cable between the rooms. Try to keep your hub/router close to your cable modem or DSL modem so they can be easily connected. If you have problems running cable, install a wireless network instead, as outlined later in this chapter.

❷ Connect the Hub/Router

Power off any of the computers you plan to connect to your home network. Then turn on the hub/router's power. For each computer you plan to network, plug an Ethernet cable into the port on the hub/router, while the computer is off, and then connect the other end of each cable to the network card on each computer. Turn on the power for each of the PCs you've connected to the network. To ensure that all the connections are working, look at the lights on the hub/router and on the network cards on the PCs. If all are properly connected, a green light should be visible on each device. If they don't all have green lights, a problem might exist, so check the cables and connections.

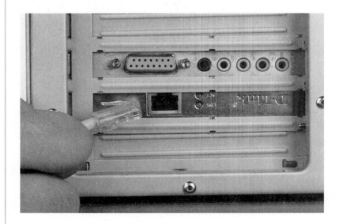

❸ Enable File and Printer Sharing

To share your PCs and printer on your network, you must enable file and printer sharing. For each computer, from the **Control Panel**, double-click **Network** and click **File and Print Sharing**. From the screen that appears, check the boxes that will let you share files and a printer; then click on **OK** twice. Your computer will install new drivers, and when a screen appears asking if you want your computer to restart, click Yes.

4 Share Your Drive

Now you have to specify which drives to share with other PCs on the network. For each computer, start Windows Explorer and right-click on the drive you want to share. Select **Properties,** the **Sharing** tab, **Shared As** and select how you want to share the drive. You can give people read-only access to the drive; you can give them full access to the drive; or you can password-enable the drive. Fill in the information, and click **OK**.

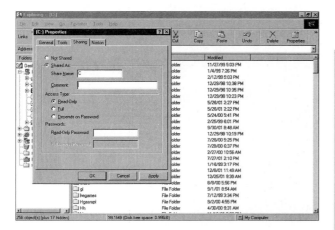

5 Explore Your Network

You should now be able to connect to other computers on your home network. Double-click the **Network Neighborhood** on the desktop, and you'll see other computers connected to the network.

6 Troubleshoot Any Problems

If all your PCs don't show up on the network, check that the cables are all securely connected, the hub/router is plugged in, and its power is turned on. If that doesn't help, turn off the hub/router and PCs and make sure the network cards you installed are seated tightly.

Watch Out!

- Be sure to use Ethernet cable and not phone line cable when putting together your network. If you use telephone line, the network won't work.

- When you first turn on your hub/router and PCs attached to it, wait a few minutes before using Network Neighborhood or My Network Places. It can take a while after the computers boot up for them all to talk to one another.

- If you want to allow PCs to share printers and other devices such as scanners, you must designate them as shared devices. Check your hub/router's documentation or Windows documentation to see how to do this. However, you should not use file sharing and printer sharing if you're connecting your network to the Internet because hackers could then possibly hack into your computers.

How to Share Your Internet Access

After the network is running, you connect it to a cable modem or DSL modem so that all the computers on your network can share a single Internet connection. In this section, you will see how to connect using a cable modem. Connecting via a DSL is similar and often identical, but not always, so check with your DSL provider about how to connect a home network to a DSL modem.

❶ Get the Hub/Router's MAC Address

Many cable companies require that you give them what's called the MAC address of a hub/router before your network can access the Internet. You'll generally find the MAC address in your router's main setup screen. Make sure that you find the WAN MAC address, not the LAN MAC address. If you provide the LAN MAC address, you won't be able to access the Internet. Write down the MAC address number, and then call your cable company and provide it to them. By the way, your network card and your cable modem also have MAC addresses. Don't confuse those with the hub/router's MAC address.

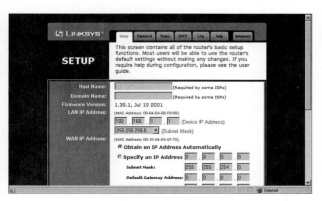

❷ Get an IP Address

In your hub/router's setup screen, be sure that you've enabled your network to get an IP address automatically from your cable company. The choice should read something like **Obtain an IP Address Automatically**.

❸ Power Down Your Cable Modem

Either find the on/off switch and switch it off, or if it doesn't have one, unplug the power cable. Wait at least 5 minutes before turning it back on. If you don't do this, the cable company's network won't recognize your network, and you won't be able to get Internet access.

4 Connect Your Cable Modem or DSL Modem

Look for a port on the hub/router called the Cascade Port, Uplink Port, or WAN Port and connect an Ethernet cable to it. Then connect the other end of the Ethernet cable to your cable modem. If a switch labeled "Cascade" is near the port, be sure it is set to the Cascade position. When that's done, power on your cable modem.

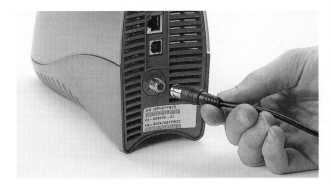

5 Verify Internet Connection

Each of the computers on the network should now be capable of accessing the Internet. If you have a problem getting connected to the Internet, first check that TCP/IP is installed properly, as outlined in the previous illustration. Then, check with your cable company for help troubleshooting the problem.

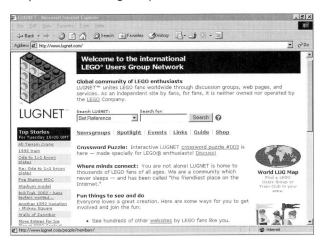

6 Install a Firewall

When you connect your network to the Internet, you potentially open it up to hackers. To protect your network and computers, install a firewall on your hub/router. Your hub/router should come with firewall software. Read the documentation to learn how to install it. Often the firewall is installed automatically, without you having to do anything.

How-to Hint

- You might have to pay extra for connecting your network of several computers to a cable modem. Some cable companies require that you pay more money if you connect a home network to a cable modem rather than connecting a single computer.

- Some hub/routers can mimic an existing MAC address that you've already given to your cable company, so you won't have to call them to give them a new MAC address. If you had to give the cable company a MAC address when connecting a computer, find that MAC address and see whether your hub/router has a MAC address cloning feature. If so, it might be on an Advanced tab in the Setup menu.

Watch Out!

- Check with your cable company or DSL provider before installing a home network in which several PCs will share an Internet connection. Some companies have restrictions or technical information you need before you can install such a network.

How Wireless Networks Work

Wireless access point (base station)

The heart of a wireless network is the wireless access point, also called base station or gateway. It is a hub/router that connects PCs with one another and lets them communicate and share resources, such as a high-speed connection to the Internet via a cable modem. It communicates using the 802.11 wireless communications protocol commonly called *Wi-Fi*. A small radio transceiver access point sends and receives data via RF frequencies in the 2.4GHz range.

Internet access

To allow people on the wireless network to use the Internet, the network must be connected to the Internet in some way. Typically in a home wireless network, the base station connects via Ethernet cable to a cable modem or DSL modem to get Internet access.

Encryption

It's possible for snoopers to read all the data being sent across a wireless network simply by using a wireless network card and special software. To combat meddlers, wireless networks can use encryption, a way to scramble data so that snoopers can't read it. The same *encryption key*, a combination of letters and numbers, needs to be used by the base station and the network cards. The three levels of encryption are 40-bit (called Wired Equivalent Privacy), 64-bit, and 128-bit. 128-bit encryption is more secure, but hardware using that level of encryption is typically more expensive than hardware using 64-bit and 40-bit encryption.

Wireless channels

The base station and wireless cards can communicate with each other over a number of different wireless communications channels. Unless each is told to communicate over the same channel, the network won't function.

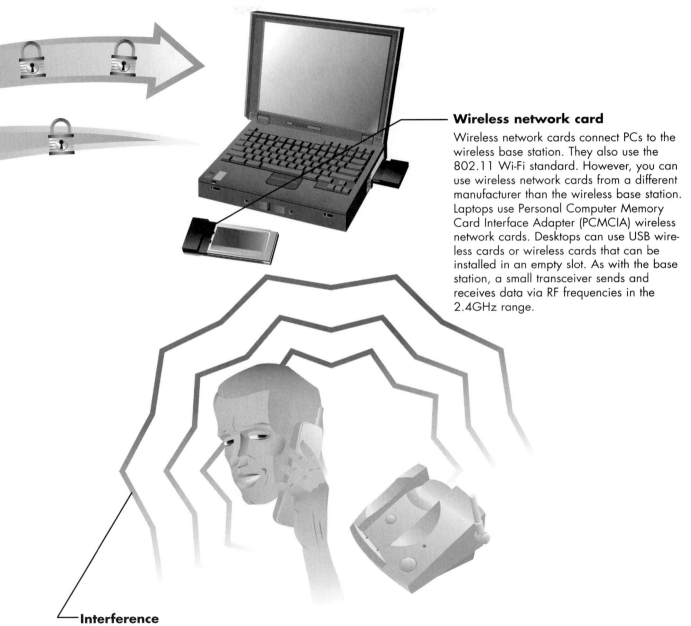

Wireless network card

Wireless network cards connect PCs to the wireless base station. They also use the 802.11 Wi-Fi standard. However, you can use wireless network cards from a different manufacturer than the wireless base station. Laptops use Personal Computer Memory Card Interface Adapter (PCMCIA) wireless network cards. Desktops can use USB wireless cards or wireless cards that can be installed in an empty slot. As with the base station, a small transceiver sends and receives data via RF frequencies in the 2.4GHz range.

Interference

Home networks aren't the only devices that communicate via RF in the 2.4GHz range. So do cordless telephones, among other devices. This results in the possibility of interference between the network and other devices. If this happens, network devices and other devices should be separated from one another. Sometimes changing the channel over which the base station and wireless cards communicate can solve the problem as well.

How to Install a Wireless Network

If you already have a home network and want to add wireless capabilities, you don't need to throw away your existing network. You can instead buy a wireless access point: You leave your existing network as is and plug the wireless access point into the uplink port on the network. You then set up computers to communicate wirelessly with the access point.

❶ Buy the Right Kit

While you can mix and match wireless base stations and network cards from different manufacturers, the easiest and most economical route when installing a network from scratch is buying a wireless network kit from a manufacturer such as Orinoco. Be sure to buy the right kit: If setting up a network of laptops, make sure all the cards are PC Cards, and if mixing laptops and desktops, get a kit with the right number of wireless PC Cards, wireless PCI cards, and wireless USB cards.

❷ Plan Your Network

Decide where to put the base station, preferably somewhere central to the locations of all the computers that will connect to it. That way, the wireless coverage will be the most consistent. Decide which computer will have primary control over the base station. That computer will get more software installed on it than the other computers on the network.

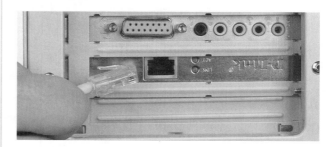

❸ Plug In the Base Station

In some base stations, you may have to take off a plastic casing in order to find the plug for the power cord.

4 Install the Software

Put the CD into the computer that will control the base station and run the installation software. This software will let you control the settings of the base station and ensure that they match the settings on each individual wireless network card.

5 Identify Your Network

Many wireless networks require that you specifically identify them in your software to work. Often the identity of the network can be found on a label on the base station. Find the label and type the identity in when prompted.

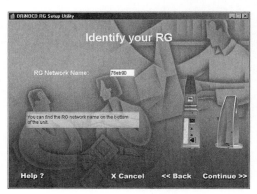

6 Choose Encryption

You should always encrypt data sent across your wireless network because it's possible for people to read every bit of data your network sends and receives if they have a wireless access card and the right software. If you encrypt it, however, your data will be much safer. Make sure you choose the option to encrypt your data. You'll choose an encryption key, essentially a password. Write it down because you'll need to use the same key with your wireless cards.

7 Choose a Channel

Wireless networks can communicate on a number of different channels. By default, a channel might be chosen for you. If so, write it down because you'll need it when installing your network card. If a channel isn't chosen, pick one.

⑧ Install Network Cards

Install a wireless network device on each computer. For information on how to install PC Cards, turn to Chapter 39, "Upgrading Notebook Computers." For information on how to install USB devices, refer to Chapter 21, "Installing USB and FireWire Devices." And for information on how to ensure that the card's network and TCP/IP settings are correct, refer to Task 1, "How to Install a Network Card."

⑨ Set Encryption and Channels

For the cards to communicate with the base station, the encryption and channel settings must be the same as those on the base station. Put in the correct encryption and channel information.

⑩ Test Your Connections

The quality of wireless connections can be affected by many environmental circumstances, including walls and interference from other devices such as cordless phones and microwaves. On each computer, use the software installed with the network card to test the strength of the wireless connection. If you detect problems, try moving the base station and the computers to see if you can make the connections better.

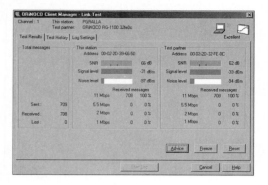

⑪ Share Your Internet Access

Connect the base station to your cable modem or DSL modem with an Ethernet cable. Then follow the instructions in Task 3, "How to Share Your Internet Access," to enable all your computers to share Internet access using the network.

- You could run into problems when enabling encryption if using wireless network cards and base stations from different manufacturers. If you already have a base station, check that the encryption of the wireless card you're considering is compatible with it.

- More than one 802.11 wireless standard exists, and you can't always mix and match wireless network cards and base stations that use different 802.11 standards. The most common 802.11 standard is called 802.11b. Hardware that adheres to the high-speed 802.11g standard will work with 802.11b hardware, but 802.11a, which also adheres to a higher-speed standard, won't work with 802.11b hardware or 802.11g hardware. However, for the foreseeable future, almost all home networks will be built using the 802.11b standard.

Task

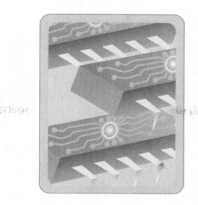

36

Installing a New CPU

The central processing unit (CPU) is essentially the brains of the PC. It does all of the computer's processing. All other things being equal, the faster the CPU, the faster the PC.

Because of that, very often the quickest way to get a faster PC is to upgrade the CPU by taking out your old CPU and putting in a new one. As you'll see in this chapter, doing the actual upgrade itself is straightforward, a matter of opening the case, taking out the old CPU, and installing a new one.

This chapter shows you how you can upgrade your PC's CPU, including how to get a CPU that matches your existing motherboard and installing the CPU itself.

Upgrade Advisor

The key to a successful CPU upgrade is making sure that the CPU you buy matches your motherboard. You must match the CPU you buy to the socket type on your PC. For a description and illustration of the different types of sockets, turn to "How CPUs Work" on the next spread in this chapter. You also have to make sure that the speeds of the front side bus (FSB), also called the system bus, in the CPU and motherboard are compatible. Voltage on the CPU should be compatible with your motherboard.

When upgrading your CPU, be aware that the absolute fastest one can cost several hundred dollars more than one that is only 20% or so slower. Plus, you won't likely notice a dramatic difference between the two. So it's often a good idea to get a slightly "trailing-edge" CPU to save money. Be sure, though, that it's enough of a performance boost over your existing CPU to be worth the price and the bother of an upgrade.

If you want a faster CPU than your motherboard can handle, you can install a new motherboard and then install the CPU onto it. To learn how to install a new motherboard, turn to Chapter 37, "Installing a New Motherboard."

How CPUs Work

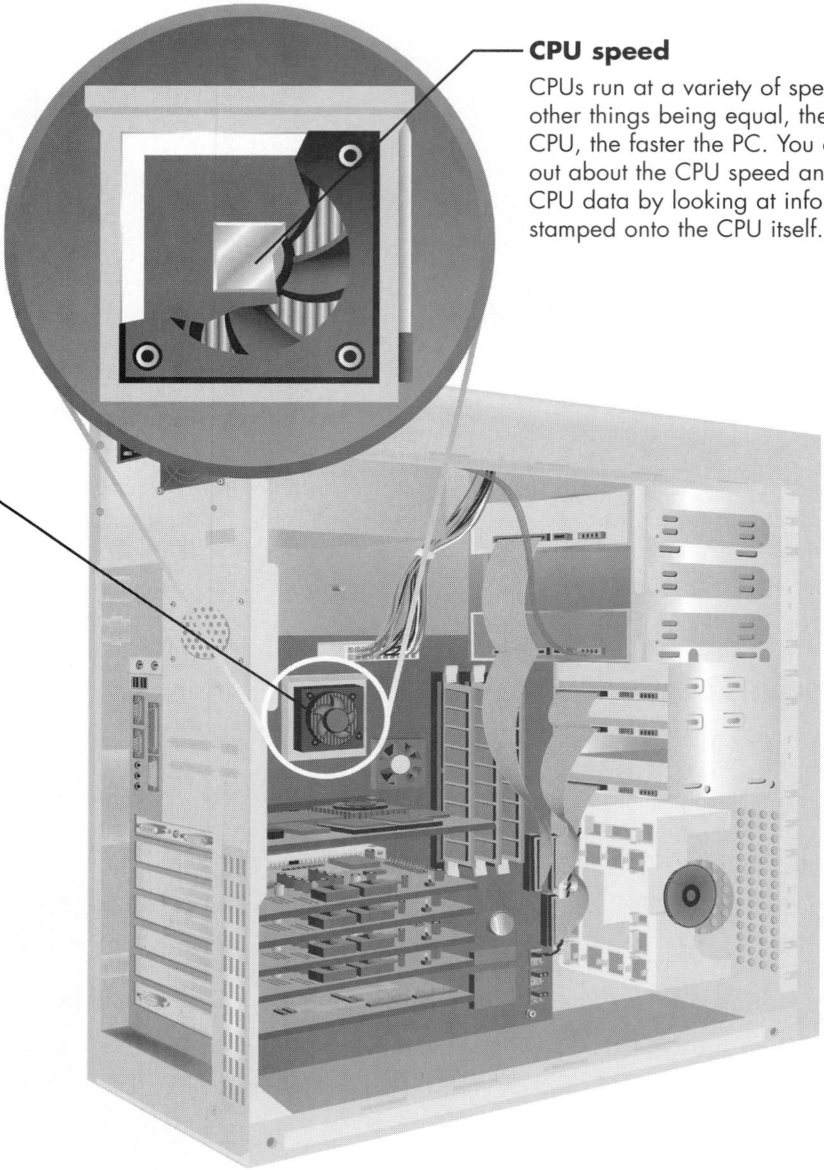

CPU speed

CPUs run at a variety of speeds. All other things being equal, the faster the CPU, the faster the PC. You can find out about the CPU speed and other CPU data by looking at information stamped onto the CPU itself.

CPU

The central processing unit (CPU), such as a Pentium III, Pentium 4, or Celeron chip, is what performs all the computer's calculations and is essentially the brains of your PC. The CPU fits into a CPU socket. The socket and the way the CPU fits into it vary according to the type of CPU. You'll have to buy the specific CPU to match the socket on your PC. So, if you have a type of socket that can accept only a Pentium chip, for example, you won't be able to put a Pentium II into it.

Heatsink and cooling fan

Because CPUs run at such high speeds, they require cooling; otherwise, they'd burn out. Heatsinks and cooling fans, sometimes in combination, cool down the CPU. A heatsink draws heat away from the CPU, much like a radiator cools a car engine. In a passive heatsink, no fan is attached, and it relies on air from the power supply fan to blow across it. In an active heatsink, a cooling fan is attached to it.

Connector types

The CPU connects to the motherboard via a socket or slot. There are many types of sockets and slots. Among the most common are

Socket 423 is for Pentium 4s.

Socket 370 is for Pentium IIIs and Celerons.

Socket 7 is for a variety of CPUs, including early Pentiums and the AMD K6.

Socket A is for AMD Athlons.

Slot 1 and Slot 2 are for Pentium IIs, Celerons, and some Pentium IIIs. These connector types are for CPUs that are packaged into cartridges, which fit into the slots and stand straight up from the motherboard.

Sockets 1, 2, 3, and 6 are for 486s.

Sockets 4, 5, 7, and 8 are for Pentiums and Pentium Pros.

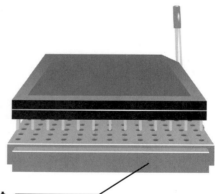

ZIF (zero insertion force) socket

CPUs are installed into their sockets in a variety of ways. The easiest and most common is the ZIF socket, in which a lever holds down the CPU into its socket. To remove the CPU, the lever is released.

Before Upgrading Your CPU

Upgrading your CPU is a bit like giving your PC a brain transplant. It can be a tricky task, but often the most important part is what you need to do before actually doing the upgrade. You need to figure out what kind of CPU your motherboard can handle, what kind of CPU will physically fit in your system, and what kind you'll buy. Before taking these steps, turn off your PC and take off its case, as outlined in "How to Open the Case" in Chapter 13, "Performing Computer Maintenance."

❶ Determine Your CPU Type

To figure out what kind of CPU you now have, check your system case and your system's BIOS. Often, a small sticker on the outside of your case will identify which processor your computer uses. When your PC boots up, your BIOS might flash information telling you the type and speed of the processor. You can also find this information on the System Information screen. To get to it, click the **Start** button, select **Accessories** from the **Programs** menu, and then select **System Information** from the **System Tools** menu.

❷ Find Your Processor

The processor usually is a large, square chip or a large, rectangular case on the motherboard. It also might have a heatsink attached to it. There are often markings that tell you the chip speed as well as other information about the chip. On many Pentiums there are four numbers separated by slashes—for example, 1.5GHz/256/400/1.7V. That tells you that the chip runs at 1.5 gigahertz, has a cache of 256KB, has a bus that runs at 400 megahertz, and uses 1.7 volts of electricity.

❸ Determine CPU Socket Type

CPUs attach to the motherboard using a variety of sockets. Most CPUs are held in by what is called a *zero insertion force (ZIF)* socket, in which a lever is used to take out and insert the CPU. Older PCs might have CPUs that are attached via a *low-insertion force (LIF)* socket, in which many small pins on the bottom of the CPU fit into a grid of holes in the socket.

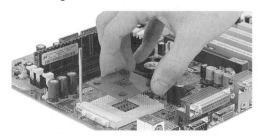

4 Determine Your CPU Upgrade

You'll often be able to upgrade to only a specific speed and make of processor. Check your system or motherboard documentation to see what your system can handle. Whether you can upgrade also depends on whether your system's bus speed can handle the new, faster chip speed. Sometimes, you will set jumpers to make the motherboard handle a faster speed, and other times you might set the system BIOS. You also have to make sure that the voltage of your new CPU matches your motherboard.

5 Consider a RAM Upgrade

Installing a new CPU while using old, slow-speed RAM won't give you the full speed boost you want. Consider buying faster RAM. In some instances the motherboard for your new CPU will require that you buy faster RAM.

6 Consider a BIOS Upgrade

Your BIOS might not be capable of handling your new CPU. Because of that, consider upgrading your BIOS before you install a CPU, especially if you have an older computer. To upgrade a BIOS, turn to the section "How to Install a New BIOS" in Chapter 37.

Watch Out!

- If you're buying a fast CPU to install, make sure you have at least a 300-watt power supply because fast CPUs need a substantial amount of power. Buy and install a new power supply if you have to.

How-to Hint

- Check your computer's or motherboard's manual to see what kind of CPU you can upgrade to.
- Verify that your motherboard is capable of handling the increased clock and bus speed of a faster CPU.
- Make sure that the new CPU you buy will fit into your existing CPU slot.

How to Install a CPU

After you've taken the preliminary steps and bought a new CPU, it's time to do the upgrade. You'll remove your old CPU and put the new one in its place, being sure to attach a cooling fan. Many kinds of CPUs and socket types can be involved in an upgrade, but in this illustration, we will look at the most common type—a CPU with a ZIF socket.

Before taking the steps in this illustration, turn off your PC and take off its case, as outlined in "How to Open the Case" in Chapter 13.

❶ Remove the Heatsink/Fan

The existing CPU will most likely have a heatsink/fan cooling combination attached to it. How you remove it can vary, but commonly you'll release metal tabs at its sides, unplug it from the motherboard, and remove it. If the heatsink/fan has a power connector, note how it is plugged in. Some connect to a power supply power connector, although some newer motherboards include a connector for the heatsink/fan right on the motherboard itself.

❷ Remove the Old CPU

Push the small ZIF lever away to the side of the CPU, and then lift up the lever. That releases the CPU from its socket. You can now lift out the old CPU by hand. If you have an older LIF socket, you'll have to use a CPU extraction tool or a chip puller to take out the CPU.

❸ Insert the New CPU

Put the upgrade CPU into the now-empty slot on the motherboard. It should fit only one way. Align pin 1 on the processor with pin 1 on the socket. Pin 1 is on the corner that lacks the corner pinhole. Align the CPU's pins with the socket's holes and slowly lower the CPU into the socket, making sure that all the pins are lined up properly. Do not force the CPU down into the socket because you could cause damage.

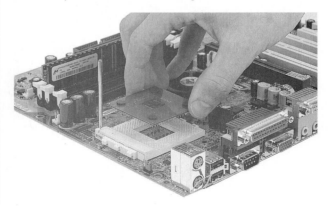

④ Secure the New CPU

Push the ZIF lever all the way down until it latches and the new CPU is securely in place.

⑤ Install the New Heatsink/Fan

Put the new heatsink/fan in place, securing it with the metal tabs at its sides. Be sure to plug in the power connector if it has one. You also might need to use thermal compound to ensure that good contact is made between the CPU and heatsink/fan.

⑥ Set Motherboard Jumpers and Restart

Depending on your motherboard and the speed of your new CPU, you might have to set jumpers on the motherboard so that it recognizes the new CPU speed. (In some instances, you might instead do this by changing the BIOS by using the CMOS setup screen.) Turn on your PC. Because things can go wrong when installing a CPU, turn on your computer before putting the case on, in case you need to reseat the CPU. After everything is working properly, you can close the case.

Watch Out!

- Check that your existing BIOS can handle your new CPU. If not, upgrade the BIOS before installing the new CPU.
- Make sure that pin 1 on your new CPU aligns with pin 1 on the CPU slot.
- Don't "overclock" your system by setting it to run faster than its rated speed. Intel and other chip manufacturers warn that doing so can damage your motherboard, particularly because it might overheat.
- Buy a CPU that comes with a heatsink/fan—if you don't use one, you can burn out your CPU.

Installing a New Motherboard

If you're not happy with your PC's performance but don't want to spend the money to buy an entirely new PC, you can upgrade its motherboard. A new motherboard will let you install a faster CPU and faster RAM and also allow all parts of the computer to communicate faster with each other. It allows them to communicate faster because it contains updated and faster buses, which are the main data highways along which information travels between all your system's components.

This chapter shows you how to upgrade your PC's motherboard and also tells you how to replace the system BIOS. An old BIOS might not support some of the newer hardware available, so if you have an old system, it's a good idea to install a new BIOS.

Upgrade Advisor

When buying a new motherboard, look for one that conforms to the ATX form factor. (First ensure that your case is an ATX case.) ATX is an industry standard, so if you buy that form factor, other common components, such as power supplies, will be compatible with it. However, if you have a computer case that doesn't conform to the ATX standard, you can either buy a nonstandard motherboard or buy a new case. Make sure that your case has enough slot openings to accommodate the number of slots on the motherboard you buy.

If you're planning on replacing your CPU—which as a general rule, you should do if you're upgrading your motherboard—make sure that your motherboard can accommodate the CPU you plan to buy. To learn how to upgrade your CPU, turn to Chapter 36, "Installing a New CPU."

Keep in mind that if you have old cards in your PC that are ISA cards, they might not work with your new motherboard, which will mostly likely have PCI slots. So, if you want to use your old cards, look for a motherboard that has ISA slots. Otherwise, plan on buying new cards.

How Motherboards Work

CPU

The central processing unit is what performs all the computer's calculations and is essentially the brains of your PC. The CPU fits into a CPU socket. The socket and the way that the CPU fits into it can vary according to the type of CPU. You'll have to buy the specific CPU to match the socket on your PC.

Ports

Parallel and serial ports allow data to be sent to and from printers, modems, and similar devices.

Slots

Many devices and add-ins, such as graphics cards and sound cards, connect to slots on the PC's motherboard. These cards plug into what is called the PCI bus on the motherboard.

Motherboard

This is the nervous and skeletal system of the PC, through which all commands pass and into which all parts connect. It is attached to the computer's case by a set of screws. The motherboard, however, shouldn't touch the case itself, so plastic spacers or standoffs sit between the screw and the case, holding the motherboard a fraction of an inch away from the case. In many cases, the standoffs take the place of the screw.

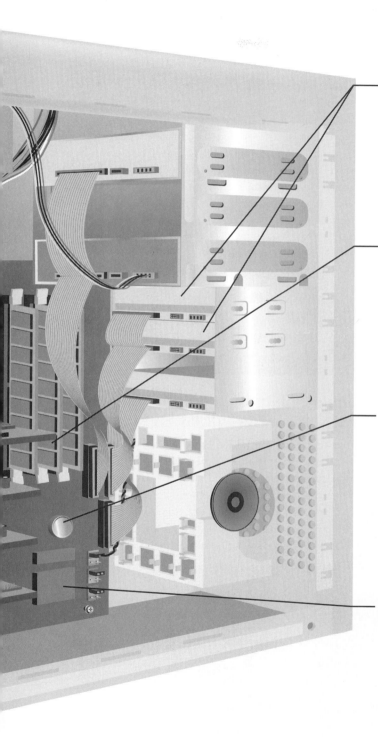

Storage devices

Hard drives, floppy drives, and CD-ROM drives attach to a controller on the motherboard via ribbon cables. Data travels back and forth between the storage devices and the CPU and other computer components along these ribbon cables.

RAM

The motherboard holds the computer's RAM (random access memory) in memory sockets. Many types of memory sockets are available to accommodate the many types of memory. Common ones include DIMMs and RIMMs, although older systems use SIMMs. You'll have to buy the specific memory type (such as DIMMs) to match the memory socket on your PC. For example, DIMMs will fit only into a DIMM socket.

Battery

Your system's CMOS needs a way to be powered, even when the computer is turned off. So, a battery on the motherboard sends a steady stream of electricity to the system's CMOS, even when your computer isn't on. CMOS contains basic information about your computer, such as the kind of hard disk it has. If power to the CMOS went off, it would forget all that information. Old batteries might eventually run out of power, but they can be replaced with a new battery. The battery also keeps system time.

BIOS chip

The basic input/output system (BIOS) handles the most basic tasks of your computer, such as configuring hard disks, transferring data to and from the keyboard, and similar tasks. The BIOS is contained on a BIOS chip on the motherboard. The BIOS can be upgraded by installing special software if it's a flash BIOS or by removing the chip and installing a new one if it's not a flash BIOS.

How to Remove Your Old Motherboard

Before you remove your motherboard, you'll turn off your PC and remove the case. To learn how to do that, turn to "How to Open the Case" in Chapter 13, "Performing Computer Maintenance." You'll be taking a lot of hardware off of your motherboard, and you'll be putting a lot of it onto your new motherboard. To make sure that you've put everything correctly on your new motherboard, it's a good idea to draw a diagram and write notes as you take out your old motherboard. Then, you can refer to it when installing your new motherboard.

If you want more in-depth information about removing cables and connectors, turn to Chapter 38, "Installing a New Power Supply," and the section "How to Remove an Old Drive" in Chapter 13.

① Remove External Connectors

Unplug your mouse, modem, monitor, keyboard, and other external devices connected to your PC or motherboard. Note which serial devices are connected into COM1 or A and COM2 or B, so you can reconnect them in the same way on the new motherboard.

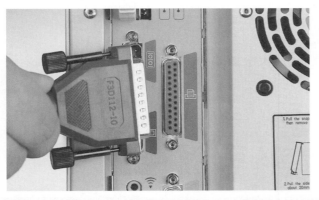

② Unplug Internal Connectors

Ribbon cable runs from your motherboard or from a controller card to devices such as your floppy drive and hard disk drive. Unplug the ribbon's connectors from the motherboard or controller card, but leave the ribbons plugged into the devices such as the hard disk and floppy drives. Finally, unplug the cables that run from the power supply to internal devices and the motherboard.

③ Remove All Cards

Cards are held in place by small Phillips-head screws. Unscrew each, and then pull out the cards by holding the card at each end and pulling them up and out. Put the cards in a safe place, preferably in special antistatic bags so that they are not damaged by static electricity. Keep the screws—you'll need them to attach the cards to your new motherboard.

④ Remove the RAM

If you have memory you plan on reusing, remove it from the old motherboard so that you can put it in the new motherboard. Use your old RAM only if it is fast enough for a new motherboard and compatible with the motherboard. For details on the different kinds of memory and how they attach to a motherboard, turn to Chapter 27, "Adding Memory to Your PC." If you're going to reuse the RAM, put it in an antistatic bag.

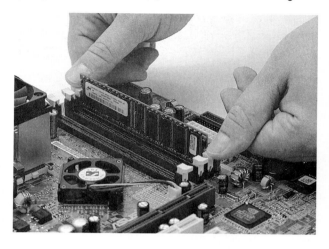

⑤ Take Screws Off Motherboard

Motherboards typically are held in place by screws and plastic standoffs that sit between the motherboard and the case. First, unscrew the screws. Next, remove the standoffs. Pinch their tops with a pair of needlenose pliers and push them through their holes, or lift the motherboard up to release them.

⑥ Remove the Motherboard

You now should be able to remove your motherboard. To remove it, hold its edges and pull it straight off the computer.

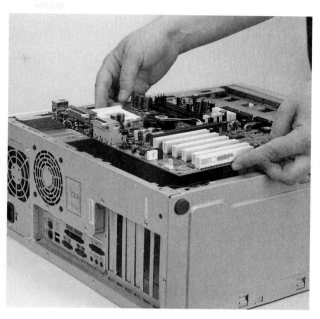

— Watch Out!

- Don't use too much force when removing your old motherboard—you could damage the case.

How-to Hint

- Look for screws that need to be removed under the power supply or behind disk drives.

- After you unplug parallel and serial cables, put masking tape on them and label them to ensure that when you put them back, you put them in the proper place.

- Check your new motherboard's manual to see whether it requires that power supply cables be plugged in differently than when they were attached to your original motherboard.

② How to Install a New Motherboard

After you've chosen the motherboard you want to install, made a diagram of where your components plug into your old motherboard, and removed the old motherboard, it's time to install the new motherboard. Exceedingly important in this procedure is that you attach the connectors properly and tightly.

① Install the CPU

If your new motherboard didn't come with a CPU, you'll have to install it. To learn how to do that, turn to Chapter 36, "Installing a New CPU."

② Install RAM

Put RAM onto your motherboard. Because it's a new motherboard, it will require some form of DIMM or RIMM. Make sure that the RAM is the right type for the motherboard. For more information on how to install RAM, turn to Chapter 27.

③ Screw In the Motherboard

Start by pushing the plastic standoffs into the holes of the motherboard where you had previously taken them out. This will keep the motherboard from touching the case. Then, fit the new motherboard into place. Screw it in, but be careful not to screw it in too tightly because you could crack the motherboard.

4 Connect Cables and Connectors

Connect the cables from the power supply to the motherboard and to devices such as disk activity lights and on/off switches. Also connect the floppy and IDE connectors from your motherboard to your floppy drive, hard drive, CD-ROM drive, and similar devices. Be sure to connect them in the same way that they were connected initially to your motherboard or controller card. Be sure to match up pin 1 correctly.

5 Install the Cards

Put the cards you've removed back into the motherboard's slots, and screw them in with the Phillips-head screws.

6 Connect the External Devices

Plug your mouse, modem, monitor, keyboard, and anything else connected to your PC or motherboard back in. Then, plug your computer back in, turn on your monitor, and turn on your PC. Your computer will go through its normal power on self test (POST). The POST test will indicate whether there are problems with the memory, CPU, video, or other parts of your system. It might take you several reboots before everything is working properly. You also might need to go into the CMOS settings to get it all to work. If problems continue, you might need to install one device at a time to make sure that the operating system recognizes all the devices attached to the motherboard. Before you close the case, you should make sure that everything works. Then, if everything works fine, put the case back on.

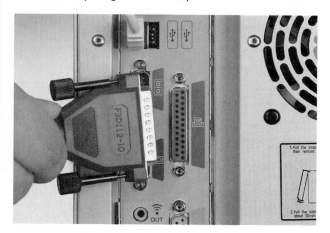

Watch Out!

- Remember to put plastic spacers between the motherboard and the case so that the motherboard doesn't touch the case.

How-to Hint

- When in doubt, follow the user's manual for connecting power and LED cables to a new motherboard.

How to Install a New Battery

Your computer's battery doesn't provide power to run your computer—your power supply does that. Instead, the battery keeps the proper time and date, even when your computer is turned off, and it powers the CMOS so that the CMOS can maintain important information about your computer, such as the type of hard disk it has.

If your battery fails, or even gets low, worse things can happen to your computer than merely forgetting the time and date. Because the CMOS wasn't supplied with the proper amount of power, it might not even recognize that you have a hard disk in your computer. You might get an error message telling you that you have `Invalid Configuration Information`. Here's what you should do to replace your battery.

① Write Down CMOS Settings

You're going to need this information after you install your battery because you will probably have to restore your CMOS settings after installing your battery. Get to the CMOS screen by pressing a special key when your computer starts. The key you press varies according to your computer, but often it is the Delete (Del), F1, or F2 key. Read your computer's documentation to find out how. Also watch your computer as it boots up because there is usually a screen telling you which key to press.

② Open the Case

For details on how to turn it off and open the case, turn to "How to Open the Case" in Chapter 13.

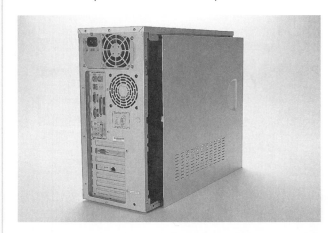

③ Find Your Computer's Battery

The most common type of battery on newer computers is the widely available lithium CR2032 batteries, which are round, are about the size of a quarter. If you have an older computer, it might be AA or AAA alkaline batteries in a battery pack attached to the motherboard via wires. Another type of battery, a real-time clock battery, is small, black, and rectangular and doesn't look like a battery at all.

4 Take Out the Old Battery

Take note of how it's attached to the motherboard so that you'll know how to install a new one. Each battery is removed differently. CR2032 batteries usually fit into a small case on the motherboard. To remove it, you usually pry it up gently from the edge.

5 Insert the New Battery

Place the battery precisely where the old one was. Make sure that the + side is facing properly.

6 Turn On Your Computer

First, put the case back on, plug the computer in, and then turn it on. Don't be alarmed if, when your computer starts up, you get an error message about your system's CMOS settings. In any case, go into your CMOS settings and restore them to what they were originally. You might be lucky and your settings might not have been changed. But in many cases, they will have changed, and you'll have to put them back to what they were originally.

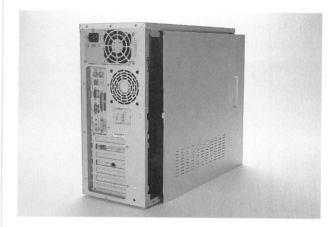

Watch Out!
- Double-check to see that you've put the + connection in the proper place on the motherboard.

How-to Hint
- Match your new battery to your old one—it'll have to fit into the location where your old battery is now plugged in.
- When you take out your old battery, pay attention to how it's connected. That way, you'll know how to put in the new one.

How to Install a New BIOS

Your computer's BIOS (basic input/output system) sits on a chip on your motherboard. It determines vital things about your computer, such as how large a hard disk your computer can handle. An old BIOS won't be able to recognize many of today's newest peripherals. And it won't be able to recognize drives over 8GB.

If you have a "flash" BIOS, you can upgrade your BIOS by running a piece of software. If you don't have a flash BIOS, you'll have to buy a new BIOS chip. When you buy, have at hand the make and model of your computer, as well as any information that comes onto your screen about your BIOS when you start your computer. You can buy new BIOSes online, at computer parts stores, and sometimes at manufacturer sites. A good place to buy BIOSes and get information about BIOSes online is www.firmware.com.

❶ Flash Upgrade BIOS

If your BIOS is flash upgradable, it means that you don't need to remove your old BIOS and install a new one—you'll be able to upgrade it using a piece of software. Go to the manufacturer's site and download the software for upgrading your BIOS. You'll run the software you downloaded to install the flash upgrade. But before installing it, be sure to read and print out the instructions on the Web site for downloading and installing the upgrade. The Web site will also give information on how to know which BIOS version is currently on your PC.

❷ Open the Case

If your BIOS isn't flash upgradable, you'll have to take it out and install a new one. To do that, you'll have to turn off your PC and open the case. For details on how to do that, turn to "How to Open the Case" in Chapter 13.

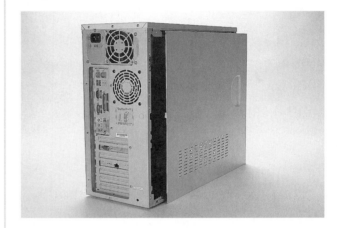

❸ Look for the BIOS Chip

Your system might have from one to five BIOS chips. They usually are small chips with a stick-on label (sometimes the label is shiny and silvery-looking) and usually have the word BIOS printed on them, as well as several other numbers. If there's more than one chip, they might have something such as BIOS-1, BIOS-2, and so on printed on them.

④ Take Out Your Old BIOS Chip

The easiest way to remove the chips is by using a chip puller. Use it to grab the chip at both ends, and gently rock it until it loosens and you can pull it out. If you don't have a chip puller, try grasping the chip with your thumb and forefinger and rocking it until it loosens; then remove it. You can also use a small screwdriver to pry out the old chip by first prying up one end and then prying up the other until it's loose enough to take it out of the socket.

⑤ Put In Your New BIOS Chips

If you have more than one chip, put the chips in the same order as your original ones. Make sure that the notched end of the chip lines up with the notched end of the socket. Before putting in each chip, be sure that the pins are straight. If they're not, you can use needlenose pliers to straighten them. Line up the pins on one side of the chip with the holes in the socket, and then with the other side. When both sides are lined up, push down with your thumb on the chip until it's firmly seated in the socket.

⑥ Turn On Your Computer

Put the case back on your computer, plug in the computer, and turn it on. Your BIOS should now work automatically. If you compare what the bootup screen said before you installed the BIOS with what it says now, you'll notice that the date has changed, along with the name of the BIOS manufacturer, if you acquired your BIOS from a new manufacturer. The CMOS won't change, unless the new BIOS adds some kind of new feature not previously available, such as giving you the choice of letting you boot from an IDE or a SCSI drive.

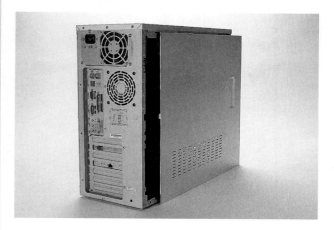

Watch Out!

- When removing the BIOS, be careful not to twist it or pull too hard so that you don't break off any pins.

How-to Hint

- If your BIOS is flash upgradable, you won't need to install a new BIOS—just download an upgrade from the maker's Web site.
- Seat the new BIOS firmly before closing up your PC.

Task

Installing a New Power Supply

Without a power supply, there is no PC. This little-thought-of workhorse takes the power from your wall outlet and transforms it into much lower-voltage direct current that can be used by your PC. It routes that current to all your PC's components so they have the power to run—think of it as your computer's energy plant.

It is often hard to know when you need a new power supply. But if your PC simply refuses to turn on and no electricity comes into it, you need a new one. Also, if the fan stops running and you can't feel air coming out of the back of your PC, you probably need a new one.

Upgrade Advisor

If you have a bad power supply, don't even think of getting it repaired. They're inexpensive enough that you should buy a new one instead. And never try to open the power supply or fiddle around with its insides because even when it's turned off and unplugged it holds electricity, and you can hurt yourself badly.

Often overlooked when buying a new power supply is making sure that it can physically fit into your case and that it uses the same types of connectors that your current power supply uses. The majority of PCs built since 1996 use what's called an ATX form factor. If you buy a non-ATX power supply, it generally won't work with a PC built to the ATX standard. So, before buying a power supply, check your PC's documentation or call technical support to find out whether it adheres to the ATX form factor. Also, open your PC's case before buying a new power supply and measure the power supply's dimensions, so that you can match the one you're buying. And to be safe, bring along the manufacturer name and model of your PC and ask whether the power supply you're buying is compatible with your PC. In fact, some systems' power supplies have proprietary designs and need to be purchased from the manufacturer.

Also consider the wattage of the power supply you're buying. There's a simple rule: More is better. With the number of peripherals in a PC today, it's a good idea to get a power supply rated at least at 300 watts. You also should consider buying a power supply from a well-known manufacturer, rather than a generic model. Generic models can put out "dirty" power, which can cause many issues with your PC. Lesser-known manufacturers might be more likely to not be as honest about the maximum output of the supplies.

How Power Supplies Work

Fan

As the power supply operates, it produces heat. To ensure that the power supply doesn't overheat and become damaged (or damage your computer's components), a fan is built into the power supply that cools it off, blowing hot air out of the rear of the computer. Be sure the fan is always running. If it stops, replace the power supply immediately.

Power supply

Your PC's power cord plugs directly into the power supply. The power supply transforms its alternating current (AC) into a lower-voltage direct current (DC) that can be used by your computer's components. Power supplies can provide from 100 to more than 300 watts of electricity. When you buy a new one, get one that produces at least 300 watts, so you can power all your computer's components and future upgrades.

Motherboard

Wires run out of the power supply and bring power to your computer's components. Several of these wires attach to the motherboard and supply power to the motherboard and the components that are plugged into it. In ATX-style systems (since 1996 ATX has become the most popular form factor for PCs), a 20-pin connector runs from the power supply to the motherboard.

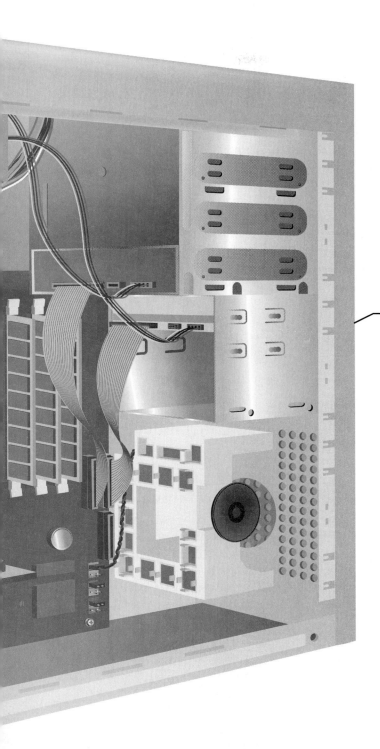

Power switch

In ATX systems, a power switch on the case is connected to the motherboard via a connector. This switch controls the on/off for the computer.

In older, non-ATX systems, A set of wires runs to the on/off switch on the front of your computer. The wires carry the signals that tell the power supply to turn on or off.

How to Replace a Power Supply

Replacing a power supply is a relatively simple matter. To begin, you must remove the case, as seen in Chapter 13, Task 5, "How to Open the Case." Once inside, disconnect all the cables that run from it to your computer's components, being careful to draw a diagram so that you know how to reattach everything. Then, take out the old power supply, put in a new one, and reconnect all the cables. As always, be sure to unplug the power supply before removing your computer's case.

❶ Unplug Power Connectors

Power connectors connect the wires from the power supply to different parts of your computer. Unplug the power connectors from the motherboard, which are usually the largest. Pull the connectors straight up and then tilt them at an angle to remove them so that you don't damage their plastic teeth. If you have an ATX connector, it has a small plastic clip on it. Pull away the plastic clip, and then pull up on the connector. Wires also run from your power supply to your PC's drives. Pull these power connectors off. Be sure to also disconnect the power supply from the case and heatsink fans.

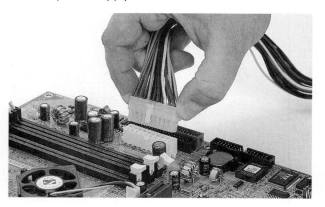

❷ Unplug the Power Switch

If your system is an older, non-ATX system, you might need to unplug the on/off switch. (In ATX systems, the power switch does not need to be unplugged to install a new power supply.) If it's a non-ATX system, four colored wires run from the power supply to the switch. Remove the wires from the switch with needle-nose pliers, if necessary. These might be all the same color. If they are, when you install a new power supply, hold the new switch next to the old one, pull the wire out of one, and connect it in exactly the same place on the new switch. That way you connect them in the same way as in your old power supply.

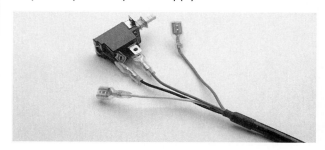

❸ Remove the Screws

Often, four screws hold the power supply in place. Don't confuse the screws that hold the power supply in place with the screws that hold the fan onto the power supply. The screws that hold the power supply are on the outside of the case, whereas those that hold the fan onto the power supply are on the power supply itself.

4   Remove the Power Supply

It should slide out relatively easily. Sometimes clips on the front of the power supply secure the power supply to the case, so you might have to first slide the power supply forward to clear the clips and then lift it out of the case. Some computer cases have a small plate built in, and the power supply fits on top of that plate.

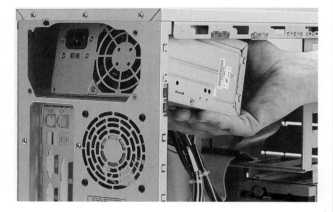

5   Slide In the New Power Supply

Touch a grounded metal object first to discharge static electricity, or use a wrist strap. If your power supply is secured by clips, you have to slide it forward into them before screwing the power supply back in. Check the back of the power supply to ensure the switch there is set to 115 volts, if you're in the U.S., or to 230 volts, if you're in a country that uses 230 volts. After you slide in the power supply, screw it in.

6   Reconnect the Power Connectors

Following the diagram you drew when you took out your power supply, reconnect all the connectors. Be careful when plugging in the connectors, especially the power switch, which is the heavy cable running from the power supply. Make sure that no cables are lying across or on top of any fans or your microprocessor. After you plug in your computer and turn it on, your system should start up. You should hear the power supply fan go on, and all your components should work.

Watch Out!
- Don't put a screwdriver into or poke around inside the power supply, even when it's not plugged in— you could get a nasty electric shock.
- Before turning on your new power supply, be sure that its switch is set to 115 volts if you're in the U.S. and to 230 volts if you're in a country that uses 230-volt power.

How-to Hint

If you don't have a free power connector, you can buy a Y cable, which will split one connector into two so that you can use the second connector. But be careful not to overload your power supply with too many peripherals.

Task

39

Upgrading Notebook Computers

At first blush, it might appear difficult to upgrade a notebook computer (sometimes called a laptop computer, as well). Notebook computers are self-contained units that have most of their capabilities, such as graphics adapters, built right into their internal motherboards. Unlike desktop PCs, they mainly use nonstandard components, so you can't mix and match components—for example, batteries often work with only one type of notebook. The same holds true for hard disks, CD-ROM drives, DVD drives, and other peripherals—you can't mix and match them.

However, there are simple ways that you can expand and upgrade your existing notebook. One of the easiest is to install what are called PC Cards—credit-card-size devices that plug into PC Card ports on your notebook, usually on the notebook's side. You can buy PC Card modems, network cards, and even hard disks, and they're all easy to install, as you see later in this chapter.

Another simple way to expand and upgrade your notebook is to buy a docking station. A *docking station* is a unit you plug your notebook into, and it expands the capability of your notebook. You can plug a monitor, keyboard, mouse, printer, modem, and other peripherals into the docking station.

Upgrade Advisor

Notebook computers are now powerful enough so that they can replace your desktop computer—no longer are they only for when you travel. Many people use them with docking stations at the office as an easy way to use them with monitors and external keyboards.

Most laptops are built using proprietary designs and might include proprietary connectors and devices, so you won't be able to buy standard, off-the-shelf hardware for them. So ensure that you buy either from the manufacturer or a third party that specifically makes compatible hardware. You might, however, be able to use a standard type of 144-pin RAM module of a type called SODIMM on most laptops—but not in all cases. So check with the manufacturer before installing RAM or any other internal devices.

One of the best upgrades you can buy for your laptop is very inexpensive but very vital: some type of security lock/cable combination and alarm. With a lock/cable combination and alarm, you can attach a cable to your laptop and wrap it around an unmovable object such as a pipe or slot built into a desk, protecting it from being stolen. For added protection, an alarm with a motion sensor can be built into the lock/cable combination.

How a Notebook Computer Works

Built-in modem and network connections
Most laptops include a built-in modem, and an increasing number include a built-in Ethernet network connection.

Mouse port
A port into which you can plug an external mouse.

Sound ports
Typically, notebooks include one or more sound ports for connecting speakers or headphones.

Monitor port
A port into which you can plug an external monitor, so that you can use one with your notebook.

Parallel port
The parallel port is the port into which a printer is plugged. It also can be used for attaching peripherals that use the parallel port, such as scanners.

Serial port
The port into which modems and mice plug.

Docking station
An excellent way to make notebooks easier to use and upgrade is to connect them to a docking station. You'll be able to attach peripherals to the docking station and install add-in cards, such as network cards, in the docking station.

Expansion bays
Most notebooks have expansion bays into which you can swap components such as batteries; floppy disks; and CD, CD-RW, and DVD drives.

PC Card slots

PC Card slots are the slots into which PC Cards attach to the notebook. There are three types of PC Card slots, corresponding to the types of PC Cards. A Type I slot can accommodate a single Type I card. A Type II slot can accommodate one Type II card or two Type I cards. A Type III slot can accommodate one Type III card or a Type I and a Type II card.

USB and FireWire ports

One of the easiest ways to expand a laptop is by adding a USB or FireWire device. Most laptops have at least one USB port, and an increasing number include FireWire ports as well.

PC Cards

One way to upgrade the capabilities of a notebook is to install PC Cards. PC Cards are credit-card-size devices that are put into special PC Card slots in the side of the notebook. Modems, network cards, external drives, and many other add-ins are available on PC Cards. There are three types of PC cards. Type I cards are typically used for adding memory to a computer. Type II cards are commonly used for modems and network cards. Type III cards can be used for hard disks, as well as other devices. Type II and Type III are the most common.

Release latch

You usually install components in drive bays simply by slipping them into the drive bay. When you slip them in, a latch usually locks into place. To remove the component, you usually press on the latch and slide the component out.

How to Install PC Cards

A notebook computer isn't as expandable as a desktop PC because it has no expansion slots. That doesn't mean, however, that you can't add capabilities to it. The main way you upgrade a notebook is via PC Cards, which are credit-card-size pieces of electronics you slide into PC Card slots built into the notebook. You can buy PC Card modems, network cards, and other peripherals for your notebook. Here's how to do it.

1 Verify You Have a Free Slot

Notebooks commonly have one or two PC Card slots. If you have an older notebook, it might have a Type I PC Card slot or slots. If that's the case, you won't be able to use newer Type II or Type III PC Cards in it. Be sure that you have one free and that it can accept a PC Card. In some instances, a PC Card takes up more than one slot. And Type II or III cards might take up two slots, so if you have only one slot free, it might not be able to accept a Type III PC Card.

2 Turn Off Your Notebook

You shouldn't install a PC Card in your notebook if it's turned on or plugged in. So, turn it off, and unplug the power cord.

3 Slide In the PC Card

Look for the end of the card with the connector on it. That's the end you put into the slot. The card should slide in easily. Be careful to align it properly so that you don't bend the notebook's internal connector pins. Be sure that the top of the card faces upward—many cards are marked at the top. When it's aligned properly, push until it's seated firmly in the slot.

④ Turn On the Notebook

Now it's time to get the PC Card to work with your computer. Plug in the notebook, or be sure that it has charged batteries in it. Then, turn on the computer.

⑤ Install the Drivers

After you turn on your computer, it should recognize that you've added new hardware and launch an Add New Hardware Wizard. Follow the steps for adding the hardware, and use the drivers supplied with the card. If your computer doesn't recognize the card, add it manually. From the **Control Panel**, double-click **Add New Hardware**. The Add New Hardware Wizard will then launch. Some notebooks come with PC Card management software, which pops up when you first install the card.

Watch Out!

- Be sure that you have free PC Card slots and that they're of the correct type for the PC Card you plan to install.

- When sliding in the card, be sure that it's aligned properly, and don't push too hard because you'll damage the internal connector pins.

- After you've installed the card, go to the manufacturer's Web site and check whether any new drivers are available for the card. If drivers are, download and install them.

- If Windows doesn't recognize the PC Card, check to see whether there is PC Card installation software on your notebook, and then run that.

How to Install a Docking Station

Perhaps the best way to make a notebook easier to use, and to upgrade its capabilities, is to get a docking station for it. A docking station has connectors for a monitor, keyboard, mouse, printer, speakers, and other peripherals. You plug your notebook into the docking station and then plug a keyboard, mouse, and other peripherals into the docking station, so that you can use them with the notebook. Many docking stations also let you install an add-in card, such as a network card, that will then work with your notebook. Not all docking stations and notebooks work the same way.

❶ Buy the Right Station

The only docking station that works with your notebook is one designed specifically for it, often available only from the notebook manufacturer. So, be sure that when you buy a docking station, it matches your make and model of notebook.

❷ Turn Off Your Notebook

After you turn off your notebook, unplug any peripherals attached to it, including the power cord. Close the display panel. You need the back of the notebook free to attach it to the docking station. And many notebooks can't be attached to the docking station while the notebook's power is on and the display panel is open.

❸ Locate the Docking Station

A connector on the back of your notebook plugs into the docking station. On many notebooks, a panel protects the connector. Slide that door open to expose the connector. There also might be panels that protect the notebook's serial, parallel, and monitor ports. Slide those closed to protect them.

④ Connect the Docking Station

On many notebooks and docking stations, a set of guide pins on the docking station line up with holes on connectors on each side of the connector on the back of the notebook. Align those guide pins first, and then gently push the computer into the docking station until it's secure. On many docking stations, you hear a click when the computer is connected.

⑤ Turn On the Notebook

Plug in the docking station's power cord, attach your peripherals, and turn on the notebook. Your peripherals should all work automatically. If, however, you get an Add New Hardware Wizard, follow the instructions for adding the hardware. After you've installed the docking station, if you install any cards into it, you'll install them the same way as you would in a desktop computer, except that you'll install them in the docking station instead of in an empty slot on the motherboard.

Watch Out!

- Never lift the notebook and the docking station when they are connected to one another—you might damage both of them.

How-to Hint

- Be sure that the docking station you buy is specifically built for the manufacturer and model of your notebook.

- Turn off your computer and close its display panel before installing it into the docking station, unless its documentation specifically tells you otherwise.

40

Installing New Software and Hardware

If your computer is connected to your company's network, a network administrator is probably responsible for adding and removing hardware and software on your computer and for keeping Windows up to date. If so, you should take advantage of his or her expertise. However, with Windows XP, adding components to your system has never been easier. If you are administering your own computer or network, this part shows how to install your own hardware and software and how to update Windows XP. This part also covers the installation of Windows XP Service Pack 1 and shows the major changes this service pack makes to your system.

How to Add a Program to Your Computer

Programs are the reason you use your computer. Almost all new programs today come on CD-ROM. When you insert the CD-ROM into your drive, Windows should automatically run the setup program for you. If this is the case, you won't need to follow the procedure in this task. If the setup process does not start automatically, or if your program is on floppy disk, the following steps show you how to start the installation yourself. If you download a program from the Internet, the setup process is much the same. You'll just have to tell Windows where the files are located. If the program is compressed (such as in a ZIP file), you'll have to expand it before installing (refer to Part 11).

① Open the Control Panel

Click the **Start** button and choose **Control Panel**. The Control Panel window opens.

② Open Add/Remove Programs

Double-click the **Add/Remove Programs** icon to open it.

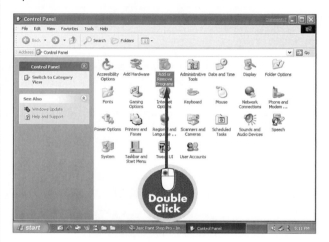

③ Add New Programs

Click the **Add New Programs** button to install a new program.

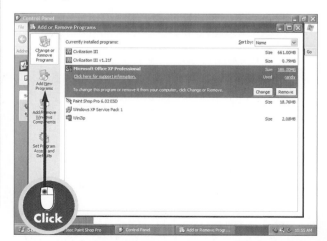

④ Choose CD or Floppy

If programs are available for installation on your network, they appear in the window. Click the **CD or Floppy** button to install a program from disk. Click **Next** to skip the initial welcome page of the wizard that appears.

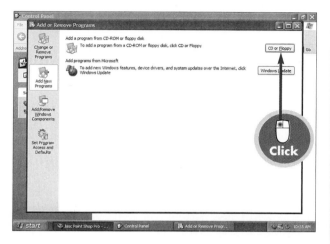

⑤ Finish

Windows searches both your floppy and CD-ROM drives for a setup program. If it finds one, the path to the program is displayed for your approval. If you think Windows found the right one, click the **Finish** button to launch the setup program. You can also click the **Browse** button to locate a setup program yourself.

How-to Hint

Installing from the My Computer Window

You can also run a setup program manually without using the Add/Remove Programs applet. Just open the My Computer window and locate the setup program yourself on the floppy or CD-ROM drive. It is almost always a program named setup.exe. If it is not named setup.exe, it will be another program with the .exe extension. If you can't figure out which program is used to start the installation, check whether the folder has a text file that explains the installation process (This file is often named readme.txt or setup.txt.) When you determine the setup program, double-click it to start.

How-to Hint

The Program Files Folder

Your C: drive has a folder on it named Program Files. Most new programs that you install create a folder for themselves inside this folder that is used to store the program's files.

How-to Hint

Restarting

Different programs have different installation routines. Some require that you restart your computer after the program has been installed. This is one reason why it is best to save any work and exit any running programs before you install new software.

How to Change or Remove a Program

Some programs, such as Microsoft Office, let you customize the installation of the program to include only the components that you want in the installation. You can then add new components later if you want. The Add/Remove Programs applet lets you change the installation of a program, and it lets you remove the installation altogether (a process sometimes called uninstalling a program).

❶ Open the Control Panel

Select the **Start** button, and then choose **Control Panel**. The Control Panel window opens.

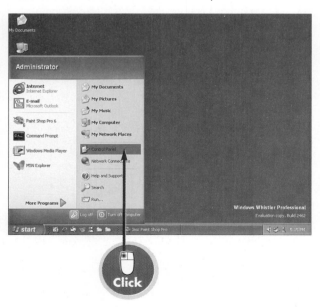

❷ Open Add/Remove Programs

Double-click the **Add/Remove Programs** icon to open it.

③ Select a Program

Choose a program from the list of currently installed programs by clicking it once. Notice that Windows lets you know how much disk space each program takes up and how often you use the program.

⑤ Follow the Program's Instructions

Every program has a slightly different routine for changing or removing the installation. Follow the onscreen instructions for the program you are using.

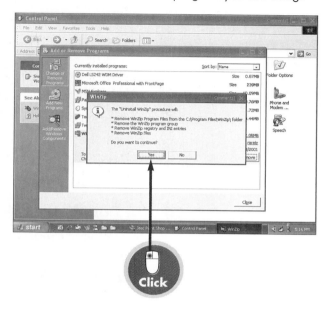

④ Click Change/Remove

Programs that do not let you change the installation show only a Change/Remove button. Programs that do let you change the installation show both a Change button and a Remove button. Click whatever button provides the action you want.

How-to Hint

Be Careful

Some programs automatically go forward with a removal without giving you a chance to confirm as soon as you click the Change/Remove or Remove button. Be sure you want to remove a program before clicking either of these buttons.

How to Add Windows Components from the CD

Windows XP comes with literally hundreds of components—and not all of them are installed during a normal installation of the operating system. You can add components from the Windows XP CD-ROM at any time after installation.

① Open the Control Panel

Click the **Start** button, and then choose **Control Panel**. The Control Panel window opens.

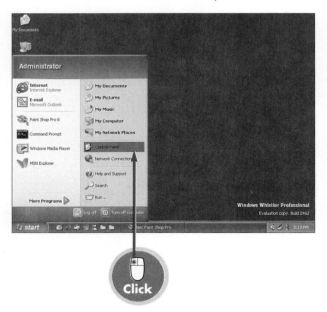

② Open Add/Remove Programs

Double-click the **Add/Remove Programs** icon to open it.

③ Choose Add/Remove Windows Components

Click the **Add/Remove Windows Components** button to display a list of the components you can install from the original Windows installation CD-ROM.

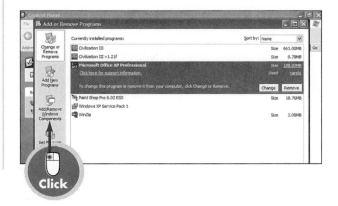

❹ Select a Component

Select a component from the list of available components by enabling the check box next to it. Some components have subcomponents that you can choose from. If so, the Details button becomes active, and you can click it to see a list of subcomponents to choose from.

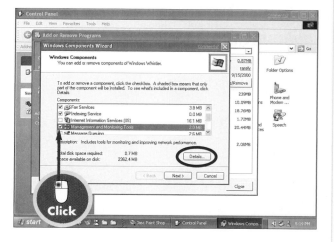

❺ Next

After you have selected all the components you want to install, click the **Next** button. Windows builds a list of files that must be installed and copies them to your drive. Windows might prompt you to insert your Windows CD-ROM during this process.

❻ Finish

After Windows has installed the components, it lets you know that the process has been completed successfully. Click the **Finish** button to finish. Depending on the components you added, Windows might need to restart your computer.

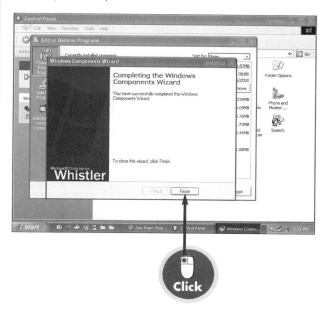

How-to Hint

Installing Windows

Many components are installed when you initially set up Windows. When you finish installing Windows, you should always check the installed components using the procedure described in this task to see what goodies you might be missing.

How to Add Windows Components from the Internet

Microsoft maintains a Web site named Windows Update that contains the newest versions of Windows components that you can download and add to your system. These components are updated versions of the components that come with Windows as well as new components and updates that Microsoft makes available. If, for some reason, the shortcut to the Windows update site does not work, you can also get there using the address `http://windowsupdate.microsoft.com/`.

① Start Windows Update

Click the **Start** button, point to **More Programs**, and select **Windows Update**. This command launches the Windows Update Web site in Internet Explorer.

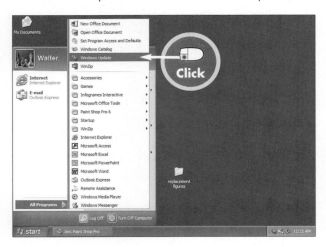

② Scan for Updates

Click the **Scan for Updates** link. The Windows Update site searches for components that you can download.

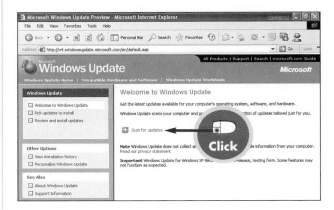

③ Review and Install Updates

Critical updates (bug fixes and security patches) are automatically selected for download. If that's all you want, click the **Review and Install Critical Updates** link. Additional non-critical updates are available in the Windows Update section on the left. Click the **Review and Install Critical Updates** link when you are ready to continue.

4 Choose Components to Update

Scroll down the Update Basket window to review the list of updates selected for download. Click the **Remove** button next to any update to remove it from the download list.

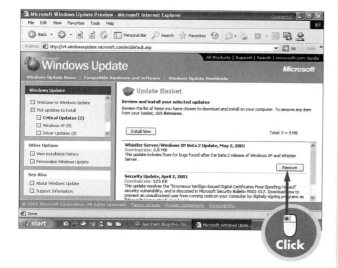

5 Install the Updates

When you are satisfied with the list of updates, click the **Install Now** button to download and install the components.

6 Accept the Licensing Agreement

Before you can download the updates, you must accept the Microsoft licensing agreement. Click **Accept** to continue. The files are then downloaded and installed to your computer. Windows will let you know when the process is finished and whether you have to restart your computer.

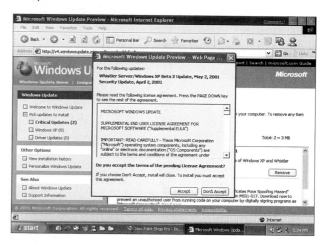

How-to Hint

Automatic Updating

Windows can automatically download and install updates when it detects that they are available—provided that you have Internet access. Turn on this feature by opening the System Control Panel applet (open the Control Panel window and double-click the **System** icon) and switching to the **Automatic Updates** tab. You can have Windows download updates and install them automatically, notify you when updates are available so that you can choose the update time, or disable the service. When automatic updating is active, an icon appears in the system tray to let you know the status.

How to Find Out About Your Installed Hardware

Windows uses a tool named the Device Manager to help you find out about the hardware on your system. You can see what is installed, what resources are used, and what devices might be having or causing problems.

❶ Open System Properties

Right-click the **My Computer** icon on your desktop and choose the **Properties** command from the shortcut menu. The Systems Properties dialog box opens.

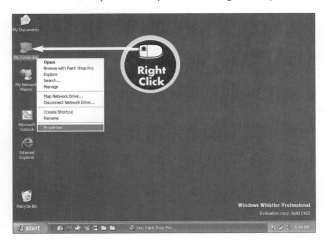

❷ Switch to Hardware Tab

Switch to the **Hardware** tab by clicking it once.

❸ Open the Device Manager

Click the **Device Manager** button to open the Device Manager window.

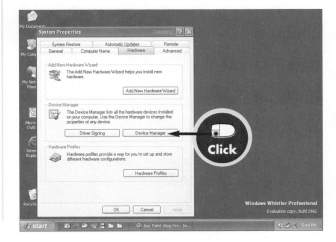

④ Expand a Category

The Device Manager window lists hardware categories for the hardware installed on your computer. Click the **+** next to a category to expand that category and show the actual devices attached to your computer.

⑥ Open Hardware Properties

You can open a detailed Properties dialog box for any device by double-clicking the device's icon. The dialog box tells you whether the device is working properly and lets you disable the device. Other tabs let you reinstall software drivers for the device and view the resources it uses.

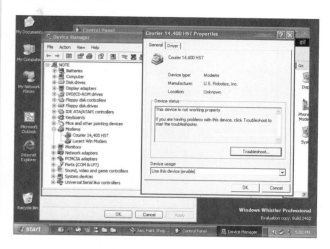

⑤ Identify Problem Hardware

Devices having problems are identified with a little yellow exclamation point. Another type of symbol you might see is a red X, which indicates a device that is turned off.

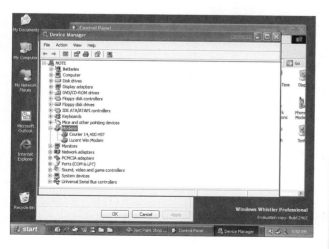

How-to Hint

Reinstalling a Device

If you see a device that isn't working, try running the Add Hardware applet (you'll find it in the Control Panel window). Windows scans your system for devices and presents a list of what it finds. The malfunctioning device should show up in the list, and you can try to reinstall it.

Installing New Software and Hardware

When you install a new peripheral, it will generally require *drivers*, which are special programs that tell Windows and your hardware how to work with the product. There are two kinds of drivers—those that Windows XP has natively available, and those that are *proprietary*, or that come directly from the manufacturer. Let's see how this works.

1 Watch Windows Load

After you install a new device and turn your computer back on, if Windows has *native drivers* for the device, you will see a message: `New Hardware Found - Windows is installing the drivers for it.`

2 Automatic Setup

If Windows has native drivers and they load successfully, you will see a prompt and a popup on the System Tray informing you that Windows has set up the drivers for the peripheral device.

3 Manual Setup

If there are no native Windows drivers, Windows will also tell you that new hardware has been found, but it will provide a dialog box that either lets you have Windows search for the best driver (which may still include previous or native drivers), or asks you to browse to where the new drivers are located.

At this point, if you have not already done so, you should locate and insert the CD or disc provided by the manufacturer. Click to change the default to **Install from a list or specific location (Advanced)**. Then click **Next**.

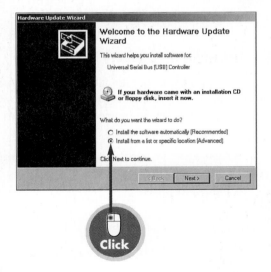

④ Access the CD

In the Add Hardware dialog box, click **Search removable media (floppy, CD ROM...)** to find the new driver. Click **Next**.

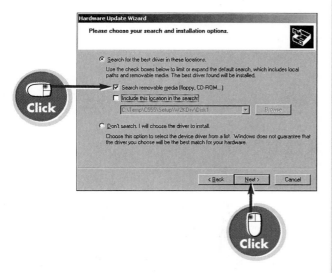

⑤ Locate It Manually

If the drivers aren't found on the CD, cancel out of the dialog box. Browse to a specific folder on the CD (usually described in the installation instructions for the product). Click **OK** and click **Next**.

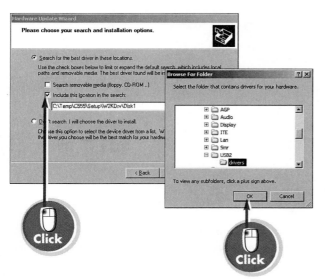

⑥ Complete the Wizard

Hopefully, the wizard will locate the driver automatically or manually and complete the installation. Sometimes you will need to reboot Windows.

How-to Hint

Driver Problems?

If your driver installs incorrectly, you might see a yellow exclamation point or question mark in Device Manager. To learn how to update the driver and fix the installation, See Chapter 14, "Maximizing System Performance," and see "Tweaking Drivers."

How to Update BIOS

The BIOS are the software drivers for the entire system. They load in a special BIOS memory chip on your motherboard that runs your Setup program before your Windows XP operating system even loads. When you call tech support, one of the first ways they will try to get rid of you is by asking whether you've "updated your BIOS." While this may or may not fix your problem, it is a reasonable first step you should take, so let's see how it's done.

❶ Open My Computer

The first thing you will need is a *bootable floppy disk*. Put a blank 3.5" disc you no longer need into your A: drive, right-click it in My Computer, and click **Format**.

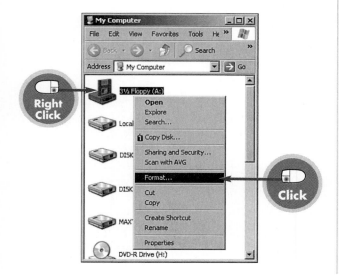

❷ Create an MS-DOS Startup Disk

Select **Create an MS-DOS startup disk**, and click **Start**. Disregard the warning about losing data and click **OK**.

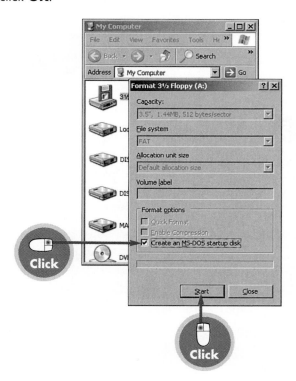

❸ Find Your BIOS Update

Generally, your BIOS update will be at the Web site of your *motherboard manufacturer*, or in some cases, the computer maker itself.

4 Download the Files

There are usually two files that you will need: the new BIOS file itself, and a Flash utility (flash.exe in many cases), which will perform the operation itself. Download both to a local folder.

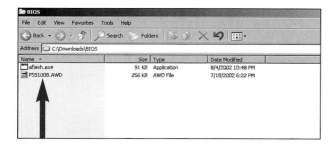

5 Copy the Files

From your Download folder, copy the files onto your floppy disk. Note the FLASH.EXE utility and the actual BIOS file.

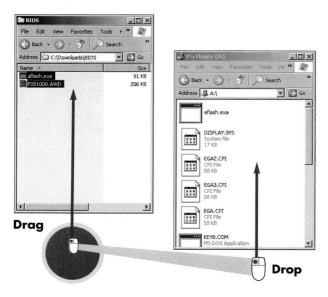

Drag

Drop

6 Reboot into DOS

Shut down your computer and restart with the floppy disk inserted. (Be sure you don't have a bootable CD in your drive, or make your floppy your first bootup choice in System setup.)

7 Run the Flash Utility

You should boot into a screen with only an A> prompt. Type **DIR** and Return. This will display the names of the files. Such as FLASH.EXE (the utility) PS1008.AWD (the new BIOS). *Write down this file name.* Type **FLASH.EXE** and Return. The BIOS program will run. *First, copy your present BIOS to the floppy.*

Then follow the prompts to FLASH the BIOS. You might need to manually type in the name of the new BIOS file—that's why you wrote it down. The BIOS should be flashed, overriding the present settings, and then you will need to remove the disk and reboot your system.

Watch Out! Use the Correct BIOS Version

Read all the instructions and make sure you are using a compatible BIOS version.

How-to Hint Back Up the BIOS

If you have a problem with the new BIOS, or during the procedure, if you have copied your present BIOS to the disk (as suggested previously), reboot and FLASH the present BIOS back into the system.

How-to Hint Read the Documentation

Different motherboard manufacturers have different BIOS upgrade procedures. The one outlined previously is very common. In all cases, read the documentation carefully and try to first copy your old (present) BIOS to the boot floppy disc before overriding it.

How-to Hint Confirmation

Once your BIOS have been flashed successfully, you should see a prompt tell you to remove your floppy and reboot. During reboot, you should see then new BIOS version ("1008") briefly on your DOS screen before Windows loads.

How to Tell Whether a Windows Service Pack Is Installed

Microsoft occasionally releases collections of updates to Windows in the form of a service pack. Service packs are numbered because more than one is normally released over the years that an operating system is in production. At the time of this writing, Windows XP Service Pack 1 is the only one that has been released for Windows XP. This task shows how to tell whether a service pack has already been applied to Windows or whether you will need to install one yourself.

① Open the Start Menu

Click **Start** to open the Start menu.

② Right-Click the My Computer Icon

Right-click the **My Computer** icon on your Start menu. If a My Computer icon is on your desktop, you can right-click that one instead.

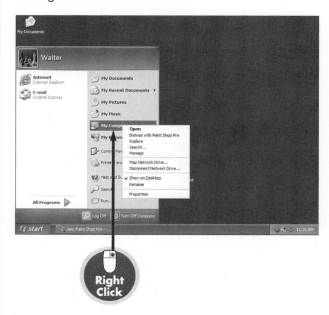

③ Open the Properties Dialog Box

Choose the **Properties** command on the My Computer icon's shortcut menu to open the System Properties dialog box.

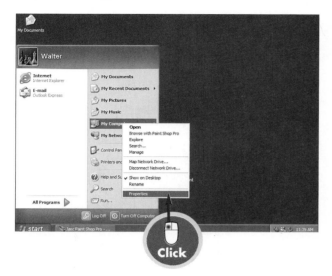

How-to Hint

Service Packs Are Cumulative

When more service packs are released in the future, you can add them to your computer with no problem. Service packs are cumulative, in that each new service pack issued contains all the features included in previous service packs. So, if you have a computer with no service pack installed, you should only apply the latest service pack available.

④ Determine Your Version of Windows

The **General** tab of the System Properties dialog box displays information about Windows and about the basic hardware on your computer. Look in the System section to find out whether a service pack has been installed on your computer. If a service pack has not been installed, you will not see this line at all.

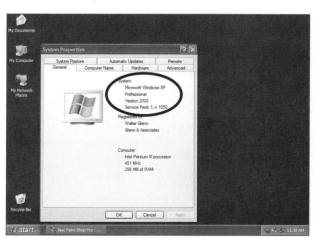

How to Install Windows XP Service Pack 1

You can obtain a service pack in a few ways. If you are part of a corporate network, your administrator might make the service pack available for you on the network (and in fact, will probably install it for you). If you are installing it yourself, you will either download Service Pack 1 (SP1) from the Windows Update site or install it from a CD-ROM. Use the steps in Task 4 of this chapter to find and start the download of SP1 from the Internet, or insert your CD and run the program XPSP1.EXE on the CD. Whichever method you choose, the steps for the installation are the same.

1 **Read the Welcome Page**

The welcome page of the Windows XP Service Pack 1 Setup Wizard has some good advice. Before installing, you should update your system repair disk and back up your computer. Steps for both of these actions can be found in Chapter 6. If you have done this, click **Next** to continue installation.

② Accept the Licensing Agreement

Read the licensing agreement for Service Pack 1. Select the **I Agree** option and click **Next** to continue installation. If you select the **I Do Not Agree** option, the setup program ends.

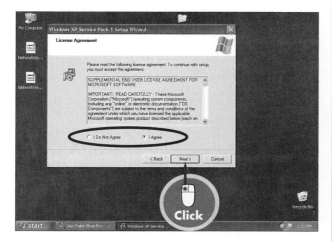

③ Choose Whether to Archive Old Files

If you want to uninstall Service Pack 1 at a later date, you must archive the current Windows files in a backup location on your computer. Archiving files takes a large amount of disk space but ensures that you can return your computer to its previous state if Service Pack 1 causes you any problems. Make your choice and click **Next**.

④ Finish the Installation

At this point, Windows begins to copy files. When it is done, you are shown the final page of the Setup Wizard. Click **Finish** to complete the installation and restart your computer. You can select the **Do Not Restart Now** option to finish the wizard without restarting, but you must restart your computer before the Service Pack 1 installation is complete.

How to Set Program Access and Defaults

Service Pack 1 includes security updates and support for new hardware devices, such as the tablet PC. The other big addition is a simple interface for letting Windows know whether you want to use built-in Microsoft programs (such as Internet Explorer and Outlook Express) or other programs installed on your computer. This is done using a feature named Set Program Access and Defaults, which is part of the Add/Remove Programs Control Panel utility.

1 Open the Set Program Access and Defaults Tool

Click **Start**, point to **All Programs**, and select **Set Program Access and Defaults**. You can also get to this tool by opening the **Add/Remove Programs** utility from the Control Panel window.

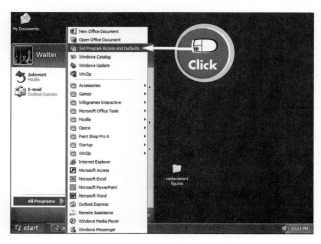

2 Use the Microsoft Windows Option

You have three choices for setting program defaults. The first is the Microsoft Windows option. When this option is set, Windows uses the built-in Microsoft programs for familiar functions: Internet Explorer for Web pages, Outlook Express for email, Windows Media Player for sounds and video, and Windows Messaging for instant messaging. There is also a setting for controlling what application loads Java applets on the Internet, but Microsoft does not provide a program for that. Click the Microsoft Windows option to use this setting.

③ Use the Non-Microsoft Option

Another choice you have is the Non-Microsoft option. This option uses whatever programs are currently set as your default programs for the listed functions. Whenever you install a new program (such as Netscape Navigator for browsing the Web), that program makes itself the default. Click the **Non-Microsoft** option to retain the default programs the way you have them set and to hide the icons for the Microsoft applications from your desktop and Start menu.

Click

④ Use the Custom Option

Click the **Custom** option to exert a little more control over your default program settings. A section for each type of program (Web browser, email, and so on) lets you select whether to use the current default program or the Microsoft program, and whether the Microsoft program should be displayed on your desktop and Start menu.

Click

How-to Hint

Why Is This Feature Here?

The Set Program Access and Defaults feature was really added to satisfy requirements set by the Department of Justice. It provides computer manufacturers a way to install programs that they choose to bundle with their computers and to hide the Microsoft equivalents from the casual Windows user. Interestingly, the program also provides an easy way for users who don't like the alternate programs that might come with a new computer to switch back to the Microsoft alternatives.

Task

41

Working on the Internet

The Internet is made up of lots of networks all connected together into one giant network. The most popular part of the Internet today is the World Wide Web, which provides pages that contain text, graphics, and multimedia to programs called Web browsers. The Internet (and especially the Web) has become an important business tool, allowing you to find information on just about anything—businesses, investments, travel, weather, news, healthcare, technology, and more. Microsoft provides a Web browser, called Internet Explorer, as an integral part of Windows XP.

When you visit a Web site, the main page of that site is called the home page. On the home page, there are usually links you can click to visit other pages in the site. Sometimes, links on one site take you to pages in other Web sites. It is this complex manner of linking pages together that gives the Web its name.

Each page on the Web has a specific address, sometimes called a URL (uniform resource locator), that tells your Web browser how to find it. For example, the URL www.microsoft.com/windows/default.asp tells a browser to load a file named default.asp in a folder named windows on a computer named www in the microsoft.com domain.

How to Start Internet Explorer

If you are on a network, your administrator has probably already configured your computer to use the company's connection to the Internet. If you are not on a network (or if your company does not have an Internet connection), you need a modem of some sort and you must sign up for an account with an Internet service provider (ISP). The ISP provides software and instructions to get you connected. When connected, your first task is to get to know your Web browser, Internet Explorer.

❶ Open Internet Explorer

Click **Start** and then **Internet Explorer** to open Internet Explorer. You can also click the **Internet Explorer** icon on the **Quick Launch** bar.

❷ Connect to the Internet

If you connect to the Internet using your company's network or using a DSL or cable modem, you should connect to a Web page immediately. If you connect using a regular modem, an extra dialog box might pop up asking you to dial your ISP. If it does, just click **Connect** or **Dial**. Your ISP should provide you with instructions on how to set up the dial-up networking connection.

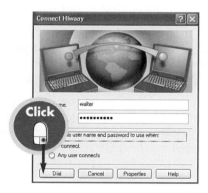

③ View a Web Page

A Web browser works like any other program you use in Windows. Along the top of the window, you find a menu bar and a couple of toolbars. The Address bar lets you enter the address of a page to visit. Use the scrollbar to move through and view the page.

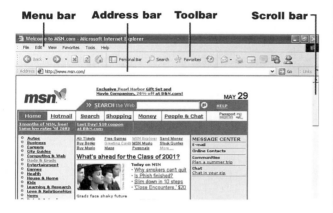

④ Select a Link

On a Web page, *links* to other pages are typically underlined and in blue text, although different pages use different schemes. Links to pages you have visited recently often appear underlined and in red text. When you move your pointer over a link, it turns into a hand pointing its index finger. Just click once to jump to that page. Normally, the page opens in the same window, replacing the page you linked from. Sometimes, pages open in windows of their own.

⑤ Refresh a Page

Some pages change frequently, especially if they contain images that are updated regularly, such as a site that has weather radar images. You can load a page in your browser again by clicking the **Refresh** button on the toolbar.

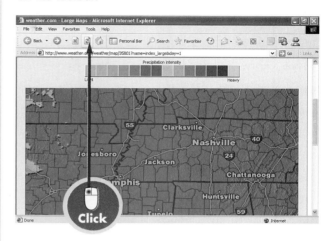

⑥ Stop a Page from Loading

If a page is taking too long to load or is having problems loading, you can stop it from loading by clicking the **Stop** button on the toolbar. Your browser displays whatever part of the page has already loaded.

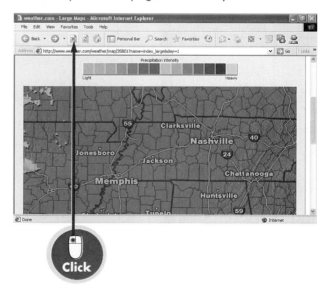

How to Get to a Web Site

If you know the address for a Web page, you can enter it into Internet Explorer's Address bar. But there are often easier ways to get to a page. You can keep favorite pages on a special Favorites menu or on a Link toolbar. You can also use your browser to quickly move backward and forward through pages you've already visited.

1 Enter the Address

If you know the URL of the site you want to visit, just type it in the Internet Explorer **Address** bar and press Enter. As you type, Internet Explorer tries to complete the address for you based on addresses you've entered before. Internet Explorer loads the page if it can find the address.

2 Open the Address List

To view a list of recently visited sites, click the down arrow next to the **Address** box, and click one of the addresses in the list to go to that page.

3 Choose a Link Button

Double-click the **Links** button to slide open the **Links** bar. Click any button on the **Links** bar to jump to that Web page.

Links button

④ Choose a Favorite Site

Internet Explorer lets you keep a list of your favorite Web sites (see Task 4, "How to Use the Favorites Menu," later in this part to learn how to add favorites). Click the **Favorites** menu to open it, and then click any page in the list to jump to that page.

⑤ Go to Your Home Page

The top page of a Web site is called its home page. The default Web page that loads whenever you open Internet Explorer is also called a home page (it's often called your home page). Return to your home page at any time by clicking the **Home** button.

⑥ Go Backward and Forward

As you use Internet Explorer, you can go backward and forward to the last pages you visited by clicking the **Back** and **Forward** buttons on the toolbar. Click the down arrows next to these buttons to open a history of sites you've visited in this online session.

How-to Hint

Adding a Link Button

You can add a button for the page you are viewing to your **Links** bar by simply dragging the icon for the page from the **Address** bar to the **Links** bar.

Making a New Home Page

You can make the page you are viewing your home page by dragging its icon from the **Address** bar to the **Home** button on the toolbar.

How to Search for a Web Site

If you don't know the address for a Web site you want to visit, you can often find it just by guessing. Try entering the name of the company (or whatever) you're looking for followed by a three-letter domain suffix. For example, if you want to find Microsoft's Web site, you can just type microsoft.com into the **Address** bar. Internet Explorer does the rest. Sometimes, however, you need to search for the information you need.

1 Open the Search Window

In Internet Explorer, click the **Search** button on the toolbar to open the **Search Companion** on the left side of the window.

2 Enter Some Keywords

Type some keywords to define what you are looking for. If, for example, you want to find Web pages that have to do with tigers in India, type **tiger india**.

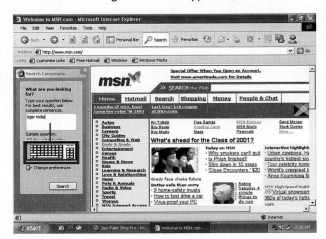

③ Click Search

After you have typed the criteria, click **Search** to begin.

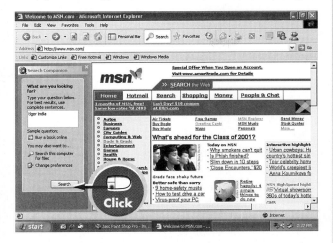

④ Scroll to View Results

Internet Explorer uses the MSN search engine to perform your search and then displays the results in the main browser window. Scroll down to view the results of the search.

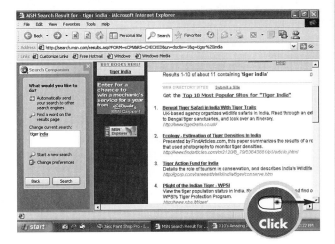

⑤ Select a Link

Hold the mouse pointer over a link for a moment to view a pop-up window that shows the first several lines of text from the Web page the link represents. When you find a link you want to explore further, click it to jump to that Web page.

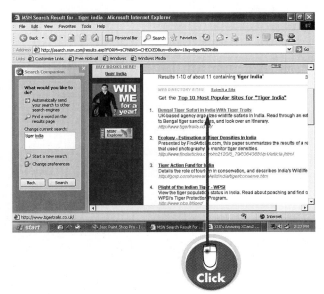

How-to Hint

Using Previous Searches

Internet Explorer remembers searches you've already performed and will automatically display them as you begin to type search terms.

Customizing the Search Procedure

From the main **Search Companion** window, click the **Change Preferences** link to open a window that lets you display advanced options to use while searching. You can change whether the **Search Companion** automatically completes words for you as you type and whether your search is automatically sent to other major Internet search engines (the default setting). If you do not want multiple search engines selected, you can choose which search engine you want the **Search Companion** to use. Choices include MSN, AltaVista, Google, and others. You may find that using only one engine speeds up your searches.

How to Use the Favorites Menu

To jump to a page on your list of favorites, all you have to do is open the Favorites menu in the Internet Explorer menu bar and choose the page you want to visit from the list. Adding a page to the Favorites list is also easy. The first step is to open the page you want to add in Internet Explorer.

1 Add a Page to the Favorites Menu

To add the Web page you are viewing to your list of favorite pages in the **Favorites** menu, open the menu by clicking it once and then click **Add to Favorites**. The Add Favorite dialog box opens.

2 Make Available Offline

If you want the page to be made available for viewing while you are not connected to the Internet, click the **Make available offline** option. Check out Task 6, "How to Make Web Pages Available Offline," for more information on doing this.

3 Rename the Page

Type a different name for the page in the **Name** box if you want. This is the name that will appear in your **Favorites** menu.

④ Create in a Specific Folder

You can organize your **Favorites** menu into folders. To add the page to a specific folder, click the **Create in** button. If you do not want to put this page in a folder, just click **OK** to add the page to the main Favorites menu.

⑤ Choose a Folder

Click the folder to which you want to add this Web page. You can create a new folder on the menu or inside any existing folder by clicking the **New Folder** button.

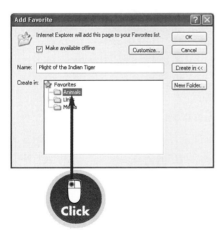

⑥ Add the Favorite

After you have configured all the previous options you want, click **OK** to add the page to your **Favorites** menu.

How-to Hint

Organizing Your Favorites Menu

If you want to move, delete, or remove pages on your **Favorites** menu, just open the menu and choose the **Organize Favorites** command.

How to Use the History List

Internet Explorer keeps track of all the pages you have visited recently (for the past 20 days, by default). When you can't remember the exact address of a site or a page you've visited before, you can use the History list to quickly find it.

① Open the History Window

Click the **History** button on the Internet Explorer toolbar to open the History window on the right side of the browser screen.

② Choose a Time Frame

By default, the History window is organized by days and weeks. To look for a site, just click the day when you think you visited it.

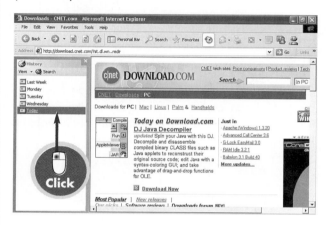

③ Choose a Site

From the list of sites you visited on the selected day, find the site you want to explore by clicking it once.

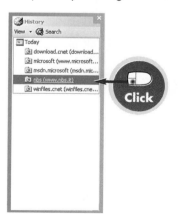

④ Choose a Page

From the list of visited pages on the site, jump to a page by clicking it once.

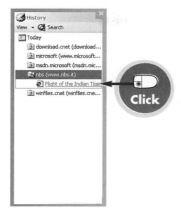

⑤ Change the View

You can view the **History** window in different ways. Click the **View** button to organize visited pages **By Site**, **By Most Visited**, or **By Order Visited Today**.

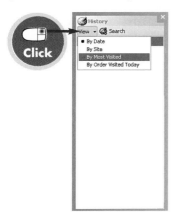

⑥ Close the History Window

Close the **History** window by clicking the **Close** button in the upper-right corner.

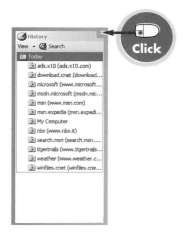

Searching Your History

Click the **Search** button at the top of the History window to search the pages in your History list by keyword.

Changing History Settings

See Task 7, "How to Change Settings for Internet Explorer," later in this part for information on how to change your Internet Explorer History settings.

History of Local Files

In addition to keeping track of Web pages, Windows keeps track of the files you've opened on your own computer. These files also appear in the History list. Windows and Internet Explorer share the same History list.

How to Make Web Pages Available Offline

Occasionally, you might want to access information on Web pages when you are not connected to the Internet. This can be useful if you are charged for connection time or if you carry your computer around with you. Internet Explorer lets you mark pages for offline viewing, which basically means that the pages are copied to your computer so you can view them without being on the Internet. You can also configure when and how the pages are updated.

❶ Make It Available Offline

First, browse to the page you want to make available offline and choose the **Add to Favorites** command from your **Favorites** menu. In the Add Favorite dialog box, enable the **Make available offline** option and click the **Customize** button. This launches the Offline Favorite Wizard.

❷ Make Links Available Offline

You can choose to make only the current page available or to make pages that the current page links to available as well. If you want to make links available, click the **Yes** option.

❸ Select the Link Depth

Choose how many links deep from the current page you want to make pages available. For example, choosing **3** makes available all pages that the current page links to and all pages that each of those pages links to. Click **Next** to go on.

④ Schedule Offline Updates

Synchronizing updates the temporary copies of offline pages on your computer with the most recent copy from the Internet. By default, pages are synchronized only when you choose the **Synchronize** command from the **Tools** menu of Internet Explorer. Create a new synchronization schedule by enabling the appropriate option. Click **Next** to go on.

⑤ Set Up a Schedule

Choose how often (in days) and at what time of the day you want the page to be automatically updated. You can also name your schedule. Click **Next** to go on.

⑥ Enter a Username and Password

If the page you are making available offline requires that you enter a username and password (as do many news sites or services you might have subscribed to), enable the **Yes** option and supply that information here. When you're done, click **Finish**.

How-to Hint

Changing Offline Settings

You can change the offline settings for a page at any time by choosing **Organize Favorites** from the **Favorites** menu. Select the page from the list and click the **Properties** button to change the offline settings.

Don't Set Your Link Depth Too High

The higher you set the link depth of pages you want to make available offline, the longer these pages will take to download during synchronization.

How to Change Settings for Internet Explorer

After you have played with Internet Explorer for a while, you might want to experiment with some of the ways in which you can customize the program using the **Internet Options** dialog box. The seven tabs on this dialog box present a lot of options. Some of the more useful ones are discussed here.

1 **Open Internet Options**

In Internet Explorer, open the **Tools** menu and choose the **Internet Options** command. The Internet Options dialog box opens.

2 **Enter a New Home Page**

The page that Internet Explorer first opens to is called the home page. You can change the home page by typing a new URL in the **Address** box.

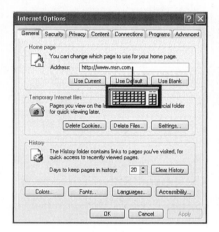

3 **Delete Temporary Files**

As you browse, Internet Explorer temporarily saves pages and graphics to your hard drive. When you open a previously visited page, Internet Explorer checks to see whether the page has changed. If it hasn't, the temporary files are opened; this way, the page loads faster. You can delete temporary files to make room on your hard disk by clicking **Delete Files**.

4 Change Temporary Settings

Click the **Settings** button to open the Settings dialog box. Here, you can change how often Internet Explorer checks for new versions of the pages stored as temporary files.

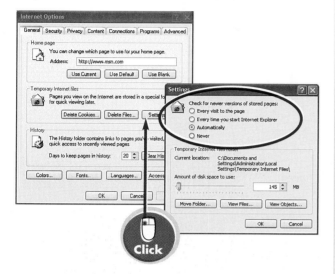

Click

5 Reduce Disk Space Used

Temporary files use up disk space—by default, as much as 2% of your hard disk. On larger drives, this can amount to quite a lot of space. However, storing more temporary files can mean quicker loading of some Web pages. Change the disk space used for temporary files by dragging the slider or by entering a specific value in megabytes.

Drag

6 Change History Setting

By default, Internet Explorer keeps track of the Web pages and local files that you have opened in the last 20 days. You can change this value using the **Days to keep pages in history** scroll buttons.

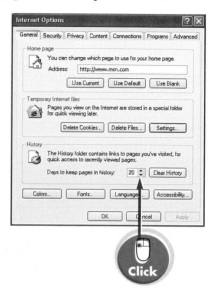

Click

7 Open the Colors Dialog Box

Click the **Colors** button at the bottom of the **General** tab of the **Internet Options** dialog box to change the colors of the text and background of Web pages you visit. Click one of the color buttons to open a palette from which you can choose a new color.

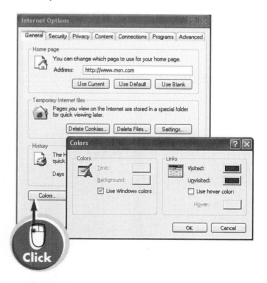

Click

How to Use MSN Explorer

Most people find Internet Explorer fairly easy to use and pretty powerful once they get used to it. Windows XP also comes with another program named MSN Explorer that features a Web browser and several other options bundled into one simple interface. To use MSN Explorer, you must be a subscriber to the Microsoft Network (MSN) or set up a free email account with Microsoft's Hotmail. The first time you use the program, MSN Explorer walks you through the process of setting up.

❶ Start MSN Explorer

On the **Quick Launch** bar at the bottom of the screen, click the shortcut for **MSN Explorer**. If you don't find it on your Quick Launch bar, you'll find it on the Start menu under **All Programs**. If you've not yet set up an account with MSN, you'll be guided through that process now.

❷ Select a User

You can set up multiple MSN accounts. Whenever you start MSN Explorer, log in to your account by clicking the icon next to your MSN user name.

❸ Enter Your Password

In the text box that appears, type your password and then click **Sign In**. If you want MSN Explorer to remember your password, enable the **Remember password** check box.

4 Browse the Web

After you sign in, a window opens that looks like a fancy Web browser. You can browse the Web using many of the same techniques you learned for Internet Explorer earlier in this part. Click a link, type an address, and even access your list of Web-page favorites.

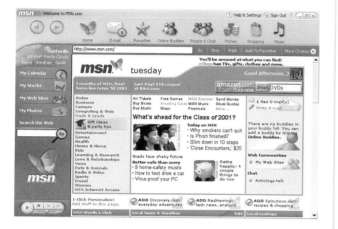

5 Check Your Calendar

Click the **My Calendar** link to create your own personal calendar. You can enter appointments, set reminders, keep track of tasks you have to do, and more.

6 Check Your Stocks

MSN Explorer lets you enter all your stocks and then track stock prices and company news. If you have a MoneyCentral portfolio, you can show it on this page. When you click the **My Stocks** link, a separate window opens with a simple list of your stocks. A link in that window takes you to the MoneyCentral site shown here.

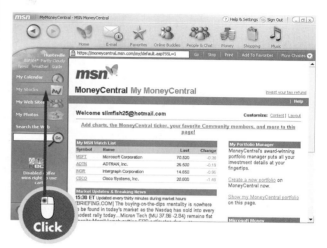

7 Create a List of Web Sites

Click the **My Web Sites** link to open a small window that lists favorite MSN sites, personal Web pages you've created, and files you've put in storage on MSN. A link in the **My Web Sites** page takes you to the **Communities** page shown here.

(8) Store and Share Digital Photos

With your MSN account, you get storage space to which you can upload your digital photos and share them with family and friends. Just click the **My Photos** link to get started. You'll find complete instructions on the PictureIt! page.

(9) Check Your Email

Click the **E-mail** button to manage your Hotmail account. You can read, write, and send email messages using a simple Web-based interface.

(10) Find and Talk to People

Click the **People & Chat** button to jump to the **People & Chat** page of MSN. From here, you can find online discussions on almost any subject. You'll also find links for playing online games and watching live videos.

(11) Manage Your Finances

Click the **Money** button to visit **MSN MoneyCentral**, where you can create and manage stock portfolios, investigate online banking, and research almost any financial decision.

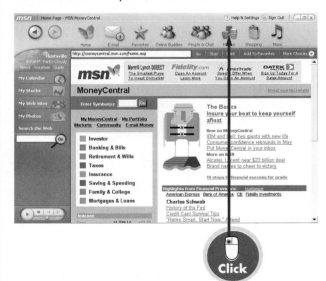

Shop

Click the **Shopping** button to visit MSN's eShops, where you can find almost anything you'd ever want to buy.

Click

13 **Find Music**

Click the **Music** button to visit WindowsMedia.com, where you can find, download, and listen to thousands of different songs.

Click

How-to Hint

Why Use MSN Explorer?

Why should you use MSN Explorer instead of Internet Explorer (or another Web browser) and Outlook Express? After all, you can get to many of the same places (such as MoneyCentral, Hotmail, shopping, and so on) by using any simple Web browser. The answer to this question is really one of taste. MSN Explorer offers all this stuff in one, simplified interface—much like the interface AOL offers with its service. If you use MSN Explorer, you can browse, check stocks, check mail, and so on all in one window without having to type in addresses.

MSN Explorer is also very easy to set up so that other people who use your computer can use it without getting in each other's way. For example, each member of your family can have his or her own account, stock list, and online photos. Many people new to using the Internet also find MSN Explorer's simplified interface a comforting introduction to being online. Although advanced users usually find the flexibility and customizability of a regular Web browser such as Internet Explorer and an email program such as Outlook Express more to their liking, MSN Explorer just offers another way to access the Internet.

How to Use Windows Messenger

Windows XP comes with its own instant messaging program called Windows Messenger. It works much like its counterparts from other companies, including AOL Instant Messenger and ICQ. To use it, you must have a Hotmail or Passport account. Windows Messenger walks you through setting up an account the first time you use it.

1 Start Messenger

On the **Quick Launch** bar, click the shortcut for **Windows Messenger**. If you don't find it on your Quick Launch bar, you'll find it on the **Start** menu under **More Programs**. If you've not yet set up your account, you'll be guided through that process now.

2 Check Your Status

The main **Windows Messenger** window shows the name of the account you are signed in with and how many messages you have in your Hotmail or Passport email account. The window also shows a list of all the contacts you've set up.

3 Add a Contact

Click the **Add** button to launch a short wizard that lets you add a new contact to your list. You'll be asked for the email address of the contact, or search the MSN directory for the contact you want to add. To send instant messages, the contact must also be using Windows Messenger.

4 Send an Instant Message

Click the **Send** button and choose a contact from the menu that drops down to open a window. Type a message to that contact, and click the **Send** button. If the contact is online, you can chat together in real time. If the contact is offline, that person will receive the message when he or she comes online again.

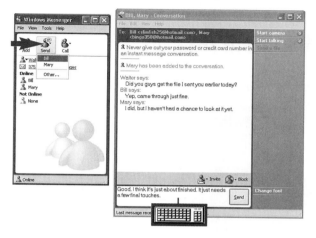

5 Invite Another Contact to Join

Use the **Invite** button to select another contact to join the conversation. The Invite button also lets you invite the contacts you are currently chatting with to start an audio-and-video chat (if the appropriate equipment is installed on your computers), run NetMeeting for collaborating on a shared document, or ask for remote assistance.

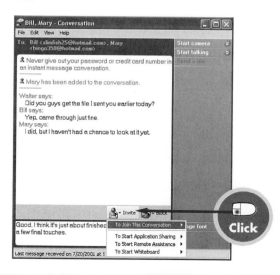

6 Block a Contact

Sometimes, you'll come across people who are sending you instant messages that you'd rather not get. Click the **Block** button to block the person who last sent you an instant message from contacting you or even seeing your name in the MSN directory in the future.

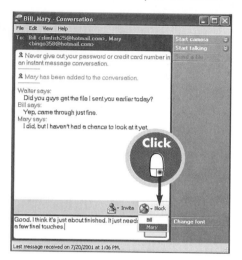

7 Set Your Status

At times, you may find it inconvenient to receive instant messages. You can change your online status to prevent people from interrupting your work online. Right-click the **Windows Messenger** icon in the system tray and point to the **My Status** command to set your current status.

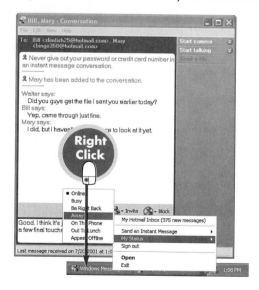

How to Publish a File to the Web

Many people maintain their own Web sites, whether those sites are served from personal space on a service, such as MSN, a business Web site, or a portion of a company intranet. Windows makes it easy to send (or publish) files to a Web site. To publish a file, you must be connected to the Internet. If you connect using a modem, Windows prompts you to make the connection if you are not already connected.

1 Find the File to Publish

In the **My Computer** window or **Windows Explorer**, find the file you want to publish to the Web and select it by clicking it once. From the **File Tasks** list on the left side of the window, click the **Publish this file to the Web** link.

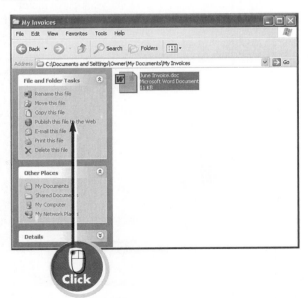

2 Click Next

The Web Publishing Wizard starts. Click **Next** to go past the welcome page.

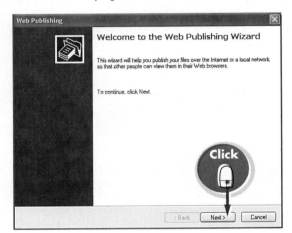

③ Choose a Network Destination

Choose the destination for your file. MSN offers free space in which you can store files. If you want to publish to another location—such as a personal Web site, an intranet, or a network location—choose **Other Network** Location. The publishing process works the same for all three options. For each option, you may be asked for a username and password to publish to the site.

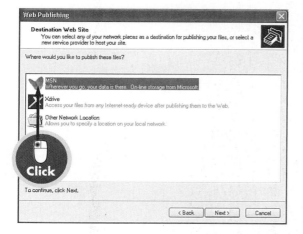

④ Choose a File Destination

Choose the location on the chosen server where you want to publish your file. This location is usually a folder you or a storage service, such as MSN, has created for your use. Make a selection and click **Next** to publish the file.

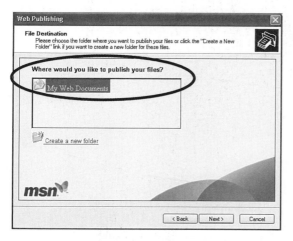

⑤ Finish

After the file has been published, click **Finish** to exit the wizard. A browser opens to display the file you have just uploaded; note that you are viewing the file from the remote server, not from your local server. Make a note of the URL that is displayed in the **Address** bar for this page so that you can share it with your co-workers and friends.

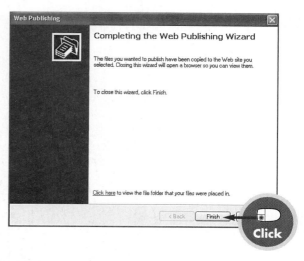

How-to Hint

Creating a Network Place

Publishing to Web sites is easier if you create Network Places for each site you want to publish your files to ahead of time. For details on how to do this, see Part 4, "Working on a Network."

Task

Having Fun with Windows XP

You can't work all the time, and when you want to have some fun with your computer, Windows XP is ready for you with several built-in "fun" programs.

Windows Media Player can play audio CDs, MP3 music files, and movies in a variety of formats. You can use Windows Media Player to search for music on the Internet and even record your own CDs.

With Windows Movie Maker, you can take still pictures, movie files, home movies, and even music and put them all together to create your own movie. You can edit and play that movie at any time and even send it to friends.

Windows also includes a number of great games, from the classic Solitaire and Hearts to fast-action Pinball. With the variety of Internet games that are available at sites all over the world, you'll never be without a gaming partner again.

How to Play Music and Movies

Unless you have set up a different player program as your default player, Windows plays music and video files using the Windows Media Player. When you insert an audio CD, video CD, or DVD into your disc drive or double-click a music or movie file stored on your computer, Windows Media Player opens automatically and begins playing. To start this task, use Windows Explorer or the My Documents window to browse to a music file (a file with the extension .mp3, .wav, and so on) or a video file (a file with the extension .mpg, .avi, .asf, and so on); double-click it to launch the Windows Media Player.

① Pause

You can pause the playback of the audio or video file by clicking the **Pause** button once. While playback is paused, the **Pause** button changes to a **Play** button; click the **Play** button to start playback where you left off.

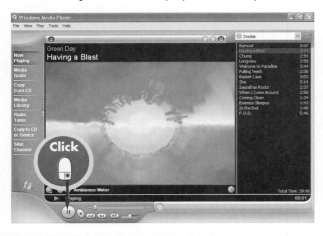

② Stop

You can stop playback by clicking the **Stop** button. When playback is stopped, the **Pause** button turns into a **Play** button.

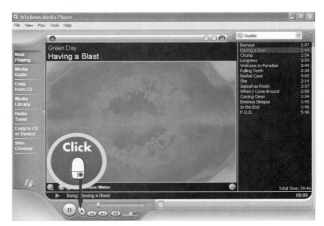

③ Play

When no music or movie is being played or when the movie or audio file is paused, a **Play** button appears. Click it once to start playback.

④ Change Volume

Change the volume for the music or video being played by dragging the **Volume** slider to the right (for louder) or to the left (for softer).

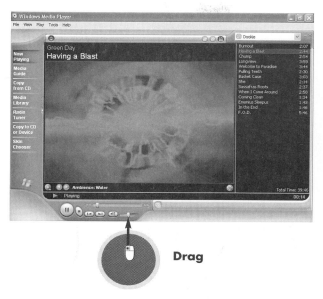

Drag

⑤ Go Backward and Forward

During playback, you can skip to the previous or next tracks by clicking the single arrows with lines next to them. During playback of some sorts of media (such as movies), you might also see rewind and fast-forward buttons which are small left and right-facing double arrows.

Rewind ⌐
Back One ⌐   ⌐ Fast Forward
Track   └ Forward One Track

⑥ Pick a Track

If you are playing a CD or DVD with multiple tracks, each track is shown in the playlist on the right side of the player screen. Click any track to begin playing it.

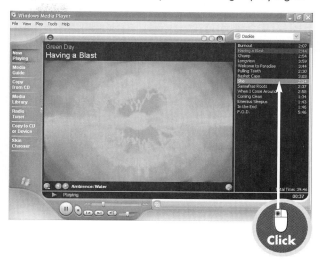

Click

⑦ Select a Visualization

Visualizations are graphics that move along with the music file as it plays. Windows Media Player includes a number of interesting visualizations. Click the left and right arrows under the visualization window to browse through the available visualizations one at a time; alternatively, click the button with an asterisk to choose a particular visualization from a drop-down list.

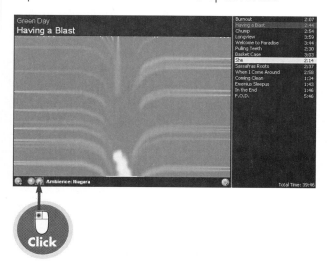

Click

How to Record Music

Windows Media Player makes copying tracks from audio CDs easy. You can record songs from an existing audio CD to a file on your hard disk or to another CD if you have a recordable CD drive. You can also convert songs to the popular MP3 format. You can even listen to songs as they're being copied. Copying music for anything other than strictly personal use is a violation of copyright laws. If you want to copy a song to a CD that you can play in your car, you're probably okay. If you want to use a song in a presentation at the office, you're on shaky legal ground.

① Start Windows Media Player

Click **Start**, point to **All Programs**, point to **Accessories**, point to **Entertainment**, and then click **Windows Media Player**.

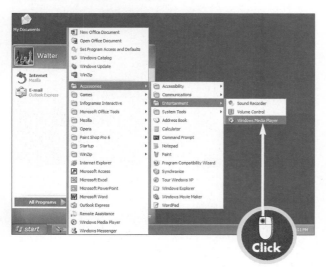

② Switch to Copy from CD

Click the **Copy from CD** button. If your CD is not in the computer's CD-ROM drive, insert it now. If the music begins playing, click the **Stop** button to stop playback.

③ Find Album Information

If **Windows Media Player** does not display the album and track information for your CD, click the **Get Names** button. A wizard opens, asks a few questions, and helps you search the Internet for album information.

4 Select Tracks to Copy

By default, all the tracks on the CD are selected to be copied. Deselect a track by clearing the check from the box next to the track (click the box once). Only tracks with check marks will be copied.

5 Open the Options Dialog Box

By default, tracks are copied to the **My Music** folder inside your **My Documents** folder. You can change this location and specify some additional settings from the **Options** dialog box. Open it by choosing **Tools**, **Options**.

6 Set Options

On the **Copy Music** tab, you can change where the tracks are copied, the file format (such as MP3 and several others) in which the tracks are copied, whether content copy protection is enabled (which basically means that the recording you make can't be further copied and shared), and the quality of the recording (higher quality takes up more disk space). When you've made your selections, click **OK**.

7 Copy the Music

Click the **Copy Music** button to begin copying the selected tracks to the location specified in the Options dialog box, with the selected options.

How to Find Music Online

Windows Media Player provides two ways to find music on the Internet. The **Media Guide** feature lets you browse for downloadable music and video files. The **Radio Tuner** lets you tune in to streaming Internet audio in dozens of different formats.

① Start Windows Media Player

Click **Start**, point to **All Programs**, point to **Accessories**, point to **Entertainment**, and then click **Windows Media Player**.

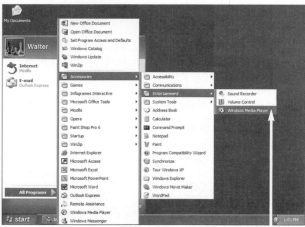

② Switch to Media Guide

Click the **Media Guide** button to open an Internet connection and jump to the WindowsMedia.com Web site.

③ Browse the Web Site

Use the WindowsMedia.com Web site to browse for all kinds of files you can play in Windows Media Player.

4 Switch to Radio Tuner

If you want to listen to a radio station across town or across the globe, switch to the **Radio Tuner** feature. Many radio stations around the world (but not all) broadcast over the Internet. Click the **Radio Tuner** button.

5 Start a Preset List

Just as you can with the radio in your car, Windows Media Player lets you create preset lists of stations. Unlike your car radio (which has a limited number of preset buttons), you can create any number of lists and fill each list with as many stations as you want. A list named **My Stations** is created for you. Switch to it by clicking its link.

6 Find a Station

To find stations to add to your list, use the list of categories on the right side of the window to browse for stations. You can also search for stations by keyword or click the **Find More Stations** link to browse a complete list of radio stations available on the Web.

7 Listen

After you have displayed a list of stations, select a station and then click the **Play** link to begin listening. Click the **Add to My Stations** link to add the selected station to your list.

How to Make Movies

Windows XP includes a program named Windows Movie Maker that lets you import pictures and movies, edit them, and put them together as a movie. Movie Maker is complex enough that an entire book could be written about it, but this task should give you an idea of what it can do.

❶ Start Movie Maker

Click **Start**, point to **All Programs**, point to **Accessories**, and then click **Windows Movie Maker** to launch the program.

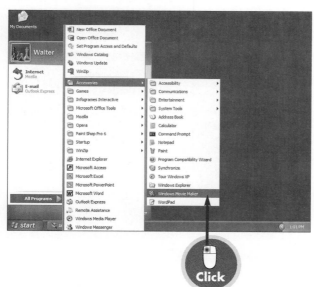

❷ Import Files

To import picture or movie files already on your computer into Movie Maker, select **File**, **Import** from the menu bar.

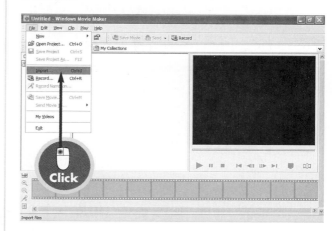

❸ Record Video

To record video from a VCR or camcorder, select the **Record** command from the **File** menu. To use this feature, you must have a video card that supports recording from an external device, and the device must be hooked up correctly to this video card.

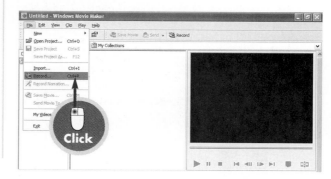

4 View a Collection

When you import pictures or record video into Movie Maker, the files are displayed as part of a collection. By default, the media files are placed into a collection named My Collection. When you select a collection from the **Collections** list on the left side of the screen, the files in that collection are displayed as thumbnails on the right side of the screen.

5 Create a New Collection

To organize the files you access in Movie Maker, you can create new collections. Right-click anywhere in the **Collections** list and choose **New Collection** from the shortcut menu.

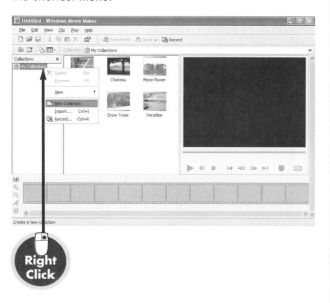

6 Name the New Collection

As soon as you create a new collection, you are given the chance to rename it. Type a name for the new collection.

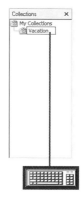

7 Move Files to the New Collection

To move files between collections, select the thumbnails of the files you want to move (the same way you do in Windows), drag them to the new collection in the **Collections** list, and drop the files.

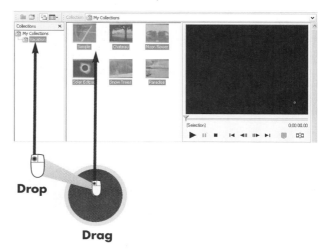

Drop

Drag

8 Move Pictures to the Storyboard

The storyboard is the filmstrip at the bottom of the Movie Maker window. It represents the movie you are currently creating. Each frame of the filmstrip is a picture in the movie. Drag each picture individually to a frame on the storyboard. This task shows the steps to make a slideshow movie out of still pictures.

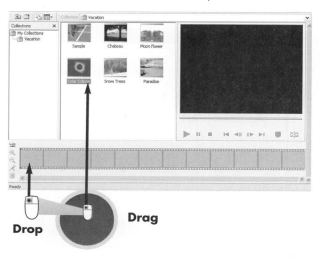

Drop **Drag**

9 Show the Timeline

After you have moved all the pictures to the storyboard, you can display the timeline for the movie. The timeline helps you adjust the length of each frame (just slide the divider between frames to adjust the size) and position an audio soundtrack should you decide to include one.

Click

10 Select All Clips on Storyboard

After you have adjusted the lengths of your frames and are ready to make your movie, select all the clips on the storyboard (hold down the **Ctrl** key and click each of the clips in turn).

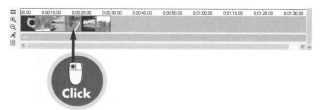

Click

11 Combine the Clips

Combining the clips tells Movie Maker that you want each picture to play in succession when you play the movie. With all clips selected, choose **Clip**, **Combine** from the menu bar.

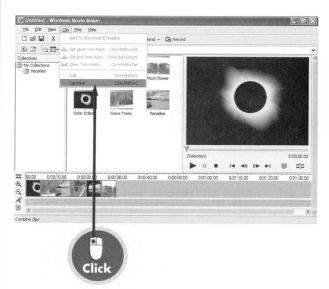

Click

12 Play the Movie

To see what your movie looks like at any time, click the **Play** button. All the frames shown in the storyboard play in sequence. You can assess the flow of the scenes and adjust the duration of the frames in the storyboard.

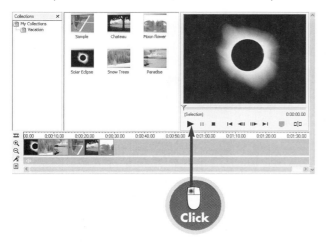

14 Click OK

Use the Save Movie dialog box to adjust the quality of the saved movie. Higher-quality movies take up more disk space. When you have made your selection from the **Setting** drop-down list and provided any labeling information, click **OK** to save the movie. Movie Maker converts all the clips and individual pictures files in the storyboard into a single movie file. After the movie is saved, you are given the chance to watch it in Windows Media Player.

13 Save the Movie

When you are satisfied with your movie, choose **File**, **Save Movie** from the menu bar. This command opens the Save Movie dialog box.

How-to Hint

Recording Audio

You can record your own narration or even include a music soundtrack for your movie. To record narration, just click the button that looks like a microphone to open the **Record Narration Track** dialog box. Click the Record button and speak into your computer's microphone to narrate your movie. To add music, click the **Change** button on the **Record Narration Track** and choose a source for the audio. You can record audio from a music CD or another audio device (such as digital tape) that you have hooked up to your computer's sound card.

How to Work with Pictures

Most Windows applications store picture files in a folder named My Pictures, which you'll find inside the My Documents folder. This folder was created to include tools that are specific to working with picture files.

1 Open My Documents

Double-click the **My Documents** icon on your desktop to open the My Documents window. If you don't see the My Documents icon on your desktop, you can find it on your **Start** menu, and you can add it to your desktop using the procedure covered in Part1.

2 Open My Pictures

Double-click the **My Pictures** icon to open the My Pictures folder.

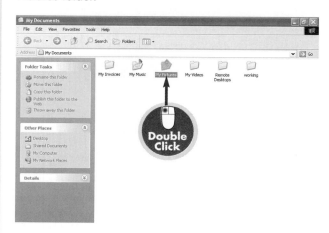

3 Select a Picture

Select any picture in the **My Pictures** folder by clicking it once.

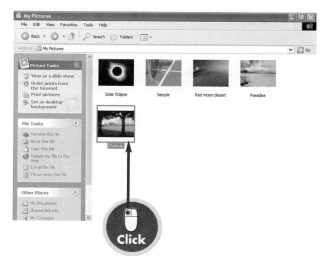

④ Print Pictures

To print the selected picture or pictures, click the **Print Pictures** link in the **Picture Tasks** list on the left side of the window.

⑤ View as Slideshow

If no pictures are selected or if multiple pictures are selected, click the **View as a slide show** link in the **Picture Tasks** list. Windows shows the selected pictures one by one in full-screen mode. You are given controls to advance, rewind, and stop the slide show.

⑥ View as Filmstrip

Select the **Filmstrip** command from the **View** menu.

⑦ Work with the Picture

In filmstrip view, the selected picture is shown enlarged. Use the tools under the enlarged picture to zoom in and out on, resize, and rotate the picture. These adjustments affect only the display of the picture and not the picture file itself. In filmstrip view, you can use the **Next** and **Previous** buttons to move through the slides one at a time.

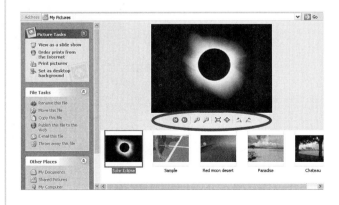

How to Play Games

Windows XP includes a number of games that you can play when you get tired of working. Some games you can play by yourself (such as the classic Solitaire); other games require you to sign on to the Internet to find other online gamers you can challenge to rounds of checkers, spades, and backgammon.

1 Start Solitaire

Click Start, point to **All Programs**, point to **Games**, and click **Solitaire**. The game opens in a new window.

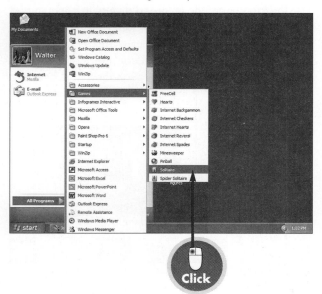

2 Move Cards

To move a card, click it with the left mouse button and drag it to its new location on the seven row stacks. Double-click a card to move it directly to one of the four suit stacks in the top-right corner of the board.

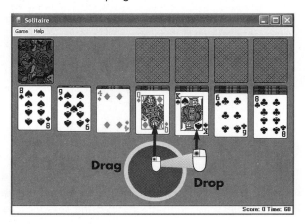

3 Get Help

To learn about the rules of the game and how to play the game, choose **Help**, **Contents** from the menu bar.

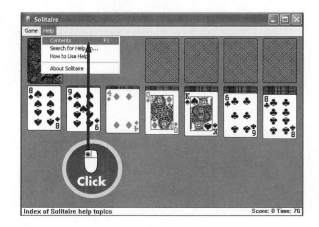

4 Start an Internet Game

Several Internet games are included with Windows. Start one the same way you would a game that can be played from your computer's hard disk: Click **Start** and choose **All Programs**, **Games**; then choose the name of the Internet game you want to play.

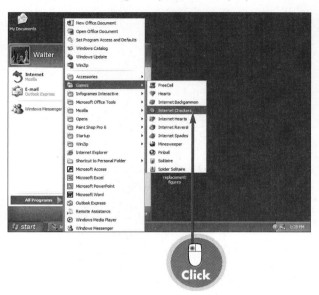

5 Enter Zone.com

To play on the Internet, you must connect to Microsoft's **Zone.com** Web site by clicking **Play**. You do not have to register or give any personal information. An opponent of your skill level will be selected for you, and the game will begin immediately. Set your skill level using the **File** menu of any open game.

6 Play

Play the game the way you would play a normal "non-computer" game. In checkers, for example, just drag a checker where you want it to go.

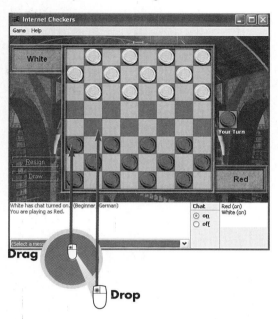

7 Send a Message

During play, you can send any of a number of preset messages to your opponent. Select one from the drop-down list at the bottom of the screen. Unfortunately, you cannot type your own messages.

Glossary

NUMBERS

3D card   A graphics card, used primarily for games, that enables realistic 3D motion.

802.11   The standard that governs how information is sent across a wireless network. Actually, several different 802.11 standards exist, not all of which are compatible with one another.

A

activate   Windows XP requires that you activate your product within a set number of days or you won't be able to continue using it. Activation is a separate process from registration. During activation, a small snapshot of key pieces of hardware on your system is sent to Microsoft. No personal information is required, and none of the hardware information can be used to identify you. In theory, activation prevents people from installing the same copy of Windows on more than one computer—an action that violates the software licensing agreement. *See also* register.

adapter card   *See* expansion card.

add-in card   *See* expansion card.

administrator   A user account created during Windows installation that gives full permission to use the computer and modify settings. Administrator is also a title given to a person who manages a computer network or system.

AGP (Accelerated Graphics Port)   A bus specification that enables 3D graphics to display quickly on a computer. The AGP bus is dedicated solely to graphics and offers more bandwidth than the PCI bus. It is required for graphically demanding applications.

antivirus software   Software that checks a computer for viruses and eradicates them if it finds them.

applet   A small program. In Windows, the programs you can access from the Control Panel window (Display, System, and Mouse, for example) are often called applets.

application   A program, such as Microsoft Word, that is separate from Windows.

archive   A collection of files copied to a specific location as a backup. When you install a Windows XP service pack, you have the option of archiving Windows files that the service pack will replace so that you can uninstall the service pack later.

associate   A document file is "associated with" the program that created it. For example, text files with the file extension .txt are associated with the Windows applet Notepad. If you double-click a file to open it, the program associated with that file type launches and opens the selected file.

attachment   A file that is inserted into an email message and sent to a recipient.

ATA   A series of standards for IDE drives and devices. It covers a wide variety of features, including how the controller is integrated onto the drive itself.

ATAPI   An IDE disk interface standard for devices such as CD-ROM or tape drives.

ATX   A commonly accepted standard for the layout and form factor of the motherboard and power supply for PCs.

audio cable   A cable that runs between a CD-ROM drive and a sound card and enables the sound card to play audio CDs.

Automated System Recovery A feature of the Windows XP Backup utility, Automated System Recovery backs up certain system files and then creates an emergency rescue floppy disk that you can use to restore your system following a failure.

automatic updating can configure Windows XP to automatically monitor the Windows Update Site for updates and even to download them automatically when it finds them.

B

back up To copy the contents of a hard drive to another storage device so that the contents can be restored if the hard disk crashes or if the data needs to be copied to a new hard disk.

backplate A metal plate that helps secure add-in cards to the motherboard.

backward compatibility The capability of hardware or software to work with older versions of the same hardware or software.

baud Formerly the prevalent measure for data transmission speed until replaced by a more accurate term: bps (bits per second).

bidirectional parallel port A parallel port enabling data to flow in two directions between the PC and printer.

BIOS (Basic Input/Output System) The system that performs all the basic functions of your computer, such as sending information from your keyboard to your PC. The system BIOS is contained on the BIOS chip.

BIOS chip A chip that contains a system's BIOS. On many systems, it can be updated with a flash utility.

bootup screen The first screen you see when you start your computer.

boot To start a computer. During the boot process, the many files that make up the Windows operating system are loaded into memory.

boot disk A floppy disk that can be used to boot your computer. Boot disks are often used to recover from a system failure or to install Windows.

briefcase A special folder designed primarily for users who want to transfer files to another computer. The briefcase contains functions for moving and synchronizing files.

broadband A high-speed connection to the Internet, such as a cable modem or DSL modem.

browser A program, such as Internet Explorer, that can display a Web page. Some browsers can display text, graphics, and frames; other browsers can display only text. Popular browsers other than Internet Explorer include Netscape Navigator and Opera.

bus A pathway in the PC over which data travels.

C

cable modem A device that enables your computer to access the Internet at high speed via the cable TV system. Although called a modem, it uses technology different from modems that use traditional telephone lines.

cache memory Random access memory (RAM) that a computer microprocessor can access more quickly than regular RAM.

cascade A way to arrange multiple windows on the screen. The multiple windows are layered, one on top of the other, so that the title bars of all the windows can be seen.

CD-R drive A CD-ROM drive that lets you write data one time per a special CD.

CD-ROM A type of optical disc that stores up to one gigabyte of data. The setup files for most applications today come on CD-ROM discs.

CD-ROM drive A device that can run CD-ROMs.

CD-RW drive A CD-ROM drive that lets you write data many times per a special CD.

chip puller A tool for removing chips from your PC.

clean installation An installation of Windows onto a blank, formatted hard disk. *See also* upgrade.

click To position the mouse pointer over a file or folder and press the left button on the mouse once. Clicking is used to select files in Windows and to follow a link on the Internet.

Close button The button with the X on it, found in the upper-right corner of most windows and dialog boxes. Click the Close button to close a window.

CMOS battery A small battery that provides power to the CMOS chip.

CMOS chip A chip containing a record of the hardware installed on your PC. The CMOS battery supplies it with power, so the data remains stored even when the computer is off. The CMOS stores the information contained in the BIOS settings as well as maintains the clock. On older systems, there will be a separate chip; on newer systems, the function is integrated onto the motherboard chipset.

CMOS setup screen A screen that enables you to change your CMOS settings.

collection A group of associated pictures or video clips in Windows Media Player. Collections are used for organizational purposes.

cold boot Starting a computer from a state in which the power is off.

color depth The number of colors displayed on your screen. Common color depths include 16 colors, 256 colors, 16,000,000 colors (24-bit), and millions of colors (32-bit). Change the color depth used by Windows using the Display Properties dialog box.

compression A way to store data so that it takes up less disk space than normal. Windows XP offers built-in compression that does not require a separate application.

computer name A name of up to 15 characters given to a computer. On a network, this name helps distinguish the computer from other computers.

COM port *See* serial port.

Control Panel A special folder that contains applets used to configure various Windows settings, such as display, mouse use, and sound.

controller A device found on an add-in card or on the motherboard that connects the motherboard to a hard drive.

controller card An add-in card that has a controller on it. *See also* controller.

CPU (Central Processing Unit) The main processor on a PC, such as a Pentium or Athlon chip.

cradle A device into which a PDA is inserted that allows it to synchronize its data with a PC's.

D

daisy-chain A configuration in which devices are connected one to another in a chain-like fashion, one attached to the next. USB devices can be connected in a daisy chain.

decryption Removing the encryption from a file or folder. *See also* encryption.

default A setting automatically selected by Windows or another program if you do not specify another setting.

defragment *See* fragmented.

defragmenter Software that allows a hard disk to run more quickly by *defragmenting* it—placing all related pieces of files next to one another so they can be called into memory more quickly.

desktop The metaphor used by Windows to display your file system. The desktop is the main screen in Windows, on which various icons are displayed.

desktop theme A coordinated collection of background colors, wallpaper, mouse pointers, and sounds used to provide a unique feel to your desktop.

device driver A file that controls and is required for running a particular type of device attached to your computer. Device drivers exist for printers, displays, CD-ROM readers, disk drives, and so on.

Device Manager An application used to control the settings for hardware on your computer. The Device Manager is used to enable and disable hardware devices, as well as to control driver versions and other settings.

DHCP (Dynamic Host Configuration Protocol) A computer protocol that assigns a different IP address to a computer each time it connects to the Internet. When you set up a home network to share a high-speed Internet connection, such as a cable modem, you often must also set up DHCP.

digital camera A camera that records and stores photographic images in a digital format that can be read by a computer.

DIMM (dual inline memory module) A type of RAM used in newer PCs, it attaches to the motherboard via a series of pins.

DIN connector A connector between the keyboard and the computer.

DIP (dual inline package)   A type of RAM used in older computers.

DIP switch   A switch on an add-in card or on the motherboard used to configure a computer or peripherals.

disable   In a list of check-box options (as in a dialog box), to remove a check mark from the check box for a particular option. In contrast, you enable an option by clicking an empty check box to place a check mark in the check box.

display adapter   *See* graphics card.

DMA (Direct Memory Access)   A way in which data moves between a device and system memory without the use of the CPU.

docking station   A piece of hardware attached to a laptop that enables the laptop to use expansion cards and devices such as external monitors and keyboards. It is sometimes called a port replicator.

domain   A way of grouping computers and users in a fairly complicated network. Domains are often used at large companies, where powerful computers called *servers* provide security, Internet access, file storage, and much more to less powerful computers called *workstations*. If your computer is on a Windows network, it will either be part of a domain or part of a workgroup. *See also* workgroup.

double-click   To position the mouse pointer over a file or folder and press the left mouse button twice in rapid succession. Double-clicking opens, or launches, a file or folder.

download   To transfer a file from another computer to your own. Downloading commonly refers to transferring a file from an Internet site to your computer.

DPI (dots per inch)   A measurement of the quality of the output of a scanner or printer, or of a computer monitor. The more dots per inch, the higher the quality.

draft mode   To print a document in a special mode offered by many programs that reduces the amount of ink used during printing and also reduces the quality of the printed document.

drive bay   A bay inside a PC into which you install devices such as hard disks, floppy disks, and CD-ROM drives.

driver   A piece of software used to enable a peripheral, such as a printer or video card, to work with your PC.

DSL modem   A device that enables your computer to access the Internet at high speed via special DSL lines. Although called a modem, it uses technology different from modems that use traditional telephone lines.

dual-boot   A computer on which two operating systems have been installed. When a computer is configured to dual-boot, you are presented with a menu when the computer first starts that prompts you to choose the operating system you want to use.

DVD decoder card   An add-in card that helps play DVDs.

DVD drive   A drive that can run DVD discs or play DVD movies.

DVD-RW drive   A DVD-ROM drive that lets you write data to special DVDs.

E

EDO RAM (extended data output RAM)   A type of random access memory.

email   Electronic mail messages sent between different users on a network, such as the Internet. Some email systems are configured only on a local network, and email messages can only be sent between other users on the network.

enable   In a list of check-box options (as in a dialog box), to place a check mark in the check box for a particular option. In contrast, you disable an option by clicking a check mark to make the check box empty.

encryption   To translate data into a secret code that only certain users can access. Windows XP provides built-in encryption. After a file is encrypted by a user, only that user can decrypt the file.

enhanced parallel port   A parallel port that offers transfer rates of up to 2 Megabytes per second. It can be used for printers and other devices.

enhanced parallel port cable   A cable you must use to take advantage of the enhanced parallel port. The numbers IEEE 1284 are printed on the side of an enhanced parallel port cable.

EPP/ECP (Enhanced Parallel Port/Enhanced Capability Port) A type of parallel port offering transfer rates of up to 2 Megabytes per second, for use with peripherals other than the printer. It enables higher data transfer rates than the original parallel port. EPP is for nonprinter peripherals; ECP is for printers and scanners. *See also* enhanced parallel port and enhanced parallel port cable.

Ethernet A standard for tying together computers in a local area network.

Ethernet card A network card that adheres to the Ethernet standard. Virtually all network cards sold for the PC are Ethernet cards.

Everyone group A special security group that includes all users of the network. By default, the Everyone group is given read access to all files and folders on your computer that you share with the network. It is best to remove this group and narrow the focus of users to whom you allow access to a resource.

event An occurrence in Windows, such as when you delete a file or empty the Recycle Bin. An event can also be an occurrence you don't cause, such as when Windows displays an error message. Most such occurrences can be associated with sounds.

expansion card Also called adapters or add-in cards, these plug into the motherboard on expansion slots and expand how your PC can be used. Video cards, disk controllers, and graphics cards are just a few of the expansion cards you can add to a PC.

expansion slot A slot on the motherboard into which expansion cards can be plugged.

Explorer *See* Windows Explorer.

extension The three-letter suffix following the dot in a filename. The extension usually identifies the type of file (for example, a .doc extension identifies the file as a Microsoft Word document; a .jpg extension identifies the file a s a JPEG image file).

extranet A company network built using Internet technologies that is available to business partners of a company as well as to the company itself.

F

FAT (file allocation table) Maintained on a hard disk by an operating system, it's a table that provides a map of the clusters (the basic unit of logical storage on a hard disk), detailing where files have been stored.

FAT32 A version of the File Allocation Table (FAT) disk format used mainly in Windows 98 and Windows Me. Windows XP can also use the FAT32 file system. When using FAT32, Windows XP cannot use several advanced features, such as encryption and compression. For that reason, it is best to use the NTFS file system with Windows XP whenever possible.

Favorites A special folder that contains links to favorite Web pages in Internet Explorer.

file A collection of data that is stored as a single unit on a disk drive and given a name. Almost all information stored on a computer, including Windows itself, is stored as files.

firewall A hardware/software combination or piece of software that protects a computer from being attacked by hackers on the Internet. Using a personal firewall is a good idea when setting up a home network connected to the Internet because it can prevent attacks.

FireWire A standard that enables devices to be easily connected to a PC without having to open the case, and that allows devices to communicate at high speeds. It is also called IEEE 1394.

Flash memory A type of memory easily updated by running a patch or piece of software. BIOS chips often contain flash memory, and so easily can be updated by running software. Flash memory is also called flash ROM.

floppy drive A drive that stores information on removable disks that hold 1.44MB of data.

floppy disk A removable disk that can hold up to 1.44MB of data. Floppy disks are commonly used to transfer information between computers and to back up small amounts of data.

folder A Windows object that can contain files and other folders. Folders are used to organize storage. (On older, nongraphical systems, folders are called directories.)

format To prepare a storage medium, such as a hard disk or floppy disk, for writing data. Windows includes utilities for formatting disks.

fragmented When data is deleted from a hard drive, the data is not actually removed. Instead, it is marked so that it can be overwritten. When new data is stored, it is written to any empty spaces on the drive. These spaces are not necessarily contiguous, which leads to a condition known as fragmentation. Fragmented drives are usable, but can slow down a system. Windows XP includes a defragmenting program that rewrites the data on a drive so that it is contiguous.

G-H

game port A port into which you plug a joystick or other gaming device.

graphics accelerator A graphics card, chip, or chipset that speeds up the display of graphics on a PC.

graphics card An add-in card that gives your computer the capability to display graphics and video on your monitor.

hard drive Where data and programs are stored, even when you turn off your computer.

hardware driver *See* driver.

heatsink A device attached to a CPU that cools down the CPU so that it doesn't overheat.

home page The top page of a Web site. The default Web page that loads whenever you open Internet Explorer is also called a home page (it's often called your home page).

I

icon A small picture on the desktop or in a folder that represents a file or folder. The icon usually helps indicate what kind of file or folder an object is.

IDE (Integrated Drive Electronics) A standard that details the way in which a computer's motherboard communicates with storage devices, such as hard disks.

IDE/EIDE hard drive A hard drive that connects to the motherboard via an IDE/EIDE controller card.

IEEE-1394 *See* FireWire.

inbox The folder in an email program to which new messages are delivered.

indicator light The light or lights on the front of the PC that show the computer is turned on, or that the hard disk or CD-ROM drive is being used.

ink cartridge A cartridge for inkjet printers.

install To load software (such as Windows or Microsoft Office) onto your computer. Most programs are installed using a setup program that guides you through the installation step by step. The word *install* is also used to refer to the process of setting up other devices and software configurations on a computer. For example, configuring a printer to work on your computer is often referred to as *installing the printer*. Hooking up a new hard drive inside your computer is referred to as *installing the hard drive*.

Internet Explorer The Web browser built into Windows XP.

intranet A local area network inside a company build using Internet technologies.

IP address A set of numbers, such as 150.2.123.134, that identifies each computer connected to the Internet. To use many Internet services, each computer must have a unique IP address.

IRQ (interrupt request) A connection between a device and a controller. Only one device at a time can use a particular IRQ.

ISP (Internet service provider) A company that provides access to the Internet. An ISP might also provide a range of other Web-related services in addition to providing access.

J–L

joystick A device for playing games that plugs into the game port.

JPEG A graphics file format that makes use of lossy compression techniques, which means that image quality is degraded when you compress the file.

jumper A small set of pins set in a particular way on the motherboard or add-in card to configure devices to work with a PC.

keyboard port A port into which the keyboard is plugged. Most often, it is a PS/2 port.

LAN (local area network) A network of computers connected together so they can share files and printers and also share a high-speed Internet connection, such as a cable modem. This enables them all to access the Internet from one connection.

lasso The dotted rectangle that follows the mouse pointer when you drag around a group of objects. The lasso encircles the objects and selects all the objects at once.

LCD (liquid crystal display) The kind of display used in laptop computers.

link On a Web page, a selection of text or a graphic that, when clicked, causes the Web browser to load another Web page.

local area network (LAN) A computer network that spans a relatively small area, such as a single building. LANs can be connected to one another to form a wide area network (WAN).

local printer A printer that is connected directly to a computer. This differs from a network printer that may be connected to a different computer on a network or directly to the network itself.

logon Because it is a secure system, Windows XP requires that you enter a username and password so that it can register you with the network and determine the permissions you have been given on a computer.

lossless compression The condition in which no elements of a picture are lost during compression, resulting in higher picture quality and often larger size of picture files.

lossy compression The condition in which certain elements of a picture are lost during compression, resulting in lower size of picture files but also reduced quality of pictures.

LPT1 The name given to the primary parallel port on a computer. The first printer attached to a computer usually uses the LPT1 port.

M

Mac address A number that identifies a network card. Each network card has a unique Mac address so that it's the only one in the world with that address. When you install a cable modem, sometimes you must tell your cable provider your network card's Mac address; otherwise, you cannot connect to the Internet.

Makebt32 The program used to make the set of floppy disks used for Windows XP installation. Makebt32 can be found in the BOOTDISK folder on the Windows XP installation CD.

map To create a shortcut to a shared resource on the network by telling your computer to treat the resource as a separate drive on your computer. Because not all programs know how to work with Network Place shortcuts, you can "fool" these programs into working with these shared resources by making them think that the resource is on a different drive on your computer.

maximize To cause a window on your desktop to grow to maximum size, filling your screen.

memory bank A series of slots or sockets on the motherboard that holds RAM.

memory socket A socket on the motherboard into which RAM is installed.

menu A collection of related commands in a program that is accessed by clicking once on the menu's title.

microprocessor See CPU.

Microsoft Network (MSN) The ISP and Web service operated by Microsoft.

minimize To cause a window on your desktop to be removed from view. After it's minimized, you can access the window using its taskbar button.

modem Short for modulator/demodulator. A device for connecting a computer to other computers or the Internet. Modems can be located outside the computer (called an external modem), or inside the computer (called an internal modem).

motherboard The main part of the PC—a very large board into which the CPU, add-in cards, chips, RAM, and many other devices are plugged.

mounting rails Rails inside a drive bay to which hard drives and other storage devices are attached.

mounting screws Screws that secure a drive into a drive bay.

mouse port A port into which the mouse is plugged.

MP3 A compressed audio file format suitable for downloading high-quality audio files from the Web. This has become a wildly popular audio format.

MP3 file   A computer file ending in the extension .mp3 that when run plays music. The MP3 standard compresses music so that the files are relatively small but still retain the high quality of the music.

MP3 player   A small portable device that can play MP3 files.

MSN Explorer   A simplified Web browser that provides quick access to many MSN-related services, such as Web-based email, calendar, and personalized Web services.

MSN Messenger   An instant messaging program, much like ICQ or AOL Instant Messenger, that can be used to communicate directly with another person on a network or the Internet.

My Computer   A special folder located on the Windows desktop that contains all the drives (hard disks, floppy disks, CD-ROM, and network drives) available on a computer.

My Documents   A special folder located on the Windows desktop meant to hold all documents and personal files you create.

My Network Places   A special folder located on the Windows desktop used to browse other computers available on the network.

My Pictures   A special folder in the My Documents folder that has special features for viewing and working with pictures.

N

nanosecond   The speed at which RAM is rated. The lower the nanosecond rating, the faster the memory. For example, a 7-nanosecond chip is faster than a 12-nanosecond chip. A nanosecond is one billionth of a second.

NetCam   *See* WebCam.

network   Several computers (and sometimes other devices) that are connected together so that they can share software, data files, and resources. *See also* local area network and wide area network.

network card (NIC)   An add-in card that enables a computer to be connected to a network or to the cable system or DSL line to get a high-speed Internet connection.

network drive   A shared resource, such as a folder, treated as a drive on your computer. A network drive gets its own drive letter and shows up in the My Computer window.

network hub   A device to which PCs are connected that enables them to communicate with one another as part of a local area network. Also, each PC can access the Internet through the hub.

Network Place   A shortcut to a resource (a file, folder, or a device) on the network. The shortcut you set up to that location works only on your computer; other computers on the network may or may not have the same Network Places you do.

network printer   A printer that is connected to another computer on the network or to the network itself and for which an icon is created in the Printers and Faxes folder on your computer.

NIC (network interface card)   *See* network card.

nonparity RAM chips   RAM chips that do not perform error checking to see if any other memory chips are not functioning properly. Most RAM sold today is nonparity.

newsgroup   An Internet-based forum in which you can participate in threaded discussions.

NTFS   The native file system format used by Windows XP. *See also* FAT32.

O

OEM (original equipment manufacturer)   A company that buys computers in bulk, customizes them, and then sells them under its own name.

object   An item on your screen (usually an icon) that represents a program, file, or folder.

offline folders   Folders that have been marked to be accessible when your computer is not connected to the network. Files in offline folders are periodically synchronized with the actual files on the network.

operating system   A program or group of programs that controls the file system, drive access, and input for a computer. Windows XP is an example of an operating system.

Outlook Express   The email and newsreader program included with Windows XP.

P

palm   A small, handheld computer commonly used for keeping track of contacts, appointments, to-do lists, and similar items. It uses the Palm operating system.

palmtop   A generic name for a PDA. *See* PDA.

parallel port   A port into which the printer is plugged. It also can be used for scanners and other external devices.

parent folder   In a hierarchical list of folders on your computer, the parent folder is the folder above (and thus the folder that contains) the folder you are currently in.

parity RAM chips   RAM chips that perform error checking to see if any other memory chips are not functioning properly. This is generally an older type of memory. Usually, 486 PCs and Pentiums use memory that is nonparity. Parity RAM chips have nine chips on them, instead of the eight found on nonparity memory.

partition   A separate portion of a hard drive. It can also be used as a verb: You divide a hard drive into sections by partitioning it.

path   The description of the location of a file or folder on your computer or on a network. A typical path might include the drive letter, folders, and name of the file (for example, C:\My Documents\invoice.doc).

pause printing   To stop a document in the print queue from printing. The document remains in the print queue but does not print until you choose to resume printing. Other documents waiting in the queue continue to print. *See also* restart printing.

PC Card   A credit-card-size add-in card that plugs into a laptop computer and gives it extra functionality. Modems and network cards are common PC cards.

PCI (Peripheral Component Interconnect)   A bus standard developed by Intel that allows for fast bus speeds.

PC Slot   A slot into which a PC card is plugged.

PCMCIA card   An older term for PC card.

PCMCIA slot   An older term for PC slot.

PDA   A generic name for a small, handheld computer, designed to keep track of contacts, appointments, to-do lists and similar items.

peer   On networks where there is no main server, all computers are part of a workgroup and are considered peers that can share their own resources and access other resources on the network.

peripheral   A general term that refers to any device, such as a printer, modem, scanner, or others, that isn't required for the basic functioning of a computer but that can be used to enhance the way it works or to give it extra functionality.

permission   On a secure system such as Windows XP, users are given specific rights (such as the ability to read or change a file) on objects.

phone jack   A connector into which you plug a telephone wire to connect your modem to the telephone system.

pickup tool   A tool for picking up small objects that have fallen into your computer.

pocket PC   A small, handheld computer commonly used for keeping track of contacts, appointments, to-do lists, and similar items. It uses a special version of Windows.

pointer   A small graphic (an arrow, by default) indicating the placement of the mouse on your screen.

port   A connection on your computer into which you plug a cable, connector, or device.

port replicator   *See* docking station.

power cable   A cable that connects the power supply and provides power to devices in the PC, such as hard drives and floppy drives.

power supply   A device inside your PC that provides power by converting the current from your wall outlet to the type of power that can be used by your PC and all its components.

print device   In Microsoft lingo, the actual printer hardware connected to a computer is referred to as the print device and the icon in the Printers and Faxes folder that represents the device is referred to as a printer.

print queue   A list of documents waiting for their turn to be printed by a specific printer.

printer   *See* print device.

priority The status a document has in a print queue. A document's priority governs when it prints related to other documents in the print queue. By default, all documents being printed are given a priority of 1, the lowest priority available. The highest priority is 99. Increasing a document's priority causes it to print before other waiting documents.

product activation New versions of Windows require that you register and activate the operating system over the Internet or by phone so that you may continue use beyond a short trial period.

product identification key The serial number found on the back of the Windows CD-ROM case and entered during the installation process that helps identify you as the proper owner of the software.

Program Access and Defaults A feature included with Windows XP Service Pack 1 that lets you control the default applications associated with certain files (such as Web pages) and activities (such as email). This feature also lets you specify whether icons for Microsoft versions of certain built-in programs are shown on your desktop and Start menu.

Properties A dialog box available for most files and folders that contains various settings relating to the object. You can access this dialog box for most objects by right-clicking the object and choosing the Properties command from the shortcut menu.

publish To upload a file from your computer to a Web server so that the file is available for viewing on the Internet.

Q–R

queue A list of the documents waiting their turn to be printed.

RAM (random access memory) Memory where programs are run and data is stored while the data is being manipulated. When you turn off your computer, any information in RAM is lost.

RAM cache Memory that sits between your CPU and your main RAM. Information is shuttled here from the main RAM to be available more quickly to the CPU. Cache is faster than normal RAM and includes intelligence. It is not part of the main memory in a PC and on most cases is not found directly on the motherboard.

RAMBUS A type of high-speed RAM.

Recent Documents A special folder available on the Start menu that contains shortcuts to the documents you have most recently opened.

Recycle Bin A special folder on your desktop that temporarily holds files you delete from your computer. When the Recycle Bin becomes full, the oldest files are permanently deleted to make room for new files to be added. You can also empty the Recycle Bin manually, permanently deleting all files inside.

register During registration of Windows, you provide certain personal information (name, address, phone number, and so on) to Microsoft so that the company can record you as the owner of a Windows license. Registering is optional. When you register, you are eligible for technical support, warranty, and software bulletins; you also may receive special promotions from Microsoft on other products. *See also* activate.

removable drive A device that stores data permanently like a hard drive or a floppy drive does, but on removable disks. These disks commonly hold several hundred megabytes or more of data.

Reset button A button that turns off your computer and then automatically turns it back on.

resolution The dimensions of your screen. Common resolutions include 640×480 pixels, 800×600 pixels, and 1024×768 pixels. You can change the resolution of your screen using the Display applet on the Control Panel.

restart printing To begin printing a paused document again from the beginning. Restarting a print job can be useful if, for example, you start to print a document and then realize the wrong paper is loaded in the printer. You can pause the document, change the paper, and then restart the document. *See also* pause printing.

restore point A special backup of system files and settings used by the System Restore application to return your computer to a particular state.

right-click To hold the mouse pointer over a certain object and click the right mouse button once. Right-clicking an object usually opens a shortcut menu that contains commands relating to the object.

ribbon cable A wide ribbon-like cable that connects a drive to a disk controller.

RIMM (RDRAM inline memory module) A form of high-speed memory used by the newest, most powerful computers.

ROM (read-only memory) Memory that is not *volatile*: It can be read but not changed, or can only be changed under specific conditions.

ROM BIOS chip A chip that holds the code necessary for starting up your computer and for basic functions of receiving and sending data to and from hardware devices, such as the keyboard and disk drives.

router A device that can connect networks and that routes information to and from the Internet. Routers are commonly combined with hubs in home networking devices to allow PCs to be networked and share an Internet connection.

S

scheduled task A job (such as launching a program or backing up files) defined in the Task Scheduler application to run at a certain time.

screen resolution *See* resolution.

screen saver A small program that displays graphics on your screen when the computer has been idle for a certain amount of time. Although designed to prevent images displayed too long from permanently burning themselves into your monitor (a phenomenon that does not often occur on newer monitors), screen savers are mainly used for entertainment and for security in conjunction with a screen saver password.

scroll To move the display in a window horizontally or vertically to view information that cannot fit on a single screen.

SCSI (small computer systems interface) A hardware interface for connecting hard disks, scanners, CD-ROM drives, and other devices to a PC.

SDRAM (synchronous dynamic random access memory) A generic name for various kinds of DRAM synchronized with the clock speed for which the microprocessor is optimized.

search engine A Web tool that compiles an index of existing sites and lets your search for pages that contain certain keywords. Some popular search engines are www.yahoo.com, www.google.com, and www.altavista.com.

secure system A computer that can be assigned a password so that unauthorized users are denied access.

select To click once and bring the focus to an object. For example, in a list of files displayed in an open folder window, you can click a file to select that file. Information about the selected object is frequently displayed.

Send to A submenu available on the shortcut menu for most files and folders that contains commands for quickly sending files to certain locations, such as the floppy drive, desktop, and My Documents folder.

serial port A port into which modems and other devices are plugged.

service pack A collection of updates and features issued by Microsoft since the original release of a Windows operating system. Service packs are numbered (Service Pack 1, Service Pack 2, and so on) and are cumulative. For example, Service Pack 3 would contain all the updates found in Service Packs 1 and 2. At the time of this writing, Service Pack 1 is the only service pack issued for Windows XP, though more recent individual updates may be found on the Windows Update site.

share To allow network access to a file or folder on your computer. After you share an object, you can define which users can access the object and exactly what they can do with it.

shortcut A small file that targets another file on your computer. Double-clicking the shortcut launches the target file.

shortcut menu The menu available by right-clicking most files and folders. The shortcut menu contains different commands that are associated with the particular object.

SIMMs (single inline memory modules) A kind of RAM. They attach to the motherboard via a series of pins.

socket The way certain Intel Pentium microprocessors plug into a computer motherboard so they make contact with the motherboard's built-in wires or data bus. A number of different socket standards include Sockets 7, 8, 370, 423, and A.

sound card An add-in card enabling your computer to play music and sounds.

Start menu The menu that opens when you click the Start button at the lower-left corner of your screen. The Start menu provides access to all your programs, special folders, and Windows settings.

standby When your computer enters a mode in which the power to the monitor, hard drive, CD-ROM drive, and most other elements is turned off or reduced. Just enough power is fed to the computer's memory so that Windows remembers what programs were running and what windows were open. When your computer leaves standby, it should return to the same state it was in before it went to standby.

synchronize To cause offline files or folders to be in unison with the actual files and folders they represent. Files in either location with newer modification dates replace files with older modification dates.

System Restore A Windows application that creates restore points (backups of certain system settings) and that can restore Windows to any particular restore point. *See also* restore points.

system tray The rightmost portion of the taskbar that contains icons representing programs running in the background. The system tray also includes the clock and volume control.

T

tape drive A drive enabling data to be copied to a tape. The tape can hold hundreds of megabytes of data and is commonly used to back up data and hard disks.

taskbar The bottom part of your desktop that contains the Start menu, Quick Launch bar, program buttons, and system tray.

TCP/IP (Transmission Control Protocol/ Internet Protocol) The basic communication language or protocol of the Internet. It also can be used as a communications protocol in the private networks called intranets and in extranets.

terminator Attaches to a device on the end of a SCSI daisy-chain and lets the chain know the device is the first or last device in the chain.

thread A group of replies to a single message in a newsreader program such as Outlook Express. When you reply to a message, your reply becomes part of the thread.

tile A way to arrange multiple windows on the screen. The multiple windows are reduced in size so that some portion of each of them appears on the screen at once. You can tile windows either horizontally or vertically on the screen.

toner cartridge An ink cartridge for laser printers.

troubleshooter A special file in the Windows Help program that walks you through steps to take in determining the cause of a problem with Windows. The troubleshooter frequently suggests resolutions to these problems or points you toward more information about the problem.

U

UART (Universal Asynchronous Receiver/Transmitter) The chip that controls a computer's serial port and the interface to serial devices such as modems.

uniform resource locator (URL) The address of a Web page. The URL for a Web page generally includes the protocol (such as http), the computer on which the file is located (such as www.microsoft.com), the folder on that computer where the file is located (such as /Windows/), and the name of the actual file (such as default.htm).

Universal Serial Bus (USB) A standard that enables devices to be easily connected to a PC without having to open the case.

upgrade To install Windows XP over an existing installation of a previous version of Windows (such as Windows 98/Me/2000/NT).

uplink port A port on a network hub that connects the hub to a cable modem or other external device for accessing the Internet.

USB hub A device that enables many USB devices to connect to a computer at the same time.

USB port A port that uses the USB standard and enables USB devices to easily connect to a PC.

V–X

V.90 A standard that allows 56 Kbps modems to communicate.

V.92 A standard that builds on the V.90 standard and adds features such those that make connections more quickly.

video port A port on the back of a graphics card to which the monitor is connected.

virus A destructive program that can wreak havoc on a PC.

volume label The name of a disk. When formatting a floppy disk, you can provide a volume label for the disk if you want; alternatively, you can leave the disk unnamed, as most people do.

wallpaper A picture displayed on the Windows desktop behind any icons.

warm boot Restarting a computer by using software rather than either turning the power off and back on or pressing a reset button.

WebCam A small, inexpensive video camera that attaches to your computer and lets other people see videos of you live over the Internet.

Web browser See browser.

Web page A document that is usually one of many related documents that make up a Web site and that is available for anyone to view with a Web browser such as Internet Explorer.

Web server The computer that serves the contents of a Web site to visitors to that site.

Web site A group of related Web pages available over the Internet for anyone to view.

Wi-Fi See 802.11.

wide area network (WAN) Two or more LANs connected together over a distance. See also local area network (LAN).

Windows Explorer A tree-based application used to browse the file system on your computer.

Windows Media Player A program installed with Windows XP that is used to display picture files, music files, and movie files of various formats.

Windows Movie Maker A program installed with Windows XP that is used to create movie files out of still pictures and recorded video and audio.

wireless base station A hub/router that connects PCs wirelessly with one another and lets them communicate and share resources and an Internet connection, using the 802.11 wireless communications protocol, also called Wi-Fi. A small radio transceiver in the base

station sends and receives data via RF frequencies in the 2.4 gigahertz range.

wireless network A network that allows PCs to communicate with one another without wires. Most wireless networks are based on the 802.11 wireless communications protocol, also called Wi-Fi.

wizard A Windows program that walks you through the steps involved in the installation or configuration of a Windows component or program.

workgroup A group of computers operating as peers on a network. See also peer and domain.

Y–Z

ZIF (zero insertion force) socket A socket that lets you insert or remove a chip without using a special device.

Zip drive A model of disk drive made by Iomega with a removable disk roughly the size of a floppy disk that holds either 100MB or 250MB of data, depending on the exact model. Zip drives have become a popular way of backing up data on home computers.

Index